DD649825

NORTHAMPTON COMMUNITY
DISCARDED
COLLEGE LIBRARY

The New Urban America

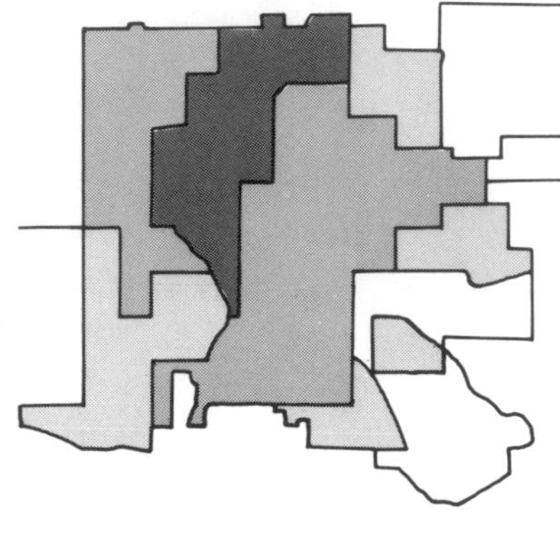

Carl Abbott

The New Urban America

Growth and Politics in Sunbelt Cities

The University of North Carolina Press
Chapel Hill

Manufactured in the United States of America

Library of Congress Cataloging in Publication Data

Abbott, Carl.
The new urban America.

Bibliography: p.
Includes index.
1. Cities and towns—Southern States—Growth.
2. Cities and towns—Southwest, New—Growth.
3. Cities and towns—Southwest, Old—Growth.
I. Title.
HT371.A25 307.7′6′0975 80-22848
ISBN 0-8078-1464-4
ISBN 0-8078-4079-3 pbk.

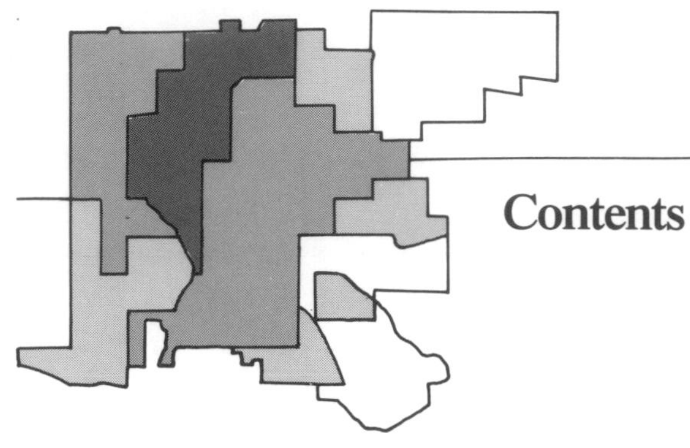

Contents

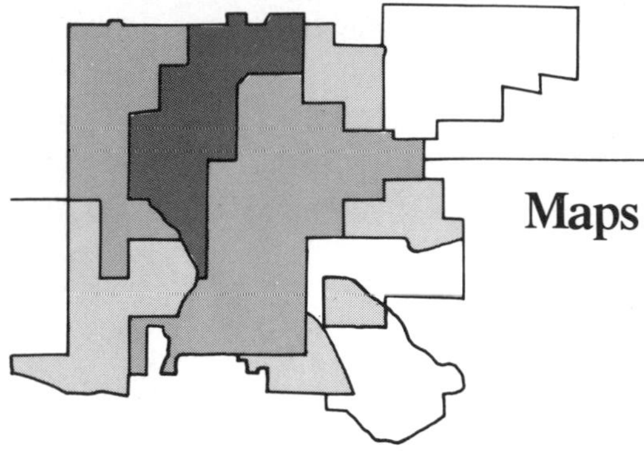

Maps

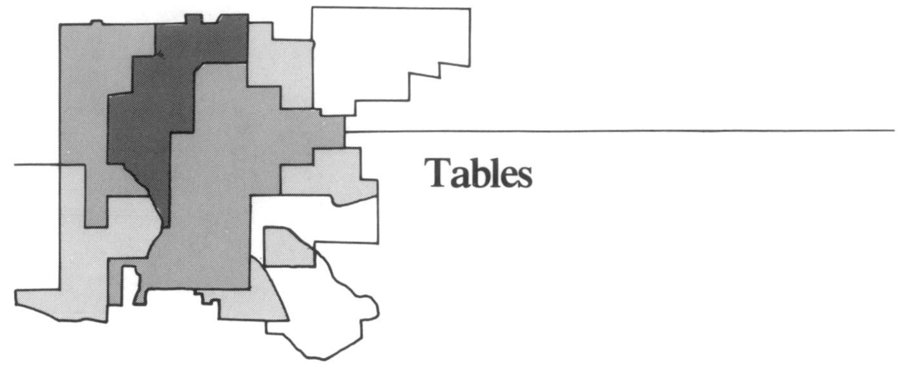

Tables

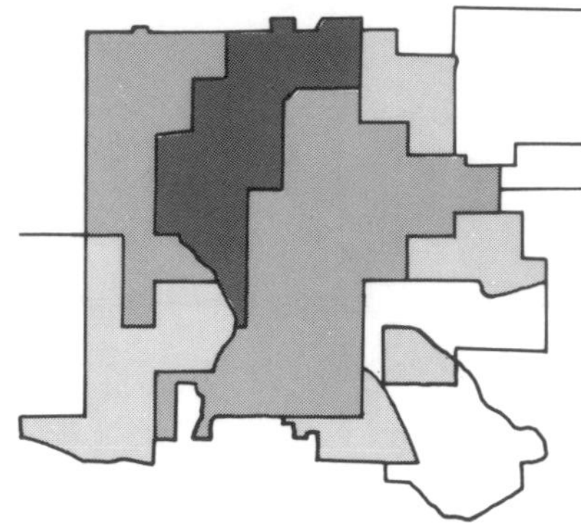

Acknowledgments

With the present book, as with most academic research, the author of record is really a front for an informal syndicate of scholarship. A number of colleagues provided comments and advice on the concept and contents of my study at various points in its progress. Among them were Gunther Barth, Blaine Brownell, Timothy Crimmins, Don Doyle, Mark Foster, David Goldfield, David R. Johnson, Roger Lotchin, Zane Miller, Gerald Nash, Norman H. Pollock, and Leo Schnore. Dozens of other professors, journalists, and public officials shared their knowledge on the spatial and political development of specific cities. They are acknowledged individually in the notes, but they deserve additional thanks for their thoughtful answers to my questions.

The progress of research has been assisted by both my former and my present university. Old Dominion University provided a semester's research leave that allowed me to draft the first chapters. The Research Committee of its School of Arts and Letters awarded a research grant that helped to secure the help of Ervin Jordan, Katie Keeton, and Joan Sulek as research assistants. The Portland State University Foundation has assisted with publication costs and its Geography Department provided help in the preparation of maps.

Portions of this book have appeared in different form elsewhere. Parts of the introduction and chapter one appeared in the *Journal of the West* and parts of chapter three in *Social Science History*, both of which journals have granted permission for use of the material here.

The New Urban America

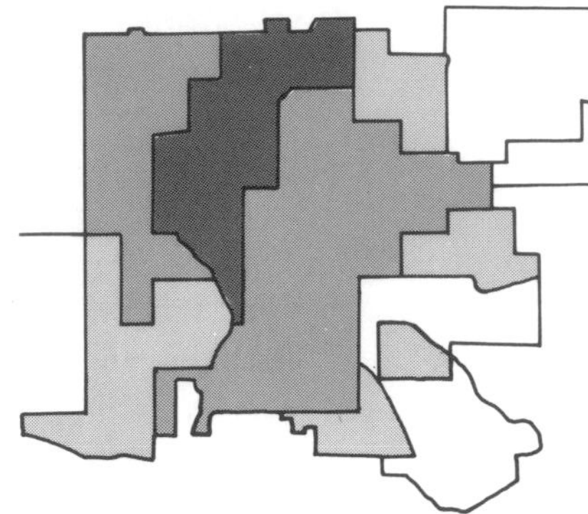

Introduction

The Sunbelt Idea

"Sunbelt" or "sun belt," the word or the phrase, the informed American in the second half of the seventies has added a new concept to his vocabulary of public affairs. In less than a decade the term has passed from new coinage to cliché. Business writers, political journalists, academic experts, and elected officials by 1976 and 1977 found it a convenient catchword, a shorthand reference for a major national policy debate. Senators and governors, the *New York Times* and *Fortune*, a college athletic conference and Jimmy Carter—all discovered "sunbelt" as a useful term for describing present and future growth patterns in the United States.

The publication of Kevin Phillips's *The Emerging Republican Majority* in 1969 marks the introduction of "sunbelt" in the analysis of national politics. In his discussion of the South and West, Phillips used "Sun Belt" and "Sun Country" interchangeably to describe a region of conservative voting habits where Republicans might expect to solidify their status as a majority party. The following year, Samuel Lubell in *The Hidden Crisis in American Politics* made a single use of the term in treating the Nixon coalition but preferred to organize his analysis of voting trends around the traditional regions of South, Mountain states, and West.[1] During the early 1970s the term remained in limited circulation but failed to make a strong impression. When surveyed in the fall of 1977, only one-third of a sample of political journalists traced their first awareness of the term to Phillips, with equal proportions unable to recall their first encounter or dating it to 1976.[2]

The response reflects the rapidly expanding attention to the idea of an emerging economic and political region across the southern tier of the United States in the second half of the seventies. Kirkpatrick Sale's *Power Shift*, a flashy and small-spirited book published in 1975, described the development of the nation's "Southern Rim" from the viewpoint of a liberal, Manhattan-based journalist. Sale found that the South and West since 1945 had developed as a "rival nexus . . . a truly competitive power base" standing in political, cultural, and economic opposition to the liberal North. Sale's ultimate concern was to explain the Nixon presidency as "the climax of the thirty-year period of increasing political power" enjoyed by the conservative states of the deep South and Southwest. A few months later the *New York Times* gave respectability and publicity to the "sunbelt" concept with a five-part series that analyzed the region's economic and demographic patterns, its urban growth and environmental problems, and its political tendencies. Here again the underlying concern was to explain the economic and financial problems of New York City and the Northeast in terms of a broad national transformation which far exceeded the reactive capacity of local governments and politicians.[3]

The *Times* series and subsequent articles in *Business Week* and the *National Journal* narrowed the concern over a "restless and historic" transformation of the American landscape to a specific question of national policy. In February, the *Times* pointed out that the balance of federal taxes and federal expenditures in 1974 had left the sunbelt states with an excess of $13 billion. The newspaper also noted that the increasing representation of southern and western states in Congress promised the maintenance of the pattern. Likewise writing at a time when the Northeast still felt the effects of the 1974–75 depression, the *National Journal* in June argued that "federal tax and spending policies are causing a massive flow of wealth from the Northeast and Midwest to the fast-growing Southern and Western regions." Its state by state comparison of federal tax revenues with federal spending on public works, defense contracts, salaries, grants in aid, and retirement programs found a net surplus in fiscal 1975 of $11.5 billion in the South and $10.6 billion for the Mountain and Pacific states. Although the article agreed that the inequities were largely "accidental," it also argued that the massive transfers of federal funds to prosperous states endangered the "economic underpinnings of the Northeast quadrant." The month before, *Business Week* had described the "flood tide" of population and industrial migration that threatened a "second war between the states" and had suggested that the nation now required a more evenhanded distribution of federal subsidies and spending in place of policies set in a previous era of southern poverty.[4]

As presented by *Business Week* and the *National Journal*, the emerging situation of structural decline in the old industrial belt and self-sustaining economic growth in the Sunbelt required redistribution of federal expenditures to aid declining eastern and Great Lakes states. Indeed, the subsequent eighteen months brought an explosion of debate in Congress and the press over the issues of balanced national growth as defined in early 1976. Both in and out of Congress, the identification of a specific policy issue triggered the organization of "antisunbelt" coalitions among elected officials. The summer and fall of 1976 thus saw the organization of a Northeast-Midwest Economic Advancement Coalition among House members led by Michael Harrington of Massachusetts, a less formal Senate coalition chaired by Howard Metzenbaum of Ohio, and regional subcoalitions of senators led by Daniel Moynihan of New York, John Culver of Iowa, and William Proxmire of Wisconsin. The Council of Northeast Governors also dates from June 1976 and helps to provide funds for the Northeast-Midwest Research Institute, a "frostbelt" research office located in the House coalition office. The Council for Northeast Economic Action in Boston and the Academy for Contemporary Problems in Columbus have also concentrated on the analysis of economic problems in the old industrial states.[5]

The limited depth of the initial northern reaction is illustrated by the reflex coinage of terms to describe the set of older states in economic difficulty: "frostbelt" and "snowbelt" for "sunbelt," "northern tier" for "southern rim." A key victory for the Northeast concerning the distribution of community development funds in which the aid formula was rewritten to favor cities with older housing stock has in turn brought charges of unfair treatment from southern states. For most of 1977, the Southern Growth Policies Board was conscripted to serve as professional staff to refute northern claims of unfair treatment. As the situation is perceived by public officials in the South and West, well-organized northern politicians have raised a false issue of federal discrimination hoping to maintain state income levels above the national average with larger and larger increments of federal aid and to mask their inability to stem the slow industrial obsolescence of their states. Typical of the sunbelt response is a resolution passed unanimously by three thousand delegates to the Texas Municipal League convention in October 1977, which called for developing accurate information on federal spending patterns, soliciting political action from sunbelt political leaders, and establishing a congressional program to represent cities in the South and West. The following month, California Congressman Mark Hannaford proposed the formation of a "Sunbelt Coalition" of House members to counteract northeastern organizations.[6]

In the political arena, the debate remained locked to the issue of equitable distribution of federal funds. President Carter, for example, enunciated the standard northern position in July 1977, when he told a group of newspeople that "there has been too much of a channeling of federal monies into the Sun Belt states." In argument and counter-argument, politicians from industrial states dwell on the special burdens of education and welfare assumed in northern cities without adequate national aid, while southern representatives such as David Boren of Oklahoma or George Busbee of Georgia attack the "myth" of the Sunbelt by citing data on the continuing poverty of the South relative to the rest of the nation. The rhetoric of such debate, of course, reverses traditional American boosterism, with each side painting its failures and economic problems in the brightest colors. Where the historic measuring rod of urban boosterism was population growth, the standard of comparison in the sunbelt funding argument has been reduced to the question of relative per capita income and wealth among the states.[7]

Several trends emerging from the debate hold promise of more sophisticated approaches in the new decade of the eighties. Academic experts increasingly emphasize that regions composed of a dozen or more states are scarcely natural economic units. Variations among individual states and between metropolitan and rural counties are often more striking than the supposed advantages of West and South over Midwest and East. They also point out that the Sunbelt's edge in federal spending results from federal purchases, especially defense salaries and procurement, while grant programs in the 1970s have favored older rather than fast-growing cities.[8] In addition, efforts to define the issues in more fundamental terms stress the identification of particular structural weaknesses in each regional economy and the development of public policies to reduce sectional tensions by dealing with such weaknesses, whether rural poverty, lack of water or energy sources, or urban unemployment. For example, the Northeast Governors Conference in November 1976 not only complained about the imbalance of federal spending but also proposed new investment in transportation, energy, and industrial facilities.[9] A series of regional economic analyses by the Economic Development Administration, a major symposium on "Alternatives to Confrontation: A National Policy toward Regional Change" held at the LBJ Library in September 1977, and a White House Conference on Balanced National Growth in 1978 were all designed to defuse the issue of federal spending by expanding the range of argument.

If attention is centered on the concept itself rather than the policy debate triggered by its reception, there is little reason to disagree with *Fortune*'s assertion that the discovery of the Sunbelt has been "a media event fogged by an uncommon number of misconceptions."[10] Frequency of use has not meant precision in its definition. The vividness that has contributed to its popularity has also helped to conceal an impressive elasticity in meaning. As used in the national press, "sunbelt" carries a basic core meaning of a fast-growth region located in the southern section of the United States. More complex definition, however, depends on each user.

As originally used by Kevin Phillips, for example, the boundaries of the sunbelt region were defined by topographical/economic subregions: "The territory stretching from the eastern Carolina lowlands down around (and excluding) Appalachia, picking up only the greater Memphis area of Tennessee, omitting the Ozarks and moving west to Oklahoma, thence virtually due west" with a possible loop northward for Colorado.[11] In the mid-seventies, however, a rough consensus developed which smoothed Phillips's irregular boundary to the enticingly continuous line of state borders running along the northern edges of North Carolina, Tennessee, Arkansas, Oklahoma, New Mexico, and Arizona. Most definitions add southern California to the thirteen states situated south of such a line. In addition, the *New York Times* and *Fortune* include Virginia, while Sale includes southern Nevada.

The poll of national political journalists taken in the fall of 1977 indicated less than complete agreement with the thirteen-and-a-half or fourteen-and-a-half state definition. Although the single most common description was the region extending from Virginia to California—a rephrasing of the *Times* and *Fortune* definition—several other commentators specified the addition of northern California, the mountain West, or the upper South. Half the writers, however, suggested a much more limited region with a focus on the Gulf Coast, with three omitting the Carolinas and Virginia, two omitting California, one omitting the entire Southeast, and another omitting the entire Southwest. Similarly, the Commerce Department has defined a "Sunbelt-South" embracing the entire census South less Maryland, Delaware, and the District of Columbia.[12]

There is equal disagreement among practicing journalists on the value of the sunbelt concept in the analysis of public events. There is roughly a fifty-fifty split among those who find it useful for describing social and economic patterns in the United States and those who do not, and a similar division about its usefulness for understanding current developments in American politics, although one columnist after another rushed to describe the "sunbelt voting" behind the presidential victory of Ronald Reagan. Even its advocates acknowledge that the term oversimplifies complex phenomena, while its detractors admit that it captures at least certain of the important characteristics of Southeast and Southwest.

The relatively narrow terms of the policy debate on federal expenditures and regional wealth to a degree obscure the original use of "sunbelt" as the name for a new cultural region. When originally adopted by Phillips in the late 1960s, the phrase "sun belt" or "sun country" seemed to capture the "cultural, political and economic essence" of the area. Phillips, Sale, and the *New York Times* series—the three sources most important for introducing "sunbelt" to the American vocabulary—all described roughly the same sets of regional characteristics. Although starting from very different ideological positions, each description argued that the economic and demographic changes of the last generation have reshaped the "social and political landscape" of the United States.[13]

Central in the regional characterization is an emphasis on the speed of economic growth. In an economy that has entered an age of affluence, the sunbelt states offer an enormous range of recreational resources to attract both retirees and highly skilled, highly educated workers. At the same time, these states benefit from enormously valuable energy supplies and a lucrative and highly productive agricultural industry. On top of the economic base provided by natural resources, sunbelt states have developed major concentrations of activity in the visible high-technology chemical, electronics, and aerospace industries. One result of the long-term economic boom in the South and West has been the movement of population from northern cities to new and fast-growing metropolitan areas. Where Sale describes an "incredible urban explosion," Phillips refers repeatedly to "booming cities," to "urban boom counties," or to "new urban complexes of Texas and Florida" that represent a "new urban America."[14]

Both suburban life-styles and a growing economy open to individual initiative and exploitation are presumed to support aggressively conservative politics as the third major characteristic of the sunbelt states. In the appalled opinion of Kirkpatrick Sale, the restless and rootless millions of new sunbelt citizens confirm the theory of the origins of the new radical right found in the work of Daniel Bell, David Riesman, and Nathan Glazer. With no strong sense of community to moderate their promotion of economic self-interest, they indulge in a politics of reaction—racism, repression, rightism, Republicanism. Phillips put the same analysis in more measured terms: "The huge postwar white middle-class push to the Florida-California Sun country . . . seems to be forging a new conservative political era in the South, Southwest and Heartland. It is no coincidence that this conservative trend is best exemplified by California, Arizona, Florida and Texas (apart from Nevada the fastest-growing states in the nation), where the very areas of greatest population explosion are the demonstrated strongholds of Reagan, Goldwater, Gurney and Tower, the vanguardmen of the new conservative sun politics."[15]

Political journalists who have not specialized in the analysis of the Sunbelt appear most certain that it is an area of rapid growth exhibiting particular cultural traits. There is general consensus that it is a region of high mobility, middle-class values, and a leisurely life-style. Equally there is agreement that it is a stronghold of political conservatism which scorns environmental legislation. There is somewhat weaker agreement on its economic character as a region of individual affluence and prosperity based on high-technology industries. In contrast, the Sunbelt's massive urban growth and metropolitan sprawl play a relatively small role in its national image. Only half of the surveyed columnists viewed urbanization or suburbanization as important to a regional definition.

Although attention to the Sunbelt as a cultural region is a valuable corrective to a narrow focus on federal taxation and spending policy, most current discussion remains limited by its concern to explain divisions within national politics. In fact, the emergence of the Sunbelt has been a complex process whose keynotes have been change and variety. Even the broad characteristics defined by most observers may mark only a stage in the region's growth. Kevin Phillips has thus noted the recent "cultural moderation" which has been brought by economic maturity, while the *New York Times* has argued that the region is still a "cultural and political experiment" whose continuing growth is likely to reduce its parochialism: "The salient impression of the Sunbelt today is that of a region in transition, with economic, political and cultural directions only now taking shape."[16]

The roots of such changes, moreover, extend more than a generation into the past. Despite the tendency of contemporary writers to emphasize the uniqueness of developments since 1970, it was the years from Pearl Harbor to Pleiku that established new directions for the sunbelt states. Recognition of the Sunbelt in the seventies has thus resulted from the passage of critical thresholds in city size, in economic independence, and in political representation rather than from the appearance of new phenomena. Understanding of the region's character requires historical description of its evolution as much as current economic and political analysis.

The first goal of the present study is to examine the development of the Sunbelt as an economic and demographic region. Although an emerging Sunbelt may also share the cultural traits discerned by Phillips and Sale, an initial analysis of the concept of a sunbelt region must center on the measurable patterns of population distribution and economic base which underlie the recognition of a new region. The first chapter therefore examines changing economic activities and growth patterns in the South and West since 1940 and explores how these objective shifts have formed the basis for the convergence of dissimilar regional images into the general idea of a "Sunbelt." It also suggests a precise definition for the Sunbelt and its constituent subregions based on growth rates, economic base, and social characteristics of states and of metropolitan areas taken as units.

The second chapter shifts attention from the growth of the region as a whole to an examination of shared characteristics among its metropolitan areas. Information on economic base, ethnic composition, social status, and governmental structure is used to evaluate the common expectation that southern and western SMSAs (Standard Metropolitan Statistical Areas) resemble each other and differ as a group from those of the Frostbelt. The discussion also introduces five cities that provide cases for detailed geographical and political analysis in the remainder of the study. The recent growth of Norfolk, Atlanta, San Antonio,

Denver, and Portland is therefore summarized within the context of regional metropolitan characteristics. Although there are clear socio-economic and governmental differences between the Sunbelt's SMSAs and those of the industrial Northeast, there are also significant differences among southern and western metropolises themselves. This latter conclusion complements the finding in the first chapter that the Sunbelt of the journalists in fact conceals a more complex regional pattern.

The second goal of this study is to use data on the five case-study cities and on other large sunbelt metropolises to examine ways in which rapid growth in total metropolitan population and rapid suburbanization have affected intrametropolitan politics in the Sunbelt.[17] The organizing idea for the analysis is the importance of social geography within metropolitan areas. The degree of concentration of economic status groups and ethnic groups and their relative location within the metropolis has obvious influence on individual life-styles. In addition, the residential location of individuals and groups helps to explain how they construct alliances to support programs and public action and how they relate to each other through the political process. Indeed, a widely accepted model of political behavior in American cities during the late nineteenth and early twentieth centuries takes internal social differentiation as a major independent variable. When the native-born middle class moved to new peripheral neighborhoods with the advent of mechanically powered transit systems in the 1880s and 1890s, a wide range of social problems could be visualized in terms of intra-urban divisions. Campaigns against liquor, immigration, and political bosses were all phrased as battles against the inner city, while needs for new services were seen as efforts to maintain social and physical order within the urban core.[18]

Since 1940, the pattern of urban land uses has undergone a second drastic change. The relatively concentrated "streetcar city" has given way to an "automobile metropolis" with widely dispersed population and decentralized economic activities. Sociologists and geographers have explored the patterns of this new social ecology at specific dates, relying largely on decennial census data. At the same time, political scientists have examined the impact of suburbanization on housing, public finance, education and other policy areas, again concentrating on current problems at particular times. The implication of these studies is that new patterns of internal metropolitan differentiation have had as much impact on politics and policymaking as did the pattern of 1880–1920.

A basic question of the present study is therefore the ways in which political issues within metropolitan areas have been defined in spatial terms. In some instances, sunbelt cities and suburbs have come into direct conflict over such issues as annexation, metropolitan government, school integration, the location of low-income housing, or the equitable provision of physical services on a metropolitan scale. In other instances, suburbs have tried to isolate themselves from core-city problems or to demonstrate their independence by separately providing a full set of services and pursuing their own aggressive policies toward growth. At the same time, several central cities have developed political patterns which increasingly revolve around the statement and reconciliation of differing interests among downtown real estate owners and a variety of local neighborhoods. In each case, the shifting balance of power on such issues can be analyzed in terms of the underlying distribution of population within the metropolitan area.

A second question that is implicit in an analysis of metropolitan growth and politics in the Sunbelt is the degree to which a specific pattern of political conflict has paralleled the distinct growth history of the modern South and West. If sunbelt SMSAs share economic and social characteristics different from those of the industrial heartland, they may also differ in styles of politics. In a suggestive article on Los Angeles, for example, James Q. Wilson argued that a distinct political culture in sunbelt cities might be tied to their age and pace of growth: "We are partly a nineteenth century nation, partly an early twentieth century nation, partly a late twentieth century nation. Our cities are differently located along the development scale, and the most important consequences of those locations are the values that animate people and which provide differing forms of legitimacy for different kinds of public action."[19] More specifically, the speed of growth and the rapid shift of socioeconomic status patterns with suburbanization may have operated to exacerbate conflict among different geographical segments of the sunbelt metropolis.

Chapter three contributes to the analysis of spatial politics by directly describing the changing social geography of sunbelt cities. Given the character of boom-city growth since 1940, the central concern is the effect of suburbanization on the distribution of socioeconomic groups and ethnic groups within metropolitan areas. The analysis uses general information for all large southern and western SMSAs divided by central city and suburban ring and detailed census tract data for Norfolk, Atlanta, Denver, Portland, San Antonio, and the super-boom cities of Orlando and Tucson. As well as defining changing patterns of social ecology, such analysis can also contribute to the ongoing debate among urban sociologists on the relative merits of several models of city-suburban status patterns.

On the basis of an understanding of aggregate growth trends and of internal social geography, the balance of the study offers detailed analysis of two interacting trends in the metropolitan politics of the South and West since 1940. The headlines in local newspapers and the occasional stories in *Time* have usually concentrated on the candidates and campaigns involved in efforts to build political coalitions committed to the promotion of urban growth. The major theme of central city politics in the postwar Sunbelt has been the rise and decline of businessmen's government in one metropolis after another. The first of three approximate and overlapping stages was a decade or more of widespread success for municipal reformers representing the downtown business community during and after World War II. Most of the fifties and sixties can be viewed as a longer period of stability and accomplishment in which ''neoprogressive'' administrations offered efficient city services and used redevelopment powers to attract outside investment. During recent years since 1965, however, previously unaccommodated interests have forced shifts in the balance of power within city politics and have weakened the influence of the postwar growth coalition.

In turn, the changing issues and alliances that first supported and then undermined the business-oriented reform administrations of sunbelt cities have centered on the problems involved in coordinating or directing rapid growth on a metropolitan scale. If attention is directed to underlying divisions of interest rather than to politicans and policies, the process of political change can be characterized as the emergence of conflict among areas of the metropolis with differing socioeconomic status and ethnic makeup. The fundamental issue of spatial politics within the metropolis has been an ongoing argument over the equitable allocation of the benefits and burdens of local government. Again, the evolution of the intrametropolitan arguments can be divided into three overlapping phases that roughly match the cycle of central city reform. From World War II into the early 1950s, vigorous leadership by central city officials postponed the effective expression of differing ambitions among outlying communities. During the fifties and sixties, most metropolitan areas witnessed increasing levels of conflict between central city and suburban governments. The seventies have added complex divisions of interest among city neighborhoods and among suburban governments to the straightforward problems of city-suburban relations.

The several aspects of this sequential model of metropolitan politics are treated in chapters four through nine. Chapter four itself describes the beginning of the ''sunbelt era'' with the impact of World War II on southern and western cities and the responses of central city leaders to the challenge of extraordinary growth. Chapters five and six discuss the development of the urban growth coalition in sunbelt cities and analyze its impacts on central city politics and growth from the mid-forties to the mid-sixties. The next two chapters shift attention to the changing political relations between the core cities and their growing suburban rings. Chapter seven analyzes the initial success and mounting failure of central city efforts to control suburban growth patterns through annexation and regional governmental agencies. Chapter eight traces the same process through the sixties and seventies and finds that recent decades have brought a system of metropolitan politics in which central cities and suburban jurisdictions interact as equals. Chapter nine describes the rise of neighborhood politics within sunbelt cities that has provided a second challenge to the postwar growth coalition to parallel that of the increasingly independent suburbs.

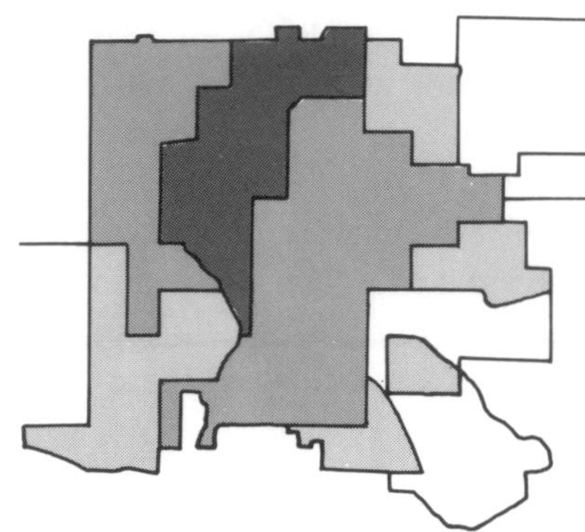

Chapter 1

The Emergence of the Sunbelt

The Sunbelt is a phenomenon of the past four decades. In 1940, the great industrial zone stretching from Boston and Philadelphia to Saint Paul and Saint Louis claimed half the nation's population, three-fifths of its personal income, and nearly three-fourths of its industrial output. The South and the West were customarily viewed as exceptions to this national norm, the one as a region of endemic poverty and social maladjustment and the other as an ongoing frontier that combined economic opportunity with cultural immaturity. Over the past generation and a half, however, real shifts of population, wealth, and productive capacity have created a new regional pattern. Today, a South that is beginning to overcome its racism and poverty and a West that is facing new problems of maturity along with continuing growth are perceived as components of a new American region.

In part, the rewriting of the popular guidebook to American regions is a simple response to the shift of economic power within the United States. Taken together, the West and South increased their share of personal income from 33 percent to 43 percent from 1940 to 1970. They increased their share of national population from 42 percent to 48 by 1970 and reached the 50 percent mark by 1976. Just as important has been the convergent development of these two historically dissimilar "hinterland" regions. Previous regional images that focused on the uniqueness of the South and the West have weakened as the two areas have grown more alike. In turn, recognition of the new Sunbelt has followed the lessening of objective differences.

The opening of the 1940s marks a clear divide in the history of the American West. With the possible exception of California, the twenties and thirties had been a long pause in which western cities and states tried to meet agricultural depression and the decline in hard-rock mining with social and political conservatism. Economically the region was a colony of the Northeast, a supplier of raw materials for eastern consumers and a distributor of outside manufactures with limited local investment capital and less than its proportionate share of industrial output.[1] It was the outbreak of war in the Pacific that brought defense contracts worth over $30 billion to the western states and federal investment in war plants of over $2 billion. By the end of the war, this impetus of defense spending seemed to have shifted the coastal and southwestern states into a new economic era, bringing industrial maturity with expanded capacity in steel, light metals, transportation equipment, and electric power and telescoping a generation of development into a decade.[2]

The continuation of wartime prosperity through the postwar decade brought a classic explanation for regional growth by Edward Ullman in 1954. Under the title ''Amenities as a Factor in Regional Growth'' he described the physical attractions of the western and southwestern states as key factors in their rapid growth. Physical amenities accounted for the concentration of activities such as recreation, aircraft manufacturing, military training, and retirement communities. The amenities of weather and recreational opportunities also helped to draw footloose manufacturing (the assembly of fabricated components and other manufacturing with low transportation costs and dependence on skilled labor), administrative headquarters, quarternary or information-processing industries, and other functions dependent on their ability to recruit and hold qualified personnel. In turn, the expanding demands for services and for capital investment in social overhead from the growing population helped to sustain the regional boom.[3]

Subsequent interpretations of western economic growth have elaborated on the same ideas. Between 1939 and 1954, according to Harvey Perloff, California accounted for 30.5 percent of the nation's net upward shift in trade, service, and government employment, Texas for 15.9 percent, and seven other western states for 14.2 percent more. At the end of the 1960s, Brian Berry described the advantages for growth found in former hinterland regions around the ''outer rim'' of the United States: ''The changes have been cumulative, for regional growth within the context of the national pattern of heartland and hinterland has brought these regions to threshold sizes for internal production of a wide variety of goods and services at the very time that changes in the definition of urban resources made their rapid advance . . . possible. Hence the explosive metropolitan growth of the south, southwest and west, led by the tertiary and quarternary sectors.''[4] Analyses of specific metropolitan areas of rapid growth similarly stress their ability to attract new activities to supplant an older focus on production and processing of raw materials. Denver and Oklahoma City have thus emerged as regional centers for federal administration; Tulsa, Dallas, and Phoenix as light manufacturing centers; and Los Angeles, Seattle, and Wichita as specialized centers of heavy manufacturing.

The public image of the West in the boom years from the 1940s into the 1960s centered on two related themes. Wallace Stegner and Earl Pomeroy, among other writers, argued that the West was the most typically American part of the nation. In particular the Pacific Coast was ''pretty much like the rest of the United States, only more so,'' a region which expressed ''the national culture at its most energetic end.''[5] It was urban, opulent, energetic, mobile, and individualistic, a region of economic growth and openness to continual change which matched America's favorite self-image. From this idea of the West as America at the extreme it was a short step to the belief that the West embodied the national future. The region in the postwar era, said historian Gerald Nash, anticipated economic and social patterns by a generation. Neil Morgan similarly found ''accelerated symptoms of national trends'' and asserted that ''the West of today is very likely a close kin of the America of tomorrow.''[6]

Regional commentators during the boom years recognized a clear gradation in both social distinctiveness and prosperity in the region. If the West was the future of America, then California was the future of the West. Carey McWilliams in 1949 argued that California had a twenty-year headstart on the rest of the region that was tipping the national balance westward, and Harvey Perloff asserted that ''the enormous growth of the California labor force is one of the most striking phenomena in recent economic history.''[7] California itself seemed to be tipped toward the San Pedro Channel, for Los Angeles was ''the center of gravity in the westward tilt.'' To journalists, to economists, and to urban planners alike, Los Angeles was ''the ultimate city'' or ''the prototype of the supercity.'' It was a ''leading city'' in a literal sense, the great exception because it was anticipating the rest of the United States in degree of decentralization, dependence on the automobile, and fragmentation of metropolitan government. Even writers skeptical about the benefits of a California future agreed it was inevitable. Richard Elman typified the attitude, a bewildered New Yorker who traveled to the Los Angeles suburb of Comptom "with the thought in mind that this was the future . . . what lies in store for all the new suburbs of all the big cities of America."[8]

The 1940s likewise brought an upturn in the economy of the South. Through the 1920s and most of the 1930s, the scattered expansion of manufacturing had not prevented the South from growing poorer relative to the rest of the United States. Although the region shared only peripherally in the wartime expansion of defense plants, its nondurable manufacturing sector and supporting activities in trade, finance, and communications were the leading sources of growth from the forties through the sixties.[9] Where the proportion of southern employment in manufacturing was only 54 percent of that in the North and West in 1940, it was 72 percent by 1960.[10] One result was a steady narrowing of the southern lag in per capita income. Another was a 4 percent annual rate of urbanization which more than doubled the 1.7 percent rate for the North and Midwest. Figures on the relative urbanization of southern and nonsouthern population show the sharp increase after 1940 (Table 1.1).

The broadening of the southern economic base since mid-century has accentuated internal differences within the region. The metropolitan areas of the Atlantic states have benefitted from the diversification of manufacturing, with expanding production in chemicals, machinery, fabricated metal products, and other durable goods. The recreational boom in Florida, the emergence of regional market centers linked by air traffic, and the expansion of federal offices in Washington and in regional centers changed Virginia, Florida, and Louisiana into white-collar states by the 1960s. In these more prosperous areas, increasing wealth and its concentration in large metropolitan markets has allowed rapid growth in local service activities during the last decade. In contrast, Arkansas, Mississippi, Alabama, and Tennessee remained tied to agriculture and to manufacturing developed in a previous generation.[11]

During the first postwar decades, these economic changes were viewed in the framework established by the propagandists for the "New South" in the late nineteenth century. According to their argument, the South was a backward region whose first goal necessarily was to close the gap which separated it from the rest of the nation. Its great task, which it seemed finally to be addressing after 1940, was to

Table 1.1. *Percentage Urban Population in South and Non-South*

	South Percentage of Population Urban	Non-South Percentage of Population Urban	Proportion Southern/ Non-Southern Urban Percentages
1900	18.0	50.0	.36
1930	34.1	66.4	.51
1940	36.7	65.7	.56
1950	44.0	65.8	.67
1960	57.7	74.4	.78
1970	64.4	77.2	.83

work its way out from the twin burdens of race and poverty that had caused Franklin Roosevelt to term the region the nation's primary social problem, to cast off outmoded cultural traditions and political values tied to a rural society and accommodate itself to national patterns of behavior.[12]

The idea of a laggard South formed the central theme of most regional social science between 1940 and 1970, with scholars concerned about analyzing "the process of social development from backwardness to modernity." Urban historians, for example, made it their first concern to explain why and how the growth of southern cities has tailed behind those of the North and West.[13] Political science and political history, from V. O. Key's *Southern Politics* in 1949 to Bartley and Graham's recent volume on *The South and the Second Reconstruction*, are organized around the effects of the postwar "bulldozer revolution" on the political and cultural institutions designed to preserve one-party and one-race politics. The overriding concern in such studies is political discrimination by race, and their region of interest is defined by the former reach of slavery. Processes that have influenced political behavior throughout the entire Sunbelt—suburbanization, the rise of a new entrepreneurial class—are of interest only as they affect the South's unique political problems.[14] Sociologists similarly focused their attention on the ways in which the outside forces of federal law, federal money, and private investment were bringing accommodation to national norms by promoting urbanization, industrialization, and the expansion of a cosmopolitan middle class with national rather than sectional loyalties. Again, the common theme of their studies was to show that the South was closing the cultural gap and "moving toward a level of modernity comparable to the nation as a whole."[15]

The real extent of change in the South is somewhat obscured by the use of data aggregated by state. For example, the slow growth in total southern population resulted from a dual process of metropolitan expansion and rural abandonment. Even for the period from 1939 to 1954, the southeastern states combined below average growth in population with above average growth in total income and per capita income.[16] The census South taken as a whole (including Texas and Oklahoma) experienced a net outmigration of 1.6 million between 1950 and 1955 and a small net immigration of three hundred thousand between 1955 and 1960. In fact, the net figures were the sum of a massive movement of black residents out of the rural South and a substantial movement of whites from other regions into the cities of Texas, Louisiana, and the South Atlantic states. The same pattern lay behind the net immigration of seven hundred thousand recorded for the 1960s.[17] Similarly, per capita income data by states underestimated the prosperity of southern cities by averaging their affluent residents with impoverished farmers of rural counties.

The South's attractiveness for new residents increased markedly in the seventies. A total immigration of 2.6 million between 1970 and 1975 has made the census South the nation's dominant growth region as it outdistanced the West for the first time both in total population growth and net migrants. The reversal is even more dramatic if the South is taken without the boom state of Florida. Such a truncated region shows an outmigration of 2.9 million in the 1950s and seven hundred thousand in the 1960s followed by a net gain of 1.2 million from 1970 to 1975. Because there has been a net positive movement of white migrants to many southern states since the 1950s, it is clear that much of the shift has involved decisions by blacks to stay or return to the South.[18]

The awareness of rapid growth in the 1970s has buoyed the southern self-image and brought changes in southern attitudes which have impressed a variety of observers. While Boston seethes with the problems of school integration and New York balks at racial balance in teacher assignments, many southerners feel a new pride in the region's racial harmony and its attractiveness to blacks. Equally there is an excited hope that many southern cities may be able to leap directly into post-industrial economic and urban patterns. Atlanta, with a burgeoning communications complex, high-rise downtown, and the nation's second busiest airport, is often cited as a symbol of the new urban America. So is the formless urban mass in central Florida that stretches between Cape Canaveral and Disney World or the 150-mile city that marches behind the Atlantic beaches from Miami to Palm Beach. Perhaps because of this new enthusiasm about the region's future, it is southern politicians who have assumed much of the defense against the Frostbelt political coalition. In particular, governors from southeastern and south central states have been most active in countering charges of unfair treatment, using data supplied by the Southern Growth Policies Board and organizing congressional caucuses to defend sunbelt interests.[19]

Rapid growth in the South during the last decade and the reversal of that region's historic outflow of population was balanced during the 1970s by a slowing of growth in the West. From 1950 to 1965, net migration into California averaged 320,000 annually; thereafter it fell abruptly to an average of only 90,000 per year for the 1965–75 decade. The city of Los Angeles actually lost 84,000 residents between 1970 and 1975 and Los Angeles County lost population for the first time in 1973. The surrounding metropolitan counties in southern California continue to grow at a reduced rate, and the period 1969–74 saw a decline in the share of United States personal income generated in metropolitan areas on the West Coast. Indeed, business commentators argue that rising labor costs, high tax levels, and progressive environmental legislation have now made California an undesirable location for new manufacturing plants. During the same period, however, other parts of the West have become increasingly attractive to new residents, particularly Colorado and metropolitan Denver, Oregon and metropolitan Portland, and Arizona and metropolitan Phoenix. As a result, net migration to the other western states passed the California total for the first time in the late sixties, with a total figure for 1965–75 greater than California's by 700,000.[20]

The retardation of population growth in Southern California in the mid-sixties coincided with changing local attitudes about the effects of the postwar westward tilt. Three books by Californians set the tone with bitter denunciations of the social and environmental effects of the boom years: Raymond Dasmann's *The Destruction of California* (1965), Richard Lilliard's *Eden in Jeopardy* (1966), and Curt Gentry's *The Last Days of the Late, Great State of California* (1968). By the early seventies, anti-California feelings had surfaced elsewhere in the West as local residents feared the destruction of their own amenities by California refugees. Denver bumper stickers in 1972 admonished "Don't Californicate Colorado," while Oregon's notorious antigrowth campaign with its emphasis on endless rain aimed to discourage migrants from the land of sunshine. Even in southern California itself, Mayor Pete Wilson of San Diego campaigned in 1971 with promises to fight off "Los Angelization."[21]

The overall result of economic growth in the last generation has thus been the convergence of South and West. They are no longer exceptions to the American standard—a charmed golden West, a South of massive resistance and rural starvation. Each region has moved toward the national average in per capita income while maintaining rapid population growth. Figures for 1969–74, the period in which Americans discovered the Sunbelt, show per capita income in the metropolitan areas of the South increasing from 93 to 98 percent of the national average, in those of the Plains-Rockies region inching upward from 97 to 98 percent, and in those of the Pacific Coast falling from 116 to 112 percent.[22] These data for the 1970s confirm the long-term trends in income by state noted by Perloff and summarized in Table 1.2. Without discounting differences among individual states, Table 1.2 indicates that the Southeast enjoyed a remarkable improvement in relative standing during the 1940s, slowed in its growth during the 1950s, and has again boomed in the 1960s and 1970s. The Mid-South region in the lower Mississippi Valley experienced strong and steady growth for the entire period while starting from a position of greater poverty. Most of the states of the southern Great Plains and Rockies made impressive gains in the 1940s and have since inched upward or held steady, while the Pacific Coast has lost much of its onetime income advantage over the rest of the nation.

The importance of the "amenities economy" for the entire rim region which arcs along the southern and western edge of the United States from Virginia to Washington is shown by its high dependence on governmental employment and private services. As Table 1.3 indicates, the South and West exceed the national average in proportion of population working at all levels of government and in the proportion employed as federal civilian workers. If the South is broken into South Atlantic and Mid-South sections, the importance of public employment in the Southeast becomes even more clear.

Table 1.2. *Per Capita Personal Income of Southern and Western States as Percentage of National Per Capita Income*

	1940	1950	1960	1970	1974
Delaware	172.8	142.5	125.1	113.7	115.7
Maryland	119.8	107.1	105.6	108.6	109.1
District of Columbia	202.4	148.4	136.4	135.3	130.2
Virginia	77.3	82.1	83.1	92.6	97.9
North Carolina	54.6	69.3	70.3	81.6	84.7
South Carolina	50.8	59.7	61.9	75.1	79.1
Georgia	56.8	69.1	73.9	84.1	87.2
Florida	85.6	85.6	87.8	93.6	99.3
Alabama	47.0	58.8	68.4	73.9	77.3
Mississippi	36.5	50.5	54.4	65.8	69.8
Tennessee	56.4	66.4	69.7	78.2	83.5
Kentucky	53.5	65.5	71.3	78.7	81.5
Arkansas	42.9	55.1	62.1	72.8	77.1
Louisiana	60.8	74.9	75.0	77.8	80.6
Texas	72.6	90.2	87.1	90.7	91.0
Oklahoma	61.8	76.4	84.2	85.0	84.2
Kansas	71.4	96.4	97.4	97.4	101.0
Colorado	91.9	99.4	102.5	97.4	101.2
New Mexico	63.1	78.7	85.1	79.1	76.0
Arizona	84.8	88.9	91.6	92.1	94.3
Utah	81.4	87.5	88.9	81.9	82.0
Nevada	150.3	134.8	128.5	112.9	110.7
California	141.0	123.8	122.0	113.3	110.7
Oregon	104.4	108.3	100.3	93.7	97.0
Washington	110.6	111.9	105.6	102.0	104.8

Sources: For 1940–70 data: *Historical Statistics of the United States*. For 1974 data: U.S. Department of Commerce, Bureau of Economic Analysis, Local Area Personal Income, 1969–74.

Information on State Economic Areas shows a similar economic pattern. As defined by the Bureau of Economic Analysis in the Department of Commerce, the United States is divided into 173 State Economic Areas, each of which consists of an SMSA or similar trade center and the surrounding counties with close economic ties; State Economic areas do not divide SMSAs or counties but may cross state lines. As of 1973, thirty-one of the thirty-four State Economic Areas

Table 1.3. *Employment and Population by Region (in 1,000s), 1975*

	United States	West	South	Southeast	Mid-South
Population	213,121	52,827	51,363	31,912	19,451
All government employment	14,841	4,011	3,744	2,491	1,253
Percentage of population	7.0	7.6	7.3	7.8	6.4
Federal civilian employment	2,744	800	926	709	217
Percentage of population	1.3	1.5	1.8	2.2	1.1

Source: U.S. Bureau of the Census, Series GE 75, No. 1, Public Employment in 1975.

Note: West includes Pacific and Mountain states, Texas, Oklahoma; Southeast includes South Atlantic states less West Virginia; Mid-South includes Alabama, Mississippi, Tennessee, Kentucky, Arkansas, and Louisiana.

most highly reliant on governmental activity were located in the South or West (including Alaska and Hawaii). Similarly, seventeen of the twenty-one State Economic Areas dependent on services were found in the same broad region. In contrast, fewer than half of the areas chiefly dependent on manufacturing were found in the South or West (thirty-five of seventy-six areas). Three of these thirty-five State Economic Areas were in the Pacific Northwest, five along the eastern borders of Texas and Oklahoma, and the remaining twenty-seven east of the Mississippi in Piedmont and Appalachian regions that industrialized in the first half of the twentieth century.[23]

Although convenience and common perception suggest the definition of the Sunbelt in terms of "South" and "West," the Sunbelt in fact is both less and more than these traditional regions. Because only parts of the West and parts of the South have experienced the types of growth seen as characteristic of the Sunbelt, more detailed examination of the extent and nature of the new region requires attention to smaller geographic areas. At the same time, the regional divisions in use by the Bureau of the Census conceal the prosperity of the Sunbelt by cutting across the north-south divide between faster and slower growing areas. The Pacific division thus includes both California and Oregon, the Mountain division both Arizona and Montana, the West

South Central division both Texas and Arkansas, and the South Atlantic division both Florida and West Virginia. Studies that attempt to determine whether the Sunbelt is myth or reality by analyzing data for such census regions build in a bias against the concept by lumping historically stagnant states with those more likely to show postwar booms.[24]

More precise analysis of the Sunbelt can start with state-level growth data. Economists and demographers in the 1950s and 1960s, who were able to draw on information for one or two growth decades after Pearl Harbor, thus noted the outstanding economic performance of California, Texas, and Florida but saw their booms as special cases within the broad historic patterns of western regional development and southern regional poverty. Indeed, the classic study of *Regions, Resources and Economic Growth* argued that the bases of growth in Florida and California were fundamentally different and asserted that Texas offered "further contrast to the two cases already examined." The impressive prosperity and growth of the eastern Great Lakes states and northeastern suburban states also helped to conceal the emergence of a special growth region across the southern United States.[25]

The availability of data for the 1960s and for 1970–75 made the long-term trends of the postwar era more evident. The western states of California, Nevada, Utah, Colorado, Arizona, and Texas and the southeastern states of Florida, Virginia, and Delaware had population growth rates that exceeded the national average in all four of the periods 1940–50, 1950–60, 1960–70, and 1970–75. Seven other states exceeded the national average in three of the four periods: Oregon in all but the 1950s; New Mexico in all but the 1960s; Washington, Maryland, New Jersey, Connecticut, and Michigan in all but the 1970s. Taken together, these states cover a Texas-Pacific triangle angled toward the southwest, the northern and southern ends of the South Atlantic coast in Florida and Virginia-Maryland-Delaware, and scattered parts of the northeast. Ohio and Indiana, which surpassed the national growth rate from 1940 to 1960, have since decelerated, while Georgia, Vermont, and New Hampshire have grown more rapidly than the nation since 1960.

A similar regional pattern emerges from the examination of growth rates of metropolitan population by states. In order to minimize the impact of the definition of new SMSAs on the percentage increase, the figures used are the 1940–50 population increase within 1950 SMSA boundaries, the 1950–60 increase within 1960 boundaries, and the 1960–70 increase within 1970 boundaries. Two sets of states surpassed the national rate of metropolitan growth in all three decades or in the 1940s and 1960s: Washington, Oregon, California, Utah, Colorado, Arizona, New Mexico, Texas, and Oklahoma in the Pacific-Southwest triangle; and Florida, Georgia, South Carolina, North Carolina, Virginia, Maryland, and Delaware along the South Atlantic coast. These two regions of above average metropolitan growth fill in more solidly the two regions suggested by total state growth data. In particular, they add the sunbelt states of Oklahoma, South Carolina, and North Carolina in which massive metropolitan growth was counterbalanced in aggregate population data by rural depopulation.

The central South's record of metropolitan expansion is scarcely more impressive than that of its total population growth. Tennessee, Kentucky, Arkansas, and Alabama exceeded the national metropolitan growth rate in only one or in none of the three decades. Mississippi and Louisiana exceeded the national average in the 1940s and 1950s but slowed in the 1960s. In Mississippi the high metropolitan growth rate from 1940 and 1960 was the result of a very small initial base of metropolitan population. In Louisiana the rate was largely produced by the prosperity of the single metropolis of Baton Rouge which outdistanced the state's other cities.

An alternative method to describe the geographic concentration of rapid urban growth areas is to examine the location of the one hundred SMSAs that had populations of three hundred thousand or more in 1970. Tables 1.4 and 1.5 confirm the distinction between high-growth zones in the ten-state West-Southwest region and in a Southeast consisting of seven states and the District of Columbia and a low-growth zone in a Middle South of six states. For all one hundred SMSAs, the median ratio of 1970 to 1940 population is 2.16. For the same period, the ratio for total metropolitan population in the United States is 1.94. (The ratios use 1970 population in 1970 SMSA boundaries and 1940 population in 1950 metropolitan area boundaries, since metropolitan areas were not defined in 1940.) The West and Southwest contain forty of the forty-nine SMSAs with growth ratios above the median figure and forty-four of the sixty-one SMSAs above the aggregate national ratio. Indeed, none of the large SMSAs of Southeast or West fell below the United States average. In contrast, 56 percent of the large SMSAs in the Mid-South and the Mid-West and 88 percent in the Northeast fell

Table 1.4. *1970/1940 Population Ratios by Region in 100 SMSAs with 1970 Population in Excess of 300,000*

	1970/1940 population ratio		
	Below 1.94	1.94 to 2.16	Above 2.16
Northeast	21	2	1
Mid-West	13	3	7
Mid-South	5	3	1
Southeast	0	2	15
West	0	2	25

below the United States ratio. The contrast is even sharper if Mobile (2.65 ratio) is placed in the Southeast rather than Mid-South and if Wichita (2.86 ratio) is placed in the West rather than Mid-West.

Recent census data do suggest that it may be necessary to widen the definition of the Sunbelt in the last quarter of the century. As measured by absolute population increases, the Sunbelt Southeast and Sunbelt West are still absorbing the bulk of new growth. Between 1970 and 1975, for example, all twenty-seven of the SMSAs that enjoyed net immigration of twenty-five thousand or more were located in the South Atlantic or western states.[26] In relative terms, however, metropolitan growth rates higher than the national average from 1970 to 1974 were recorded not only in the six states of the Sunbelt Southeast and ten states of the Sunbelt West but also in the Mid-South states of Tennessee, Louisiana, Arkansas, and Mississippi. The new vitality was especially marked in the hill country of northern Mississippi, in the city and hinterland of Memphis, and in the Ozark Mountains of Arkansas.

A historical definition of Sunbelt that recognizes state and metropolitan population growth patterns from 1940 to 1970 clearly results in the delineation of two distinct regions. In terms of state boundaries, the Sunbelt consists of a Sunbelt-Southeast running from Delaware to Florida along the Atlantic Coast and a Sunbelt-West of Texas, Oklahoma, Colorado, New Mexico, Arizona, Utah, Nevada, California, Oregon, and Washington. This definition, of course, does not follow the transcontinental line along the thirty-sixth parallel commonly used by journalists. It extends northward to include the environs of Chesapeake Bay, the Columbia Basin, and Puget Sound, which are major centers for outdoor recreation, but omits the cotton states of the lower Mississippi Valley.

Table 1.5. *1970/1940 Population Ratios by City for 100 SMSAs*

	West		Southeast		Mid-South	
	Anaheim	10.83				
	San Bernardino	7.10				
	San Jose	6.09				
	Oxnard	5.37				
	Phoenix	5.20				
	Tucson	4.84				
	Sacramento	4.73				
	San Diego	4.70				
	Albuquerque	4.62				
	Dallas	3.90	Fort Lauderdale	15.50		
	Houston	3.75	Orlando	6.11		
	Fort Worth	3.39	Miami	4.73		
	Denver	3.01	West Palm Beach	4.36		
	Seattle	2.84	Tampa	3.72		
	El Paso	2.74	Columbia	3.08		
	Salt Lake City	2.63	Washington	2.96		
	Oklahoma City	2.63	Charlotte	2.69		
	San Antonio	2.56	Atlanta	2.68		
	Los Angeles	2.52	Norfolk	2.63		
	Tulsa	2.47	Jacksonville	2.52		
	Honolulu	2.44	Charleston	2.51		
	Bakersfield	2.44	Baltimore	2.42		
	Fresno	2.31	Wilmington	2.24		
	Tacoma	2.26	Greenville	2.19		
median,	Beaumont	2.18	Greensboro	2.16	Mobile	2.
100 large SMSAs						
					Memphis	2.
	SF-Oakland	2.13			Nashville	2.
average,	Portland	2.01	Richmond	1.95	Little Rock	2.
all SMSAs						
					New Orleans	1.
					Louisville	1.
					Knoxville	1.
					Birmingham	1.
					Chattanooga	1.

Mid-West		Northeast	
sing	2.88		
hita	2.68		
ton	2.57		
anapolis	2.41		
umbus	2.41		
nd Rapids	2.19		
t	2.18	Hartford	2.24
y	2.16	Syracuse	2.16
edo	2.01		
on	2.00	Rochester	2.02
n-St Paul	1.93	Paterson	1.89
waukee	1.83	York	1.85
sas City	1.83	Binghamton	1.82
enport	1.83	Bridgeport	1.78
roit	1.77	Harrisburg	1.63
cinnati	1.76	Trenton	1.54
aha	1.66	Albany	1.54
ouis	1.65	Philadelphia	1.51
veland	1.63	New Haven	1.48
ria	1.61	Springfield	1.45
ton	1.58	Buffalo	1.41
cago	1.54	Allentown	1.37
ngstown	1.13	Worcester	1.36
		Providence	1.35
		New York	1.32
		Utica	1.29
		Boston	1.26
		Newark	1.17
		Pittsburgh	1.15
		Jersey City	.93
		Wilkes-Barre	.77

Fast-Growing Metropolitan Areas: 1940–1970

The American Sunbelt: 1940–1975

However, such regions do coincide roughly with geographical features and with spheres of metropolitan dominance. Overall, it has been the warm coasts of the Pacific, the Gulf of Mexico, and the Atlantic Ocean southward from Chesapeake Bay that have exerted the strongest pull on the American population. The Sunbelt-Southeast can be considered as the South Atlantic slope, for all its fast-growing metropolitan areas lie southeastward of a line drawn parallel to the Appalachian front from the Mason-Dixon Line to the Gulf of Mexico. Indeed, this line recognizes growth differences within Alabama by splitting Mobile from the less prosperous cities upstate. Analyses of metropolitan influence by Vance and Smith in 1954 and by Duncan in 1960 indicate that this South Atlantic region matches fairly closely the commercial and financial sphere of Atlanta in Georgia, Florida, South Carolina, and Alabama and of Richmond and Baltimore in North Carolina and the Chesapeake Bay states.[27]

The Sunbelt-West embraces two geographic subregions. The South Plains subregion is delimited to the south and west by the Rio Grande, on the east and north by a line north-northwest from the mouth of the Sabine River, skirting the edge of the Ouachita-Ozark mountains, and bending west along the fortieth parallel. Such borders include Oklahoma and Texas cities, the plains fringe cities of Albuquerque and Denver, and the prosperous south Kansas city of Wichita, all of which have historically had strong ties to Dallas merchants and bankers created through the growth of ranching, energy production, and real estate investment. With the exception of geographically isolated Salt Lake City, the remaining metropolitan centers of the Sunbelt-West lie on the Pacific slope in Washington, Oregon, California, and southern Arizona. From the 1850s to the 1960s, commercial and financial activity in this far western area has focused on the metropolis of San Francisco.[28]

The definition of Sunbelt suggested above obviously places more importance on the census than on sunshine. If "Sunbelt" is anything more than a striking metaphor, the region has to be described in uniform and objective terms. It is not enough to describe the Sunbelt by pointing to Phoenix or Miami and arguing that the larger region includes those areas which resemble such extreme cases. Nor is it any better to take the alternative frequent among contemporary politicians and assume that "Sunbelt" is simply a new terminology for the familiar and comfortable political regions of South and West. Instead, the Sunbelt in historical perspective is a pair of regions oriented toward the southeastern and southwestern corners of the United States that have shared similarities of economic development and demographic change since the 1940s. What remains to be explored in the following chapters is the extent to which this common growth experience over the last generation has produced common patterns and problems in local governmental efforts to direct these powerful forces of metropolitan growth.

Chapter 2

The Growth of the Sunbelt Cities

Houston is the new symbol of the American future. At the start of the seventies, space-age corporations discovered its possibilities as a headquarters city and *Business Week* and *Fortune* gave star billing to its management boom. By mid-decade, it seemed to many observers to epitomize the new Sunbelt. Its free-form growth uninhibited by zoning, its single-function downtown, its fabled political conservatism, and its business spinoffs from the NASA space center suggested it as the logical center for the emergent region. Like the state of Texas, Houston was neither precisely southern nor precisely western, but rather typical of what was new in both South and West—a "Soulless Los Angeles of the Gulf Coast."[1]

During the last few years in particular, national journalists have found Houston a convenient place to seek the essential character of the Sunbelt. The *New York Times* in its 1976 series devoted an entire article to "Houston: Booming Even by Sunbelt Standards." According to Lynn Ashby in the *Saturday Review*, it is "the last word in American cities . . . rushing hell-bent into tomorrow without much thought about the day after," while a sober academic study by the Urban Institute took it as typical of fast-growing metropolitan areas. Ada Louise Huxtable summed up the new consensus: "Houston is the place that scholars flock to for the purpose of seeing what modern civilization has wrought. Correctly perceived and publicized as freeway city, mobile city, space city, strip city, and speculator city, it is being dissected by architects and urban historians as a case study in new forms and functions. . . . Houston is *the* city of the second half of the 20th century."[2]

Houston is the latest in a long series of "shock cities" which have symbolized the pace, excitement, and human costs of economic change for a decade or a generation. In the 1830s and 1840s, the world's shock city was Manchester, the setting for *Hard Times* and the source of data on *The Condition of the Working Class in England in 1844*. In the 1890s Chicago was the shock city that seemed to be ushering in a dubious new century. As the epitome of American industrial urbanization, it was a sprawling encampment of barbarians to a visitor like Rudyard Kipling, an amalgam of social misery and new opportunities for novelists and reformers from W. T. Stead and Upton Sinclair to Jane Addams and Theodore Dreiser.[3]

Contemporary imagery that seizes on Houston (or Los Angeles, Phoenix, Atlanta, or Miami) to represent the emerging Sunbelt recognizes the basic fact that southern and western growth in recent decades has been metropolitan growth. Indeed, data prepared by Brian Berry and John Kasarda indicate that the 1930s was the decade in which the percentage share of national metropolitan population growth attributable jointly to the South and West jumped from the 20 to 40 percent range to a plateau of 55 to 60 percent maintained for the 1940s, 1950s, and 1960s. During the thirties the gain in percentage share was explained by the fact that the numerical increment in metropolitan population fell more sharply in the North and Middle West than in the South and West. Since 1940, however, the latter regions have held their high percentage share because of huge increases in the absolute additions to their metropolitan populations.[4] Figures on the increases in total metropolitan population between 1940 and 1970 provide an even more vivid summary of major city and suburban growth, with gains of 13,480,000 in California, 5,808,000 in Texas, 3,837,000 in Florida, and 2,078,000 in Virginia.

Beyond summarizing the importance of metropolitan growth, however, focus on a Sunbelt shock city begs the question of representativeness. Even if most Sunbelt residents and almost all new migrants are urban or suburban, it is necessary to develop precise data to determine whether their lives match the journalistic image. The present chapter therefore undertakes to explore characteristics of the economic, social, and governmental environment of sunbelt SMSAs. For example, what is the degree of similarity among the metropolitan areas of the South and West? Do mobile families who move from Marietta, Georgia, to Arlington, Texas, or from Tempe, Arizona, to Bellevue, Washington, in fact change anything more than license plates and landscapes? Can they expect the same range of job opportunities, the same sorts of neighbors, and the same structures for political activity? Another consideration is whether the SMSAs of the Sunbelt differ significantly from those of the Northeast and Middle West in these economic, social, and political traits.

Within the context of these summary data on the metropolitan environment of the Sunbelt, the chapter also sketches the growth of the five metropolises that have been chosen for detailed political analysis. As the discussion indicates, the cities are representative rather than exceptional of sunbelt SMSAs. Most directly, they represent different geographical regions—Norfolk and Atlanta the Southeast, San Antonio both the Gulf South and the Southwest, Denver the Mountain states, and Portland the West Coast. None of the five is a supercity in the class of Washington or Los Angeles, but each is a freestanding metropolitan area that has developed an extensive independent hinterland. Their growth rates for 1940–70 were substantially above the national average but in the middle range for the Sunbelt. The 1970 population figures place Atlanta ninth among southern and western SMSAs (1,390,000), Denver twelfth (1,228,000), Portland seventeenth (1,009,000), San Antonio nineteenth (864,000), and Norfolk twenty-fifth (681,000).

In broad outline, the common element in the growth histories of Norfolk, Atlanta, San Antonio, Denver, and Portland from the 1930s to the 1970s is the gradual achievement of metropolitan independence. The growing prosperity of the Sunbelt has been tied to the development of a set of cities with aspirations to regional leadership. In each case, economic diversification has sustained population growth by substituting local sources for goods and services that were previously imported. At the same time, differences in the activities that are performed for regional and national markets have influenced the relative success of these and other sunbelt cities when measured against each other. Southern and western cities that have retained a dependence on military bases or on trade and processing of regional resources have grown more slowly in recent years than those that have developed as headquarters for public and private administration, business services, and the information industries. Among the five cities, it was Atlanta that made the greatest contribution to the change in location of metropolitan growth in the 1930s. Its annual population increment of ten thousand and overall growth of 20 percent for the decade (Table 2.1) reflected in part its enthusiastic self-promotion during the booming twenties.[5] The other cities had much more conservative leadership and less exuberant economies during the interwar years. Norfolk failed to find a replacement for naval activity and shipbuilding after demobilization and the arms limitation agreement of 1922.[6] Portland gained a reputation in the same years as a "spinster city" that took its cue from Calvin Coolidge, Denver as a "city prematurely grey," and San Antonio as a stodgy "mother-in-law of the army." Local bankers and capitalists were largely interested in finding a safe haven for money earned by a previous generation in south Texas ranching and farming, Colorado mining, or trade in Oregon timber and wheat.[7] As a result, San Antonio, Denver, Portland, and Norfolk each grew by only 10 to 13 percent during the 1930s with annual increments of three to five thousand residents.

Despite their differing careers in the twenties and thirties, four of the five cities showed signs of economic and political vitality at the end of the depression decade. San Antonio's rambunctious new Mayor Maury Maverick forced attention in 1939 and 1940 to slums and public health problems that the local elite had preferred to ignore. The election of Mayor William Hartsfield in 1937 similarly promised efforts in Atlanta to modernize an outmoded structure of local government. More active businessmen in Portland looked with interest at the possibilities of cheap electric power from Bonneville Dam, which became available in 1940. Norfolk enjoyed the first stages of economic recovery after the passage of the Naval Expansion Act in 1938.

Mobilization for national defense in 1940 and 1941 confirmed the arrival of a new era in metropolitan growth. Rates of population increase for the 1940s ranged from 30 percent to 65 percent and the annual population increment between sixteen and twenty thousand. The story was the same as in Mobile and Charleston, Fort Worth and Wichita, San Diego, Albuquerque, Seattle, San Francisco, and smaller sunbelt cities. The construction of defense plants and expansion of military bases before and after Pearl Harbor raised employment, shattered the relative calm of the thirties, and opened further opportunities for economic growth. The influx of war workers and military personnel in turn broadened local perspectives and stirred the complacency of entrenched civic and business elites.

Norfolk was one of the country's prime examples of the impact of rearmament and war, especially since its convenience to Washington and New York attracted congressional investigators and roving journalists. Population and employment in the Norfolk area in fact expanded

Table 2.1. *Population Growth in Metropolitan Atlanta, Denver, Norfolk, Portland, and San Antonio*

	Atlanta	Denver	Norfolk
1930	462,384	395,048	262,436
1940	558,838	445,206	293,041
Percentage Increase 1930–40	20.9	12.7	11.7
1950	726,989	612,128	483,777
Percentage Increase 1940–50	30.1	37.5	65.1
1960	1,017,188	929,383	622,482
Percentage Increase 1950–60	39.9	51.8	28.7
1970	1,390,164	1,228,529	725,624
Percentage Increase 1960–70	36.7	32.2	16.6
1975	1,532,500	1,474,000	763,000
Percentage Increase 1970–75	10.2	20.0	5.2

Note: Atlanta = Fulton, DeKalb, Cobb, Clayton, and Gwinnett counties.
Denver = City and County of Denver, counties of Adams, Arapahoe, Boulder, and Jefferson.
Norfolk = Cities of Norfolk, Portsmouth, Chesapeake, Suffolk, and Virginia Beach.
Portland = Multnomah, Clackamas, Clark, and Washington counties.
San Antonio = Bexar and Guadalupe counties.

in several waves which spread new growth over the entire war period. With the initial necessity of enlarging military bases, construction jobs were most numerous in 1940–42 with a top figure of 34,000 workers. Employment in the Norfolk Naval Shipyard in the twin city of Portsmouth climbed more slowly to a peak of more than 40,000 in 1943 and 1944. The Newport News Shipbuilding and Dry Dock Company, a ferry ride away on the north side of the James River, accounted for 30,000 additional workers. To the surprise of local leaders, who had expected a local slump to match that of 1919–20, direct military employment continued to grow through the entire decade under the impetus of the cold war. Between 1940 and 1950, civilian government employment in metropolitan Norfolk grew from 23,610 to 48,856 and military employment from 6,425 to 60,532.[8] Total metropolitan population shot upward by more than 100,000 between 1940 and 1943,

Portland	San Antonio
455,037	321,458
501,275	363,772
10.2	13.2
704,829	525,852
40.6	44.6
821,897	716,168
16.6	36.2
1,007,130	864,014
22.5	20.6
1,081,000	935,500
7.3	8.3

held at around 400,000 in 1944 and 1945, and climbed by another 80,000 in the second half of the decade.[9]

The impact of mobilization was equally spectacular in Portland. Within the space of two years, Henry J. Kaiser created a new shipbuilding industry that accounted for defense contracts totaling $2.4 billion. The Kaiser Company Portland, the Kaiser Company Vancouver, the Oregon Shipbuilding Company, and several independent firms along the Willamette and Columbia rivers employed nearly 120,000 workers at their peak production, drawing tens of thousands of new migrants from the depressed states of the northern Rockies and northern Plains.[10] Since more than half of the workers hoped to remain after the war, local leaders worried particularly about postwar unemployment and relief burdens.[11] To their surprise, the metropolitan area was able to hold three-quarters of its new population with postwar diversification of manufacturing, a growing aluminum industry, and expanded trade in grain and lumber.[12]

Although Portland and Norfolk received greater attention in national publications, San Antonio and Denver nearly matched their metropolitan growth. Much of the growth of the Rocky Mountain metropolis was based on a broad mixture of defense activities, including the expansion of Lowry Field and Fitzsimmons Hospital, the establishment of the Rocky Mountain Arsenal and Denver Ordnance Plant, and military orders for rubber goods and fabricated metals.[13] With a smaller manufacturing base, San Antonio's growth was dependent on the expansion of military payrolls at Fort Sam Houston, Randolph Air Force Base, and Lackland Air Force Base and the employment of thirty thousand civilians at the Kelly Field aircraft repair facilities and other bases. Viewed from a longer perspective, the availability of federal jobs was particularly important for opening an avenue for the integration of Mexican-Americans into the urban economy.[14]

Since 1950, Denver has grown most rapidly of the five metropolitan areas, with an average annual gain of over thirty thousand in the 1950s and 1960s and forty-nine thousand in the early 1970s. The city's amenities of climate and scenery have brought a tenfold growth in the tourist business and have attracted scientific research establishments and high-technology manufacturing. The most spectacular example was the decision of Martin Marietta Aerospace Corporation in 1956 to build a plant for Titan missiles in the suburb of Littleton, in part because the location would ease the recruitment of highly trained scientific and engineering personnel. Hewlett-Packard, IBM, Honeywell, Sundstrand, Ball Brothers Research, Johns Manville, and Beech Aircraft are some of the other high-technology firms attracted by life near the mountains. From defense industries and science-oriented corporations, it is a short step to the research divisions of the University of Denver and University of Colorado and to federal research agencies —the National Bureau of Standards, the National Oceanic and Atmospheric Administration, and the National Center for Atmospheric Research.

At the same time that Denver followed Massachusetts and the San Francisco Bay area in the development of a science-based economy, it remained a white-collar as well as a lab-coat city. Continuing development as a regional center for federal agencies has been matched by the growth of private business headquarters that occupy office space created in a downtown building boom of the fifties and early sixties.[15] Its centrality to the High Plains and Rockies has also supported its continuing importance as a commercial and financial center. The energy boom brought a surge of forty thousand new residents a year in the second half of the seventies and turned fast growth into explosive growth. Demand for office space in a dozen new towers has turned the central business district into what Calvin Trillin calls a "rookery for the Twenty Story Crane." Imposing office parks in the south suburbs now compete for the same market.[16]

Atlanta has almost matched Denver with growth that accelerated steadily through the forties, fifties, and sixties. During the war years, greater Atlanta gained fifty thousand residents with the expansion of Fort McPherson and the location of a huge plant for B-29s in nearby Marietta.[17] However, its postwar growth rate more than matched that of the war years as the city and the Southeast passed the size threshold to support automobile assembly facilities and scores of other branch plants for the regional market.[18] Beyond the diversification of manufacturing, Atlanta's sustained prosperity has built on its historic role as a center for distribution, finance, and services. Its boosters can cite thousands of warehousing and wholesaling operations, dozens of regional offices for federal agencies, and a Federal Reserve bank. Its network of rail lines is complemented by the busiest airport south of New York and three interstate highways that make it the hub for southeastern trucking. Even though speculative overbuilding in downtown office space and worries over the transition to a black mayor brought a short-term crisis in 1974–75, the annual population increment of twenty-eight thousand for the early seventies matched that for the fifties and fell only a little short of the extraordinary sixties. The most recent years have seen a resurgence of the real estate market and a renewed attractiveness for corporate offices.[19]

Portland, in contrast with Denver and Atlanta, experienced its slowest postwar growth in the 1950s. Although it retained its role as the commercial center for Oregon, Idaho, and eastern Washington, it failed to expand the manufacturing base of the 1940s. In response, SMSA per capita income dropped from 113 to 114 percent of the United States average in the fifties to 99 percent in 1965. During the last dozen years the trend has again reversed. The continuing importance of agricultural exports, the attractiveness of Oregon in an age of ecological awareness, and the employment of twenty thousand by Tektronix Corporation brought relative success in the longstanding competition with Seattle during that city's Boeing depression. Annual population growth for the metropolitan area averaged twenty-five thousand in the years around 1970 and per capita income climbed to 109 percent of the national level by 1974.[20] In the later seventies, the area's image of livability has helped to attract branches of several major electronics firms and an aggressive Port of Portland has continued to expand the city's commercial functions.

Postwar prosperity in Portland and Denver has been closely tied to the fortunes of extensive agricultural and mining hinterlands, for both cities are major regional centers. San Antonio and Norfolk in comparison are clearly "second cities" that operate in their regions within the commercial and financial shadows of Dallas and Richmond. Typically in both cities, the growth of local finance and business services was sufficient in the 1970s to support the expansion of suburban office space, but the lack of regional dominance left a limited demand for similar space downtown. At the same time, however, Norfolk and San Antonio are among the nation's primary centers for the industry of national defense. Growth in San Antonio was thus particularly rapid during the Korean and Indo-Chinese mobilizations of the early fifties and later sixties, whereas 1955–64 and the middle 1970s showed a somewhat slower pace of economic expansion and higher unemployment. Indeed, the wartime boom of the sixties and the excitement of HemisFair in 1968 helped to conceal otherwise serious weaknesses in the local economy. San Antonio has developed as a tourist city and a medical center, but it has failed to establish extensive wholesaling or a major manufacturing base and has had a slow decline in its rate of population growth.[21]

In the other military center, Norfolk, the economic structure filled in around the basic defense industries after 1950. With the number of jobs on the military bases, at the Naval Shipyard, and in shipping relatively stable, above-average employment growth has come in finance, construction, retailing, education, and other services. Despite active development efforts, however, the Norfolk area has shared only slightly in the growth of manufacturing characteristic of the sunbelt South. As in San Antonio, one result of patchy economic growth has been a slow decline in the rate of population increase of the metropolitan area. More positively, the expansion of tertiary activities (trade, services, and government) and diversification of the local economy has allowed a slow rise in relative per capita income. Where the area's per capita income ranked 192 among SMSAs in 1959 after a period of relative decline, it had moved to 158 by 1973. Even so, Norfolk remains characteristically a lower-middle-class metropolis with few major sources of wealth under local control. Indeed, by 1977 figures, military and civilian employees of the Navy Department constituted one-third of the total jobs in the metropolitan area. Direct and indirect effects of the navy payroll and purchases accounted for more than half of the area's income.[22]

Comparative analysis of quantitative data on the dominant industries of sunbelt cities confirms the existence of this basic division between two types of metropolitan economy by the end of the wartime decade. Using 1950 census data, Otis Duncan and his coworkers grouped fifty major American cities into categories by economic function. Denver, Portland, Atlanta, Seattle, San Francisco, Dallas, and Kansas City were categorized as regional metropolises because of their substantial commercial and financial activity. Ten other southern and western cities were "regional capitals," metropolitan centers of more limited hinterland and lesser financial importance than Atlanta, Denver, or Portland but with basically similar functions within their particular regions. In contrast, San Antonio and Norfolk as military centers were classed as "special cases" along with the other government cities of Washington, Knoxville, and San Diego and the resort cities of Tampa, Miami, and Phoenix.[23]

Growth during the next quarter century maintained these differences among the four metropolitan economies. Data on sources of personal income for 1975 confirm the earlier finding that the five cities are representative of the major economic types in the urban South and West. Use of the location quotient allows the determination of economic activities in which a particular SMSA specializes. Since the location quotient is calculated by dividing the proportion of total SMSA income generated in a given activity by the proportion of total national income attributable to the same activity, a figure greater than 1.00 indicates that the metropolitan area has more than its proportionate share of that activity. As Table 2.2 indicates, forty-three of the fifty-two large southern and western SMSAs showed one of three economic patterns in 1975: a specialization in government services, a specialization in trade and private services, or a dual concentration in tertiary ac-

Table 2.2. *Economic Base of Large Sunbelt SMSAs, 1975*

	West	Southeast	Mid-South
Commerce/services	7	5	4
Government/commerce/services	5	5	2
Government	11	4	—
Government/manufacturing	—	—	2
Manufacturing	2	3	1

Source: Bureau of Economic Analysis, United States Department of Commerce, location quotients based on sources of personal income, 1975.

Note: The Location quotient data are provided in the standard industrial categories: farm, manufacturing, contract construction, wholesale/retail trade, finance/insurance/real estate, transportation/communication/utilities, services, all government, federal civilian, military, state and local government. Cities were allocated to the several groups in Table 2.2 according to the following criteria:

(1) commerce/services—LQ > 1.00 in at least three of the four categories of trade, finance, transport, and services and LQ < 1.20 for each government category.
(2) government/commerce/services—LQ > 1.00 in at least three of the categories of private trade and services and LQ > 1.20 for at least one category of government employment.
(3) government—LQ > 1.40 for all government employment and no more than one category of private trade and services with LQ > 1.20.
(4) government/manufacturing—LQ in manufacturing > 1.20 and LQ in at least one government category > 1.20.
(5) manufacturing—LQ in manufacturing > 1.20 and higher than LQ for any other category.

The Bureau of Economic Analysis data combine Dallas and Fort Worth as a single metropolitan economy. Fresno does not appear, because its only concentrations of activity were in farm employment and "other industries."

tivities in both the public and private sectors. Norfolk and San Antonio were among the fifteen government cities, Portland and Atlanta among the sixteen whose strongest sectors were trade and services, and Denver among the twelve that combined commerce and private services with government.[24] Trade and service cities are found throughout the South and West but government is of major importance only for cities in the core sunbelt subregions.[25]

The social characteristics of sunbelt cities have been influenced both by their economic base and by their regional location. Among the five case studies, for example, Denver and Portland show striking similarities in social status and ethnic composition. Both have a wide range of white-collar positions in banking, education, personal services, business administration, and public administration that result in levels of education and proportions of professional and managerial workers that are above the average for all metropolitan areas in the United States (Table 2.3). Their commercial economies also support average family income levels and relatively low percentages of poverty families. High rankings on status indicators are also related to low minority populations. Portland is located off the main paths of black and Hispanic migration in the twentieth century and Denver has been only a secondary target for minority migrants.

In contrast, San Antonio and Norfolk have large minority populations. San Antonio has served as a funnel and staging ground for Mexican immigrants since the beginning of the century. Norfolk is surrounded by a large rural black population that has viewed the city as a way station on the route to Philadelphia and New York. Both groups have failed to share fully the opportunities of sunbelt economic growth and are one of the reasons that the two military cities fall below the national average in levels of income, education, and high-status employment. The difference in the character of the two types of city is apparent even to the casual visitor in their cultural facilities, entertainment, and retailing. Denver and Portland, for example, have major full-service department stores, viable downtown shopping and entertainment centers, and a broad range of upper-price specialty retailing. San Antonio and Norfolk can best be described as "Sears-Penneys" markets with a "PX mentality."

Atlanta falls somewhere between the other two types of cities. Its high proportions of white-collar and professional-managerial employment in 1970 reflect the booming trade and service sectors of its economy. However, it also has a lower educational level and a higher poverty level than either Denver or Portland. Atlanta's varying rank on the several indicators in effect indicates the existence of a dual society. The city has a large, mobile white middle class including a number of northerners who have moved to serve its myriad branch offices and business headquarters, and a smaller, black middle class tied to a number of important black businesses and to the Atlanta University complex. As the metropolis of a relatively impoverished state, it has also attracted a large number of relatively undereducated migrants of both races from the farms and small towns of Georgia.

Sunbelt cities as a group clearly differ in their social patterns from those of the North, but there are equally clear differences among

Table 2.3. *Socioeconomic Characteristics of Metropolitan Atlanta, Denver, Norfolk, Portland, and San Antonio, 1970*

	Atlanta	Denver	Norfolk	Portlan
Ethnicity:				
Percentage black	22.3	4.1	24.7	2.3
Percentage Spanish-surname	1.0	11.3	1.2	1.4
Percentage foreign stock	3.9	13.5	6.8	17.0
Employment:				
Percentage workers white collar	57.9	59.2	50.6	52.8
Percentage population in professional-managerial jobs	10.9	11.9	6.8	9.9
Percentage black population in professional-managerial jobs	3.7	8.7	4.7	6.6
Percentage Hispanic population in professional-managerial jobs	14.1	6.2	4.7	9.0
Income:				
Median income families	$10,693	$10,774	$8,704	$10,45
Percentage families below poverty level	9.1	6.8	13.4	6.9
Education:				
Median years education, persons 25 years or older	12.1	12.5	11.8	12.4
Percentage high school graduates, persons 25 years or older	53.4	67.4	48.3	62.9

Note: N. A.: not available.

the component sections of the Sunbelt itself. In their location adjacent to large minority populations, for example, San Antonio, Atlanta, and Norfolk are more typical of sunbelt cities than is Denver or Portland. In the Southeast and Mid-South, twenty-two of the twenty-six large SMSAs in 1970 had nonwhite populations greater than the 13.5 percent found in all United States metropolitan areas taken together. The median proportion of nonwhite residents was Little Rock's 18.7 percent for the Mid-South and Atlanta's 22.6 percent for the Southeast. In the West, Hispanic residents form the important minority group. Nineteen of the region's twenty-seven large SMSAs exceeded

n Antonio	All SMSAs
6.9	12.0
44.6	6.1
20.8	20.0
52.4	52.4
5.7	9.5
6.0	N.A.
4.6	N.A.
$7,979	$10,469
16.0	8.5
11.6	12.2
46.8	55.3

the national metropolitan figure of 5.5 percent Spanish-surname population. The regional median was Denver's 11.3 percent. Five major cities—Miami, Houston, Dallas, Los Angeles, and San Francisco–Oakland—recorded more than the national average of both minorities.

If sunbelt cities tend to have more important black and Hispanic populations than frostbelt cities, they also tend to have fewer residents with an identifiable European ethnic background. In 1970, foreign-born residents and persons with foreign-born or mixed parentage constituted 20 percent of the population of all American metropolitan areas. The median for the large Mid-South cities, in contrast, was 3.0

percent. The median for the SMSAs of the Southeast was 7.65 percent. The three southeastern cities that exceeded the national average were Miami, Fort Lauderdale, and West Palm Beach—in each of these, large numbers of Cuban refugees and retired New Yorkers contributed to the population total. The median for western SMSAs was 19.0 percent. The cities with above average proportions of foreign stock included the genuinely cosmopolitan centers of Honolulu and San Francisco, the northwestern cities of Seattle and Tacoma with large numbers of Canadians, and southwestern border cities with large Mexican populations. Since Mexican immigrants and their children are also counted among the Spanish-surnamed population, they can be deducted from the figures for western cities to give a better measure of the European ethnic communities. Such an operation reduces the regional median from 19.0 to 12.4 percent.

The socioeconomic characteristics for all sunbelt cities as summarized in Table 2.4 also reflect the different histories of the South and West. From 1950 through 1970, the SMSAs of the relatively affluent Southwest and Pacific Coast as a group remained above the national level in educational attainment and white-collar employment, although the advantage has been narrowing as the western states have converged toward national economic averages. These western SMSAs also show an increasing margin over the national norm in median family income. In comparison, Portland in 1970 fell precisely at the regional median, Denver somewhat above, and San Antonio considerably below. In the metropolitan areas of the Southeast, in contrast, social status indicators have reflected the region's overall poverty. Educational levels dropped below the national average in the 1960s, family income hovered just under the national figure, and white-collar employment held at 3 percent above the national level. Norfolk fell squarely in the middle range among these southeastern cities and Atlanta somewhat above the middle. At the same time, the SMSAs of the Sunbelt Southeast maintained a lead over slower-growing Mid-South cities similar to that shown in state level data.

Data on social characteristics indicate that it is western cities that differ most extensively from those of the established industrial belt. They have smaller European ethnic populations and much larger Mexican-American communities. Their citizens are more affluent and better educated and more likely to hold a high-status job. Such a conclusion for metropolitan areas parallels a recent analysis of state level data

Table 2.4. *Comparative Social Characteristic Data for 1950–1970 from Sunbelt SMSAs as Defined at Each Census*

	Percentage High School Graduates	Median Years Schooling 25+ Years	Median Family Income	Percentage White-Collar Workers
1950:				
United States	34.3	9.3	$ 3,073	N.A.
West (22 SMSAs)	45.95	11.4	3,455	N.A.
Southwest (14 SMSAs)	35.4	9.8	2,990	N.A.
Mid-South (9 SMSAs)	31.8	9.0	2,722	N.A.
1960:				
United States	41.1	10.6	5,660	41.1
West (25 SMSAs)	50.2	12.0	5,950	47.0
Southwest (16 SMSAs)	41.2	10.85	5,219	44.3
Mid-South (9 SMSAs)	37.9	10.2	5,103	42.2
1970:				
United States	52.3	12.1	9,586	48.1
West (27 SMSAs)	62.9	12.4	10,190	53.2
Southwest (16 SMSAs)	49.5	11.95	9,120	51.6
Mid-South (9 SMSAs)	47.6	11.6	8,511	48.9

Source: *County and City Data Book*, 1952, 1962, 1972.

Note: Regional figures are medians for 300,000+ SMSAs in each region (1970 population). N.A.: not available.

by Clyde Browning and Wil Gesler that finds the greatest regional contrast in the United States between the Northeast and the West.[26] Southern cities are set apart both by their relative poverty and by the importance of blacks as the most prominent minority group. However, the convergence of southern and western cities on measures of socioeconomic status from 1950 to 1970 fits the pattern of regional convergence described in the preceding chapter.

Spectacular growth of cities in the postwar Sunbelt affected the structure of metropolitan government as well as social characteristics and economic base. The same expanded populations that provided the market to support increasingly diversified tertiary sectors also spilled across city boundaries to force changes in governmental forms. Prewar city limits had confined San Antonio to thirty-six square miles, Atlanta to thirty-seven, Denver to fifty-nine, Portland to sixty-two, and the twin central cities of Norfolk-Portsmouth to thirty-eight square miles. When new housing projects and subdivisions sprouted beyond the old boundaries in the wartime and postwar booms, the amount of land devoted to urban uses increased to an average of ninety-five square miles in the four metropolitan areas in 1950 and more than three hundred square miles by 1970. With little preparation, political leaders faced the problem of providing services to a growing suburban population and harnessing suburban revenue sources to regional needs. Each city had to develop its own solution to this central crisis of metropolitan government by adapting existing governmental forms and creating new institutions within the context of state law. The widely varying results of such organizational improvisation have made the framework of governmental institutions one of the important variables affecting metropolitan politics.

The most straightforward governmental response to the deconcentration of population is the annexation of peripheral territory to the central city. Because annexation fully captures outlying residents and revenue sources for the annexing municipality, it has often been taken as a symbol of civic vitality. As chapter seven will explore in detail, annexation programs were an important element in the revitalization undertaken in a number of sunbelt cities after World War II. One of the most spectacular examples has been San Antonio, which grew to 69 square miles in 1950, 160.5 in 1960, 184.1 in 1970, and 253.7 square miles in 1974. Because the city also controls subdivisions and land-use planning for five miles beyond its borders and is counterbalanced only by a weak Bexar County government and a scattering of small suburban towns, San Antonio effectively has acquired the power to coordinate metropolitan growth. Atlanta similarly added 82 square miles and one hundred thousand residents in a massive annexation in 1952, and Norfolk added seventy-seven thousand residents with two annexations totaling 25 square miles in 1955 and 1959. Portland cautiously added only 4 square miles in the first fifteen years after the war, but a population decline recorded in the 1960 census shocked conservative leaders into more active efforts that added 27 square miles from 1960 to 1974. The pace of expansion accelerated in Denver during the same years as the city tried to absorb undeveloped land before it was incorporated into suburban municipalities. The city's annexations jumped from 13 square miles for the 1940s and 1950s to 42 square miles for the 1960s and early 1970s.

Such extensive annexation has been particularly characteristic of sunbelt cities in the postwar era. A statistical analysis by Thomas Dye and a historical study by Kenneth Jackson have both shown that annexation is most likely in smaller and younger cities where local loyalties have not yet crystalized around suburban governments. Social and cultural differences between city and periphery may be relatively small in such cities. A casual stranger to metropolitan New York can easily distinguish between Flatbush and Manhasset, but one study shows that residents of Oklahoma City find little difference between inner and outer neighborhoods and therefore have little reason to defend suburban integrity. In addition, state law in the Sunbelt during the immediate postwar decades made annexation relatively easy. Texas, Oklahoma, and North Carolina allowed virtually unilateral expansion and Virginia relied on the judgment of special judicial panels rather than referenda. A number of sunbelt cities therefore showed spectacular territorial gains in the fifties and sixties that matched San Antonio. Memphis, Oklahoma City, Tulsa, Houston, Dallas, Fort Worth, Phoenix, San Diego, and San Jose all added more than one hundred square miles between 1950 and 1970, with Atlanta, Mobile, and El Paso adding over ninety. In the early seventies, the most important annexations continued to come in southern and southwestern cities such as Houston, Memphis, Charlotte, and Chattanooga.[27]

In recent years, however, increasingly influential suburban politicians and residents have begun to alter state annexation policies. Responding to vigorous growth programs in the 1960s and 1970s, they have followed the lead of the Frostbelt in erecting barriers to easy municipal expansion. In a relatively mild step, Texas placed certain restrictions on the rate of and procedures for annexation, while Oregon and California established boundary commissions to test annexation proposals against standards of efficiency and equity before allowing the actions to proceed. Colorado voters in 1974 approved a pair of constitutional amendments which effectively block further annexations by Denver. After extending an annexation moratorium year by year from 1972 to 1977, the Virginia General Assembly enacted a further ten-year prohibition. Aggregate statistics show that annexation had begun to decline in importance before the enactment of many of these measures.[28] Where 21 percent of the population growth of central cities in the South and 14 percent in the West came from annexation in the 1950s, the figures declined to 13 percent and 7 percent for the 1960s.[29]

The logical extension of annexation is the consolidation of a central city and a suburban county into a single new governmental unit. Although scarcely as common as urban specialists might hope, consolidation has been used most extensively in the South, where the chief examples are Baton Rouge (1947), Hampton (1952), Newport News (1955), Nashville (1962), Jacksonville (1967), Columbus, Georgia (1970), and Lexington, Kentucky (1972). Because consolidation requires the submergence of particular interests into a larger whole, explanations of its popularity in the South usually point to the relative simplicity of the political system in southern SMSAs. According to one facet of the argument, the average southern metropolitan area has fewer independent suburbs and special districts than do those of other regions and therefore fewer public employees and officials who could be expected to protect their spheres of influence. At the same time, the existence of areawide political elites and one-party dominance reduce the number of political factions and organizations that "lose" in consolidation.[30] Both consolidation and annexation also can be used in southern cities to maintain the political status quo by balancing a growing black or Hispanic population with white suburbanites.[31]

In the Norfolk-Portsmouth SMSA, city-county consolidation has had the special effect of creating major suburban municipalities rather than combining core city and periphery. Three new suburban cities with substantial populations have been produced from the consolidation of a small outlying city and a suburbanizing county. The new city of Virginia Beach, with a 1975 population of 214,000, dates from the merger of Princess Anne County and the oceanfront resort town of Virginia Beach in 1963. The merger of the industrial suburb of South Norfolk with Norfolk County in the same year created the city of Chesapeake, with a 1975 population of 104,000. The new city of Suffolk, with 48,000 inhabitants in 1975, was born in 1974 from the consolidation of Nansemond County and the farm market center of Suffolk. A major motivation behind each merger was the desire of county politicians to preserve their jurisdictions from Norfolk and Portsmouth annexations.[32] Because cities of over 10,000 inhabitants in Virginia are independent governmental entities that combine city and county functions, local government in virtually the entire metropolitan area since 1963 has been the responsibility of a handful of municipalities along with a scattering of special districts for port operations and sanitation.

In Denver, Portland, and Atlanta the government of outlying areas beyond expanded city limits is shared by relatively vigorous counties and growing suburban cities. The most active governments outside Portland are Multnomah County, the industrial satellite city of Vancouver, Washington, north of the Columbia River, and the suburban towns of Gresham, Lake Oswego, and Beaverton. Vigorous efforts by Atlanta area counties to acquire urban services have brought conflict with a half-dozen middle-size suburbs (East Point, Marietta, College Park, Decatur, Smyrna, and Forest Park). New residents to the Denver SMSA who prefer a suburban location can choose among the substantial suburbs of Littleton (28,000 in 1975), Englewood (36,000), Northglenn (35,000), and Wheatridge (29,000), the independent university city of Boulder (79,000), and the supersuburbs of Arvada (74,000), Aurora (118,000), and Lakewood (120,000). Although Denver itself is a consolidated city-county whose creation dates from the last century, suburban cities must share governmental authority with the suburban counties of Boulder, Jefferson, Adams, and Arapahoe and with a massive array of special districts.[33]

One way to summarize the effects of these several types of governmental reorganization on the framework for metropolitan politics is to measure the percentage of metropolitan area population in all municipalities of 50,000 or more. The regional tendency toward institutional innovation has given many sunbelt SMSAs a highly organized political environment. All five SMSAs with 80 percent or more of their population in large cities, seven of nine with 70–79 percent, and six of eleven with 60–69 percent were in southern or western states. Norfolk topped the list at 100 percent because of its suburban consolidations. In the San Francisco Bay area, the combined population of San Francisco, Oakland, and San Jose (1,553,000 in 1977) is almost balanced by the 1,183,000 residents of fifteen suburban cities with populations of 50,000 or more. The four large suburbs of Arvada, Aurora, Boulder, and Lakewood hold a quarter of the population of metropolitan Denver and the suburbs of Tempe, Mesa, Glendale, and Scottsdale account for 30 percent of the residents of greater Phoenix. In these and similar areas, the parceling of most metropolitan residents among several major municipalities can be expected to increase the competitiveness of regional politics. In San Antonio, Albuquerque, El Paso, Memphis, and other metropolitan areas that have experienced extensive annexation, a single municipality is likely to make problems of metropolitan growth into issues for city politics.

At the same time it should be pointed out that many sunbelt cities share the pattern of government fragmentation that is most fully developed in the Frostbelt. The same SMSAs of Los Angeles and Dallas that have a large portion of their population in large cities and suburbs also lead the Sunbelt in *total number* of municipalities. The Sunbelt cannot match the extreme fragmentation of seven frostbelt metropolises that each counted more than one hundred separate municipalities in 1970. However, the fifteen SMSAs that had from fifty to ninety-nine separate municipalities included eight in the northern states and seven in the South and West—Dallas (ninety-six), Los Angeles (seventy-seven), Louisville (seventy-three), Houston (sixty-eight), Washington (sixty-one), San Francisco-Oakland (fifty-eight), and Birmingham (fifty-five). Regional medians for number of municipalities in large SMSAs are fifteen for the Mid-South, twenty-one for the Southeast, and twenty-four for the West, figures that do not differ sharply from the median of thirty for the Northeast and forty-four for the Middle West.

In comparison with the Northeast or the Middle West, the Sunbelt is striking for the shared characteristics that set it apart within the United States. For nearly forty years it has been the area of most rapid growth at the state and city level, with its exceptional prosperity keyed to the rise of the national defense industry and the evolution of an information-system economy. Indeed, it is hard to overstate the impact of World War II in stimulating regional growth and altering the national image of the sunbelt states. To a significant degree, both southern and western cities are still working out the effects of wartime changes on their economic structure and their political climate.

Within the Sunbelt, in contrast, it is important to note major differences that may be obscured by regional data. Specific cities show wide variations in wealth and in social status. The relative poverty of Norfolk and San Antonio, for example, reveals the underside of the sunbelt experience in which population growth has failed to restructure metropolitan economies. Along with Charlotte, Greenville, and El Paso and other cities of the Southeast and Gulf states, they continue to function as outposts whose contribution to the national economy is location and cheap labor. Many of their important decisions are made outside the region and battles for union organization remain central issues in local politics. At the other extreme, Denver and Portland are typical of the sunbelt environment of journalistic cliché. Like Seattle, San Francisco, San Diego, Salt Lake City, or the cities of Florida, they offer the attractions of a spectacular physical setting and the amenities of a white-collar society. In addition, their relatively small minority populations allow them to escape a common problem of sunbelt cities that is frequently ignored in popular commentary. A wider contrast within the SMSA places Atlanta somewhat between the two groups of cities. Its white-collar economy results in high median incomes but its large and poor black population lowers educational achievement and increases the level of poverty.

The same sort of analysis is also applicable to changes in political structure in response to suburban sprawl. In comparison to cities in older parts of the United States, sunbelt SMSAs have been relatively open to changes in governmental institutions through annexation, city-county merger, and suburban consolidation. On more detailed examination, however, they are equally impressive for the variety of solutions that have been devised. As Table 2.5 indicates, the largest central cities in each southern and western SMSA contain widely differing shares of metropolitan area population. On the one hand, the feasibility of extensive annexation and the popularity of consolidation

Table 2.5. *Distribution of Percent of Metropolitan Population in Largest Central City by Region, 1970*

Percentage	West	Southeast	Mid-South	Mid-West	Northeast
81–100	2	1	1		
61–80	5		1	3	1
41–60	7	4	4	4	2
21–40	10	9	3	16	13
1–20	3	3			8
Medians:	41.9 (Denver)	26.4 (Washington Miami)	43.8 (Knoxville Louisville)	36.3 (Cleveland)	25.3 (Utica Hartford)

US Median (100 largest SMSAs): 37%

explain most of the metropolitan areas where the proportion is above fifty percent.[34] On the other hand, many of the cases with low shares in the chief central city are Florida and California metropolises in which particularly rapid growth has outrun governmental reorganization.[35] Several others are urbanized regions where peripheral sprawl has linked two or three originally independent core cities.[36] Working together, these contrary influences have produced a broader range of central city percentages for the Sunbelt than for other parts of the country but have left regional medians close to the nationwide figure.

The foregoing conclusions support two related suggestions for the study of metropolitan growth in the Sunbelt. As already stated, differences among southern and western cities can be as important as regional similarities. The following discussion of the political impact of postwar growth therefore examines the full range of types of cities characteristic of the Sunbelt. By extension, the importance of differences from city to city makes it necessary to analyze individually the physical and institutional structure of each city. Where the present chapter describes and compares the development of SMSAs as units, the next explores effects of economic and population growth on the distribution of socioeconomic groups within metropolitan areas. The remainder of the study then examines the dual impacts of growth and of changing social geography on the evolution of political issues, leadership, and conflict in the sunbelt metropolis.

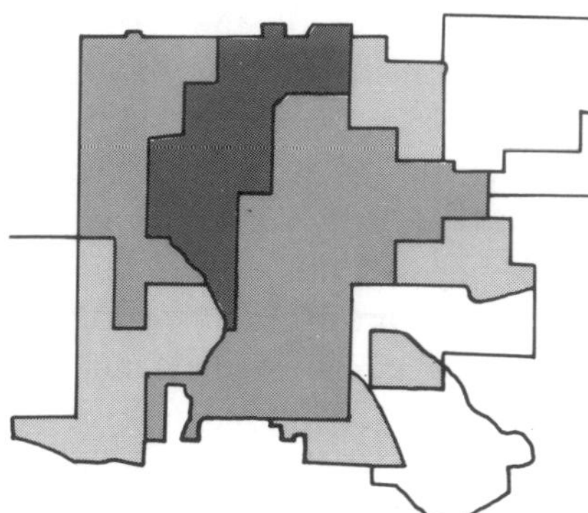

Chapter 3

Suburbanization in the Sunbelt

The United States Census has provided historians with convenient symbols of our changing society. In 1890, the Eleventh Census proclaimed that it was no longer possible to distinguish a distinct frontier line across the American West. Thirty years later, the new census of 1920 showed that for the first time there were more urban than rural residents. Together these two dates mark the end of the nineteenth-century era of westward movement and extensive resource exploitation and the emergence of the crowded industrial city as the typical American environment. In the two statistics we can see the disappearance of the log cabin and the sod house, and the spread of Philadelphia row houses, luxury apartments on Chicago's lake front, and Manhattan tenements.

The census of 1970 marked yet a third period of American growth, for it revealed that the United States had become a suburban nation. With 37.2 percent of the total, suburban rings held a larger share of national population than did central cities (31.4 percent) or nonmetropolitan areas (31.4 percent). In everyday experience, the changing percentages symbolize the replacement of steel towns and trolley cars by sunshine cities and two-car families, of corner groceries and downtown movie houses by air-conditioned shopping malls. Summarizing a shift that had been underway for a generation, the census statistic on population distribution also anticipated further deconcentration of activities. By 1973, employers had followed population to bring a majority of metropolitan jobs into the suburbs. By 1975 demographers were remarking the rapid growth of population in the exurbs beyond even the distant suburbs of SMSAs.[1]

The era of the Sunbelt in the years since 1940 has equally been the age of suburbanization. The census benchmarks of the early 1970s are the product of massive population shifts over the last generation. Although the total numbers involved were relatively small, the 1930s marked the first decade in which a majority of metropolitan growth occurred in suburban rings rather than central cities (Table 3.1). Approximately the same ratio held for the 1940s, followed by a further spectacular shift in the 1950s which brought virtually all of recent metropolitan growth into suburban rings. Because of the acceleration of total metropolitan growth in mid-century, the proportions for the 1950s and 1960s involve huge numbers of new suburban residents. Data prepared by Brian Berry and John Kasarda give the increase of suburban population as 3,518,000 for the thirties, 10,484,000 for the forties, 23,200,000 for the fifties, and 23,784,000 for the sixties. If adjusted to include residents of suburban areas annexed to central cities in each decade, the suburban totals are even more impressive: 3,854,000 for the thirties, 11,872,000 for the forties, 27,283,000 for the fifties, 27,311,000 for the sixties, and 7,655,000 for 1970–76.[2] Both in proportionate and absolute terms, there is little question that the 1950s was the pivotal decade in the suburban transformation of metropolitan America.

Urban scholarship follows the census much as the Supreme Court eyes the election returns. As the opportunity for suburban residence opened to the majority of Americans in the fifties, popular writers reacted with a sharply critical literature. Ignoring earlier studies that had seen suburbs as the solution to the crisis of the overcrowded city, the new pop sociology of the mid-fifties described a tawdry physical environment which fostered false values and social disorganization. Beyond "slurb" and "sloburb," behind titles like "The Suburban Sadness," *The Crack in the Picture Window*, and *The Split Level Trap* was a common indictment. Critical summaries by Scott Donaldson and William Dobriner picked out the common adjectives: transient, conservative, conformist, child-centered, homogeneous, middle-class, materialistic, superficial in values.[3] More serious journalists and scholars in the 1950s tended to accept the terms of debate set by this "suburban myth," investigating family relationships, Republican voting, and the problems of the "other-directed" life. In the terminology of Maurice Stein, the growth of suburbs was the central element in the "eclipse of community" that threatened to sterilize American life.[4]

During the last decade, scholars have returned with new interest to break past the suburban stereotype. With Herbert Gans's study of *The Levittowners* as a keynote, there is a more sophisticated recognition

Table 3.1. *Relative Shares of Metropolitan Growth, 1920–1970*

	1920s	1930s	1940s	1950s	1960s
SMSA Growth: Adjusted for Annexation					
All US SMSAs					
Share in central cities	50%	34%	30%	2%	0%
Share in suburban rings	50%	66%	70%	98%	100%
Southern SMSAs					
Share in central cities	62%	47%	30%	7%	7%
Share in suburban rings	38%	53%	70%	93%	93%
Western SMSAs					
Share in central cities	50%	37%	33%	17%	16%
Share in suburban rings	50%	63%	67%	83%	84%
SMSA Growth: Unadjusted for Annexation					
All US SMSAs					
Share in central cities	58%	40%	39%	21%	19%
Share in suburban rings	42%	60%	61%	79%	81%
Southern SMSAs					
Share in central cities	80%	53%	52%	45%	40%
Share in suburban rings	20%	47%	48%	55%	60%
Western SMSAs					
Share in central cities	57%	43%	37%	34%	28%
Share in suburban rings	43%	57%	63%	66%	72%

Source: Berry and Kasarda, *Contemporary Urban Ecology*, pp. 172–73, 186–88.

that the popular taste for suburban living is scarcely compatible with a vision of suburbs as inferior social and physical environments. Sociologists place new emphasis on the variety of suburban communities and on the consequent opportunities for self-expression through residential location, while political scientists emphasize the increasing political influence of suburban voters in Congress and state legislatures. Brian Berry's model of the metropolitan mosaic in which residents choose among all communities in the metropolitan area for the one most appropriate for their life-style, income, and ethnicity provides a recent summary of the new thinking.[5]

Reflecting this new scholarship, journalistic analysis of the 1970 census has produced a new popular image of suburbia not as an exception but as the norm for American life. With shopping centers, office parks, manufacturing plants, sports arenas, and universities, suburban zones offer all the amenities for a full life independent of the central city and have "exchanged suburbanity for self-sufficiency."[6] The theme was stated by a series in the *New York Times* in 1971: "Rapidly, relentlessly, almost unconsciously, America has created a new form of urban settlement. It is higher, bolder and richer than anything man has yet called city. . . . Suburbs are no longer just bedrooms. They are no longer mere orbital satellites. They are no longer sub. They are broad, ballooning bands, interlinked as cities in their own right."[7]

Americans since the war have found suburban growth in the Sunbelt particularly striking. Because most core cities in the South and West were relatively small at the beginning of the suburban era, the dispersed or sprawling metropolis has seemed especially characteristic of these regions. California, of course, provided the prime examples for commentators in the fifties and sixties with what William H. Whyte called its "vast smog-filled deserts that are neither city, suburb nor country." An influential article by Whyte in 1958 offered San Jose and Santa Clara County as the epitome of sprawl. In Victor Gruen's parade of synonyms, "spread city" and "scatterization" marched together with sprawl to define "today's pattern of the 'anti-city'" in the Los Angeles basin. Even the sober *New York Times* in 1955 described Los Angeles as a "violently aggressive organism" without form, pattern or focus and two years later warned easterners about the "crazy pattern" of "helter-skelter municipal growth."[8]

In the last decade, a fuller understanding of Los Angeles and that city's convergence toward national social norms have reduced its prominence as the bad example and shifted attention to other sunbelt cities.[9] Denver to one commentator now looks like "a lumpy pancake" draped over the Colorado plains and foothills, and Phoenix is variously a "sprawling metropolitan unit" and a "huge unplanned urban complex."[10] In the southeast, complexes of smaller cities sprawl toward each other to form emerging urban regions in central Florida and the Carolina Piedmont.[11] Most generally, however, it is Houston that has captured the imagination. It is described as a "nowhere city" that is "all process and no plan" where residential development is "a spin-the-wheel happening that hops, skips and jumps outward" with each project "seemingly dropped from the sky."[12]

The popularity of the term indicates that "sprawl" is a compelling figure of speech, but it is one without precise definition. At times it may imply extensive or dispersed development that produces a monotonous and undifferentiated residental landscape. At other times it may imply the disorder of helter-skelter growth. Among the consequences of such a lack of preplanning of locational decisions is a disordered spatial pattern that lacks clear distinction between dominant and subordinant centers. In turn, this geographical jumble may result in a fragmented governmental structure and a formless, incoherent social system.

In fact, two complementary approaches can be used to give more precise content to the popular metaphor. One possibility is to examine sprawl as a process of extensive development by defining aggregate characteristics of a metropolitan landscape that can be taken as objective indicators of dispersal. The second alternative is to explore patterns or order within such dispersed metropolitan areas, for it is unlikely that residents actually make random locational choices. Even in the metropolis of popular imagery where thousands of tract houses march toward the horizon with occasional interruption by freeway interchanges and shopping centers, the residents seek access to employment, public facilities, neighbors of a certain ethnic background and life-style, and a neighborhood with a particular reputation and status. In particular, if we are to step beyond simple complaints over governmental fragmentation to understand the nature of political relations within metropolitan areas, it is necessary to examine the effects of these individual choices on the distribution of groups within the metropolis. Because the concern of the present study is the impact of rapid population growth and suburbanization on intrametropolitan policies, the focus with both approaches is residential patterns and the residential environment.

It is relatively straightforward to decide on specific aggregate characteristics that indicate the relative degree of sprawl when defined as dispersal of population. Brian Berry, for example, has implicitly offered such measures by referring to the "low-slung and far-flung form" of the new metropolitan regions in the South and West. Thomas Muller has suggested that the sprawling metropolis can be seen as "essentially groups of contiguous, low-density communities consisting of relatively new housing stock." A comparison of the extensiveness of suburban sprawl among different metropolitan areas can therefore examine data on housing type, housing age, population density, and dependence on automobiles.[13]

Southern and western cities in fact show the characteristics associated with a dispersed suburbanized metropolis. As of 1970, for example, 49 percent of the housing units in metropolitan America had been built during the last two decades. The median figure for large SMSAs was 64.4 percent in the West, 63.3 percent in the Southeast, and 55.4 percent for the Mid-South, with only Baltimore, San Francisco-Oakland, and Portland falling below the national percentage.[14] Such a concentration of new housing indicated both rapid new growth and the rapid replacement of old housing. The result, of course, has been the creation of a modern urban landscape of tract ranch houses, split-levels, and townhouse complexes.

Similarly, western metropolitan areas since 1950 have had a higher than average proportion of single-unit dwellings. During the 1950s, all three regions on the outer rim gained single-family houses more rapidly than the nation as a whole, with the shift especially rapid in the South (Table 3.2). Taken together with the huge increases in suburban population totals, the shift toward single-family housing confirms the importance of the fifties for the creation of a suburban environment. Although a nationwide trend toward apartment living in the sixties brought a reduction in the proportion of single-unit housing, the sunbelt cities remained substantially above the figures for the nation as a whole and for all metropolitan areas as a group.

Since single-family housing requires space, it is scarcely surprising that the density of population also thinned in southern and western metropolitan areas. Again using median values for the large SMSAs of West, Southeast, and Mid-South, the population density of urbanized areas in each region declined most rapidly in the 1950s and somewhat more slowly in the 1960s (Table 3.2). On this measure too, it was western cities that sprawled most loosely over the countryside in the immediate postwar years. More rapid deconcentration in the metropolitan areas of the South, however, brought their average density below that of the metropolitan West by 1970.

A landscape of dispersed population in new single-family houses is

Table 3.2. *Population Density and Housing Patterns in Sunbelt SMSAs*

	1950	1960	1970
Western SMSAs			
Median population density per square mile for urbanized areas	4,106	3,008	2,818
Median percentage of one-unit dwellings	71.2	84.4	73.7
Southeastern SMSAs			
Median population density per square mile for urbanized areas	4,782	3,296	2,567
Median percentage of one-unit dwellings	64.1	80.3	72.2
Mid-South SMSAs			
Median population density per square mile for urbanized areas	4,588	3,096	2,236
Median percentage of one-unit dwellings	62.7	83.3	76.0
All SMSAs			
Overall population density per square mile for urbanized areas	5,438	3,837	3,376
All USA			
Median percentage of one-unit dwellings	64.0	76.3	69.1

Source: *County and City Data Book*, 1952, 1962, 1972. *Seventeenth Census: 1950*, Vol. I: *Population*, Table 17.

Note: For number of SMSAs, see Table 2.4, with following exceptions for number of cases for median population density for urbanized area: West 1950, 21; West 1970, 26; Southeast 1950, 13.

of course a landscape dependent on automobiles. In the popular literature, Los Angeles is again the epitome of the auto town whose residents are distressingly eager to stage an internal combustion revolution and rearrange the structure of their city into Autopia.[15] In fact, only 84.9 percent of Los Angeles households in 1970 had access to automobiles, a figure below the western metropolitan median of 89.0 percent. The highest degree of automobility in the United States was recorded in southern California's supremely suburban SMSAs of Oxnard (93.8 percent) and Anaheim (94.5 percent). Both the Southeast with a median of 85.0 percent and the Mid-South with a median of 83.1 percent also ranked above the 81.4 percent for metropolitan America as a whole.[16]

Analysis of patterns in the residential geography of metropolitan areas is a more complex undertaking. The basic concern of this study is to examine subareas within individual SMSAs to discover patterns and changes in the distribution of total population and of specific ethnic and socioeconomic groups. The remainder of the chapter therefore provides detailed comparative description of the social geography of seven sunbelt metropolises. Omitting the four SMSAs over 2 million inhabitants (San Francisco–Oakland, Los Angeles, Baltimore, Washington) and the constellation of metropolitan areas surrounding Los Angeles in southern California, it examines three southern and four western cities whose growth rates range from moderate (Portland) to rapid (Norfolk, Atlanta, San Antonio, Denver) to extraordinary (Orlando, Tucson). In each case, the historical analysis combines information on neighborhood characteristics and perceptions with available quantitative data on small areas.

The resulting description of the social ecology of Sunbelt SMSAs can illuminate intrametropolitan politics in particular communities by indicating the changing character of the central city and of suburban jurisdictions. It can also assist understanding of metropolitan policies by contributing to a broader debate on the evolution of city-suburban status patterns. Some scholars stress that suburban rings are following a natural differentiation from central cities in which "the upper strata might be expected to shift from central to peripheral residence, and the lower classes might increasingly take up occupancy in the central area." Others argue that metropolitan areas outside central city boundaries have increasingly shown the same variety of neighborhoods, of economic activities, and of social, ethnic, and racial groups as does the city itself.[17] For clarity, the following section examines quantitative data in terms of urban core and rings of suburban growth. The final section presents evidence for urban heterogeneity within suburban areas.

The hypothesis that the status of suburban areas has been increasing relative to their central cities is based on the commonsense view of postwar suburbia as the goal of upwardly mobile urbanites. It is also based on a historical understanding of the long-term impacts of improvements in transportation technology since the mid-nineteenth century.[18] On the basis of detailed cross-sectional analysis of the 1950 and 1960 censuses, Leo Schnore has proposed that American cities are in the process of evolution from a "traditional" or "preindustrial" to a "modern" land-use pattern. As he has described the evolutionary sequence:

> (1) smaller and younger central cities in the United States tend to be occupied by the local elite, while their peripheral suburban areas contain the lower strata; (2) with growth and the passage of time, the central city comes to be the main residential area for both the highest and lowest strata . . . and (3) a subsequent stage in this evolutionary process is achieved when the suburbs have become the semi-private preserve of both the upper and middle strata while the central city is largely given over to the lowest stratum.[19]

Analysis of changes in city-suburban status patterns during the postwar era also support the evolutionary hypothesis. Schnore found that 82 percent of the metropolitan areas studied for the period 1950–60 maintained the same city-suburb status differential or shifted in the direction of higher suburban status. Using data for twenty metropolitan areas from 1950 to 1970, Norval Glenn found that the urban fringe experienced a net gain in relative status as measured by family income in sixteen cases, by occupation in seventeen cases, and by education in eighteen cases. After finding similar patterns among fifteen cities, Reynolds Farley pointed out that the inability of central cities to attract the higher status white migrants to the metropolitan area accounts for much of the social differential.[20]

A number of independent studies indicate that it is the older, large SMSAs of the industrial heartland that were most likely to have reached the third of Schnore's three stages by the 1950s. Suburban zones in smaller SMSAs, younger SMSAs, or SMSAs in the South and West have been more likely to show the process of transition from low to high status during the decades of rapid growth after 1940.[21] A first step in measuring the degree of status reversal in sunbelt metropolises is to follow the majority of published studies and compare socioeconomic indicators for central cities and suburban rings for all the large southern and western SMSAs. Table 3.3 shows the number of metropolitan areas for West, Southeast, and Mid-South in which central city values exceeded suburban values on several such indicators in 1950, 1960, and 1970. It also shows the median values for central city and metropolitan area for the SMSAs of each region. The data provide at best partial support for the status reversal hypothesis. The experi-

Table 3.3. *Socioeconomic Indicators for Sunbelt Central Cities and SMSAs by Region*

	1950		
	West	South-east	Mid-South
Median years education			
SMSA	11.40	9.80	9.0
Central city	11.70	10.05	9.2
Percentage of cases central city higher than SMSA	64	50	67
Median family income			
SMSA	\$3,455	\$2,990	\$2,7
Central city	\$3,533	\$3,005	\$2,8
Percentage of cases central city higher than SMSA	77	43	56
Percentage workers white collar			
SMSA	N.A.	N.A.	N.A
Central city	N.A.	N.A.	N.A
Percentage of cases central city higher than SMSA	N.A.	N.A.	N.A

Note: For number of SMSAs by region at each census, see Table 2.4. N.A.: not available.

ence of western cities follows the expected pattern most closely. The region's central cities as a group held a slight lead on the four indicators in 1950 and 1960. During the following decade, however, western suburbs gained the advantage in educational levels and income although still lagging in white-collar employment. In both the Southeast and Mid-South, the reversal of central city advantage is less marked. Suburban rings gained a clear lead only in income levels. On indicators of education and employment, in fact, the central cities of the Mid-South during the 1960s appear to have regained an advantage lost in the 1950s.

The measures used in Table 3.3 have two major weaknesses which limit their usefulness for testing the status reversal hypothesis. First, the use of medians for groups of metropolitan areas blurs the distinctions among individual cities. Second, the measurements are controlled by the political boundary between central city and suburban ring. No

1960			1970		
Vest	South-East	Mid-South	West	South-East	Mid-South
2.00	10.85	10.20	12.40	11.95	11.60
2.00	11.05	9.60	12.30	12.00	11.90
36	50	22	22	44	56
,950	$5,219	$5,103	$10,190	$9,120	$8,511
,135	$5,219	$4,915	$ 9,789	$8,390	$8,092
52	31	33	30	19	44
7.0	44.3	42.2	53.2	51.6	48.9
1.3	45.6	42.1	55.5	50.8	51.2
92	50	44	67	56	56

distinctions are made between older and younger suburbs, residential and industrial suburbs, or densely settled and sparsely developed city neighborhoods. Since the data are not adjusted for central city annexations, changes in the relative position of city and suburbs over a decade may reflect boundary changes rather than population shifts. The relative gains shown by Mid-South cities during the 1960s, for example, may result from the addition of high-status areas through consolidation in Nashville and annexation in Memphis.

The evolutionary model can be tested more precisely by detailed examination of individual cities. It is useful both to explore differences in social status among suburban jurisdictions in each metropolitan area and to divide the metropolis into growth zones on the basis of age of housing stock. Census tract data allow the definition of areas with pluralities of housing built before 1950, from 1950 through 1959, and from 1960 through 1970. In some cases, the first of these zones can be further divided into areas of standard and substandard housing as of mid-century.[22] The development of metropolitan social geography can then be explored using medians for census tracts within each growth zone. In the present study, the variables used are: (1) median years of school completed for persons twenty-five years or older; (2) median income of families and unrelated individuals; (3) percentage of population in professional and managerial jobs; (4) percentage of population black; and (5) percentage of population with Spanish surname.

Detailed analysis of data for Denver provides the fullest support for the status reversal model of metropolitan social geography.[23] Each of the five major jurisdictions in the SMSA experienced absolute increases in educational attainment and proportion of professional-managerial workers in the decades from 1940 to 1970 and absolute increases in median income from 1950 to 1970 (Table 3.4). In relative terms, however, Denver fared less well than its suburbs. In 1940 and 1950, the city ranked ahead of all the surrounding counties on the occupational and educational indicators and ahead of two suburban counties in income level. Despite substantial annexations, the city by 1970 had dropped behind all four counties in income and behind three of four on the measures of occupation and education, with the greatest relative shift coming in the 1950s.

Use of housing age zones allows a more precise description of the changing status of inner city and outer city. Table 3.5 indicates the relative ranking of the several zones in 1960 and 1970 by showing the ratio of zone medians in each of five categories to the individual-based figures for the entire five-county SMSA; these ratios provide a measure of change in the relative ranking of zones within the metropolitan area.[24] In the most straightforward analysis by cross section at each year, minority group distribution and socioeconomic status show the patterns suggested by Schnore's theory and by the county-level analysis. In both 1960 and 1970, black and Hispanic population was most predominant in Zone 1 and least predominant in the suburban zones. Income, educational attainment, and professional-managerial employment, in contrast, increased steadily from older to newer growth zones. The only deviation in this latter pattern is the unexpectedly low figure for percentage of population in professional-managerial jobs for Zone 3 in 1960.

Again, the basic pattern of increasing status with increasing distance from the central city can be modified on closer examination. From

Table 3.4. *Socioeconomic Indicators by County and County Subareas for Denver, 1940–1970*

	1940	1950	1960	1970
Percentage of population in professional-managerial jobs				
Denver	8.5	10.1	9.6	11.3
Adams	4.5	4.8	7.2	7.7
Arapahoe	4.8	6.8	10.0	13.5
Boulder	6.8	8.2	12.5	14.7
Jefferson	5.8	8.3	12.3	13.7
North Tracts	N.A.	N.A.	12.3	13.1
South Tracts	N.A.	N.A.	12.9	14.3
Median years school for persons 25 years or older				
Denver	10.3	12.1	12.1	12.4
Adams	8.6*	10.5*	12.1	12.3
Arapahoe	9.1*	11.5*	12.4	12.7
Boulder	9.5*	12.0*	12.5	12.8
Jefferson	9.5*	11.9*	12.5	12.7
North Tracts	N.A.	N.A.	12.3	12.7
South Tracts	N.A.	N.A.	12.6	13.4
Median income families and unrelated individuals				
Denver	N.A.	$2,846	$4,938	$ 6,920
Adams	N.A.	$2,637	$5,985	$ 9,428
Arapahoe	N.A.	$3,095	$6,341	$10,623
Boulder	N.A.	$1,782	$4,111	$ 7,023
Jefferson	N.A.	$3,094	$6,713	$10,998
North Tracts	N.A.	N.A.	$6,440	$10,540
South Tracts	N.A.	N.A.	$7,407	$11,900

Note: North Tracts figures for Jefferson County are median values for tracts 98–111, 113–115. South Tracts figures are medians for tracts 112, 116–120. N.A.: not available.

*Average of medians for males and females weighted by numbers of males and females 25 years or older.

1960 to 1970, according to the ratios in Table 3.5, both Zone 2 and Zone 3 lost ground in relative terms on all three status measures although Zone 4 either showed a relative gain (income, occupation) or no change (education). The discontinuity in status level which lay between Zones 2 and 3 in 1960 fell between Zones 3 and 4 by 1970. At least part of the status gain in new suburbs in the 1960s thus appears

Table 3.5. *Ratios of Zone/SMSA Medians for Socioeconomic and Ethnicity Indicators by Age Zone and City, 1960–1970*

	Denver		San Antonio		Portland		Tucson	
Zone	1960	1970	1960	1970	1960	1970	1960	197
Median Years Education								
1	.71	.72	.53	.61	.88	.91		
2	1.00	.98	.91	.85	.94	.98	.76	.8
3	1.02	.99	1.15	1.02	1.03	1.02	1.02	1.0
4	1.03	1.02	1.16	1.08	1.01	1.01	.97	1.0
Percentage Population in Professional-Managerial Jobs								
1	.26	.26	.22	.25	.82	.78		
2	.90	.79	1.02	.67	.87	.78	.87	.
3	1.01	.76	1.10	.99	1.09	1.27	1.13	1.1
4	1.20	1.28	1.17	1.36	1.02	1.10	1.15	1.1
Median Income, Families and Unrelated Individuals								
1	.53	.41	.74	.68	.56	.42		
2	.96	.85	.97	.87	1.00	1.01	.79	.
3	1.26	1.16	1.41	1.27	1.25	1.24	1.17	1.
4	1.30	1.40	1.46	1.31	1.15	1.24	1.08	1.
Percentage Population Black								
1	.71	.82	.02	.07	.25	.54		
2	.09	.05	.07	.10	.05	.13	.33	.
3	.03	.12	.02	.06	0	.04	.06	.
4	.03	.05	.03	.09	0	.04	.23	.
Percentage Population Spanish-Surname								
1	4.28	4.32	2.37	2.12				
2	.41	.81	.53	1.13			1.11	2.
3	.29	.66	.28	.61			.43	.
4	.33	.30	.41	.36			.44	.

Note: Ratios shown are zone medians divided by individual-based figures for SMSA as of 1970 definition (San Antonio ratios based on figures for Bexar county only). Zone 1 was not defined for Orlando and Tucson. Figures for Zone 2 for Orlando and Tucson are equivalent to Zones 1 and 2 taken together in other cities.

*Because of marked changes in census tract boundaries in Orlando between 1960 and 1970, it is not possible to define 1960 equivalents to Zones 3 and 4 as delineated using 1970 data. As given here, the rough equivalent for 1960 to Zones 3 and 4 taken together is the areas which in 1960 had a plurality of housing built in the 1950s.

Norfolk		Orlando		Atlanta	
960	1970	1960	1970	1960	1970
.76	.75			.69	.69
.02	.94	.92	1.00	1.03	.91
.14	1.03	1.05*	1.00	1.11	1.01
.03	1.03		1.00	.96	1.01
.55	.31			.16	.23
.13	.88	1.16	.79	1.06	.65
.13	1.10	1.05*	1.05	1.15	.97
.10	1.32		1.07	.81	1.03
.77	.61			.51	.36
.36	1.12	.80	.64	.91	.79
.68	1.53	1.25*	1.12	1.38	1.15
.43	1.63		1.16	1.15	1.21
.54	4.01			3.62	4.40
.03	.11	.02	.06	.08	.29
.04	.05	.01*	.01	.14	.21
.46	.25		.01	.25	.06

to have come at the expense of the high-growth region of the previous decade. Using the analogy of a wave, the outward movement of high-status population involves a two-way displacement in which the movement of the crest into Zone 4 also involves a following trough in Zone 3.

The changing distribution of Hispanic population within metropolitan Denver also indicates a growing similarity of Zones 2 and 3. Within the deteriorated core area with its already heavy concentration there was a relatively small increase in the percentage of the population with Spanish surname during the 1960s. In Zones 2 and 3, the ratio of median tract percentage to the SMSA percentage roughly doubled, but in Zone 4 the ratio actually declined. On the basis of this analysis, one can expect that the outward movement of Hispanic population will help to create some of the same problems and needs in the older suburbs as now exist within the city of Denver.

Finally, Table 3.5 suggests a change in the relative attractiveness of inner-city neighborhoods for high-status persons. Although Zone 1 showed a decline in relative income level, it maintained a stable position on the measures of education and high-status occupations. Changes of relative status can also be assessed since 1940 for Zone 1 and for that portion of Zone 2 lying within Denver's city limits in each census year (Table 3.6). The data indicate that both areas have been declining in relative income since 1950. Again for both areas, sharp declines in relative educational achievement and high-status occupations from 1940 to 1960 were followed by stabilization in the 1960s. The pattern of the three indices probably reflects the settlement in the central city of large numbers of well-educated professional persons at the start of their careers. Migration figures by age group support this suggestion that Denver itself has had a special attraction for young adults in their twenties.[25]

Other sunbelt cities analyzed in terms of growth rings can be ranked more briefly in comparison with Denver. In Schnore's studies based on 1950 census data, Tucson was offered as a typical example of a traditional city in which high-status residents concentrated in the central city. With the aid of massive annexations that increased the central city population from 45,454 to 212,892, Tucson in 1960 continued to outrank the remainder of Pima County. By 1970, in contrast, the city had fallen behind in income, maintained equal rank in education, and held only a narrowing lead in high-status occupations (Table 3.7). Analysis of growth rings similarly shows the area of fastest growth in the fifties had the lowest proportion of minority residents and the highest socioeconomic position in 1960. As also occurred in Denver, however, Zone 4 moved into first place and Zone 3 fell back on status measures relative to the total metropolitan area during the sixties (Table 3.5).

The analogy of an outward wave of high status with crest and trough is applicable to Atlanta and Norfolk as well as to Denver and Tucson. Taken as a whole, Atlanta outranked the surrounding suburbs in 1940, matched the rest of the metropolitan area in 1950, and fell increasingly behind by 1960 and 1970. Census tract data for the area within Atlanta's 1950 city limits (Table 3.6) show that core city slum areas dropped in socioeconomic status relative to the entire SMSA during the fifties and sixties and that Zone 2 plunged spectacularly. For the area within Norfolk's current city limits, core slum areas also lost status, established neighborhoods slipped from first to second rank, and the suburbs of the 1950s assumed first place in social rank within the city.

The outward ripple of high-status residents is even more apparent in figures for the entire Atlanta and Norfolk SMSAs (Table 3.5). In 1960, Zone 3 held the highest status rank in each metropolis, followed by Zones 2 and 4 at roughly equal rank and Zone 1 showing the lowest status. The next ten years brought massive growth in suburban Virginia Beach and Atlanta's suburban counties of DeKalb, Cobb, and Clayton. One result was to surround the rural black population of these outlying areas with new white residents. The area of most recent suburbanization also surged into first place in social status in both SMSAs. Only this zone of most rapid growth in the sixties showed gains relative to the entire metropolitan areas, with even the comparatively new neighborhoods dating from the fifties losing ground in relative terms.

San Antonio is the fourth city where the status patterns by growth rings are similar to those of Denver. San Antonio's black population is too small to figure meaningfully in zone medians, but Mexican-American population is heaviest in the older sections of the metropolis (Table 3.5). In addition, each measure of social and economic status increases as housing becomes newer. Both in 1960 and 1970, there were clear discontinuities in income and education levels between Zones 1 and 2 and between Zones 2 and 3, with the two areas of

Table 3.6. *Ratios of Zone/SMSA Medians for Education, Employment, and Income by Age Zone in Atlanta, Denver, Norfolk, and Portland, 1940–1970*

	Median years education				Percentage of population in professional-managerial jobs			
	1940	1950	1960	1970	1940	1950	1960	1970
Atlanta								
Zone 1	—	.75	.69	.69	—	.40	.16	.23
Zone 2	—	1.15	1.05	.88	—	1.31	1.06	.61
Denver								
Zone 1	.83	.73	.71	.72	.66	.48	.26	.26
Zone 2	1.09	1.02	.99	.98	1.71	1.37	.90	.85
Norfolk								
Zone 1	—	.82	.75	.73	—	.66	.46	.25
Zone 2	—	1.21	1.10	.99	—	1.43	1.38	1.04
Zone 3	—	1.13	1.14	1.03	—	.94	1.22	1.18
Portland								
Zone 1	.96	.92	.88	.92	1.10	1.01	.74	.78
Zone 2	1.06	1.06	.99	.98	.96	1.13	.88	.82

Note: Ratios shown are zone medians divided by individual-based figures for each metropolitan area. Geographical coverage for Atlanta is area within 1950 city limits, for Denver is area within city limits at each census, for Norfolk is area within 1970 city limits, and for Portland is area within 1940 city limits.

more recent development (Zones 3 and 4) being relatively close. Especially in 1970, however, Zone 4 shows a clear margin over Zone 3 in occupational status.[26]

Another similarity between Denver and San Antonio is the outward movement of Hispanic population in the 1960s. The ratio in Zone 2 doubled during the decade from .53 to 1.13 percent as Mexican-Americans moved out of long-established slum areas in the urban core into blue-collar Anglo neighborhoods in southeast San Antonio, into newer low-rent housing on the southern edge of the city, and into middle-class housing in northwestern San Antonio. The latter movement is reflected in the increase in the median percentage of Hispanic population in census tracts on the north side of the city from 7.6 percent in 1960 to 14.3 percent in 1970 (Table 3.8). The spread of low-income Hispanic residents to the south and southwest may also

Median income, nilies and unrelated individuals		
50	1960	1970
6	.51	.36
5	.85	.67
5	.53	.41
3	.96	.82
5	.72	.60
6	1.42	1.09
9	1.86	1.53
0	.55	.42
9	1.01	1.01

help explain why Zones 3 and 4 declined in status relative to the metropolitan area as a whole between 1960 and 1970.

In two other sunbelt cities the weight of evidence falls against the full applicability of the status reversal model. Although county-level data in metropolitan Portland show evolution toward a high-status suburban ring and a lower-status core city (Table 3.9), data aggregated by growth zones do not fully confirm the expected pattern (Table 3.5). Both in 1960 and 1970, it was the fast-growth areas of the 1950s that ranked highest on status indicators, followed in order by newer outlying suburban areas, by older neighborhoods, and by center city slums. Although the suburban counties stretch more than fifty miles into the mountains from the central business district, the values for Zone 4 are not held down by the inclusion of rural backlands. Since Zone 4 has four times the population of Zone 3, it is more likely that its

Table 3.7. *Socioeconomic Indicators for Pima County and Subareas of Tucson and North/East Tracts, 1940–1970*

	1940	1950	1960	1970
Percentage of population in professional-managerial jobs				
Pima County	6.7	4.3	8.2	9.5
Tucson	8.2	6.7	8.6	9.7
Ratio	1.22	1.56	1.05	1.02
North/East Tracts	N.A.	N.A.	12.4	14.85
Ratio			1.51	1.56
Median years school for persons 25 years or older				
Pima County	9.2	11.2	12.1	12.4
Tucson	10.1	11.8	12.1	12.4
Ratio	1.10	1.05	1.00	1.00
North/East Tracts	N.A.	N.A.	12.6	12.7
Ratio			1.04	1.02
Median income families and unrelated individuals				
Pima County	N.A.	$2,373	$4,762	$ 6,983
Tucson	N.A.	$2,155	$4,800	$ 6,764
Ratio		.91	1.01	.97
North/East Tracts	N.A.	N.A.	$6,455	$10,726
Ratio			1.36	1.53
Percentage of population Spanish-surname				
Pima County	N.A.	19.3	16.7	23.6
Tucson	N.A.	24.1	16.8	23.9
Ratio		1.25	1.01	1.01
North/East Tracts	N.A.	N.A.	3.8	8.5
Ratio			.23	.36

Note: Ratios are median values for North/East tracts or individual-based values for Tucson, each divided by individual-based values for Pima County. N.A.: not available.

lower medians result from the inclusion of a wide range of suburban communities at all income levels. The decline of areawide per capita income levels during the sixties also suggests that migrants to the SMSA during that decade were of lower socioeconomic rank than those in the fifties.

Status changes for the entire wartime and postwar period can also be traced for the neighborhoods located within Portland's 1940 city limits. Such sections of Zone 2 include the bulk of the east side and a few

Table 3.8. *Socioeconomic Indicators for Bexar County and Subareas of San Antonio and North Tracts, 1940–1970*

	1940	1950	1960	1970
Percentage of population in professional-managerial jobs				
Bexar County	8.3	6.2	6.3	7.3
San Antonio	8.1	6.4	6.3	7.2
Ratio	.98	1.03	1.00	.99
North Tracts	N.A.	N.A.	12.3	13.7
Ratio			1.95	1.87
Median years school for persons 25 years or older				
Bexar County	6.3	9.1	10.0	11.6
San Antonio	6.5	9.0	9.6	10.8
Ratio	1.03	.99	.96	.93
North Tracts	N.A.	N.A.	12.4	12.8
Ratio			1.24	1.10
Median income families and unrelated individuals				
Bexar County	N.A.	$2,196	$3,764	$6,346
San Antonio	N.A.	$2,373	$4,069	$6,563
Ratio		1.08	1.08	1.03
North Tracts	N.A.	N.A.	$6,305	$9,259
Ratio			1.68	1.46
Percentage of population Spanish-surname				
Bexar County	N.A.	35.3	37.4	45.3
San Antonio	N.A.	39.3	41.3	52.2
Ratio		1.11	1.15	1.10
North Tracts	N.A.	N.A.	7.6	14.3
Ratio			.20	.32

Note: Ratios are median values for North Tracts or individual-based values for San Antonio, each divided by individual-based values for Bexar County. N.A.: not available.

West Hills neighborhoods. Zone 1 includes the central business district, Northwest Portland, and immediate cross-river commercial areas; between 1950 and 1970, massive land clearance for expressways, the civic center urban renewal project, and the Lloyd Center complex helped to reduce its population from seventy to thirty-five thousand. As of 1940, Zone 1 outranked Zone 2 in occupational patterns and lagged in educational level (Table 3.6). From 1950 to 1970, Zone 2 maintained a small margin in education, established a small edge in occupations, and held a greatly increasing margin in income levels. As in Denver, it is possible that the slight narrowing of the gap in occupations and education during the 1960s came from a renewed attraction of older parts of Portland for young professionals at the start of their

Table 3.9. *Socioeconomic Indicators in Portland, Surrounding Counties, and County Subareas, 1940–1970*

	1940	1950	1960	1970
Percentage of population in professional-managerial jobs				
Washington County	4.9	7.1	10.5	12.3
Clackamas County	5.3	6.6	9.3	9.7
West Tracts	N.A.	N.A.	14.2	15.0
Multnomah County	8.7	9.4	8.5	9.7
Portland	9.2	10.2	9.0	9.8
Other Multnomah	5.5†	6.5	7.8	9.5
West Tracts	N.A.	14.2	14.8	17.2
Clark County	5.1	4.5	6.6	8.0
Median years school for persons 25 years or older				
Washington County	8.8*	10.9*	12.2	12.6
Clackamas County	8.8*	10.6*	11.9	12.4
West Tracts	N.A.	N.A.	12.6	13.0
Multnomah County	10.0*	11.6*	12.0	12.3
Portland	10.2	11.8	12.0	12.3
Other Multnomah	9.1†	N.A.	12.0	12.3
West Tracts	N.A.	N.A.	12.8	13.6
Clark County	8.9*	9.6*	11.6	12.3
Median income families and unrelated individuals				
Washington County	N.A.	$2,964	$5,863	$10,083
Clackamas County	N.A.	$2,862	$5,525	$ 9,400
West Tracts	N.A.	N.A.	$6,920	$11,184
Multnomah County	N.A.	$3,077	$5,205	$ 7,527
Portland	N.A.	$3,051	$4,918	$ 6,701
Other Multnomah	N.A.	N.A.	$5,926	$ 9,582
West Tracts	N.A.	N.A.	$6,823	$10,996
Clark County	N.A.	$3,046	$5,572	$ 8,947

Note: West tract figures for Clackamas County are median values for tracts 201–207. West tract figures for Multnomah County are median values for tracts 46, 58, 60–71. N.A.: not available.

*Average of medians for males and females weighted by numbers of males and females 25 years or older.

†Average of rural-farm and rural-nonfarm weighted by population.

careers. In Portland, however, such a trend is countered by the continuing role of Zone 1 neighborhoods as places of residence for blacks, American Indians, and other ethnic migrants.

Despite the fourth highest growth rate in the nation from 1940 to 1970, metropolitan Orlando also showed only limited consistency with the status reversal model. Within Orange County, the status differences among different sections were relatively slight. In 1970, Zone 4 and Zone 3 had roughly the same values on all three socioeconomic indicators, while Zone 1 and 2 taken together matched the outer rings in educational level. Because of drastic changes in census tract boundaries, it is not possible accurately to define the four zones for 1960. A rough equivalent to Zones 3 and 4 together, however, are the areas that in 1960 had a plurality of housing built in the last decade (see Table 3.5). As of 1960, this area of more recent growth outranked older sections of Orange County in education and income but not in professional-managerial occupations. In contradiction to the expected pattern, the recent growth ring in 1960 had a higher status relative to the metropolitan area than did Zones 3 and 4 in 1970. The only strong shift in status over the decade came from rapid urbanization in Seminole County, where a drop in black population from 25 to 17 percent and major gains in socioeconomic status reflected the arrival of thousands of middle-class white migrants.

Despite the importance of concentric growth rings, local residents are more likely to view their cities in terms of immediately obvious divisions between richer and poorer neighborhoods. The evolution of such divisions creates a second sort of orderliness in the social geography of metropolitan areas that is a product of local circumstances rather than national trends in locational decisions. Indeed, data on the cities under consideration provide continued support for the work of Homer Hoyt, who demonstrated in the 1930s that different types of land use tend to spread outward from the central business district in distinct wedges or sectors of differing economic function and status. Specific circumstances of landscape and industrial siting determine the location of the several residential sectors, which tend to grow outward without regard to municipal boundaries. The result, as Hoyt's contemporary William F. Ogburn realized, was that "the suburban movement is simply an expansion of parts of the city outward and the suburbs are thus diversified just as are the wards within the city."[27] In the terminology of current scholarship, this pattern of sectoral growth

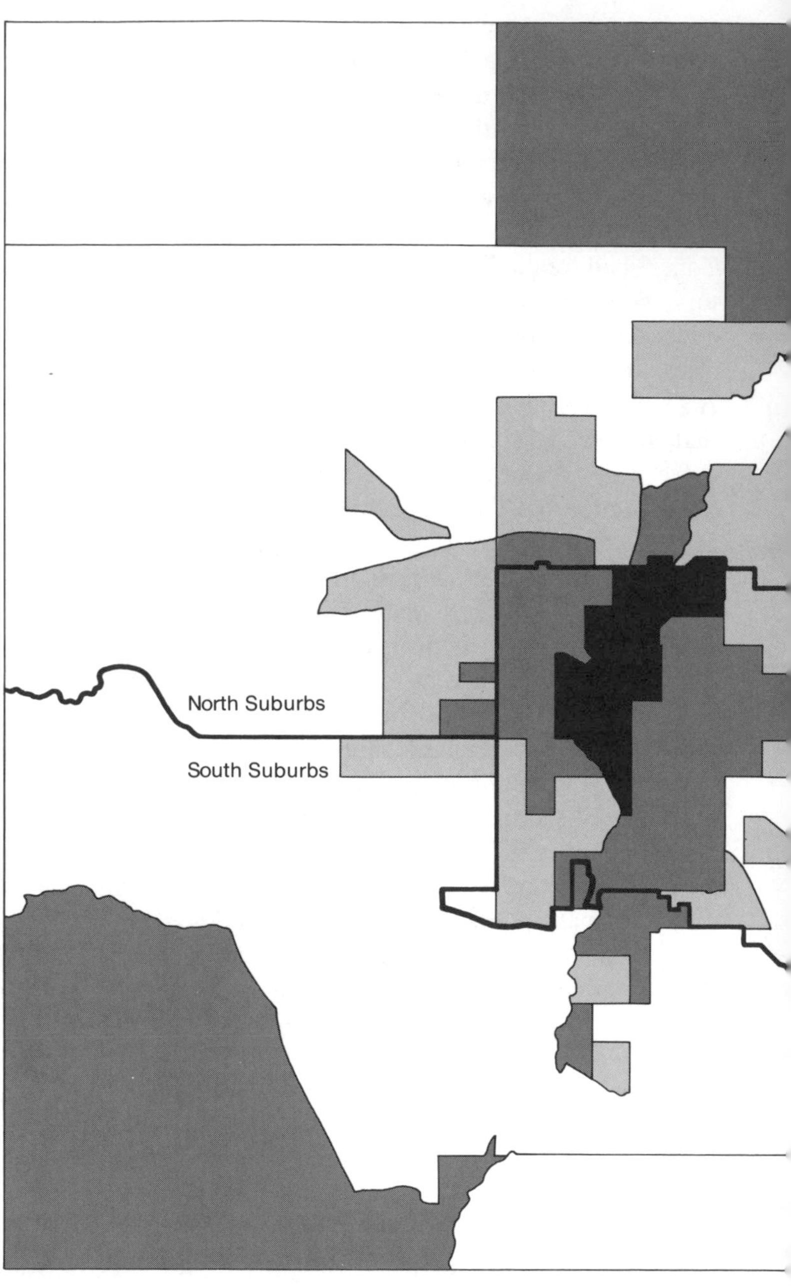

Housing Age Zones: Denver, 1970
Adams, Arapahoe, Denver, and Jefferson counties

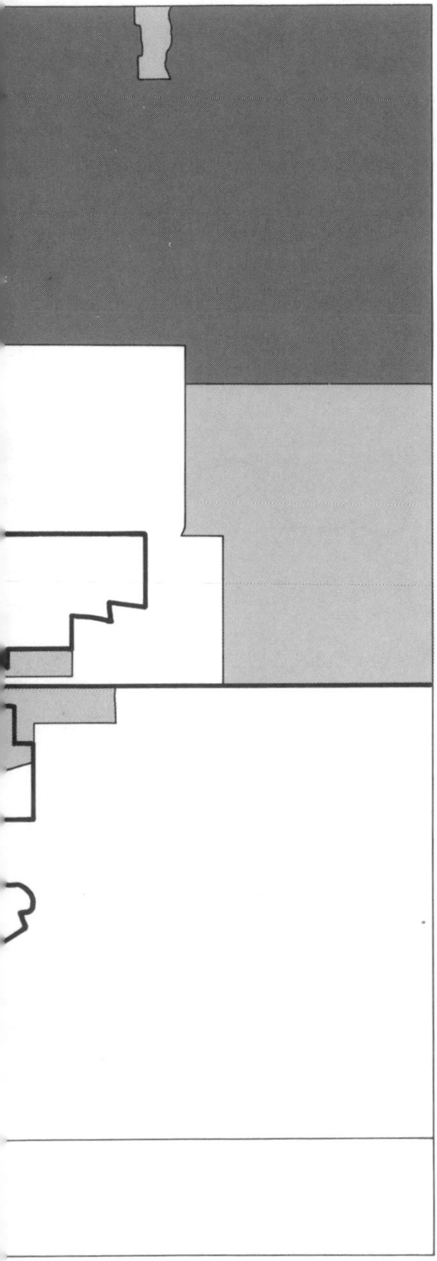

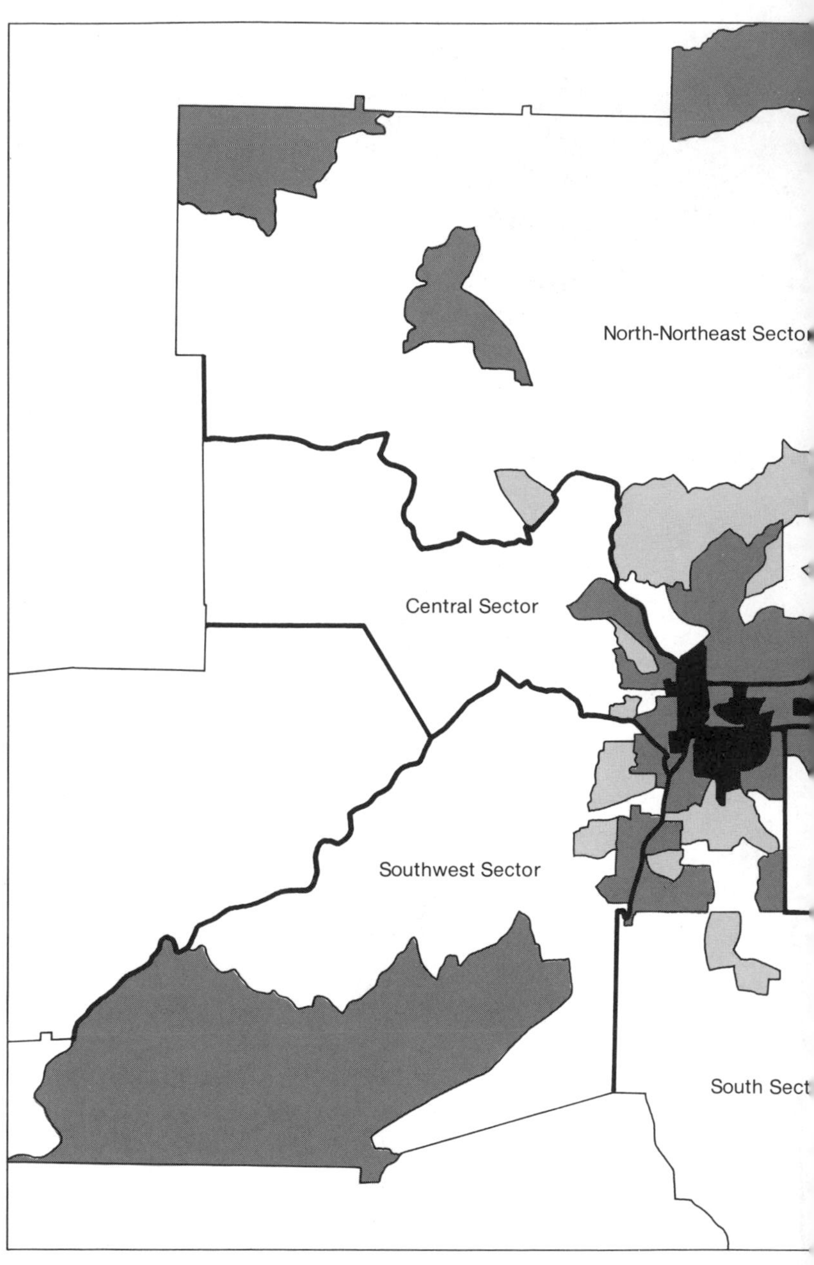

Housing Age Zones: Atlanta, 1970
Clayton, Cobb, DeKalb, and Fulton counties

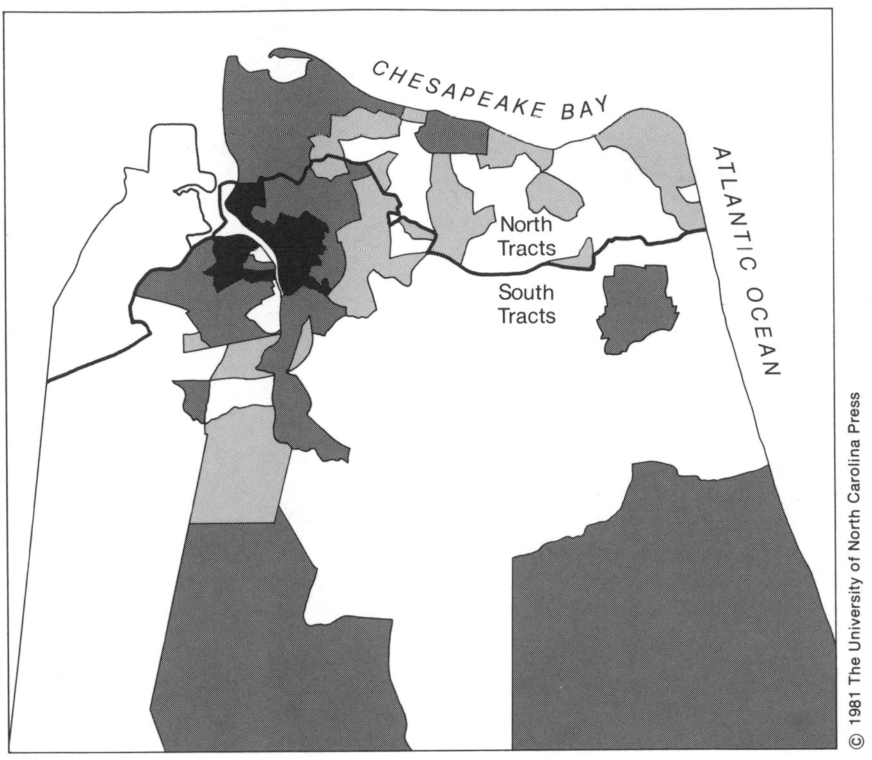

Housing Age Zones: Norfolk, 1970
Chesapeake, Norfolk, Portsmouth, and Virginia Beach

and suburban diversity is summarized as "the urbanization of the suburbs." According to Louis Masotti's analysis of employment, multifamily housing, and population movements, "suburbia . . . is rapidly becoming a highly competitive and increasingly attractive, although more loosely organized, alternative to the historic city for economic activities and population groups. In major metropolitan areas, there is now scarcely an urban function, activity, or group which cannot also be found in suburbia."[28]

Examination of sectoral patterns in cities and suburbs also reveals an important difference between southern and western SMSAs that was not apparent in the analysis of growth rings. In the South, the heritage of rigid social lines and a racial caste system has allowed social dis-

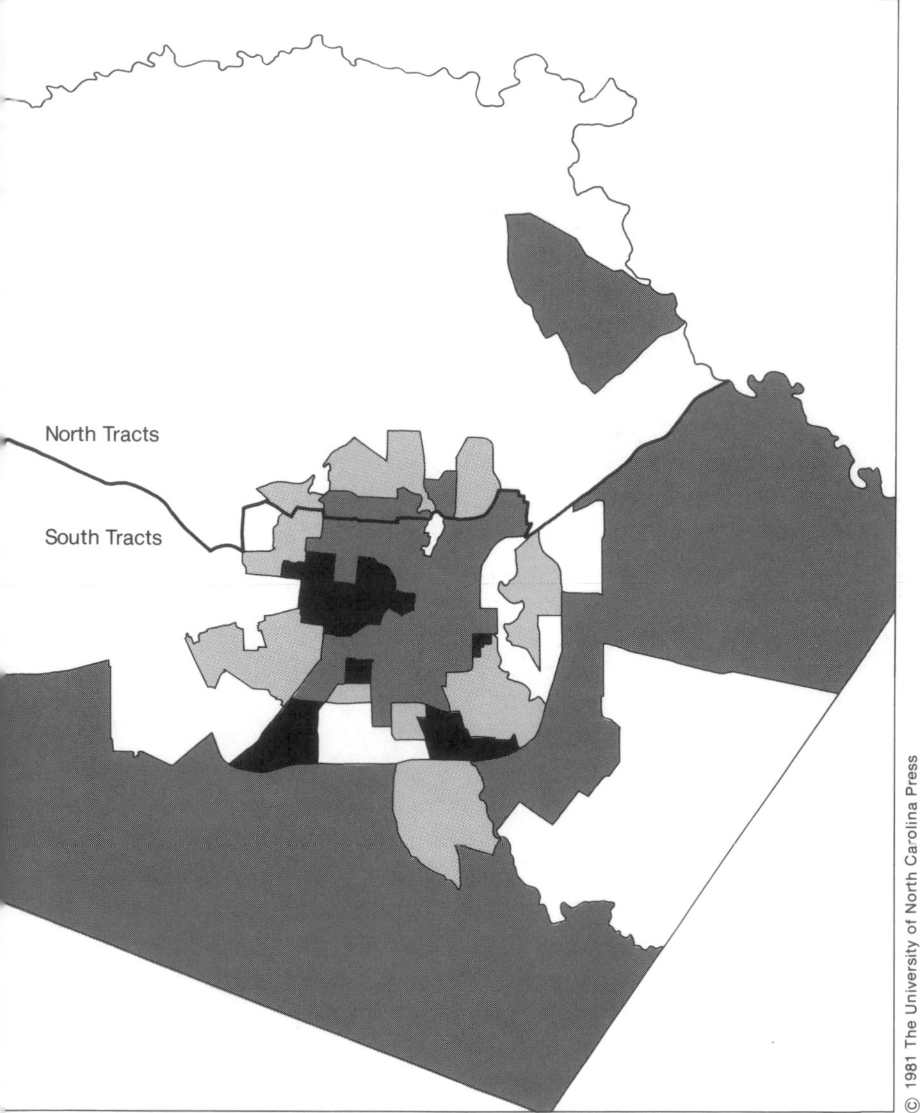

Housing Age Zones: San Antonio, 1970
Bexar County

Housing Age Zones: Portland, 1970
Clackamas, Clark, Multnomah, and Washington counties

tance to function without the reinforcement of physical isolation. Especially in older southern cities, the result was the development of a close-grained pattern of racial and social segregation in which black and white and rich and poor neighborhoods jumbled together in close proximity and in which attention focused on the social status of small groups of blocks rather than large sectors of the city.[29] Even rapid growth in sunbelt boom cities such as Norfolk and Orlando has not erased this typically southern style of social geography that finds both minority neighborhoods and high-status white neighborhoods scattered relatively equally through the entire metropolitan area.

Western cities, in contrast, have a much simpler social geography. Working without the guidance of long established community patterns or of rigid social codes, westerners in the late nineteenth and early twentieth centuries built new cities in which social distinctions were maintained by a clear division between better and poorer sides of town. Two generations later, Denverites still agree that the south side of their city holds more prestige and social status than its northern half, while Tucson residents recognize the higher status of the north and east sides. A similar perception of social differences between the east and west sides of the Willamette River in Portland has created open social rivalry and tacit political conflict over the location of public facilities. In the most extreme case, politics in San Antonio for the past decade has centered on a bitter dispute between the northern and southern halves of the city over the equitable distribution of city investment and services.

San Antonio's split between north and south sides has been shaped by the city's location on the southern edge of the Edwards Plateau. Southward toward the Gulf of Mexico and the Rio Grande are poor farming counties with large Hispanic populations. North and northwest are limestone hills attractive to German immigrants in the nineteenth century and retirement communities in the later twentieth century. Within Bexar County, the old Spanish settlement of San Antonio and the American city that developed around it were located just below the southern edge of the plateau country. With the development of streetcar suburbs and early automobile suburbs between 1880 and 1940, upper-status residents sought higher land to the north of the city. Community names such as Alamo Heights, Olmos Park, Terrell Hills, Los Angeles Heights, Castle Hills, and Balcones Heights indicate the topography. Lower land around the central business district was reserved for blacks to the east and Mexican-Americans to the south and west. The middle-class community of Highlands on an isolated ridge to the southeast was the only exception to the pattern.[30]

Growth since World War II has exaggerated the city's bifurcation. As Hispanic population has grown from 177,000 in 1950 to 460,000 in 1975, it has filled in empty land to the west and south, much of it flat, ill drained, and close to airbases, sewer facilities, and steam plants. Peripheral growth on the south and west edges of the city has involved the scattered location of mobile homes and other low-cost housing and is inadequately served by commercial facilities. The interpenetration of low-rise slums with the crop and grazing lands of southern Texas provides a symbol of San Antonio's historic role as refuge and reservoir for Spanish-speaking farm workers. North-side development, in contrast, has reached frantically for the hills. At the same time that high-status Hispanic residents have moved into neighborhoods in the near northwest, the Anglo middle class has sought housing adjacent to the circumferential expressway.[31] The strongest surge in the 1950s was toward the northeast, where Randolph Air Force Base and a cluster of small suburbs in Bexar and Guadalupe counties form a semi-independent complex.[32] More recently the tide of development has turned toward the northwest where the new insurance offices of the United Services Automobile Association, the South Texas Medical Center, and the University of Texas at San Antonio have served as growth poles in the seventies. Indeed, explosive suburbanization north of the I-410 loop has created a current crisis over the acceptability of urban growth on the recharge zone for the aquifer which provides San Antonio's water.

Census tract data for 1960 and 1970 clearly define the difference between north-side and south-side San Antonio. Table 3.8 shows individual-based figures for Bexar County as a whole and median values for census tracts north of Hildebrand Avenue (the northern boundary of San Antonio until 1940 and the accepted metropolitan dividing line). The north side maintained a sharp advantage through the decade in its share of professional-managerial workers. The narrowing of the gap in income and education resulted more from improved educational and employment opportunities in the central city than from any reversal in the relative attractiveness of the two areas. It is especially impressive that the north side held its advantage in socioeconomic status while absorbing 94,850 new residents or two-thirds of the Bexar

County population increase. It is equally important that the division between north and south sides is sharper than that among the several growth zones. Because of the bifurcation of the metropolis, recent growth areas have absorbed both rich and poor, Anglo and Mexican. As a result, the north side as a whole shows an advantage over the highest status outer zone on every indicator for both 1960 and 1970 (Tables 3.5 and 3.8).

In Portland the original axis of development ran north and south along the Willamette River, with the first settlement and the evolving central business district sited on a sloping terrace of level land on the west bank. The Tualatin Mountains or ''West Hills'' confined growth on the west side to an area scarcely more than a mile deep, with a scattering of expensive homes struggling up the slopes. Construction of bridges and the growth of the streetcar system opened flatter land east of the Willamette to more extensive development in the latter part of the nineteenth and early twentieth centuries. The east side rapidly developed with a mixture of wholesaling and light industry, blue-collar and white-collar neighborhoods, and Italian, Slavic, and Anglo communities.[33]

The growth induced by World War II had its most immediate impact on the east side. The bulk of wartime public housing was located in east-side neighborhoods and most of the city's new black residents settled in older housing just east of the river. With undeveloped and buildable land and easy access to centers of industrial employment, the east side absorbed much of the area's lower-income and middle-income housing between 1945 and 1960 as tract ranch homes in new neighborhoods filled the role played earlier by the ubiquitous bungalow.[34] Beyond the city limits, eastern Multnomah County showed the highest growth rate among suburban counties, with a share of metropolitan area population that climbed from 9.9 percent in 1940 to 18.3 percent in 1960 before dropping in the sixties. Multnomah County in the 1950s and 1960s was in many ways a classic suburb. It counted a high percentage of workers who commuted to Portland, and its percentage of residents who had moved from the central city was twice that of the other SMSA counties. Such rapid growth was supported by a county government willing to assume urban functions.[35]

When intensive residential development came to the west side after 1945, the higher social status of the West Hills was already well established as a product of the expense of hillside construction and

Table 3.10. *Socioeconomic and Ethnicity Indicators for Atlanta and Metropolitan Subareas, 1940–1970*

	1940	1950	1960	1970
Percentage of population in professional-managerial jobs				
SMSA	6.0	7.4	7.6	10.0
Atlanta	6.5	7.4	7.4	8.8
Central Sector	N.A.	N.A.	4.3	3.6
Southeast Sector	N.A.	N.A.	4.4	4.4
Southwest Sector	N.A.	N.A.	8.3	10.6
North Sector	N.A.	N.A.	11.7	14.9
Median years school for persons 25 years or older				
SMSA	6.9	9.7	11.1	12.1
Atlanta	8.6	9.5	10.5	11.5
Central Sector	N.A.	N.A.	8.7	10.1
Southeast Sector	N.A.	N.A.	9.5	10.3
Southwest Sector	N.A.	N.A.	11.7	12.3
North Sector	N.A.	N.A.	12.5	12.6
Median income families and unrelated individuals				
SMSA	N.A.	$2,477	$4,901	$ 8,769
Atlanta	N.A.	$2,191	$3,938	$ 6,257
Central Sector	N.A.	N.A.	$3,480	$ 4,806
Southeast Sector	N.A.	N.A.	$4,714	$ 7,618
Southwest Sector	N.A.	N.A.	$5,429	$ 9,626
North Sector	N.A.	N.A.	$6,155	$10,350
Percentage of population black				
SMSA	26.8	23.8	22.8	22.3
Atlanta	34.6	36.6	38.3	51.3
Central Sector	N.A.	N.A.	37.2	93.2
Southeast Sector	N.A.	N.A.	5.1	10.5
Southwest Sector	N.A.	N.A.	6.7	18.7
North Sector	N.A.	N.A.	2.4	0.6

Note: N.A.: not available.

transportation and the proximity of downtown offices. The westward flow of new development reached Washington County in turn during the 1950s, creating new suburban communities that took their social tone from the adjacent Portland neighborhoods. Although the county's share of total SMSA population rose only from 7.8 percent to 8.7

percent during the forties, it reached 15.7 percent by 1970. If Multnomah County's suburban communities have retained close ties to the central city, those in Washington County have been considerably more independent. Among the several suburban jurisdictions it had the highest proportion of residents arriving directly from outside the metropolitan area both in 1960 and 1970. With the exception of Clark County, where cross-river commuters are confined to a single bridge, Washington County also had the lowest percentage of workers who commute to Portland and the highest percentage working in their county of residence.[36]

The resulting contrast of east side and west side shows clearly in measurements of social status. Omitting Clark County because it is an independent industrial center with limited out-of-state commuting, Table 3.8 shows that Washington County in 1940 ranked below Clackamas County, Portland, and the remainder of Multnomah County on all three standard indicators. After making slight relative gains to 1950, Washington County surged ahead of the rest of the metropolitan area in 1960 and widened its lead by 1970. The difference between the eastern and western halves of the metropolitan area is further clarified if the West Hills census tracts in western Portland and Multnomah County and the Clackamas County tracts west of the Willamette River are grouped as separate subareas. In both 1960 and 1970 the median values for the tracts in each of these west-side areas far exceeded the values for the entire county of which they are a part.

County level data for Denver show the development after 1940 of a similar split between northern and southern suburbs. In particular, Adams County by 1970 lagged behind the other suburban counties and Denver in education and occupational status and behind Arapahoe and Jefferson counties in median income, with the low income level in Boulder County attributable to its large student population.[37] A more detailed analysis of regional differences can be introduced by dividing Jefferson County into northern and southern segments along Sixth Avenue. Adams and north Jefferson counties constitute that part of the suburban ring encircling the northern half of Denver, and Arapahoe and south Jefferson counties complete the ring around the southern half of the city. As measured by mean census tract values, the southern suburbs in 1970 outranked the northern on all three status indicators, strengthening a differential already apparent in 1960 (Table 3.4).

At least in part, the status differential between north and south suburbs reflects the division of metropolitan Denver by ethnicity. The bulk of the black population of Denver proper lives within the northeast quadrant of the city and the bulk of the Hispanic population lives in the northwest quadrant.[38] Each minority group has followed these same directions of residential expansion since the 1940s as metro area black population rose from 10,000 to 50,164 and Hispanic from 30,000 to 140,000.[39] Although only 3,154 blacks lived in the suburban ring as of 1970, the Spanish-surname population at that date totaled 86,345 in Denver, 32,930 in Adams and north Jefferson counties together, and 11,361 in Arapahoe and south Jefferson counties together. It has been argued elsewhere that the Hispanic population of Denver since World War II has been experiencing a process of assimilation similar to that of European immigrants in a previous era.[40] The northern suburbs of Denver thus have lower status than the southern suburbs in part because they are the region of upward mobility and assimilation for Hispanic residents of the metropolis.

In turn, ethnic patterns within Denver reflect a more general division of the city traceable to the nineteenth century. Since the valley of the South Platte River in Denver opens toward the north, the broad bottomlands northwest and north of the original settlement provided the logical location for railroad tracks and freight yards, stockyards, and smelters. Literally "on the wrong side of the tracks," north Denver communities in the late nineteenth and early twentieth centuries developed as blue-collar and ethnic neighborhoods, with Italians immediately north of the Platte, Slavic immigrants in Globeville adjacent to the Globe Smelter, and Germans, Welsh, Irish, and Cornishmen in Elyria near the Argo Smelter.[41] As the city's black and Mexican populations grew rapidly after 1940, the low-cost housing in such older working-class communities seemed the reasonable location for their settlement. Over the last generation, the expansion of minority population has therefore involved the displacement of previously established working-class communities.[42] Environmental drawbacks of recent decades including airport noise and water supply problems have worked to reinforce a relatively lower reputation for north Denver and adjacent suburbs.

Residents of the smaller western city of Tucson also commonly refer to the social divide that separates the affluent and Republican north and east ends of the metropolis from the poorer and Democratic south and west sides.[43] The older sections of the metropolis, which extend roughly north-south along the Santa Cruz River and include the town of South Tucson, are the areas of Hispanic residence in mid-century. Anglo population in the 1950s pushed eastward into new neighborhoods beyond the University of Arizona and north of Davis Mountain Air Force Base. In the following decade higher-status Anglos continued to settle in increasingly distant east-side areas and in new north-side communities. As a result, 62 percent of the population increase in metropolitan Tucson in the 1960s was absorbed in the area lying north and east of I-10, the Rillito River, Alveron Way, and the air force base. Both in 1960 and 1970, this northeast side outranked the highest growth ring. Indeed, the northeast side diverged upward from the SMSA average in income and occupational status during the 1960s (Table 3.7).

Norfolk provides a sharp contrast to the bifurcated western metropolis. Both topography and the social patterns peculiar to the South have strongly modified any tendency toward a north-south split of the metropolitan area. The key to local geography is the attractiveness of waterfront locations for both commercial-industrial and residential uses. The city in the early twentieth century was a waterfront metropolis. The north-south axis of the Elizabeth River served as the axis for business activity, with factories, wharves, and the central business districts of Norfolk and Portsmouth along the main channel and its Eastern Branch. Through the 1940s, the main areas of residential growth lay to the north toward the Naval Operating Base and to the south around the Norfolk Naval Shipyard in Portsmouth.[44] Upper-status neighborhoods sought waterfront locations along several smaller tributaries of the Elizabeth, particularly the West Branch in Portsmouth and the Lafayette River in Norfolk. As in many southern cities, black population occupied a half-dozen pockets scattered among white communities.

Since 1950, explosive suburban growth has shifted the axis of the metropolitan area from north-south to east-west, with major development eastward into Virginia Beach and westward into Chesapeake and Suffolk.[45] In the new suburbanized metropolis, many upper-status neighborhoods have developed to the north around tributaries and extensions of the James River, Hampton Roads, and Chesapeake Bay, including the Nansemond River, the West Branch, Lake Smith and Lake Whitehurst, Lynnhaven Bay, Broad Bay, and Linkhorn Bay.

Along the entire northern edge of the region, however, higher-price residential areas have had to compete for waterfront access with the Naval Base, Naval Air Station, Little Creek Amphibious Base, and Fort Story (all with associated military housing), with new manufacturing in Portsmouth and Suffolk, and with existing black communities.

The resulting split between northern and southern sections of the SMSA is most obvious if the large suburban city of Chesapeake is compared with the remainder of the area. Chesapeake is the most "interior" of the metropolitan municipalities and has its major waterfront along the Elizabeth River lined with factories and tank farms. In 1960, the Chesapeake area (at that time Norfolk County and the city of South Norfolk) ranked below Virginia Beach in housing values and below Virginia Beach, Portsmouth, and Norfolk in educational level and professional-managerial employment. Its only improvement in relative standing over the next decade was to pass Norfolk in occupational status.

Because of the fragmentation of the region by tidal inlets, Norfolk residents tend to think in terms of individual communities rather than an areawide division. However, it is also possible to draw an arbitrary dividing line that marks off sixty tracts in the northern parts of Chesapeake, Portsmouth, Norfolk, and Virginia Beach. Even though the line is designed to mark off the maximum of high-status white neighborhoods on the north side of the metropolis, they are intermixed with military facilities and isolated black communities.[46] Between 1960 and 1970, this northern sector showed a slight decline in status relative to the metropolitan area as a whole. In comparison, it stood roughly equal to Zone 3 with above average but not exceptional status.[47]

In Atlanta, the definition during the early twentieth century of radial sectors of differing status determined socioeconomic patterns within surrounding suburbs through the postwar decades. The establishment of several planned upper-class neighborhoods around the turn of the century fixed the north side as the city's prestige section for white Atlantans. More recent growth in the same direction has brought high-status residents to Buckhead and West Paces Ferry in northern Fulton County and to the suburban communities in DeKalb County stretching north from Druid Hills and Emory University. The old black neighborhood which centered on Auburn Street east of the business district grew rapidly eastward in the 1960s and 1970s toward a smaller black community in the town of Decatur. A second black sector also developed in the first decades of the century around the Atlanta University complex on the west side. In turn, an area of middle-class black residence has grown southwestward from this community and a lower-status black area northwestward. The remaining southeast quadrant of the city has developed with a relatively close mixture of industrial activities and lower-status black and white neighborhoods.[48]

Census tract data for 1960 and 1970 confirm the importance of Atlanta's sectoral pattern. For analysis, Fulton, DeKalb, Cobb, and Clayton counties can be divided into southeast, southwest, northside, and central sectors (the last stretching from Decatur to southern Cobb County across the central business district).[49] In both years, the sectors ranked in the same order, with the north side and the southwest quadrant above the metropolitan average and the southeast and central sectors below. There was a slight decline in the contrast among the sectors as a result of the huge wave of suburbanization in the 1960s, but the difference between the four sectors in both years was greater than that between the pre-1950 and post-1960 housing age zones. In accord with the common southern pattern, the southern half of the city shows a relatively close intermixture of black and white population on the scale of census tracts.

The social geography of Orlando can be described even more directly as an abstract mosaic of individual communities distributed without a larger pattern. Again as in many other southern cities, black residents are scattered through the metropolis in several small communities. In 1970, there were seven noncontiguous sets of census tracts in the metropolitan area with 30 percent or more black populations. High-status populations were found in an inner ring around downtown Orlando and in a half-dozen corridors leading outward from that ring to the northwest, north, northeast (through Winter Park), east, south, and southwest (toward Disney World).

The foregoing analysis supports two fundamental criticisms of the concept of metropolitan sprawl. Although the term implies the random distribution of land uses, sunbelt cities possess clearly defined patterns of residential geography. Gas stations and fast-food franchises may be jumbled among schools and homes within specific neighborhoods, but there is readily apparent order in the distribution of population groups on the scale of the metropolitan area. The metaphor as applied to Houston or Los Angeles also implies newness in addition to disorder, for sprawl is seen as a product of the postwar plunge into automobility.

In fact, historical analysis of small-area statistical data and of information on neighborhood perceptions demonstrates the impressive consistency of residential geography. The most striking characteristic of social geography in the huge tracts of land absorbed into sunbelt SMSAs over the last four decades is the reproduction of old patterns in the new landscape.

In the Southwest and West, broad sectoral divisions that antedate World War II have continued to guide residential choices in the era of explosive suburbanization. Such basic north-south and east-west divisions are based in part on parallel reactions to local geography and in part on a spillover effect that causes previously undeveloped segments of the suburban zone to take on the social coloration of adjacent sectors of the core city. The long-standing social gap between the two halves of the metropolitan area in Portland, Denver, and Tucson in fact widened during the 1960s. In the southeastern cities of Norfolk and Orlando, where geographical segregation has been less needed to preserve social distinctions, suburbanites have copied the city by mixing a variety of neighborhood types on a small scale. As is true farther west, however, local physical features have been as important in determining the character of specific neighborhoods as have national attitudes toward city and suburban living.

In the evaluation of alternative descriptions of metropolitan social geography, these findings suggest that the model summarized as the "urbanization of the suburbs" provides the most accurate description of the growth process. Whether the particular city shows the outward extension of growth sectors or the propagation of an urban mosaic, its characteristic prewar pattern has continued strongly to influence contemporary residential choices. Socioeconomic differentiation by growth zone, which appears as a recent addition to residential patterns, has so far failed to reduce the importance of these previously established patterns. In western cities, indeed, it has yet to create suburban rings whose margin above SMSA averages matches that of north-side San Antonio, west-side Portland, or south-side Denver. The extension of Orlando's mosaic pattern into the suburbs has similarly prevented the emergence of a clear differentiation by growth rings.

The description of variations in socioeconomic status patterns within sunbelt SMSAs also carries implications for metropolitan political relations. Most obviously, the outward movement of high-status neighborhoods through the several growth rings has accentuated the political power of suburban areas. By the 1960s, suburban jurisdictions in most sunbelt cities could rely not only on their growing strength in numbers but also on the political resource represented by their affluent residents. Increasingly, the political influence of new suburbanites within the metropolis has been disproportionately weighted by their greater than average wealth, their education, and their contacts in business and the professions. In consequence, we can expect to find that suburban leaders in the last fifteen years have displayed new confidence in battles with the central city.

Equally important, however, are emerging differences within the suburban rings. In several SMSAs, the continued advance in the relative status of the outermost suburbs has left older suburban communities to face growing problems of physical deterioration and the accommodation of minority populations. These older stranded suburbs will more and more find that their interests lie close at hand with the central city rather than with new neighborhoods that march relentlessly toward the horizon. Indeed, the president's task force on suburban problems concluded a decade ago that "the already vast and rapidly growing suburbs of the United States are in a state of quiet, slowly building crisis. . . . The suburban crisis is an indivisible part of the urban crisis."[50]

The emerging geographical patterns that support the thesis of the urbanization of the suburbs also promise increasing political conflict within suburbia. There is no reason to expect frequent cooperation between poor and rich suburban counties nor permanent alliances between outlying Anglo and Hispanic communities. Without discounting the fundamental differences that remain between central cities and suburbs, the increasing variety of suburban environments suggests the importance of viewing metropolitan politics as a multilateral process.

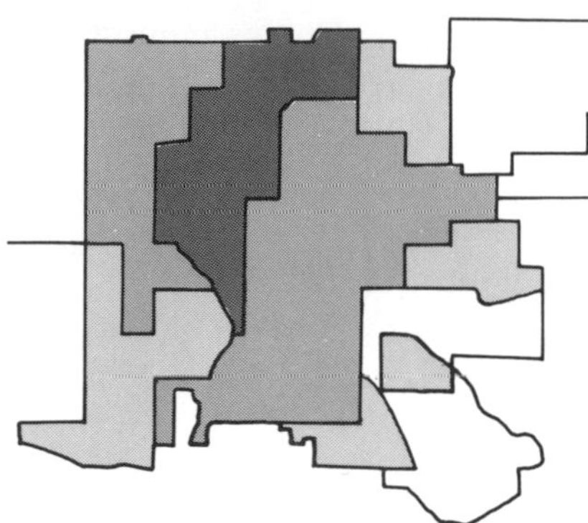

Chapter 4

The Sunbelt Cities in World War II

In November 1943, the editors of *Fortune* took time out from World War II to discuss the "battle of the approaches" in American city planning. Borrowing a military metaphor, the magazine contrasted the approach to urban planning that guided specific tactics by a larger strategy with the approach that was concerned only with the tactics necessary to solve specific problems. Lewis Mumford was offered as the leading spokesman for comprehensive planning that tried to match physical development to social needs and to balance the location of activities and land uses within entire metropolitan areas. The contrasting figure was Robert Moses, the archetype of the realistic planner whose concerns were "beautification, spectacular piecemeal attacks on specific problems, and half-baked public works programs." The discussion left little doubt that *Fortune* hoped to persuade its readers that comprehensive metropolitan planning was an essential tool for promoting the rational growth of the postwar American economy.[1]

In the majority of southern and western cities, wartime growth meant new problems as well as new opportunities. Staggering demands on housing and public services forced municipal officials and business leaders to make specific decisions on the same sorts of issues that *Fortune* had raised in general terms. In the short term, most of the wartime boom cities discovered that they lacked the resources, the institutional tools, and the agreement on basic policy goals effectively to meet the crises of 1941 and 1942. By the second half of the war, however, a clear pattern emerged in which political and economic leaders in city after city agreed that the primary function of urban planning and public action was to assist in maintaining and expanding the business and employment gains of the war years. In the longer run, this consensus on a practical agenda for municipal planning and policy helped to set the themes that would dominate political discussion in sunbelt cities for at least two postwar decades.

Decisions about the character of urban planning efforts in the early 1940s were especially important for the cities of the South and West. More than any other single factor, it was the American mobilization for World War II that marked the emergence of the Sunbelt. The expansion of defense production in 1940 and 1941 and the organization of a huge military enterprise in 1942 and 1943 accelerated previous regional growth patterns and shifted the balance within the national economy toward the South Atlantic, Gulf, and Pacific coasts. The pattern of differential growth that bypassed many of the older cities of the northern industrial belt simultaneously added new layers to the urban economies of the South and West. Small cities like Phoenix, Albuquerque, and Charleston became important urban centers within half a decade. The uneventful development of larger cities from Richmond and Norfolk to Denver and Portland similarly was interrupted by new growth and new roles as regional and national metropolises.

The basic needs of the war economy determined the regional distribution of population growth in the early forties. The War Department and Navy Department concentrated new military facilities in warmer states which allowed year-round training and in ports with direct access to the European and Pacific Theaters. Roughly three-fourths of all defense production contracts went to sixty corporations, among which aircraft and shipbuilding firms were obviously prominent.[2] Estimates by the Census Bureau based on registration for ration books showed that the Pacific and Southeast census regions enjoyed a net increase in civilian population from 1940 to 1943, even though the growth of the armed forces cut the country's total civilian population by three million. The states with the highest rates of population growth were California, Oregon, Washington, Nevada, Utah, Arizona, Florida, Virginia, and Maryland. The 152 counties that recorded civilian population growth of 15 percent or more from April 1940 to November 1943 likewise clustered along the Middle Atlantic, South Atlantic, Gulf and Pacific coasts and in the southwest interior.[3]

If wartime migration previewed the emergence of the Sunbelt Southeast and the Sunbelt West, it also involved a shift in relative fortunes among America's metropolitan areas. At the start of mobilization in 1940 and 1941, it was possible to pick out a list of cities where the impacts of growth were most obvious. The highest growth rates between April 1940 and October 1941 were felt by San Diego (27 percent) and Wichita (20 percent). The highest total increases during the same months were forty thousand in Seattle, fifty thousand in Washington, and one hundred fifty thousand in Los Angeles. Other cities whose populations increased by at least 10 percent included Newport News, Norfolk, and Portsmouth, Virginia, Wichita Falls and Corpus Christi, Texas, and Long Beach, California.[4]

By 1942 and 1943, the acceleration of migration made it easier to describe the patterns of metropolitan growth in summary than in detail. From the 1940 census to the fall of 1943, 81 of the 137 metropolitan areas in the United States gained civilian population and 56 lost population. Region by region, 13 of 15 metropolitan areas in the West and 43 of 49 metropolitan areas in the South gained population but only 25 of 74 metropolitan areas in the North. A few boom cities like Hartford and Philadelphia were found in the Northeast and a few more like Detroit and Saint Louis in the Middle West. Many more were strung along the coastal zones of the South and West—Richmond, Charleston, Savannah, Jacksonville, Mobile, New Orleans, Baton Rouge, Houston, Los Angeles, San Francisco, and Portland in addition to towns already mentioned. In the interior of the Southwest were other burgeoning metropolises around air bases and aircraft plants—Dallas, Fort Worth, Tulsa, San Antonio, Albuquerque, Denver, Salt Lake City, Phoenix, and Tucson. In aggregate for 1940–43, metropolitan counties in the Mountain and Pacific states gained 920,000 civilian residents, those in the South Atlantic states gained 791,000, and those in the South Central region gained 603,000. By way of contrast, the metropolitan counties of the North Central region gained only 331,000 civilian residents and those of the Northeast lost 1,023,000.[5]

In many of the southern and western cities, the war not only brought immediate crowds of newcomers but also laid the basis for continued prosperity. Shipbuilding could expect a severe recession after the war, but the establishment or expansion of military bases and other manufacturing facilities promised long-term additions to the local economic base. Population growth also meant enlarged metropolitan markets that would demand substantial increases in services, retailing, and local manufacturing once wartime restrictions were lifted. An analysis of postwar expectations by Census Director Phillip Hauser in 1943 grouped metropolitan areas into those that were likely to hold their wartime growth with little trouble, those that would need special exertions to hold wartime gains, and those that had not benefitted from the war. The first category included thirteen northern cities and forty-seven from the South and West. The second category included six northern and five southern and western cities. The last group included fifty-five northern cities and only eleven southern and western cities.[6]

The flush times that came with rearmament and full mobilization brought a common set of problems to southern and western mayors and city managers. The booming cities of the South, Southwest, and Pacific coast had to act fast and think big if they were to cope with the influx of war workers, soldiers, and sailors. Articles in *American City* and *Business Week*, papers at meetings of the American Society of Planning Officials, and publications of the National Resources Planning Board all describe frantic action by local governments in 1941 and 1942. In the opinion of City Manager C. L. Cookingham of Kansas City, the essential problem of the boom towns was to stretch limited resources to serve an exploding population with almost no lead time for preparation. First on everyone's list was the difficulty of rapidly expanding the housing supply. Close behind were the need to provide trolley and bus service to connect housing projects to war plants, bases, and downtown stores and theaters and worries about the interrelated problems of recreation, prostitution, and crime. Beyond the daily crises of overcrowding and strained utilities, city officials faced the extra problem of dealing with a new federal bureaucracy. They needed to learn the proper approach to assure larger allocations of defense housing, larger subsidies for expanded water mains, and draft deferments for cadres of police and firemen. In cities where the expansion of federal facilities removed land from the tax rolls, they also had to find alternative revenues to balance their inflated budgets.[7]

The immediate response to these problems of unanticipated growth was painfully inadequate in most southern and western cities. With a few exceptions, local governments had neither the institutional mechanisms nor the political will to take fast and constructive action. At the most obvious level, the planning function in sunbelt cities was severely limited at the start of the 1940s. A major exception was the Los Angeles area, where the Los Angeles County Regional Planning Commission from the mid-twenties had undertaken major subdivision, zoning, and highway planning for the booming metropolitan area with a staff of several dozen engineers and draftsmen. More typical were municipalities where citizen planning commissions were lucky to secure the services of a single full-time planner. Dallas, Oakland, Spokane, Nashville, Memphis, and Portland limped through the thirties with a single professional planning engineer to deal with daily zoning problems and to implement consultants' reports. Indeed, Portland's Planning Commission survived economy moves only because of the interest of Public Works Commissioner Ormond Bean, an architect who had been involved in local planning efforts since the 1910s. In Norfolk and in many other cities, the volunteer members of the planning commission were scarcely more than an advisory board to the public works department. San Antonio had no planning commission or planning function whatsoever. As late as 1939, only seven major cities in the future Sunbelt had used federal work relief money to sponsor local planning projects. Thirteen of the fifteen projects were first-step efforts to gather basic land use and building inventory information or to prepare traffic plans.[8]

The weakness of planning institutions reflected the confirmed opposition of local leaders in a number of sunbelt cities to municipal governments that went beyond the minimum of protective and custodial services. For example, ideological opposition to New Deal activism and fears of unbalanced city budgets had combined to produce a tepid response to public housing at the end of the thirties. William Hartsfield tried to limit Atlanta's public housing program after his election as mayor in 1937. In contrast, San Antonio's first housing projects were the outcome of Maury Maverick's single enthusiastic term in city hall rather than the result of broad support. Despite pleas by Ormond Bean and by visiting officials from the United States Housing Authority, Portland in 1938 responded to the National Housing Act by voting thirty-two thousand to eighteen thousand against the creation of a city housing authority to carry on local slum clearance and public housing programs. Pressures from local real estate interests in Norfolk delayed the establishment of a housing agency until the needs of shipyard workers and navy families could no longer be ignored; only in July 1940 did the city council reverse its previously negative stand. With fewer pressures for defense housing, Birmingham's business community pursued the goal of cheap government with even greater tenacity and pushed a total prohibition on the use of federal money for low-income housing through the Alabama legislature in 1944.[9]

Federal assistance to defense cities in 1940, 1941, and 1942 was as confused and inadequate as were local programs. The functional division of labor in Washington meant that field offices of federal agencies were interested chiefly in accomplishing their specific tasks without wasting time on interagency and intergovernmental coordination. Disagreements over basic policies also crippled the efforts of several new agencies whose job was presumably to coordinate the federal response to problems of wartime growth. For example, the Division of Defense Housing Coordination relied on private construction and ignored local housing authorities to the open dismay of public housing advocates in the United States Housing Authority. Only in February 1942 was a compromise defined by the creation of the National Housing Agency as an umbrella for federal housing programs, which continued to rely on an improvised combination of private construction and temporary structures. The Office of Civilian Defense similarly defined a limited function when it rejected suggestions to develop neighborhood councils that could deal with social services and community morale as well as physical protection. Also in 1941 and 1942, Congress defeated two proposals for financial assistance to localities for the preparation of public works plans.[10]

The following examples provide more detailed illustrations of the urban crisis of the early 1940s and of the troubled local responses. From 1940 at least through 1942, the common pattern was a pyramiding cycle in which overpriced and insufficient housing forced new residents to locate haphazardly through the metropolitan area and thereby placed extra burdens on already overcrowded transit systems. The dislocation of massive migration placed special burdens on schools and social services, whose inadequacy helped to raise the levels of tension and conflict. The several cases also show various sources for the inadequate response by public officials. Local leaders in Norfolk and Mobile seemed unwilling even to try to take control of their cities' growth. San Diego took several years to adjust its decision making to the extraordinary pace of change, while the San Francisco-Oakland metropolitan area lacked the institutions necessary to coordinate a response to regional problems. Portland's political and business establishment made a conscious decision in 1941 to make only short-term responses and to ignore existing planning institutions in favor of expedient and improvised actions.

In the summer of 1941, San Diego became one of the first widely recognized examples of a mobilized city when the House Committee on

National Defense Migration (Tolan Committee) made it the first stop on a tour of war centers. Reporters for *Life*, the *Saturday Evening Post*, *Business Week*, the *New Republic*, and *Fortune* all inventoried the crowded schools, overpacked hotels, raucous night life and other problems of the "rip-roaringest Coast boom town." According to testimony by the Chamber of Commerce, the city had added fifty-five thousand immigrants during the last twelve months and counted ninety thousand civilian defense workers and thirty-five thousand military personnel. Continued growth of the city's aircraft industry and its complex of naval air station, training base, supply depot, hospital, and destroyer base promised an equal increase in the following year. As Catherine Bauer Wurster described the transformation, San Diego in 1939 "was still a Utopian haven for tourists and retired people, with a few sailors for local color. By 1940, airplane workers were already crowding into auto courts and make-shift trailer parks. In 1941 the Tolan Committee found it a seething boom town, with housing as the core of every problem and controversy."[11]

The San Diego boom initially seemed as unmanageable to municipal officials as it did to journalists. Although the city had a comprehensive plan sitting on the shelf that had been prepared by consultant John Nolen, it was largely ignored in the rush of 1940 and 1941. Operating on their own hurried schedules, federal agencies exacerbated the city's problems by locating new defense plants and emergency housing on isolated sites that forced extra service costs and created painful traffic problems. At the start of 1942, only half the city's new families had found separate and permanent housing. The other half were crowded into trailers and hotels or doubled up with a second family. San Diego's city manager summarized the limited success of the municipal response when he argued that "this sudden growth . . . has meant a disorganization of practically all municipal services. Our plans were laid for orderly growth. Suddenly we find ourselves with a disordered growth, and we have to step up the tempo of every community function."[12]

Norfolk was another military center which was nearly overwhelmed by growth from 1940 through 1942. Civilian population in the Norfolk-Portsmouth area shot from 259,000 in 1940 to 323,000 in 1942 and 365,000 in 1944. Military personnel added 128,000 additional residents by 1944, while uncounted dependents of servicemen crowded the hotels and rooming houses and placed further burdens on stores and streetcars.[13] Because national rearmament restored prosperity to its shipyards and bases two years before Pearl Harbor, the metropolis matched San Diego as a detailed object lesson on the pains of rapid growth. Beneath titles like "Norfolk Night," "Our Worst War Town," and "Growing Pains of Defense" Americans could read stories about inflated prices, rampant gambling and prostitution, trailer cities and crammed apartments in which "hot beds" rented in twelve-hour shifts.[14]

The metropolis's unwillingness to deal with its housing shortage and other problems disturbed planning professionals as much as journalists. With long memories of real estate deflation after the previous war, the Norfolk Real Estate Board and local savings and loans had formed a joint committee in 1940 to limit new construction for defense workers and to deny the existence of a housing crisis.[15] Both in Norfolk and in Portsmouth, city officials similarly worried about overbuilding public facilities for a temporary population and the possible impact of a postwar housing glut on local taxes. As early as March 1941, Mayor Joseph Wood of Norfolk therefore asserted with remarkable lack of foresight that current construction was sufficient to solve the city's housing problems. Adamant inaction by Portsmouth simultaneously forced Admiral Manley Simons, the commandant of the Navy Yard, to act as his own entrepreneur in the construction of a housing project funded by the Reconstruction Finance Corporation. Three years later, Portsmouth City Manager Arthur Owens argued against new housing on available outlying land by asserting that "Portsmouth is faced with the problem of the possibility of the break-down of its tax structure, after the war, which is dependent on 55 percent of its income from real estate. The egress of people to outlying territories after the war will leave many of the old sections of the city in such condition that tax revenue from them will be impossible."[16] The result of timidity on the part of local officials and businessmen, as Phillip H. Klutznick told the American Society of Planning Officials in 1942, was an entire metropolitan area preparing to repeat its mistakes from World War I. In November of the same year, Robert Moses led a special task force that reviewed the area for Navy Secretary Frank Knox. Leaks from Washington indicated that Moses's secret report was a broad indictment of confused local officials, competing federal agencies, and uncoordinated housing policies that had combined to produce shoddy buildings, unusable streets, and woeful services.[17]

A fuller exploration of Norfolk area problems came in testimony to a visiting delegation from the House Naval Affairs Committee in the spring of 1943. The federal housing officials, admirals, and city managers who appeared before the subcommittee agreed that the immediate edge had been taken off the housing shortage by navy base housing projects, the construction of eleven thousand private houses and apartments, and the opening of ten thousand units by the Federal Public Housing Administration. However, local officials expressed a lingering sense of grievance that Norfolk and Portsmouth had been saddled with what were properly national burdens. Arthur Owens, for example, complained to the committee about city personnel shortages, overcrowded buses, inadequate recreational facilities, and overburdened sewer plants and requested federal aid for a new jail, a new fire house, and law enforcement.[18] Norfolk officials added their own concerns with delays in hospital construction, difficulties in the control of prostitution, and an undermanned police force, although the latter had been eased by the recent establishment of a permanent shore patrol by the navy.[19] Although a vehement enemy of the New Deal, Mayor Wood also bent serious efforts from 1940 through 1944 to excusing local inaction and shifting responsibility to the federal government. "It is true there is much to be desired," he wrote Congressman Edward Izac after the Naval Affairs Subcommittee visit, "but the demands due to the war are overwhelming and there is no doubt that some of our ills will have to be endured during this very trying crisis."[20]

Norfolk's city manager matched the mayor's negativism with his own reactive approach to wartime problems. Like many other Norfolk leaders, H. C. Borland was haunted by the fear of rapid demobilization and the memories of the depression at the end of World War I.[21] The result was a consistent policy that the city should strive barely to match current demands for expanded services and facilities rather than anticipating future growth. City planning therefore operated on a bit-by-piece philosophy and a one- or two-year time scale—a school here, a new water main, bridge repairs there, more asphalt on the roughest streets. The bottom of the city's priority list was crowded not only with health centers, parks, and recreation facilities but also with pipe and concrete projects like a new sewage disposal plant.[22]

By 1942 and 1943, it was Mobile rather than San Diego that seemed for many itinerant journalists to typify the social dislocation that came at the height of the war boom. An air base, army supply depot, Alcoa plant, and two major shipyards made Mobile the fastest growing city in the United States with a 67 percent increase in population by 1943. Overtaxed city services were further strained by overflow from the shipyard city of Pascagoula located forty miles west across the Mississippi border. Within months of Pearl Harbor, Mobile's mayor admitted the city's inability to supply adequate housing, control traffic jams, meet demands for water, or enforce the law. A year later, Agnes Meyer reported to the *Washington Post* that Mobile was still "up to its ears in trouble."[23] John Dos Passos, another visitor during the chaotic spring of 1943, offered eloquent testimony to the transformation of the "mouldering old Gulf seaport" by the wartime gold rush:

> Sidewalks are crowded. Gutters are stacked with litter that drifts back and forth in the brisk spring wind. Garbage cans are overflowing. Frame houses on treeshaded streets bulge with men in shirtsleeves who spill out onto the porches and trampled grassplots and stand in knots at the streetcorners. . . . The trailer army has filled all the open lots with its regular ranks. In cluttered backyards people camp out in tents and chickenhouses and shelters tacked together out of packingcases. In the outskirts in every direction you find acres and acres raw with new building, open fields skinned to the bare clay. . . . Over it all the Gulf mist, heavy with the smoke of soft coal, hangs in streaks, and glittering the training planes endlessly circle above the airfields.[24]

Dos Passos's portrait was bleak enough, but it omitted additional problems of racial relations. In Mobile as in other southern cities, the crisis of growth was accentuated by the resistance of shipyards and unions to the employment of blacks. Skilled black shipyard workers in Mobile, New Orleans, and Jacksonville in fact found themselves squeezed out of their jobs by closed-shop agreements made out of expediency between the shipyards and segregated unions. One result of the job discrimination that was especially pronounced in Houston, Jacksonville, and Savannah as well as in Mobile was to pyramid population growth, since available black workers sat idly on their front porches and watched white newcomers crowd the streets on the way to their shift at the yards. When Mobile's Alabama Dry Dock Company replied to pressures from the Fair Employment Practices Commission by abruptly integrating its work force at the end of May 1943, white workers responded with two days of rioting which required federal troops before calm returned.[25]

The central theme in Portland's reaction to wartime growth was not inaction but pragmatic improvisation to meet immediate ends. Henry Kaiser opened three huge shipyards between the spring of 1941 and the spring of 1942 to bring 30,000 new residents to the metropolitan area even before Pearl Harbor. By 1942 and 1943, the Kaiser yards were importing workers by the train load from Chicago and New York. At the peak of war employment in late 1943 and early 1944, metropolitan Portland counted 92,000 workers in the Kaiser yards, 23,000 in other shipyards, and 25,000 in other war industries. The metropolitan population had grown by 32 percent since 1940, from 500,000 to 660,000.[26]

The journalist who claimed that "Portland neither likes nor knows how to accommodate its Virginia City atmosphere" was speaking as much for its local leadership as for the average citizen.[27] The response of the city government to the surge of growth in 1941 and 1942 was conditioned by a conservative bias against government action and by a desire to limit the development of strong planning institutions that might develop their own programs and constituencies. The Planning Commission tried to fill the initial void in 1941 by developing plans for new transportation facilities and public housing sites, but it moved too slowly for the emergency and showed too much concern with the social impact of growth. When Mayor Earl Riley led the creation of a Housing Authority in the week after Pearl Harbor to preempt direct action by federal "carpet baggers," the Planning Commission found itself effectively shouldered out of important decisions. By the following July, the Housing Authority had five thousand public housing units in operation or under contract in the metropolitan area, most of them on the North Portland peninsula near the shipyards. Like the Planning Commission the year before, the Housing Authority also found itself torn between the desire to build quality housing and the demands for immediate action.[28]

The ad hoc solution to the housing shortage in fact came from the private sector rather than the city. To the astonishment of the Housing Authority, the Kaiser Corporation and the United States Maritime Commission broke ground in September 1942 for a massive development on the Columbia River flood plain north of the city limits. The first residents moved into the instant city of Vanport on 12 December and the project reached its maximum population in 1944 with the occupation of over nine thousand apartments. Title to the community was taken by the United States Public Housing Authority as segments were finished, with management contracted to the Portland Housing Authority. By the summer of 1943, Vanport was functionally a complete city, with schools, a post office, cafeterias, community buildings, five shopping districts, a 150-bed hospital, fourteen playgrounds, an independent fire district, and a 750-seat theater that provided three double bills each week. At the same time, however, the imperative of rapid construction had overwhelmed any opportunities for quality in design or for social planning. One reporter called Vanport a glorified auto camp multiplied a hundred times over, with two-story apartment blocks in grey paint rising out of a sea of Oregon mud. The former city manager who served as project director and his staff struggled to keep pace with demands for basic social and recreational services, let alone to carry out plans to organize neighborhood councils or otherwise to promote community identity among transient residents.[29]

The San Francisco Bay region provides a final example where extraordinary pressures from wartime growth elicited an inadequate response in the first years of the war effort. The Bay area cities that had worked persistently and successfully during the 1920s and 1930s to secure naval facilities found themselves with more than they had bargained for in 1940 and 1941. The federal government pumped millions of dollars into the expansion of the Mare Island and Hunters Point shipyards, Moffett Field, the Naval Operating Base and new Naval Air Station at Alameda, naval supply depots, and new facilities on Treasure Island. Federal contracts also funded the expansion or establishment of a half-dozen huge private shipyards—General Engineering and Drydock Corporation in San Francisco, Western Pipe and Steel in South San Francisco, Bethlehem Shipbuilding in South Alameda, Moore Drydock Company in Oakland, Todd-Kaiser in Richmond, and Marinship in Sausalito. Manufacturing employment in the Bay area rose from 100,000 in June 1941 to 175,000 in June 1942 and 275,000 by June 1943. In aggregate, the San Francisco–Oakland area had a larger increase in civilian population than any other metropolitan area in the United States, with a growth of 278,000 by the end of 1943.[30]

Different cities within the metropolitan area developed different sets of problems. San Francisco became a huge dormitory housing war workers, servicemen between assignments, and their dependents. Despite serious overcrowding, it was better able to handle the war boom than were smaller communities. The population of Vallejo and adjoining areas more than tripled from 30,000 to 100,000 residents, more than a quarter of whom made do with temporary housing. With four Kaiser shipyards and fifty-five other war industries, Richmond made everyone's list of severely impacted cities. When population increased from 23,000 to more than 100,000 and employment from 15,000 to 130,000, it was impossible to build apartments, schools, hospitals, and jails fast enough to meet demand. Beyond the difficulties of individual communities, the entire Bay region also suffered from massive transportation problems. The housing shortage made the basic inefficiency of the region's land transportation system glaringly obvious by forcing workers to live wherever they could with little reference to the location of their jobs. The Mare Island yard in Vallejo had a commuting shed of fifty miles, with hundreds of workers using rationed gasoline to drive two or two and a half hours each way. Richmond was unable to find enough ferries to serve commuters from San Francisco, and imported old El cars from New York for a new rail line to Oakland.[31]

The Bay area cities and counties met both their individual and common problems without significant assistance from professional planning. No Bay area city in 1941 had a completed general plan that could be used to guide the location of wartime facilities. Attempts to use the emergency to promote a metropolitan planning agency also failed. An effort in 1941 by the California State Planning Board to designate the area as a planning region under existing state legislation stalled at a preliminary hearing when local jurisdictions objected to any limitations on their land use planning authority. The State Planning Board tried again on 8 December 1941 by suggesting a temporary advisory Regional Development Council to make recommendations on a permanent regional agency. Local politicians again preferred to ignore even such a tentative first step.[32]

Many cities in the war growth regions found that employment and population reached a plateau in the second full year of the American war effort. As lessened growth pressures allowed slightly more time for the development of public policies, more and more cities turned to postwar planning in 1943, 1944, and 1945. Speakers at conventions of the American Municipal Association and the American Society of Planning Officials urged bold and comprehensive planning on delegates. Publications of the National Resources Planning Board in 1943 and of the American Society of Planning Officials in the following years kept up the encouragement by citing long lists of defense towns that had tied their worries about wartime growth and public services to systematic planning efforts for peacetime needs. *American City* also offered consistently strong support for postwar planning to its readership of municipal bureaucrats. Indeed, planning historian Mel Scott has argued that the wide range of activity in the last years of the war constituted a "renaissance" for local planning in the United States.[33]

The achievements of postwar planning at the local level were important and concrete in most southern and western cities, but they were also narrow in conception and results. Mayors, city councils, or chambers of commerce typically established postwar planning efforts to work toward a limited set of goals. One concern was to ward off the postwar depression that most Americans expected to hit the boom cities by calling attention to the need for new jobs for returning veterans and assisting war industries in their conversion to peacetime markets. The second goal was to develop efficient programs for the construction of utilities, transportation systems, and other public facilities that would help to promote economic diversification and growth. In short, concern about patterns of postwar development in cities from Atlanta to San Francisco was not so much a revival of city planning as a comprehensive tool for local government as it was a pragmatic effort to solve a specific set of anticipated problems.

Certainly the federal government by the last years of the war was encouraging cities to take a limited approach to planning both by example and by precept. The only federal assistance to the war boom cities that matched *Fortune*'s prescription for comprehensive metropolitan planning came from the National Resources Planning Board (NRPB) between 1941 and 1943. Working through its regional offices and through affiliated state planning boards, NRPB staff performed significant background work in inventorying metropolitan resources and defining metropolitan economic structures. Efforts to coordinate specific planning efforts on a metropolitan or regional scale, however, showed a mixed record. The more successful examples involved technical assistance to locally initiated projects. In the Seattle-Tacoma area, staff from the NRPB and the Washington State Planning Council helped the organization of a twelve-county Puget Sound Regional Planning Commission. As part of the Wasatch Front project, the agency assisted in data collection for Salt Lake City and for Utah's industrial development and social service offices. More ambitious demonstration projects to show the efficacy of comprehensive economic, social, and land-use planning in three selected cities during 1942–43 had a very mixed record that ranged from failure in Tacoma to partial success in Corpus Christi. Unfortunately, NRPB planners never had the time to build on their successes and learn from their failures, for a conservative Congress killed the agency in the summer of 1943 at the same time it was curtailing rural electrification, crippling the Farm Security Administration, and otherwise phasing out New Deal initiatives.[34]

Other federal intervention to assist local governments in defense centers took the form of short-term troubleshooting. The Navy Department thus dispatched Robert Moses to several coastal cities in the fall of 1942 for a quick once-over and some instant advice. The executive also established a President's Committee on Congested Production Areas in April 1943 at the suggestion of the House Naval Affairs Committee. The committee's charge was to help cities cope with immediate problems, not to assist comprehensive planning for growth. Its local representatives in eighteen overburdened cities worked to expedite federal aid for the immediate improvement of housing, transportation, child care and recreation centers, hospitals, clinics, and other facilities whose inadequacy led to high labor turnover.[35]

At the same time, Congress clearly defined the national concern about the postwar era as planning for economic survival rather than planning for social betterment. Repeated suggestions for the establishment of a federal agency to promote urban planning and redevelopment met opposition from private real estate interests and from city officials such as Robert Moses whose main interest was the expansion of public works programs under their own control. A detailed study by Phillip Funigello has also found that House and Senate Special Committees on Postwar Economic Policy and Planning during 1944 and 1945 had a bias against any sort of planning that went beyond capital improvements budgeting. Indeed, Congress reduced an administration request in 1945 for assistance to local public works planning through the Federal Works Administration from $78 million to $17.5 million and blocked serious consideration of a national urban redevelopment effort.[36]

Most sunbelt cities were quite willing to follow the tacit suggestion from Washington, drawing together public agencies and private business interests to cooperate on a narrowly defined postwar planning effort. In several cases, in fact, it was local business organizations that took the lead. Chambers of commerce in Birmingham and a number of other cities surveyed their membership to determine postwar expansion plans and to encourage thinking about reconversion problems and the employment of veterans. The new Committee on Economic Development, which represented the commitment of large corporations to rational growth, also organized state and local affiliates around the country. The CED chapter that was organized in Portland in July 1943 built on the work of other business organizations and included representatives from the largest bank, the gas and electric companies, and local manufacturers on its executive committee. More active younger businessmen also used the Chamber of Commerce to attract new industries in 1944 and 1945, despite the preference of many older Portlanders that all the city's newcomers should go back where they came from.[37]

Many southern and western cities also established or reorganized their planning agencies in the last years of the war in order to be prepared to make rational decisions on the location of new industrial and residential growth and public investment. Charleston and Birmingham developed planning commissions with the help of NRPB staff in 1943. San Antonio created a zoning commission in 1942 and a planning board in 1944 to study and promote postwar development. Seattle reorganized its Planning Commission and relocated it within the executive department after wide public discussion. Portland had virtually suspended its Planning Commission at the height of the war crisis in 1942, but reactivated it with an expanded staff in 1943 to work on master planning and housing.[38] In Norfolk, however, the strongly conservative city manager and city council refused the suggestions from the Norfolk Association of Commerce and other business leaders that the city's planning commission be reorganized as a separate city department with professional staff.[39]

The most typical form for postwar planning was the appointment of an ad hoc committee to develop a program of public works projects to relieve postwar unemployment and to equip the metropolis for further growth. In Portland, for example, deep worries about the city's ability to accommodate its new population and hold its windfall growth began to surface as the city met the immediate needs of housing, transportation, and law enforcement. At the direction of Mayor Earl Riley, Commissioner of Public Works William Bowes in February 1943 organized a Portland Area Postwar Development Committee "composed of forty-seven of Portland's leading citizens representing labor and industry, public and private utility interests, real estate and business interests, architects, engineers, leaders of civic and religious groups, the press, regional planning interests, and members of the City Planning Commission." The chairman was David Simpson, a real estate broker who was current president of the Chamber of Commerce and past president of the local Realty Board and the National Association of Real Estate Boards, and the membership overlapped the board of the local Committee for Economic Development chapter. The committee's charge included planning for improved transportation, industrial expansion, and suburban development in order to take advantage of opportunities for regional growth, and it borrowed staff advisors from the Bonneville Power Authority, the National Resources Planning Board, and the Northwest Electric Company. After several months of indecision, the committee accepted the suggestion of Edgar Kaiser that it obtain one hundred thousand dollars from the city, county, dock commission, port authority, and school district to hire the advice of Robert Moses on postwar public works.[40]

Moses dispatched his advance team of a dozen planners and engineers to Portland at the beginning of September and spent six hectic days in the city at the end of the month. The resulting plan for *Portland Improvement* which Moses presented in November was a $60 million public works program designed to "stimulate business and help bridge the gap between the end of the war and the full resumption of private business." The program covered the entire metropolitan area and promised to employ a maximum of twenty thousand workers during the first two postwar years. The list of projects included $20 million for a freeway loop around the central business core, $20 million for capital improvements to sewers, schools, public offices, and airport, $12 million for upgrading existing parks and streets, and $8 million for highway construction outside the city. As in a previous era of "City Beautiful" planning, the new program placed greatest stress on the design of an efficient citywide system of arterial highways and on the enhancement of Portland's physical appearance by landscaping the Willamette waterfront, modernizing the railroad depot, and building a civic center to link existing city and county offices.[41]

Portland Improvement on one level served as one more blow in the argument among different concepts of city planning that *Fortune* was simultaneously describing. Writing with a well-worn chip on his shoulder, Moses had asserted that "among ivory-tower planners who will accept nothing short of a revolution in urban life, this report is bound to be disappointing" because it recommended only limited public improvements. Responding from his home base at the Harvard School of Design, Martin Meyerson called the report a grab bag of unrelated projects. Christopher Tunnard similarly attacked its narrow vision, its negative forecasts about postwar industry, and its neglect of planning for housing, health, community facilities, and other social needs.[42]

Within Portland, however, the reception was enthusiastic. The *Oregonian* and the *Oregon Journal* both applauded the recommendations, the *Journal* reprinted thousands of copies, and the widely respected City Club issued a favorable evaluation. Commissioner Bowes, in a radio talk on 15 November described the origins of the report and gave special credit to Edgar Kaiser, who had helped to persuade Moses to undertake the Portland contract. The next day Bowes wrote Moses that there was "a real disposition on the part of the agencies to do all possible to make full use of all the recommendations." Over the next several months, Bowes and the Postwar Development Committee worked to coordinate the response of the several agencies. The result in May 1944 was the overwhelming approval of $19 million in bonds for new sewers, roads, and docks and a special $5 million school levy.[43]

The worst of the wartime growth crisis was also over in San Diego by the start of 1943. The completion of twenty thousand new houses and apartments by the end of 1942 relieved the most severe housing pressures. The city was also finding enough lead time to direct $10 million in local investment and $15 million in federal aid to the construction of sewers and other capital facilities according to the existing master plan. In August of 1943, the first step toward a coherent strategy for postwar development was a report on "Planning for the Peace Era of San Diego County" issued by the county planning commission. The second step was the creation of a Postwar Planning Committee that represented the city and county governments, utilities, and business interests. With the assistance of the Chamber of Commerce, the committee bought a thirteen-hundred-page blueprint for postwar industrial reconversion from Day and Zimmerman, Inc. San Diego spokesmen proudly argued that the seventy-two-thousand-dollar report was the most comprehensive analysis of postwar opportunities available in any city since it added concerns about economic diversification to the sort of public works program that Robert Moses had devised for Portland. Rather than worrying about comprehensive area planning in the traditional sense, the committee also defined a specific agenda of economic development projects including the establishment of a port authority, downtown renewal, and waterfront improvements.[44]

A third example of metropolitan planning for postwar growth was the Denver Metropolitan Planning Project. Since the 1920s, Denver had enjoyed a relatively active planning commission. Organized with the support of major bankers and the Real Estate Exchange, the commission's central concern was to preserve downtown property values through a capital improvements program embracing roads, freeways, and parks. The end of the thirties had seen efforts to extend physical planning to the metropolitan area through the five-county Upper Platte Valley Regional Planning Commission, while the Denver Planning Commission stepped forward to deal with housing and construction problems in the peak growth years before and after Pearl Harbor.[45]

A further step came with the establishment of the Denver Metropolitan Planning Project in August 1942. The new agency was a cooperative effort by the Denver Planning Commission, the Colorado State Planning Commission, the NRPB, and the University of Denver to preserve the city's expanded manufacturing base. Reorganized as the Denver Regional Association with Rockefeller Foundation funds in 1943, the group directed its attention to land use, employment, industrial development, and economic reconversion. Its pamphlet on *Facing the Challenge of War and Post-War Problems* stressed the need to provide adequate electric power and to lay claim to scarce water supplies in order to prepare for postwar growth.[46]

Wartime planning received the consistent backing of downtown businessmen in several other cities as well. Since 1937, the Dallas City Council had read the script written by the Citizens Council, a coterie of bankers, merchants, and publishers that handled virtually every important decision. Speaking for the city's business community, Mayor Woodall Rogers in 1942 urged members of the American Municipal Association to prepare comprehensive postwar development plans. Practicing what he preached, Rogers in 1943 oversaw the preparation of a master plan calling for $40 million in public improvements in anticipation of cutbacks in aircraft production. Local officials and the

Morning News worked together to publicize the needs for capital investment and continued annexation. In response, Dallas voters in December approved a $15 million bond issue to cover the first steps in the master plan.[47] Atlanta acted somewhat more slowly, appointing a committee of citizens and businessmen in 1945 and approving their recommendations for a bond issue in 1946. With the backing of the newspapers and the Chamber of Commerce, Norfolk's advisory Planning Commission and its Public Works Department submitted a list of needed highway improvements, schools, health facilities, and flood control measures to the city council in 1944, although the council declined to designate a formal postwar planning effort.

The experience of the San Francisco Bay area epitomizes the tendencies toward pragmatic postwar planning with active business participation that have been described for cities from Atlanta to Portland. The California legislature signaled the prevailing attitude in 1943 by replacing the State Planning Board with a Reconstruction and Reemployment Commission whose specific charge was "to prevent unemployment . . . promote development of new industries, create new markets, promote the reemployment of discharged servicemen and readjustment of war workers, and the conversion of industry and commerce from war to peace standards."[48] A commission-sponsored meeting on postwar problems of the Bay area in August 1944 drew more bankers, utility company representatives, and chamber of commerce officers than public officials to the sessions in the Oakland council chamber. One outcome was the establishment of the Bay Area Council, a private organization headed by executives from the Central Bank of Oakland and Pacific Gas and Electric and drawing most of its members from local businesses. Starting with a broad interest in the promotion of areawide economic growth and areawide planning for physical services, the Bay Area Council evolved into a powerful lobby and an important decision making forum as its corporate members learned to translate its goals into specific projects that culminated with the Bay Area Rapid Transit system.

At the same time during the last war years, the cities of Oakland and San Francisco appointed ad hoc committees to recommend public works projects. The San Francisco committee held fifteen public hearings during 1945 and recommended capital improvements costing $177 million. The list included $20 million for the San Francisco airport, $23 million for streetcars, and huge amounts for street and highway construction. The Oakland committee also submitted a shopping list of new public investment, although it did also recommend that the Planning Commission be strengthened as the coordinating agency.[49]

If anyone had been keeping score, there would have been no doubt who was winning in *Fortune*'s battle of planning styles by 1945. The difficulties of rearmament in 1940 and 1941 and full mobilization in 1942 and 1943 required local government actions largely unknown in the previous decade. Especially in southern and western cities, where the interwar years had been relatively quiet and the wartime boom especially pronounced, municipal leaders and governments chose policies that added up to vigorous pragmatism. Even if they had desired, local governments lacked the technical resources for comprehensive planning and the time to develop them. Planning and public investment from 1940 through 1942 were therefore scarcely more than a scramble to keep up with growth by any means possible. Indeed, the immediate reactions in cities like Norfolk and Portland may have weakened rather than strengthened planning institutions. By 1943, 1944, and 1945, worries about employment for discharged war workers and veterans kept attention on specific issues of economic growth. Planning for peace focused on the realistic problems of new jobs, industrial reconversion, public works for stopgap employment, and public facilities to support economic diversification.

The long-term impact of postwar planning was in fact more significant than its immediate accomplishments. The process itself helped to legitimize the idea of urban planning for conservative politicians like Portland's Earl Riley, who admitted in 1946 that the war had begun "a new era in municipal administration" in which it was impossible to return to the "customary way of running municipal affairs."[50] The planning effort also helped to achieve one of the aims of the Committee on Economic Development and of *Fortune* by bringing large local corporations into active cooperation with local government. The results included ongoing organizations like the Bay Area Committee and continuing alliances for progress among businessmen and bureaucrats in such cities as Portland and Atlanta.

The choice among specific urban goals also anticipated the major thrust of public policy in sunbelt cities during the next two decades. Agreement on the need to make the encouragement of growth an explicit aim of city government reaffirmed a traditional American attitude that had faded in a number of cities. Further agreement on the importance of metropolitan land use and transportation planning as tools for directing that growth to the benefit of local businesses and investors widened the acceptance of ideas that had long been advocated by planning professionals. Together, these broad goals constituted a framework for postwar agendas in the majority of sunbelt cities. As the following chapters will describe, central city politicans and decision makers in the later 1940s and 1950s filled out the strategy by defining specific objectives for channeling regional growth to the benefit of the central city and its downtown core.

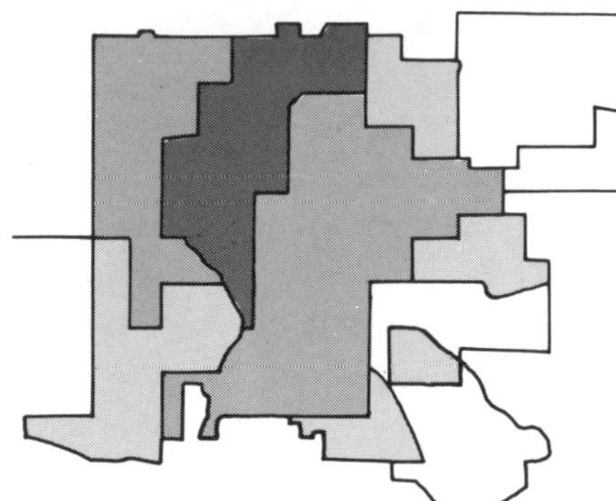

Chapter 5

The Politics of Growth in Sunbelt Cities

If the war years had been a shock for sunbelt cities, the first years of peace were an exciting surprise. Many civic leaders had been uncomfortable about the growth of 1942 and 1943 because they fully expected that boom would be followed by bust. It had therefore been the problems of postwar transition and employment rather than crises in wartime services that had justified experimentation with large-scale planning efforts. The bigger the wartime boom in a metropolitan area like Portland or San Francisco–Oakland, the more important it had seemed to promote active planning to help cushion the coming recession.

In fact, the initial peacetime months and years brought continued prosperity. In the nation as a whole, the drop of $90 billion in federal spending from 1945 to 1946 was largely counterbalanced by private demand for automobiles, houses, and refrigerators purchased with bottled-up savings from defense jobs. With a prosperous national economy and with only partial mobilization, few of the boom towns of the South and West suffered the feared crisis of reconversion. Sunshine cities such as Denver, Tucson, Phoenix, and Albuquerque enjoyed a veterans' boom as GIs returned to settle in cities they had first visited on weekend passes from nearby bases. Continued defense spending and the onset of the cold war helped to maintain the population of military cities like Norfolk, Mobile, San Antonio, and El Paso. At the same time, new manufacturing and services filled the demands of expanded metropolitan markets in other boom cities. The number of new or expanded manufacturing plants in Los Angeles, for example, was 50 percent higher for the 1945–48 period than for the war years 1942–44. The Pacific states, Mountain states, and South all received a disproportionate share of new investment in manufacturing facilities as judged against prewar industrial capacity, with especially spectacular increases in Texas and Oklahoma.[1]

On a regional basis, the reaction to continued prosperity in the later forties included a series of books analyzing the new opportunity for the South and West to declare their independence of a quasi-colonial economic pattern. In the war years, traveling journalists had concentrated on the problems of boom towns and had summarized their observations as "Trouble on the Northwest Frontier" or *Journey through Chaos*.[2] Now a more typical title was *Economic Freedom for the West* or *America's New Frontier*. New possibilities for the southern economy were analyzed by journalist A. G. Mezerik and by economists Calvin Hoover and B. U. Ratchford.[3] Western states where postwar prosperity was not diluted by rural poverty attracted even more attention. Wendell Berge in 1946 advocated industrialization based on the West's new War industries. Coloradoan Morris Garnsey described the invidious influence of special economic interests on western states and argued for a new regional liberalism based on economic growth and resource conservation.[4]

With this background of renewed excitement about regional growth, residents of more than a dozen sunbelt cities undertook major changes in municipal government in the first decade after World War II. From Augusta to Albuquerque, reformers defined the obstacle to headlong growth as satisfied and sleepy municipal leadership.[5] Depending on local conditions, they advocated changes ranging from the election of a new mayor or council to the formal organization of a civic reform league to the adoption of a new chapter. As the remainder of this chapter describes, the common element in the various efforts was the desire to replace the small-time politics of city hall croneys with administrations of growth-oriented businessmen and bureaucrats. In one city after another, the new politicians lambasted entrenched cliques of officeholders as corrupt "machines," promised to crack down on vice and end police corruption, and argued for efficient planning and budgeting. Their campaign platforms called for the modernization of outmoded municipal governments and the provision of adequate public services.

Beyond the immediate desire to win the key elections and to implement the goal of efficient city government, the local businessmen who dominated postwar reform efforts shared two further substantive aims. One of the underlying motives for political revolution and structural reform was the desire to mobilize public and private resources to provide the necessary physical facilities for business and commercial growth. The list included new docks, airports, highways, expanded water supply, and more electric power, but the central item on the agenda was usually the provision of adequate office space and transportation for downtown business districts. Another and more complex goal was to manage the process of suburbanization for the benefit of central city business interests, broadening the progressive era concern for orderly growth to cover the entire metropolitan area. As discussed in chapter six, the goal of physical improvements and downtown renewal lay largely within the capacity of the postwar municipal reformers. Despite repeated efforts, as chapter seven and chapter eight indicate, the hope of harnessing suburbanization to central city interests has grown increasingly elusive and illusory.

As an approximate rule, the strength of reform varied inversely with each city's success in meeting the challenges of the war itself. Cities that had failed to mobilize significant planning efforts in the early 1940s or that had relied on emergency aid from federal agencies found that postwar prosperity compounded wartime chaos. Choked streets and schools, overburdened bridges and sewers all demanded quick and decisive action if local businesses were to take advantage of new opportunities. Norfolk, San Antonio, Denver, and similar cities were fertile ground for political reform efforts precisely because of their earlier inaction. In contrast, partial reforms between 1935 and 1940 were one of the factors that accounted for the constructive responses to World War II in such cities as Atlanta, Dallas, San Diego, and Seattle. In these cities and in others such as Portland where unreformed regimes had been able to transform an initial "crisis" into manageable "problems," the pressures toward municipal upheaval were relatively weak.

With its strong record of wartime accomplishments, for example, Portland lurched uncertainly toward a halfway revolution. Despite the city's prosperity in 1946 and 1947, Earl Riley in 1948 faced revival of charges that his police department shared a corrupt partnership with gamblers and prostitutes. His successful challenger was Commissioner Dorothy McCullough Lee, who had made good use of reports on vice by a special grand jury and by the reform-minded City Club.[6] Beyond energetic measures to reinvigorate the vice squad, the new mayor took on the question of structural reform of Portland's government. Asserting that the city's rapid growth required the more efficient organization of municipal administration, she appointed a group of businessmen and civic leaders to a Committee on Municipal

Reorganization in August 1949. Unfortunately for reformers, the city council balked at placing the committee's city manager charter on the ballot by a vote of three to two, as individual commissioners defended their semiindependent satrapies. Lacking the support of the daily papers, which argued that Portland enjoyed quite a satisfactory administration, the city manager movement failed when proponents were unable to secure enough signatures to place the proposal on the ballot by petition.[7]

After Portlanders refused Dorothy Lee a second term in 1952, city politics moved on two levels for a decade and a half. Day-to-day decisions were dominated by three men who became local institutions. Public Works Commissioner William Bowes (1939–69) modeled himself after Robert Moses and snorted at the disastrous notions of Lee and other liberal reformers. Finance Commissioner Ormond Bean (1948–66) was a curious combination of crotchety liberal and pragmatist who liked to clarify issues with pedantic memos for other members of the city council. With an eye to public relations, Mayor Terry Schrunk (1956–72) walked the line between fiscal conservatism and the attractions of city projects. Whether the leadership provided by this mixed council seemed temperate or plodding depended on the critic's own point of view. At a measured pace the city attempted to implement the standard agenda of postwar projects, building a coliseum after bitter debate on its location, enacting a modern zoning ordinance, promoting industrial development and port expansion, and preparing the way for freeway construction.

During the same years, citizens who had been disappointed by the failure of the city manager movement in 1950 could take heart from the continuation of a "line of municipal reform that had been bubbling for a decade or more."[8] An impressive array of reports by legislative study commissions, the City Club, and the Public Administration Service all pointed to shortcomings in city politics.[9] In response, a Committee for Effective City Government revived the idea of a city manager charter in 1957–58 with support from the City Club, League of Women Voters, Junior Chamber of Commerce, Young Democrats, *Oregonian*, and *Oregon Journal*. Determined opposition from Bowes, Schrunk, and labor unions helped to defeat the proposal by a narrow margin of seven thousand votes.[10] In pursuit of the same end of a centralized executive to replace the five independent commissioners, the same groups through a Citizens' League for Effective City

Government introduced a proposal for a strong mayor charter and suffered a similar defeat in 1966.[11] After nearly twenty years of effort with the same issues and the same actors, Portland still justified description as a city whose leaders hoped for steady growth and preferred placid prosperity either to machine politics or to political reform.

The precondition to political revolution in Denver was stifling control by a small business elite even more narrow than Portland's. In what was perhaps a self-fulfilling prophecy, most residents agreed that Denver emerged from the war years with local decisions in the hands of three or four men.[12] Denverites usually agreed that Claude Boettcher, John Evans, and Gerald Hughes had set the lead for the local business community since the 1920s. As conservators of family fortunes established by parents or grandparents, the three held interlocking investments in the Great Western Sugar Company, banks, utilities, railroads, and real estate. A procession of journalists who inventoried the city in the immediate postwar years shared the same conclusion that Denver had sustained the pressures of mobilization with remarkable stability at the top. John Gunther summed up the general impression that Denver was "immobile . . . Olympian, impassive, and inert. It is probably the most self-sufficient, isolated, self-contained and complacent city in the world."[13]

The central goal of Denver's dominant elite was the preservation of wealth earned in previous decades and of the comfortable life that it supported. They found nothing wrong with increases in white-collar government jobs, expanding tourism, or the export of raw materials to eastern producers. They balked at the growth of manufacturing because they feared environmental pollution, the possibility of strong labor unions, and the growth of economic interests independent of their own control. Henry Kaiser, who had employed more than a thousand workers at the federally owned Denver Ordnance Plant during the war, thus found a solid wall of opposition to any ideas for peacetime operations in the city. The major banks on Seventeenth Street preferred to place their funds in safe and certain bond issues rather than in loans, which totaled only 20 percent of assets.[14]

It was modern carpetbaggers attracted to Denver by wartime and postwar opportunities who provided the initial impulses for change. Through the forties, respectable Seventeenth Street tycoons shuddered at the thought of Elwood Brooks, a Kansan who bought the tottering Central Bank in 1942 and revived its fortunes with expanded hours, liberal loans, and advertising. A few years later, the local establishment used protracted litigation in an unsuccessful effort to block the downtown building plans of New York real estate promoter William Zeckendorf. The public voice for the new entrepreneurs came from Palmer Hoyt, who moved from the Portland *Oregonian* in 1946 to edit the *Denver Post*. As the model of the modern, moderate Republican booster, Hoyt enlisted the *Post* in the cause of Denver development and broadcast the city's claim to be the leader of the Rocky Mountain Empire.[15]

The most vulnerable target for Denver reformers was not the establishment triumvirate but its junior partner Ben Stapleton. Mayor since 1923 (with one four-year vacation), "interminable Ben" maintained himself in office through his authority to appoint virtually all city employees and his efforts to adapt the city tax structure to the suggestions of businessmen. In many ways an effective administrator who had taken good advantage of federal funds for parks and parkways, Stapleton was also an easy target for caricature. Readers of *Time* or *Inside USA* found a portrait of Stapleton "gliding on his oars," mumbling through press conferences, sleeping in meetings, and marching determinedly toward the 1920s. As returning veterans and new migrants crowded the city in 1945 and 1946, the mayor's solution was simple: "If all these people would only go back where they came from, we wouldn't have a housing shortage."[16]

Stapleton's opposition in the 1947 election came from James Quigg Newton, a thirty-five-year-old Denverite returning to the city after years at Yale, as clerk to William O. Douglas, and in the navy. Newton provided everything that Stapleton lacked—youth, dynamism, cosmopolitan background, ambitions for himself and his city. With the strong backing of the *Post*, he campaigned against the incompetence of Stapleton's administration for allowing dirty and rutted streets, awarding contracts to croneys, and contributing to the housing shortage with archaic building codes appreciated only by the craft unions. His general promise to take advantage of Denver's golden chance for growth was broad enough to appeal to new migrants and veterans, smaller businessmen, liberals, and labor unions. The result on 20 May was a smashing victory with the largest plurality in the history of Denver.[17]

Quigg Newton's major impact during his two terms as mayor was the modernization of municipal government in Denver. Although voters rejected a new city charter, Newton under the old charter was able to import a "Michigan Mafia" of young professional administrators. He implemented competitive purchasing and civil service, pushed through a sales tax, and reorganized city health services and Denver General Hospital. Although Newton reached to broaden his coalition to the left by appointing George Cavender of the Colorado Education Association to a City Council vacancy, his sympathies clearly lay in the very successful growth of Denver as a white-collar metropolis. The two mayors who followed Newton were the heirs of the same reform ideology. Will Nicholson was a real estate man who had been Newton's chief lieutenant on the Republican side, and he ran an openly partisan campaign against George Cavender in 1955 with the support of Newton's backers. Richard Batterton, deputy mayor and manager of public works, carried on businessmen's government with an easy victory in 1959.[18]

By the middle fifties, the old establishment began to discover that making additional money was not quite so unpleasant as had been feared. Under the lead of banker Thomas Dines and Cris Dobbins, who managed the Boettcher enterprises, the Chamber of Commerce and the U. S. National Bank began to produce booster literature of a sort unimaginable in the 1940s. Although the number of decision makers expanded, the dominant voices in the early sixties remained the incumbent mayor, the newspapers, and businessmen working through the Chamber of Commerce and downtown organizations.[19] The same excitement about the possibilities of growth pervaded the state and helped to support far-reaching projects to expand possibilities for metropolitan growth. Successive administrations fought long court battles with agriculturalists and the west slope counties over the diversion of Colorado River water through the Blue Mountain Reservoir and Dillon Lake into the Denver water system. Governor Ed Johnson and Will Nicholson also combined their efforts to gain the addition of a Denver–Salt Lake City link to the interstate highway system. The recently opened Eisenhower Tunnel beneath Loveland Pass commemorates the decision.[20]

Across the continent, Norfolk during the 1940s was as much a "second city" as Denver. If citizens of the Rocky Mountain capital knew that the big money was controlled from New York and referred to one of their prewar representatives in Washington as "the third Senator from Pennsylvania," Norfolk's businessmen were equally aware that the important decisions were made in Navy Department offices, legislative committee rooms, and the halls of Richmond's Commonwealth Club. At the top of the scale in Norfolk there were families with wealth and influence, but no aristocrats of industry and real estate to match the Dukes of Durham or the Reynoldses of Richmond. At the bottom of the scale, Norfolk's military population and lack of manufacturing pulled its income levels well below the regional and state averages.

By the end of the war, Norfolk's slow-moving municipal government had left a city more than ready for political reform. The daily papers carefully described a dilapidated city of worn-out streets, sputtering buses, shabby airport, and crowded slums. They also found a second-rate council whose majority had close ties to the political organization of Senator Harry Byrd and a tendency to defer to Byrd's viceroy, Clerk of Courts William Prieur. At the same time, many residents sensed a new opportunity to remake the city without the heavy hand of federal directives. There was already substantial interest in reforming city government when the resignation of City Manager H. C. Borland in December 1945 after a disagreement with the city council provided the immediate occasion for action. The "People's Ticket" that challenged three incumbent councilmen in the spring of 1946 consisted of three political newcomers—Pretlow Darden, an automobile dealer recently returned from service in the navy, attorney Richard Cooke, and John Twohy, owner of a sand and gravel business. Running on a platform of clean government, police reform, and industrial development, Darden, Cooke, and Twohy attacked machine politics and claimed independence from special interests. In fact, they enjoyed the backing of the newspapers, the support of most local businessmen, and the endorsement of Colgate Darden, brother of the candidate and Virginia's wartime governor. Prieur activated organization supporters behind the incumbents and secured their unanimous endorsement by Norfolk's legislative delegation. Nevertheless, a record turnout on 12 June swept the People's Ticket to victory by a two to one margin. The newcomers carried all but the black precincts, but they accumulated 60 percent of their margin in a half-dozen voting districts in the high-income neighborhoods of Ghent, Larchmont, and the North Shore.[21]

The victory of the People's Ticket marked the triumph of a group of local leaders who had begun to work together before the war. As early as 1936, the city council had appointed a Committee on Slums that publicized the high crime rates and service costs associated with deteriorated neighborhoods at a crime study conference in March 1937. Three years later, committee members led the agitation for a local housing authority and supplied the members for the first Norfolk Housing Authority board. At the same time, a more inclusive group of businessmen had joined as a matter of civic pride to salvage the city's faltering United Fund drive.[22] Names from among these active business leaders reappeared in 1943 as advocates of an expanded planning commission, in 1944 as special grand jurors empaneled to investigate charges of corruption in local law enforcement, and in 1946 as supporters of Darden, Cooke, and Twohy.[23]

As Newton had done in Denver, the reform council worked to modernize Norfolk's city administration. Perhaps their most important step was to seek out the best city manager available and to hire Charles Harrell. In turn, Harrell pushed through new building and zoning codes, established a Personnel Bureau and Department of Parks, reorganized the Planning Commission to include professional staff, and directed capital improvements for streets and water system. Darden and his associates simultaneously pressured their backroom supporters to take public positions on appointive boards and commissions. The new council worked to shut down the open prostitution, bootlegging, and numbers games that had flourished in downtown Norfolk during the war and shook up the police department in 1948. It also established a Norfolk Port Authority to serve as an economic development agency. The following year, the expanded Norfolk Redevelopment and Housing Authority launched an impressive effort to build a "New Norfolk out of old" by constructing 3,428 new units of low-income housing on 190 acres north of the central business district.[24] Local leaders took special pride that Norfolk was one of the first cities to execute a loan and grant under the 1949 Housing Act.[25]

Darden, Cooke, and Twohy in 1946 had advertised that they intended "to serve only one term as an effective means of driving politics out of the conduct of city affairs." In fact, Norfolk's reformers in the early months of 1950 struck a bargain with the political professionals. In a series of meetings with Billy Prieur, the reform leaders agreed to destroy their precinct voter card files and to remain neutral in legislative and statewide elections. They also agreed to share the selection of council candidates with Prieur and expected a favorable climate for economic development in return. The immediate result was the election of a "Harmony Ticket" with closer ties to the Byrd machine than to the local elite.[26] Over the next several years, the compromise brought a slow erosion of business participation in city government through the realignment of appointive boards and the resignation of Charles Harrell in 1952 after continued disagreements with Mayor Fred Duckworth.[27]

At the same time that he represented the interests of the local political organization and won the favor of Harry Byrd, Duckworth gave Norfolk businessmen much of what they wanted. An executive at the city's Ford assembly plant, Duckworth shared the central aim of rescuing Norfolk from its limited economic base. In the back of his mind was a vision of metropolitan Norfolk as a major financial center able to compete equally with other South Atlantic cities. On his own terms, he also continued to implement the development strategy detailed by Harrell. New housing, new business investment, a new airport, a four-year college, new highways, new tunnels to Portsmouth and Hampton—all promised to supplant sour wartime memories with the shining steel and solid concrete of new Norfolk.

The crisis that reassembled the reform leadership emerged out of state rather than local politics. Harry Byrd's reaction to the 1954 Supreme Court school desegregation decision was to engineer the passage of a set of laws that committed Virginia to a course of "massive resistance" to federal policy. The key measure required that the governor seize control and close any public school that was threatened with integration by local or federal action. In Norfolk, the ponderous machinery of massive resistance clanked into action in the fall of 1958 when the U.S. District Court ordered the admission of 17 black students to three junior and three senior high schools. Governor Lindsey Almond officially assumed state control of the affected schools on 27 September, locking the doors on 9,950 white and 17 black students. Although 21,000 other white children and 15,000 other black children continued their education in segregated schools, attention during the next months focused on "the lost class of 1959." Neither requests by the school board nor petitions by Norfolk's small liberal community were able to alter state policy through the last months of 1958. Indeed, the Norfolk City Council offered outspoken support for massive resistance and blamed the city's problems on the ingratitude of blacks. In the background, Fred Duckworth and Billy Prieur consulted regularly on strategy with Harry Byrd.[28]

The Norfolk crisis peaked during two weeks in the middle of January. On the thirteenth, the city council voted to spread the burdens of massive resistance by cutting off local funding for segregated black junior and senior highs. On the nineteenth, the U.S. District Court and the Virginia Supreme Court both invalidated the state's massive resistance legislation. After listening to an emotional segregationist outburst by Lindsey Almond over a statewide radio network on 20 January, Norfolk residents eagerly switched on their televisions the next night to watch Edward R. Murrow analyze the city's problems on CBS Reports. While Duckworth and other organization stalwarts still mulled alternative plans for continuing resistance to federal law, the Norfolk business community finally moved to public action. On 26 January, the morning *Virginian-Pilot* and the evening *Ledger-Star* carried a short statement signed by one hundred leading business and professional men offering strong support for the preservation of public schools: "While we would strongly prefer to have segregated schools, it is evident from the recent court decisions that our public schools must be either integrated to the extent legally required or abandoned. The abandonment of our public school system is, in our opinion, unthinkable, as it would mean the denial of an adequate education to a majority of our children. Moreover, the consequences would be most damaging to our community. We, therefore, urge the City Council to do everything within its power to open all public schools as promptly as possible." In an accompanying editorial, the previously segregationist *Ledger* commented on the "tremendous weight" carried by the advertisement. The more liberal *Pilot* rejoiced that "a new clear voice speaks in Norfolk" and applauded the action of "an impressive group of men of large responsibilities and of effective leadership." A week later, the six schools reopened with the addition of seventeen black students.[29]

In local historiography, the Committee of 100 is given major credit for resolving the school crisis and pointing Norfolk back toward its primary goal of economic development. Certainly the men who recruited the signers of the advertisement represented the Norfolk establishment. Charles Kaufman, as director of the National Bank of Commerce, general counsel for the daily papers, and chairman of the Redevelopment and Housing Authority, was a key figure in numerous local decisions. Pretlow Darden had helped to guide the growth in Norfolk since 1946 as councilman, mayor, and member of the Redevelopment and Housing Authority board. Frank Batten was the publisher of the two metropolitan newspapers and vice-president of the largest radio and television station. During the same months, he had joined several other Norfolk businessmen to work against massive resistance through an informal committee directed by Richmond attorney Lewis Powell and Norfolk and Western Railroad president Stuart Saunders.[30]

Analysis of the Committee of 100 membership offers a chance for a closer look at the sorts of people involved in municipal reform movements in sunbelt cities. The men who joined in the statement are best described as "respected citizens." The newspapers made much of the fact that the list included two former mayors [and one future mayor] and nine men who had been honored as "first citizens" of Norfolk. The average member, however, was a man of means and position but not of extraordinary wealth. Three-quarters lived in the city's three stable and established upper-middle-class neighborhoods. In a city where the median value of owner-occupied homes was $11,500 in 1960, two-fifths lived in census tracts with median house values of over $25,000, two-fifths in tracts with medians in the $15–25,000 range, and one-fifth in tracts with medians under $15,000. Most of the businesses represented on the Committee of 100 shared a chamber-of-commerce orientation toward Norfolk markets and the health of Norfolk real estate. Only six of the signatories represented important manufacturing firms, seven were involved in port operations and transportation, and eight were officers of banks or savings and loans. The remaining members of the group worked in the local sector of the economy with business or professional horizons confined to the metropolitan area; ten were physicians, ten were lawyers, seventeen sold insurance, stocks or real estate, sixteen owned or managed retail firms, and twenty-three worked in the broad area of local business support services and wholesaling.[31]

Despite the bitter feelings from the long fall of 1958, new political forces mobilized by the school crisis forced a rapid reconstruction of the alliance between businessmen and politicians on terms somewhat more favorable to the good government contingent. The object of mutual distaste was Henry Howell, a liberal activist who capitalized on support from the Norfolk Education Association and the Norfolk Committee for Public Schools (the two consistent proschool voices during the 1958 crisis) to win a seat in the House of Delegates in 1959. The next spring, Howell and the proschool groups directed a challenge of city council members that unseated one incumbent. In 1961, Howell's faction overreached itself by challenging Billy Prieur's thirty-six-year tenure as clerk of courts. Where businessmen feared Howell as an economic liberal who had targeted high utility rates, Prieur and the Democratic party worried about unreliable voters brought into political activity by the uproar of 1958. With the strong backing of the newspapers, the organization candidates held their offices with the help of 60–80 percent margins in the genteel west-side precincts that had housed the core support for the old People's Ticket and the Committee of 100.[32] Two weeks after the election, the *Virginian-Pilot* ran a ten-thousand-word series of retrospective articles that argued in detail that "the business core of the city has been the key force in the making of the new Norfolk. It has acted with cohesion, direction and remarkable unanimity."[33] Norfolk was ready to forget the aberrant past and turn again to the important matters of economic growth.

The reform revolution in the last example of San Antonio involved extraordinary extremes even in comparison with Norfolk. From start to finish, it required seventeen years of wide-open Texas politics in which personal ambitions were often more important than issues or ideologies. Especially during the early 1950s, alliances among reformers and machine politicans formed and dissolved so rapidly that local reporters were scarcely able to keep the score. If the city proved particularly reluctant fully to accept the well-advertised benefits of municipal reform, however, it also ended its decade of turmoil with the good government advocates holding a degree of control over city affairs unsurpassed in other sunbelt cities.

The first prerequisite for municipal reform was to crack the power of San Antonio's professional politicians. With a brief interruption in the 1910s that allowed the establishment of commission government, San Antonio politics since the nineteenth century had been dominated by a self-perpetuating city hall machine. Benefitting from the disinterest of military personnel and low turnouts among the Anglo-German middle class, the city hall clique built its majority with well-disciplined black votes from the east side and scattered Mexican votes from the west side barrio. Through the 1930s, only 6 to 10 percent of the potential electorate participated in city elections, with the majority of San Antonians willingly overlooking the normal machine problems of election frauds, protection of illicit businesses, and favoritism in city business.[34]

The first important challenge to this machine dated from the end of the 1930s. After joining in an ultimately unsuccessful reform effort in 1930–31, Maury Maverick had served two bumptious terms in Congress as an outspoken New Dealer. A primary defeat at the hands of a machine candidate in 1938 brought him back from Washington to take on the scandal-ridden administration of Mayor C. K. Quin. Self-consciously emulating Fiorello La Guardia, Maverick ran on a Fusion ticket that appealed both to respectable reformers and to Mexican-Americans. Maverick's impressive victory in May 1939 brought the largely alien New Deal to the dusty streets of South Texas. In the space of two years he reformed San Antonio's public health and sanitation services, obtained WPA funds to build the elegant Paseo del Rio along the disreputable San Antonio River, used the National Youth Administration to preserve a section of the original Mexican town as La Villeta, and opened the way for the construction of a twelve-hundred-unit public housing project on the west side.[35]

Maverick's political coalition was built in part on the appeal of national liberalism and in part on the backing of a group of businessmen interested in council-manager government. Unfortunately for San Antonio, the mayor's aggressive personality, his defense of free speech, and his refusal to honor a commitment to push a city manager charter lost him much of his middle-class support. He simultaneously alienated black voters and failed to create an organization to consolidate popularity on the west side. The result in 1941 was a sound defeat for Maverick, victory for Quin and the city hall gang who quickly put a lid on efforts to analyze San Antonio's growing social problems and to cope creatively with wartime growth.[36]

The defeat of Maury Maverick was the first of several conspicuous failures in the effort to reform municipal government in San Antonio. The second came in the immediate postwar years. In order to refurbish their public image, local bosses in 1943 eased C. K. Quin into a judgeship and replaced him with Gus Mauerman, a respected attorney from an established San Antonio family. Like Martin Kennelly in Chicago a few years later, Mauerman took his position more seriously than the bosses intended. The mayor not only tried to give the city a competent government but also responded to the growing spirit of civic activism by pushing through an annexation of twenty square miles in 1944 and appointing Chamber of Commerce president Alex Thomas to chair an informal planning commission in 1946. The annexation unfortunately turned out to be political suicide for Mauerman because it promised higher taxes both for the annexed neighborhoods and for the core-city property owners who would need to finance extended services. He recruited several young veterans to run for city commission on the Greater San Antonio ticket and campaigned for the implementation of a modern civil service, expanded services, and capital improvements, but he finished a distant third in the May 1947 election. Maury Maverick, who ran largely on his reputation and who drained off liberal votes, lost the runoff to Tax Commissioner Alfred Callaghan, son and grandson of previous San Antonio bosses.[37]

The Callaghan election was a short-term victory but a long-term disaster for the San Antonio machine. With none of the political savvy of his ancestors, the new mayor proved himself a clown and a fool. On one day he could propose to cut the city budget by stuffing the three hundred animals at the zoo and saving their food bills. On another he might refer to a rash of shootings by the police as "seven measly deaths" or refuse to spend $180,000 budgeted for industrial development. On still another he dared a delegation advocating a council-manager charter to take direct action. In reply, savings and loan executive Walter McAllister raised $50,000 to back the mayoral candidacy of A. C. "Jack" White. With the support of the Chamber of Commerce (of which White was president), the Citizens Committee for Council-Manager Government, Mauerman, and other reformers who had been interested in manager government since the 1920s, White won in a landslide with 80 percent of the vote in May 1949.[38]

The 1949 election was more a reaction to Callaghan's ineptness and an expression of pious hopes for good government than the product of a well-organized reform coalition. Within a few months, the new mayor was feuding with the four independently elected commissioners who retained close ties to the machine. A charter revision committee appointed in the fall also split down the middle to produce rival programs for reforming the city's antiquated government, with one proposed charter backed by Jack White and the other by the Chamber of Commerce reformers. The result was a standoff election in which the entire array of charter amendments was defeated. It seemed clear from the returns that the good government leadership held the support of middle-class Anglo voters, that the San Antonio machine held the loyalty of black voters, and that White had gained considerable support on the west side through the advocacy of district elections.[39]

For the single year of 1951, the various advocates of municipal reform were able to forget their charges and countercharges about gerrymandering and "special privilege leeches" and to close ranks around a coherent program. In May, Jack White was reelected over a machine candidate and helped to carry reformers to victory in contests for the four city commission seats. At the same time, voters approved the appointment of a new charter review committee. Five months later, voters at a special election agreed with the *Express* that they needed "better parks, better streets, better garbage collection, [and] more efficient and businesslike administration" of city services and voted in a council-manager charter by nineteen thousand to ten thousand votes. In November, a "Citizens Committee" ticket representing the good government advocates swept aside a weak challenge by professional politicians to take every seat on the first city council under the new charter.[40]

Unfortunately for San Antonio, declining vote totals during 1951 were a forecast of new trouble for the reformers beyond their immediate success. Although forty-eight thousand voters had turned out in May to reelect Jack White and approve the charter commission, only twenty-five thousand bothered to choose the new council that took office on 1 January 1952. Again, it took only a few months in 1952 for the appearance of open hostility between White and City Manager Charles Harrell, hired away from Norfolk at $27,500 per year. Accustomed to the powers and publicity of the active mayoral role allowed under the old commission charter, White found that Harrell was determined to organize San Antonio's first efficient and professional bureaucracy as Newton had done in Denver and Harrell himself had done in Norfolk. By the next election in April 1953, White had broken completely with the other reform councilmen, formed his own ticket of "San Antonians," and attacked the reform coalition in the Citizens Committee as the tools of the city's Big Ten property owners. Citizens Committee candidates in turn defended the record of Charles Harrell, accused White of consorting with pimps and gamblers, and argued that the "alarming surge of strength in the old-line machine areas will once again arouse the old crusading spirit that carried good government forces to six previous victories." Although the contest was close enough to require a runoff, the San Antonians outpolled the reformers for all nine council seats.[41]

If 1952 was a bad year for city manager government in San Antonio, the next two years were excruciating for middle-class reformers. Elected with minority votes delivered by old-line politicians, White and his allies seemed determined to revive the era of Alfred Callaghan by opening the city offices to traditional spoilsmen and shady dealers. A recall campaign organized in the summer of 1954 quickly deteriorated into a game of musical chairs. Just before each recall petition could be officially presented, the affected councilman resigned so that other members of the council could appoint a like-minded successor. As the city swept through four city managers following Harrell's quick resignation and through councilmen by the half dozen and the dozen, fifty of the original advocates of charter reform met in December 1954 to plan a final effort that they hoped would assure "retention of the Council-Manager system, creation of good city government geared to community progress with efficient nonpartisan administrations, an end to factionalism, sectionalism, patronage politics, and maneuvering for special selfish interests."[42] With city business nearly at a halt, the new Good Government League easily raised forty thousand dollars, recruited eight council candidates, and won easily by a margin of two to one.[43]

Municipal reformers in Norfolk and Denver during the fifties and sixties were eventually satisfied to moderate their success by sharing power with the established partisan leadership. San Antonio leaders were unwilling to take a similar risk after a decade of bitter factional fights. The Good Government League quickly evolved into the functional equivalent of a political party. It advocated a well-defined set of measures for San Antonio, maintained continuity of organization, used an anonymous nominating committee to choose candidates for the city council, and spent one hundred thousand dollars every two years to secure their election. From 1955 through 1971, seventy-seven of San Antonio's eighty-one city councilmen were recruited and endorsed by the Good Government League.[44] As Robert Lineberry has described it, the league was "not a casual, 'crowd at the civic club,' political clique" but rather a "sort of upper-middle class political machine, officing not in Tammany Hall, but in a savings and loan association, whose electoral wonders are impressive to behold."[45]

In its own definition, of course, the Good Government League was not a political party but an advisory committee that sought to persuade leading citizens to devote their time to public service. From 1955 the league was careful to present "balanced" slates that included at least one Mexican-American. From the mid-sixties it also slated a black candidate and token spokesmen for liberal causes. Even so, the results were remarkably homogeneous councils. Between 1955 and 1969, twenty-nine of the forty-nine individuals who served as league councilmen were entrepreneurs or business executives and eighteen others were lawyers, doctors, accountants, and other professionals. Thirty-nine of the council members lived in census tracts with median incomes greater than the San Antonio average, with twenty-six of these in the five highest income tracts. More than half of the Good Government League directors in 1969 lived in the same five San Antonio tracts or in the elite northern suburbs. Roughly two-thirds of the league councilmen lived on the affluent north side and another quarter in the middle-class Anglo southeast. By another measure, only twenty-five of San Antonio's 113 census tracts had direct councilmanic representation. The same sections of San Antonio provided the bulk of Good Government League votes and furnished the large majority of members for the powerful independent utility and transportation boards appointed by the city council.[46]

The business leadership that worked through the league had a clear idea of its city's needs. In the first decade under the new charter, the municipality made initial efforts to solve its tremendous drainage problems and built one thousand miles of storm sewers, paved two thousand miles of streets, bought six hundred acres for parks, connected ten thousand homes to the water system and sixteen thousand to sewer lines, acquired and expanded the bus system, installed street lights, and opened new libraries and fire stations. A long series of bond referenda for such capital improvements climaxed in January 1964 with the approval of a $30 million issue with majorities in every precinct.[47]

The related goal of improved transportation was a special interest of Walter McAllister, who provided continuity for the Good Government regime as mayor from 1961 to 1971. At the start of the decade, complaints from the commander of Kelly Field about poor highway access supplied a major argument for a $10.5 million bond package to pay for arterial roads into the base and a controversial north expressway through the edge of Brackenridge Park. By 1966, the city manager could boast that the completion of 98.3 miles of freeway placed San Antonio second to Los Angeles in freeways within city limits. After protracted court battles, the north-side freeway opened as the final link in the San Antonio system in 1978, now carrying the name of Walter McAllister.

The postwar politics of a number of other sunbelt cities show similar patterns of reform. The small city of Augusta, Georgia, for example, provides a set piece for the description of the G.I. revolt. During the war years, the town lay under the tight control of the "Cracker Party," a local machine run by the commissioner of public safety. Following the standard model, the Crackers used city patronage and city services to protect illicit businesses, reward friendly voters, and harass opponents. Between 1943 and 1945, good government advocates in Augusta built a case against the inefficiency of the city administration and the corruption of local voting practices. The case for reform was restated by Augusta novelist Berry Fleming in *Colonel Effingham's Raid*, a 1943 Book-of-the-Month Club selection that satirized the Cracker leadership. As in Norfolk, the spring of 1946 brought concerted action from concerned businessmen. The Independent League for Good Government offered slates of candidates for the state legislature and county commission elections in April. Five of the six candidates were returning veterans and all were members of the upper middle class: newspaper publisher, substantial farmer, insurance executive, lawyers. Their campaign promise was to attract new manufacturing to Augusta by offering dignified and efficient local government. Their solid victory effectively uprooted the Cracker machine and introduced Augusta to two decades of businesslike booster government.[48]

On the political stage of New Orleans, de Lesseps S. Morrison played the same role that Quigg Newton filled in Denver. The close of World War II found New Orleans under the thumb of Mayor Robert S. Maestri, a protégé of Huey Long and the leader of the Regular Democratic Organization. Especially since his reelection in 1942, Maestri had given New Orleans a government of favoritism, payroll padding, and routinized graft without any effort to solve large problems. The response of many of the city's business leaders was to organize a citizens committee to challenge Maestri in the 1946 election. The final choice as a standard-bearer was the thirty-four-year-old Morrison, a returning army officer, incumbent state legislator, and dynamic campaigner. Morrison's platform of civic reform and economic progress rallied a coalition of businessmen, women's organizations, and veterans eager to see New Orleans share in the postwar prosperity. After a narrow victory in January 1946, Morrison's first administration implemented budgetary reform, reduced operating costs, established housing and recreation departments, and extended streets and storm sewers into new neighborhoods. Less than two years after the election, *Time* declared that Morrison "symbolized as well as anyone or anything the postwar energy of the nation's cities."[49]

In the Southwest, the Phoenix Charter Government Committee and the Albuquerque Citizens Committee both bore striking resemblance to San Antonio's Good Government League. Phoenix voters in 1948 responded to blatant corruption in city government by amending the charter to provide at-large elections and to strengthen council-manager government. When established politicians made it clear that they intended to maintain their influence on the city administration, prominent business and professional men in 1949 organized the Charter Government Committee and assembled a full ticket of reform candidates including department store executive Barry Goldwater. The committee swept the election in 1949 and repeated its success every two years for the next two decades. In Albuquerque, the immediate wave of postwar reform in 1946 had ended the reign of Clyde Tingley, an old-line politico who had converted the position of city commission chairman into that of a partisan boss. Eight years of fragmented politics and "government by crisis" persuaded middle-class reformers in Albuquerque's "Heights" neighborhoods to organize the Citizens Committee to back candidates who would return the city to the ideal of neutral, businesslike administration. The Charter Government Committee and the Citizens Committee both functioned as informal political parties. They chose candidates, raised funds, consistently supported the idea of nonpartisan city manager government, and won elections with votes from affluent precincts.[50]

As previously mentioned, several other cities that initiated political changes in the late thirties offer partial fits to the historical model. After adopting council-manager charters at the start of the 1930s, San Diego, Dallas, and Charlotte each found that structural change had brought chaotic factional battles among city employees, neighborhoods, and amateur politicians rather than the expected efficiency in city administration. The response of civic leaders in each community was to launch an emergency rescue effort to save city manager government. The substantial business and professional men of San Diego formed a Civic Affairs Conference in 1935 to elect upper-middle-class councils and to provide support for their decisions. The mercantile oligarchy of Dallas bankers, builders, and retailers similarly formed the Citizens Council in 1937 to set policy for the city manager and city councilmen. Without organizing a formal committee, the businessmen of Charlotte also staged an electoral counterrevolution against factional politics in 1938 and 1939. The city's business establishment reconfirmed its influence in the aftermath of World War II by ending a short experiment with ward voting and encouraging the participation of younger entrepreneurs to help implement its ambitious growth strategies. Both the success of large-scale planning from 1943 to 1945 and the desire to enlist city government in the cause of postwar growth held San Diego and Dallas businessmen together as the controlling force in city politics long beyond the normal life of municipal reform coalitions. Through the 1950s, every observer in San Diego agreed that important decisions for the city were made behind the scenes in board rooms and by chamber-of-commerce committees. Descriptions of Dallas politics in the same years could start and end with the Citizens Council and its subordinate Citizens Charter Association, that took on the task of recruiting and electing suitable city councils.[51]

Seattle nudged toward reform in the 1950s somewhat in the manner of Portland. As early as 1938, Mayor Arthur Langlie had undertaken to clean up what had historically been one of the country's wide-open towns. Langlie's work was continued by William Devin, who presided over the wartime boom and postwar readjustment between 1942 and 1952. His dull, honest, and inactive administration drew the backing of downtown real estate and business interests that feared rapid growth and refused loans to outside entrepreneurs. Like the "spinster city" of Portland or the "prematurely grey" Denver of 1946, Seattle in the early fifties was a "collection of complacent little empires." The first impetus toward change came from Mayor Allen Pomeroy (1952–56), who defeated Devin by promising to revitalize the city with industrial development and capital improvements. Failure to carry a majority of the city council for his program reduced Pomeroy to headline seeking and bickering and made him a one-term mayor. As his successor, however, Gordon Clinton between 1956 and 1964 was able to respond to a new surge of growth in Seattle with a major public works program.

As attitudes among Seattle businessmen also changed, he was able to work with the Central Seattle Association representing the "Big Ten" of the city's economic elite to begin major downtown redevelopment.[52]

In a final example, Atlanta began a thirty-year alliance between city hall and the downtown business community with the new administration of Mayor William Hartsfield in 1937.[53] After campaigning on the issue of police corruption, he worked particularly during his first term to update Atlanta's creaky governmental arrangements with modern budgeting procedures. In 1938, the city, Fulton County, and the Chamber of Commerce jointly sponsored a report on local government by Thomas Reed of the National Municipal League. In response to Reed's recommendations, the city and county established civil service systems and consolidated several overlapping services. The city also adopted at-large voting for council members and undertook a substantial public housing program in 1940. Immediately after World War II, the same elements in the community turned more directly to economic development, pushing through a $40 million bond issue for highways, airport, sewers, and schools and sponsoring a major consultant's report on expressways. By the later forties, in other words, the Atlanta business community had already taken care of internal housekeeping and was prepared to turn its attention and energy to the problems of suburban growth.[54]

In the larger perspective of American urban growth, the younger businessmen and professionals who led the political revolts were motivated by the same tenets of urban boosterism that had been prominent in popular thought about cities from the pioneer years of the nineteenth century to the decade of *Babbitt* and *Middletown* in the 1920s. Boosterism is primarily an ideology of businessmen oriented toward the local market and its basic urge is toward rapid population growth—more illnesses for the doctor, more litigation for the lawyer, more policies for the insurance agent, more customers for the retailer, more sodas from the soft drink bottler, and more subscribers and advertisers for the daily paper. In essence, only the rhetoric has changed over a century and a half. Their great-grandfathers had hoped to build New Eden on the Mississippi and New Chicago on the high plains. In phraseology still relevant for the late 1970s, postwar boosters preferred the formulation of the Portland *Oregon Journal*: "big league city or sad sack town."[55]

The returned veterans and other ambitious urbanites who stood heir to the tradition of boosterism were more likely to describe themselves in the time-honored rhetoric of "good government." Developed in response to explosive immigration and urban growth in the decades around the turn of the century, the good government approach to municipal affairs emphasized economical and businesslike city government. The standard set of measures had included commission and city manager forms of government, nonpartisan elections held at large, planning and zoning, and city home rule charters. More broadly, it had emphasized the need to impose order on the chaos of rapid growth by delivering control of the city to the established middle class. Under a reform administration, the residents of outlying residential neighborhoods could hope for low taxes, effective services, and vigorous law enforcement. The gainers had been the homeowner and the local businessman, the losers were supposedly utility tycoons, corrupt politicans, saloon keepers, and immigrant voters crowded into downtown slums.[56]

In the second half of the 1940s, the excitement of previously unsuspected growth possibilities resulted in the updating of the good government agenda. Because mid-century cities had fewer vice kings and traction magnates to serve as symbolic enemies, the rhetoric and goals were more positive than in the progressive era. In cities that had failed to act in the 1910s and 1920s, the first accomplishment was often the adoption of the city manager system. From coast to coast, as this chapter has shown, municipal efficiency meant buttoned-up bureaus run by button-down bureaucrats trained in schools of planning or administration. As the following pages will describe, political coalitions led by eager businessmen and supported by professional administrators were consistently able to assist economic growth. After initial success in a number of cities, they have been less able to achieve the other long-standing progressive goal of regulating metropolitan growth in the interests of central city business interests and property owners.

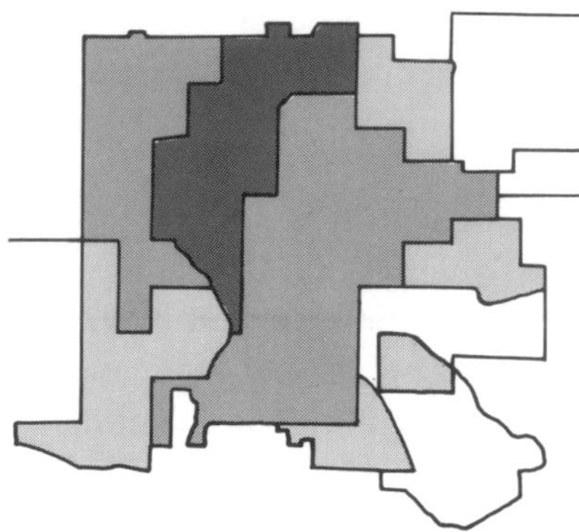

Chapter 6

The Renewal Era

Downtown Atlanta rises above its surrounding city like a walled fortress from another age. The citadel is anchored to the south by the international trade center and buttressed by the municipal stadium. To the north, the walls and walkways of John Portman's Peachtree Center stand watch over the acres of automobiles that pack both flanks of the city's long ridge. The sunken moat of I-85 with its flowing lanes of traffic reaches around the eastern base of the hill from south to north, protecting lawyers, bankers, consultants, and regional executives from the intrusion of low-income neighborhoods.

The business traveler and the conventioneer discover the same result in other sunbelt cities. Houston's central blocks of high-rise hotels and oil company offices take pride in their isolation, towering above a wilderness of dusty parking spaces and an encompassing loop of freeway concrete. At five o'clock, its workday crowds drain away through its streets like water from a sudden rainstorm. By nightfall it seems to float on the humid Gulf air, an abandoned luxury liner in a dark sea. Its masts and towers from a distance are alight with invitation, but its streets are as empty as the decks of the *Mary Celeste*.

Dallas, Los Angeles, Denver, Houston, Atlanta—the fast-growing American cities from one ocean to the other have built interchangeable cores. The uniform environment of high-rise offices, convention centers, sports arenas, and girdling freeways is an expression of shared values among urban leaders in our boom-time cities. The phenomenon in Calvin Trillin's phrase is a spreading infection of municipal "domeism"—the tendency in sunbelt glamour cities to focus civic pride on a single project of pharaonic scale.[1] Cities have worked to top the Astrodome with the Kingdome and the Superdome, the Regency-Hyatt in Atlanta with the Crown Center in Kansas City, and Century City in Los Angeles with the Dallas-Fort Worth Airport. In larger perspective, the central business core of most sunbelt cities is a concrete dream of the 1950s realized in the 1960s and 1970s by private speculators and government agencies tapping public funds for one downtown project after another.

The planners and businessmen who copied each other's blueprints for massive downtown development were involved in implementing a key element in the program of neoprogressivism in the sunbelt cities. In most southern and western cities, efforts to rebuild and expand the central business district came as a second step following charter changes or political upheavals and the modernization of city administrations. From the mid-fifties through the sixties, the redevelopment of city centers showed the strengths and weaknesses of businessmen's government and helped to define the sources of its political support. In particular, it involved the use of the federal urban renewal program to assist private investment directly by assembling developable land at low cost and indirectly by providing necessary public facilities in downtown areas. In the urban renewal alliance, it was impossible to separate public and private interest, to untangle private real estate booms and surges of public construction, and to differentiate between the goals of bureaucrats and businessmen.

The rebuilding of downtown districts was intended to secure two related economic goals. On the broad scale, urban renewal became a tool in intercity rivalries for economic advantage. Where nineteenth-century cities had competed to acquire the best railroad connections, those of the twentieth-century Sunbelt worked to provide the facilities for metropolitan activities of regional finance, public administration, business headquarters and distribution, and professional services. In city after city, the postwar leadership worked to facilitate the construction of abundant modern office space. The list of common projects also included a trade center, a convention-exhibition center with appended hotels, and a public university campus to train technical and managerial staff for the new white-collar enterprises. In the best tradition of urban boosterism, a successful redevelopment program became a selling point in itself as a symbol of civic unity and modernity. New sports arenas and stadiums were intended to confirm the new image of a "major league city."

It would be easy to list the themes of interurban rivalry that motivated downtown redevelopment in dozens of younger cities. The Oakland Planning Commission introduced major redevelopment plans in 1959 with the forecast that Oakland could become the regional metropolis for central California. At the same time, the cross-Bay establishment was working on plans to reassert San Francisco's role as a metropolis with national influence. Advocates of renewal in Denver argued in the middle 1960s that massive downtown redevelopment would make it a continental city that could finally throw off the rankling dominance of Kansas City and Dallas. Portland initiated its renewal projects to aid in countering the 1958 recession and to restore lost ground in its perennial battle with Seattle. Even if Norfolk residents did not believe the consultant who promised that they would soon live in the "Manhattan of the South," they did expect the new office space available in a renewed downtown to help make them the dominant city on the South Atlantic coast.[2] In a chain of competing ambitions, Charlotte likewise viewed urban renewal as a tool for establishing primacy as a distributing center among other North Carolina cities and for competing with Richmond, Norfolk, and Atlanta. In turn, renewal in Atlanta helped that city hold first place in its commercial and financial competition with Birmingham.

The second essential goal of postwar renewal programs was to sustain the predominance of established central business districts against the growing challenge of suburban areas. The expectation was that downtown land values could be held and increased if the attractiveness of that land was increased through public investment. Such attractiveness could be enhanced by improved access and parking facilities for automobiles, by the assembly of land at low cost for private developers, and by the construction of facilities that might increase levels of transient activity (auditoriums, stadiums, convention centers, hotels) or the supply of permanent customers (downtown high-rise apartments). By extension, the renewal of the business area was an important element in efforts to maintain the primacy of the core city within the metropolis by making it the focus for the entire population of the SMSA. In the morning, suburbanites would speed over the new downtown freeway to the high-rise offices of banks, insurance companies, and other firms with areawide concerns. In the evening, they would return to enjoy the symphony in the civic center theater, to finish a degree at the downtown university, or to cheer their ABA basketball team at the new coliseum. In most cases, obviously, a single coordinated renewal effort could be expected to achieve both broad goals simultaneously by centralizing metropolitan functions within a core district.

For the present study of political responses to metropolitan growth, three questions in relation to the urban renewal era are of particular interest. As just suggested, one concern is how the residents of specific cities expected downtown redevelopment to affect aggregate metropolitan growth and patterns of development within their metropolitan area. A second subject of concern is the sources of political support and opposition for core area renewal efforts. The third question is the actual impact of renewal programs on the appearance and structure of sunbelt cities. The following section therefore defines three broad stages in the process of urban renewal and describes the common patterns in its evolution as a political issue. The second half of the chapter examines downtown redevelopment in Denver, San Antonio, Norfolk, and Atlanta and compares their experiences to those of other southern and western cities.

The urban renewal era that provided the climax for the good government impulse in many sunbelt cities spanned the presidencies of Eisenhower, Kennedy, and Johnson. The basic legislation that made urban redevelopment a municipal responsibility was the Housing Act of 1949, which provided federal assistance to local agencies for the assembly, clearance, site preparation, and sale or lease of land for "predominantly residential uses" to private developers or housing authorities. The arena for municipal action expanded with amendments added in 1954. Where the 1949 law had envisioned a slum clearance and public housing program, the new provisions allowed 10 percent of federal capital grant funds under the program to be used for nonresidential projects. Additional amendments in 1959 expanded the nonresidential allocation to 20 percent and also removed a previous requirement that projects include the demolition of large numbers of substandard buildings. In response to complaints about the disruptive effects of renewal projects, the first legislative limitations came in the middle and later 1960s with increasingly stringent requirements for relocation programs. After twenty-five years, the urban renewal program was effectively terminated when categorical grants for redevelopment were superseded by community development block grants under the Housing and Community Development Act of 1974.

In combination with the evolution of internal city politics, the changes in legislation keyed three stages in the downtown redevelopment of sunbelt cities. The initial stage in the early and middle 1950s was marked more by start-up problems than by accomplishments. Cities like Atlanta, Norfolk, and Portland, which had active public housing programs dating from the thirties or forties, already possessed a mechanism for planning redevelopment programs. At the same time, their initial proposals were likely to be relatively small in scale and to involve unresolved conflicts between housing and development goals. Especially when project initiatives came through a housing agency, residents of neighborhoods that were slated for redevelopment found it hard to understand why their own substandard housing had to give way to new commercial uses. There was also scattered opposition to federal participation in municipal affairs. In Richmond, the *News Leader* helped to kill a small redevelopment project in 1952 by invoking the "shadow of Marx." Efforts to develop an urban renewal program for Tucson in the late fifties also foundered on noisy political controversy over the acceptability of federal funds. Dallas was a third city in which local business leaders tested the political winds in 1956 and decided not to try the citywide referendum that Texas law required before an urban redevelopment agency could be established.[3]

Portland provides a good example of the factors behind false starts toward core area renewal in the early 1950s. In the spring of 1952, the planning staff of the Housing Authority of Portland submitted a "Vaughan Street" redevelopment plan for a forty-four-block area of mixed housing and commercial use in the dreary northwest industrial zone, a mile and a half from the business district. The proposal was to remove 500-odd residential buildings housing a thousand households in order to make the entire area available for warehousing and light industry. With strong support from the Chamber of Commerce, City Club, Building Trades Council, League of Women Voters, and other civic groups, the city council put a $2 million bond issue to cover the city cost share on the November ballot. Despite the impressive list of endorsements, the proposal to tear down several hundred frame cottages from the turn of the century was unable to engage the public imagination. It was also attacked by conservative politicians such as County Commissioner Frank Shull for disrupting an established neighborhood and for inviting the federal octopus into Portland. On election day, the margin for a substantial defeat came from east side working-class and middle-class neighborhoods whose residents were worried about their own housing costs in the face of growing tax bills and Korean War inflation.[4]

If concerned taxpayers and political conservatives defeated the Vaughan Street project in 1952, it was protest from the neighborhood itself that blocked its revival the next year. In the first months of 1953, the housing authority attempted to revive the project using its own funds from the sale of surplus war housing. The authority weakened its own case, however, by adding provisions for new public housing, which implicitly contradicted previous claims that project area residents could easily find new homes on the private market. Continued pressure from the Chamber of Commerce and the Building Trades Council was now balanced by protest from the first and second generation Croatians who constituted a stable core of homeowners in the Vaughan Street area. After receiving a petition with the signatures of 953 northwest area residents, even a development-minded city commissioner like William Bowes took the safe position of protecting neighborhood stability and joined the rest of the city council to kill the project.[5]

The heart of the urban renewal era in southern and western cities stretched from the late 1950s through the 1960s. In ambitious cities all over the country, the Eisenhower administration amendments were taken as an invitation to disinfect the fringes of downtown office districts. Planners carefully drew thick black lines around blocks of sleazy bars, cheap apartment hotels, and crumbling houses. Unveiled with front-page headlines and commendatory editorials in the metropolitan dailies, proposals to buy and clear underutilized core area land and make it available for new projects elicited strong local support. Blue-ribbon committees of civic leaders and businessmen issued favorable pronouncements, city councils voted necessary approvals, and citizens usually supplied support in special elections.

Rising interest in the use of urban renewal tools was intimately associated with local booms in downtown real estate. In lagged response to the increases in size and wealth of regional and metropolitan markets since 1940, private investors in the middle 1950s began to offer their own schemes for downtown construction. In many cases, the new offices, stores, and hotels which they undertook in Atlanta or Denver or San Francisco were the first major downtown construction since the end of the 1920s. This initial proof that old downtowns retained their attractiveness for private entrepreneurs helped to convince residents that large-scale redevelopment projects could attract the private capital necessary for success. Only in the Texas boom cities of Houston, Dallas, and Fort Worth did extraordinary prosperity and fears of creeping socialism combine to prevent the use of urban renewal to reinforce private investment.

Since support for downtown redevelopment in the 1960s came in the first instance from the business interests which had the most to gain, the backers of the strategy constituted a familiar cast. What Harvey Molotch has characterized as the "growth machine coalition" included utilities, major retailers, print and broadcast media, universities, and other organizations whose futures are tied to the expansion of local markets. Specialists in business and professional services ranging from law to data processing also expected to profit very specifically from the arrival of new corporate tenants for downtown high rises. At the same time, core area renewal promised to aid central department stores, downtown property owners, and financial institutions with large portfolios of downtown mortgages.[6] The sorts of people who do not benefit from downtown redevelopment include small shopkeepers with neighborhood clienteles, factory workers, and residents of inner-city neighborhoods that may be disrupted by renewal bulldozers.

Coalitions of downtown businesses and investors therefore took the lead in selling urban renewal programs to city councils and to voters in a number of cities in the years around 1960. In Portland, Tucson, and Richmond, leading local businessmen were largely responsible for the revival of urban renewal several years after initial defeats. Typical business coalitions were Downtown Denver Incorporated (1955) and the Downtown Denver Master Plan Committee (1961), the Greater Baltimore Committee (1962), and Downtown Tulsa Unlimited (1955). With the backing of bankers and department store owners, the latter group helped to secure city approval and to pass bond issues in 1959 and 1965 for a $55 million civic center. It was also a consistent supporter of an adjacent renewal project that cleared land for a hospital, junior college, apartments, and offices.[7]

San Francisco offers another example of the steps involved in mobilizing and holding support for downtown renewal. The key project was the Golden Gateway Center, which replaced the old wholesale produce market near the ferry terminal with high-rise upper-income housing, the Embarcadero complex of four huge office buildings, and a Hyatt Regency Hotel. The project also provided for a Bay Area Rapid Transit station to bring suburban commuters to the Embarcadero Center and nearby financial district. With a somewhat inactive city administration in the mid-fifties, it was industrialists C. B. Zellerbach and Charles Blyth who provided the necessary support for the project in its planning stage by forming a businessmen's committee in 1955 to advance funds for planning to the redevelopment agency. Although adjacent building owners raised specific complaints about unfair competition, the redevelopment agency, planning commission, and board of supervisors took less than six weeks to approve the final plans in the spring of 1959. Both their decisions and the speedy project implementation were strongly backed by the new San Francisco Planning and Urban Renewal Association (PURA) that was formed out of the Blyth-Zellerbach committee in 1959 to represent the city's business establishment. The appointment of M. Justin Herman in the same year gave the redevelopment agency an energetic director whose economic rationale for urban renewal matched that of the PURA.[8]

The Golden Gate development during the 1960s helped to trigger a private construction boom in the San Francisco financial district. The neo-Egyptian obelisk of the Trans-American tower is the most conspicuous among more than a score of buildings that added 10 million square feet of space for banking, corporate headquarters, and other functions appropriate to a national metropolis. While local-market businesses enjoyed the rising land values and economic activity, international corporations with San Francisco bases benefitted from the growing concentration of attorneys, accountants, advertising agencies, and other business services. The tacit trade-off for general acceptance of this financial district redevelopment was the construction of almost three thousand units of subsidized housing in the oriental and black neighborhoods of the western addition. By the end of the decade, the same coalition building and bargaining became explicit in arguments over the Yerba Buena project, through which the redevelopment agency hoped to replace eighty-seven acres of cheap hotels, parking lots, and warehouses south of Market Street with a convention center and additional offices. City bureaucrats saw an annual tax increment of $5.2 million to add to the $3.4 million gain from Golden Gateway, large corporations saw extra facilities for the metropolitan economy, members of the Convention and Visitors Bureau saw flush times for owners and employees of hotels, restaurants, entertainment, and professional sports, and the Building and Construction Trades Council saw more jobs. Community activists saw the eviction of three thousand low-income elderly and transient residents and the disruption of a natural neighborhood. Public protests and extensive litigation starting in 1968 blocked federal funds for several years and resulted in a public agreement whereby the redevelopment agency proceeded with the Yerba Buena project but added twelve hundred units of low-rent housing for the elderly and rehabilitated fifteen hundred units of low-rent housing elsewhere in the city.[9]

As the San Francisco experience suggests, the 1970s have brought a third stage in which downtown renewal programs have wound down and the typical project character has changed. The median starting date for major downtown renewal projects in southern and western cities was 1967, and almost no major land clearance programs for commercial or institutional use were started after 1970. In part, the change has resulted from the completion of urban renewal agendas. No city needs two new stadiums, convention centers, or downtown universities. In the real estate slump of the early seventies, a number of sunbelt cities also found themselves with temporary surpluses of downtown offices and hotel rooms. The Housing and Community Development Act of 1974 is therefore doubly appropriate as the end point of the urban renewal era because it changed the terms of federal redevelopment aid at a time when interest in massive core area renewal was fading. Although renewal in the style of the 1960s can still be paid for with community development money, it must compete for limited funds with programs for upgrading existing communities.

The result has been to shift the interests of local redevelopment agencies from commercial and institutional programs to housing rehabilitation and the encouragement of private housing on in-town sites, both for lower-income residents and for upper-income customers for renewed downtown businesses. In Tucson, for example, the Pueblo Center project in 1968 provided office space, public buildings, and a community center; three years later, the university and Manzo projects focused on housing rehabilitation and mixed-income apartments. Tulsa followed its massive Downtown Northwest project of 1965 with a Westbank project for residential improvement and an extensive Neighborhood Development Program in 1970. The most recent projects of the San Francisco Redevelopment Agency have involved either the preparation of peripheral industrial land or new low- and moderate-income housing. As the following section describes, there have been similar shifts in cities like Atlanta and Norfolk. In larger context, the renewed emphasis on public housing assistance is one manifestation of the rising political influence of local neighborhoods that will be the subject of chapter nine.

The goals and politics of urban renewal can be shown in more detail through a closer examination of San Antonio, Norfolk, Denver, and Atlanta. In the first two cities, the renewal process was tightly controlled by the new establishment of municipal reformers and local market businessmen. In the latter two cities, redevelopment programs were more subject to open debate but survived controversy largely intact. In each case, the career of downtown redevelopment shows the character of the supporting interests and the ways in which a set of projects could be designed simultaneously to promote metropolitan growth and prestige and to enhance downtown activity. Despite their differences in economic base and in previous politics, the results of redevelopment in the several cities were also remarkably similar.

In San Antonio, the initial goal of the Good Government League was simply to reduce administrative chaos, but the second and substantive aim was to vitalize the central business district and refurbish the image of the city through urban renewal. Although other Texas cities were reluctant to participate in federally funded renewal, San Antonians approved a general city program in December 1957. Starting in the early sixties, the Central West project took sixty-eight acres of dilapidated Mexican housing west of the courthouse and city hall for commercial reuse. In Rosa Verde to the north of Central West, renewal involved a combination of housing rehabilitation and spot clearance for new apartments in the vicinity of major hospitals. However, Rosa Verde soon took second place to the preparation of a site for HemisFair, the minor league international exposition held in 1968. The renewal authority acquired 149 acres southeast of the Alamo for $28 million and resold it to the city for $3 million, evicting sixteen hundred residents and a number of active businesses. In turn, the city used a large portion of a 1964 bond issue to finance a civic center consisting of theater, arena, and exhibition building and leased the remaining land to the HemisFair company.[10]

HemisFair itself was a classic example of civic boosterism. In the public arena, support ranged across the political spectrum. West-side

Congressman Henry B. Gonzales first publicized the idea in 1962. Senator Ralph Yarborough helped to secure federal participation necessary for designation as an official international exposition. Governor John Connally was responsible for a multi-million dollar appropriation for state participation. Behind the scenes, the operating corporation was financed by $4.5 million from a consortium of twenty-six local banks. The loan was secured by pledges from 480 businessmen. A pledge of $25,000 secured membership on the board of directors, a commercial who's who of Good Government leaders and the old German families that dominated local business. The board chairman was H. B. Zachry, owner of the largest construction and land development business in South Texas, and the president was industrialist Marshall Steves. Other leaders included Mayor Walter McAllister and banker Tom C. Frost, Jr.[11]

Timed to precede the Mexico City Olympics, HemisFair itself emphasized the cultural and commercial ties between the United States and Latin America. It was intended to impress its 6 million visitors with the unique heritage of San Antonio and to mark its coming of age as a modern metropolis. After the fair closed, the site remained in use for the convention center, a federal building, and tourist attractions to supplement the Alamo such as the Institute of Texas Cultures and the Tower of the Americas. More recently, a major effort of city policy has been to promote the construction of additional hotels near the site to allow an expanded tourist and convention business.

Urban renewal in Norfolk also involved the two aims of direct economic stimulus and the revision of the city's popular image. The major renewal projects undertaken from 1955 through 1958 had two targets —a biracial working-class neighborhood of six hundred families that blocked highway improvements, and the dives and burlesque houses of East Main Street that every American sailor had visited in story if not in person. In the place of an old Norfolk with roots in the age of wooden ships would rise a new steel-ribbed city. The projects constructed through the sixties involved the standard components from the tinker-toy box of urban designers. Adjacent to the old center of the city are new high-rise offices to house the major banks, a new library, and a new set of municipal buildings. To the northeast are public housing units and a drive-in shopping center for displaced black residents, to the northwest two luxury apartment towers and a complex of medical buildings. Linking the scattered pieces of new Norfolk is a six-lane road looping around the waterfront. North from the First Virginia and Virginia National bank buildings across still vacant land are a separately financed auditorium and sports arena that float in isolated splendor on an elevated plaza that offers views of brick heaps, a Holiday Inn, and the Greyhound station.[12]

With the hindsight of the 1970s, it is easy to criticize urban renewal in a city like Norfolk. The bill of indictment is especially detailed because of the haphazard siting and design of individual structures and the barrier highways that have effectively destroyed any potential for natural interaction in the urban core. Twenty years ago, however, the renewal program enjoyed almost complete support as the symbol of a city on the make. With Pretlow Darden and Charles Kaufman as dominant figures, the Redevelopment and Housing Authority Board spoke for the same establishment of businessmen who participated in the reforms of 1946 and the Committee of 100 in 1959. Both the board and the city council placed full confidence in Executive Director Lawrence Cox, who provided continuity in program and implementation by serving from 1943 until 1969, when he moved to an assistant secretary's desk at HUD. Indeed, both Fred Duckworth and his successor Roy Martin placed urban renewal at the center of their strategies for Norfolk and helped to assure unanimous council backing through the fifties and most of the sixties. The editors of the *Pilot* and the *Ledger* joined in supporting every step of the program and proudly analyzed the "benevolent contagion of redevelopment and its renewal of spirit in Tidewater." The majority of black leaders and the widely read weekly *Journal and Guide* similarly applauded the "magnificent job" in return for significant accomplishments in the provision of public housing.[13] The only vocal opposition came from a single black lawyer and from Main Street tavern owners and small businessmen. None of these critics belonged to the Tidewater Yacht and Country Club and none were taken seriously by the local decision makers.

If urban renewal was intended to transform downtown Norfolk into a regional financial center, it was also valuable as a municipal advertisement to overcome the bad memories of the forties. For local leaders, the school crisis was therefore especially unwelcome because it distracted attention from the approval and commencement of the major downtown project that was considered crucial to the city's future.[14] In reaction, the Norfolk Redevelopment and Housing Authority in 1959, 1960, and 1961 stepped up its efforts to sell an image of "vision in Virginia" to counteract the national impact of massive resistance. The agency sponsored journalistic junkets and received glowing write-ups contrasting the "old" and "new" Norfolk in the Richmond *Times-Dispatch*, Louisville *Courier-Journal*, Dallas *News*, Chattanooga *Times*, Cincinnati *Enquirer*, Milwaukee *Journal*, Miami *Herald*, and the *New York Times*. Norfolk also won praise for its renewal accomplishments from the Urban Land Institute, the National Municipal League, and the National Association of Housing and Redevelopment Officials.[15]

In more recent years, Norfolk has been an example of efforts to fill out a downtown renewal scheme with provisions for new middle- and upper-income housing. The hope of city officials in the 1970s has been that new in-town residents will complement commercial redevelopment by supporting downtown retailing and entertainment. In the Ghent neighborhoods, between one and two miles northwest of downtown, the redevelopment authority has used a combination of rehabilitation for two thousand housing units and demolition of a black neighborhood to make room for several hundred middle-cost townhouses. The project for the 1980s is the resuscitation of an abandoned downtown dock area for trendy commercial and residential uses.

Unlike Norfolk or San Antonio, where public money was the necessary catalyst, redevelopment in downtown Denver began with private investment in the 1950s. Expansion of metropolitan functions in the postwar years triggered outside interest in the lucrative possibilities of Denver real estate. Clint Murchison of Dallas built the Denver Club Building for $7 million in 1954 and the First National Bank Building for $10 million in 1957. William Zeckendorf constructed the Mile Hi Center office tower in 1954, a department store for the merged May Company–Daniels and Fisher in 1957, and the Denver Hilton in 1961. Local banks and utilities followed with more new buildings that tripled the available office space by the mid-sixties and pushed the focus of the shopping and financial districts "up the hill" toward the capitol. A new round of private building in the late seventies has continued the pattern with a half-dozen new high rises on Seventeenth Street and blocks to the east.[16]

In 1955, seventy-five local businessmen took up the cause of the core area by organizing Downtown Denver Incorporated and contracting for a study by the Urban Land Institute. The next year, 176 companies including all major downtown banks and retailers formed the Downtown Denver Improvement Association. The city council responded with the creation of an Urban Renewal Authority in 1958 and a Downtown Denver Master Plan Committee in 1961, the latter including both private and public members charged with writing a basic urban renewal plan and selling it to the electorate. The resulting *Development Guide for Downtown Denver* argued for public investment in buildings and transportation to support the Denver economy. Despite favorable publicity and the formation of Forward Metro Denver as yet another lobbying group, voters in 1964 reacted to a crowded ballot by narrowly rejecting an $8 million bond issue for the local share of the Skyline Renewal Project.[17] The solution was to expand the project boundaries to allow the city to credit the costs of the independently financed Currigan Exhibition Center as the required local contribution. In transcontinental diplomacy, Palmer Hoyt lobbied Lyndon Johnson and Senator Gordon Allott negotiated with Senator Harry Byrd. The result was the last of the big urban renewal pork barrel bills that allowed Norfolk, Denver, and six other cities to receive major grants without matching cash. In a new referendum in 1967, voters approved the Skyline Project to redevelop thirty-seven blocks of outmoded office and warehouse buildings in the city's original business district. Without significant opposition, the project passed in every district and gained a margin of five to two overall.[18]

Denver's second major renewal project included twenty-two blocks of nineteenth-century housing west of Cherry Creek. Although the site of the original Denver settlement, Auraria had been left behind by the trend of downtown growth and stranded between Cherry Creek, the Platte River, and railroad tracks. The proposed replacement was an education complex to house Denver Community College, Metropolitan State College, and the University of Colorado-Denver. The Auraria Project aroused greater debate than Skyline because it required the dislocation of Chicano residents and the demolition of old houses. Despite erosion of black and Chicano support, however, voters approved the project by two to one in 1969. Indeed, it is safe to say that a thorough airing of the issues of urban renewal in Denver had left public support largely intact at the end of the 1960s. Not until the recent energy boom, however, did sufficient private capital become available to use the Skyline blocks for more than parking lots. To quote Denver Urban Renewal Authority Director J. Robert Cameron in 1979, "what's happening now is what we dreamed of when we sent the bulldozers in. . . . A new era, a twenty-four-hour lifestyle in downtown Denver is taking shape."[19]

The takeoff for urban renewal in Atlanta coincided with the arrival of the 1960s. In order to consolidate business support and meet editorial criticisms, William Hartsfield had begun to advocate downtown renewal in 1955 and 1956 as a logical step to follow the establishment of a metropolitan planning agency and extensive annexations (see chapter seven). He had also created a Department of Urban Renewal in 1957, but legal challenges to the state renewal law had delayed any action to 1959. Even then, the protests of specific neighborhoods in 1959–60 persuaded the board of aldermen to ignore the downtown business kings and to adopt only a portion of an already limited first-stage project. In the private sector, a twenty-six-story tower built for the Fulton National Bank in 1955 stood alone as the only major downtown office construction in the 1950s.[20]

The new decade brought a natural succession in the city's power structure by which younger businessmen in their forties and fifties who had served their apprenticeships running the community chest campaigns stepped in for members of the previous generation. Under the presidency of Ivan Allen, Jr., the Chamber of Commerce in 1960 upgraded its staff and revived the historic slogan of "Forward Atlanta." Over the next six years, the Forward Atlanta program raised $3.2 million in private funds to publicize the city and attract new businesses. The chamber also provided consistent support for a six-point Forward Atlanta agenda that called for a new stadium and auditorium-coliseum, accelerated freeway construction, a rapid transit system, economic diversification, and downtown renewal. At the same time, the construction of a Chamber of Commerce building and a National Bank of Georgia building in 1961 marked a surge of private construction that quickly put pressures on the supply of buildable downtown land.[21]

If there had been any question, the Forward Atlanta program became city policy when Ivan Allen walked into the mayor's office with an overwhelming victory in the 1961 election. During his first term from 1962 through 1965, Allen worked to set in motion the processes and projects that would improve access to the central business core and provide the facilities needed by a regional and national metropolis.

The results of urban renewal and public investment included expansion space for Atlanta University, Georgia State University, and Georgia Tech, an auditorium and convention center, new hotel space, new apartments, and a city stadium built in a single year for the Milwaukee Braves. Urban renewal land clearance also opened enough land for a total of forty-eight thousand downtown parking spaces by 1970. The results of core area renewal in Atlanta were in fact so spectacular that Allen could feel justified in 1966 to claim that "Atlanta is riding the crest of a four-year wave of progress unmatched . . . in the history of any American city."[22]

Allen's enthusiasm was the result not only of successful municipal renewal projects but also of an astounding wave of downtown construction by private entrepreneurs backed by Atlanta banks. By removing low-value commercial uses and pushing black residents away from the fringes of the business district, providing useful public facilities, and focusing national attention on Atlanta's progressivism, Allen and his renewal bureaucrats made the city particularly attractive to investors. The most exciting of the new construction was John Portman's Peachtree Center, where the spectacular Hyatt Regency Hotel is the centerpiece of an office complex that has expanded to include a second seventy-floor hotel. In addition to a score of freestanding office towers, the projects of the sixties included the micropolis of Colony Square north of the business district, a Peachtree Summit transit mall over a planned subway station, and the World Congress Center finished in 1976. The latter is tied to the Omni megastructure at the southern end of the business district with its own hotel, offices, retailing, theaters, and coliseum. Together, the new projects stretch in a 2.5-mile line that runs north and south through and beyond the old business core.

The obvious beneficiaries and backers of the new business district were the major local corporations that head every description of the Atlanta power structure—Rich's department store, Coca-Cola, Southern Bell, Georgia Power, Georgia Trust, Citizens and Southern Bank, First National Bank—along with the 150 other large firms that constituted the Central Atlanta Association. Nevertheless, the public sector components of the redevelopment program needed support at the voting booth as well as at the Commerce Club. To secure one element of his urban renewal coalition, Allen continued to work through the two thousand businesses in the Chamber of Commerce to hold the backing of the white middle class on the north side. Atlanta's enthusiastic participation in federal public housing programs since the 1930s helped to cancel arguments about the evils of federal interference. The city's commitment to major capital improvements as shown in bond issues in 1946 and 1957 also made appeals for new public spending less shocking than in some other sunbelt cities.[23]

To complete the coalition, Allen also had to sell urban renewal to black voters. The outlawing of Georgia's white primary in 1946 had changed the basis of city politics by allowing community organizers to increase the black voter registration from three to twenty-five thousand in a single year. Thereafter, William Hartsfield had carefully negotiated with conservative black leaders to provide for the hiring of black police officers, extensive public housing on the west side, calm school desegregation, and the suppression of race-baiting in a "city too busy to hate."[24] In a direct continuation of Hartsfield's policy of intracity diplomacy, Allen and his business allies offered relatively high levels of city services for black neighborhoods, ongoing attention to public housing, and a constructive response to retail boycotts in 1960–61. The other side of the bargain continued to be black votes for the urban renewal program and its advocates as defined and chosen by the white establishment.[25]

Voting patterns in the first half of the 1960s show the urban renewal coalition in practice. In 1962, a key bond issue for the city share of renewal costs went down to defeat with 58 percent of the black vote but only 47 percent of the upper-status white vote and less than 30 percent of the working-class white vote. The next year, Ivan Allen submitted a less ambitious bond issue whose terms had been carefully defined to be more acceptable to white business interests and to blacks. This second issue passed with 81 percent of the black vote and 61 percent of the north-side white vote balanced against 45 percent support from other white voters. In his 1965 reelection campaign, Allen received over 90 percent of the black vote, 67 percent of the north-side vote, and 41 percent of the vote in lower-status white precincts on the south side. Even though black voters were the infantry of the coalition, however, the north side continued to supply the officers. The purpose of the political maneuvering through the early and middle sixties was always to secure black support for projects desired by bureaucrats and businessmen, not to supply white support for black community interests. As chapter nine will indicate, it began to fall apart when Atlanta blacks refused to continue an alliance of unequals.[26]

Increasing black independence was in fact shown in the protracted decision to build the Metropolitan Atlanta Rapid Transit system as the climax of the urban renewal era. At the same time that Ivan Allen was implementing plans for downtown renewal in the early sixties, a handpicked board of white businessmen were meeting as the Metropolitan Atlanta Transit Study Commission to plan ways in which to focus the metropolitan circulation system on the rebuilt downtown. The successor of the study commission was the Metropolitan Atlanta Rapid Transit Authority (MARTA), appointed in 1966 with Richard Rich as chairman and other members representing local banks, downtown business, and Emory University. After two years of largely closed planning that ignored input from black Atlanta, MARTA announced a referendum for November 1968 at which Fulton and DeKalb county citizens could vote on a sales tax to support a forty-mile and $750 million subway/rail transit system. In a bungled campaign, MARTA and its citizen's committee refused to commit to service improvements for west-side neighborhoods, dismissed a group of younger black activists, and ignored the working-class white communities in the southern half of the metropolitan area. The proposal was supported by white "civic progress" voters in north-side Atlanta and northern DeKalb suburbs but attracted only 42 percent of the total vote in the city and 34 percent in the Fulton County suburbs.[27]

As it had after the 1962 defeat of urban renewal bonds, the redevelopment coalition took steps to assure success at the second try in 1971. The local establishment added blacks to the MARTA board and staff and set up a black advisory committee. The new plan for a fifty-mile transit system combining subterranean, elevated, and street-level lines included an additional line to the Perry Homes housing project on the west side. The new MARTA package also included a promise of equal employment opportunities for blacks on MARTA construction, public acquisition of the private bus system, new buses and crosstown routes, and a fifteen cent bus fare while the rapid transit lines were under construction. Even though the 1969 election of Sam Massell as mayor and Maynard Jackson as vice-mayor was commonly viewed as the end of the old urban renewal coalition, the Atlanta business leadership was able to reassemble for one more time the combination of black and affluent white voters who provided the MARTA sales tax with a narrow victory.[28]

Indeed, by the late sixties and the seventies, the changing political balance within Atlanta brought significant modifications to renewal goals and procedures. An example of the transition has been the redevelopment plans for the Bedford-Pine renewal area in the old "Buttermilk Bottoms," a black slum east of the business district. In the mid-sixties, downtown interests pushed for redevelopment of the 270-acre area as an extension of the existing Butler Street renewal project with a civic center and commercial structures. Unlike earlier projects, however, the Bedford-Pine proposal met serious opposition from the community itself. The result was a compromise in 1968 to devote the western third to downtown uses and the eastern section to housing. The city immediately proceeded to build a civic center and a public housing project, but action on the heart of the area was delayed for another ten years by court challenges, the environmental impact process, and continued community complaints about the residential development plans. The result appears to be a delicate balance among competing interests. The community has gained a major housing rehabilitation program and 750 subsidized housing units, Georgia Power has acquired a site for a new office building, and downtown banks and Central Atlanta Progress have acquired control of Park Central Communities that will build the 750 subsidized apartments and 2,250 units for the private market.[29]

With the implementation of the bulk of the Forward Atlanta agenda by the early seventies, the downtown establishment is now more concerned with filling its new facilities than with new construction. The Chamber of Commerce during the 1970s advertised Atlanta as "the New International City" or "the world's next great city." Attention has focused on securing international air traffic, keeping the new world trade center in continuous use, and attracting the national headquarters of major corporations rather than their regional offices. The city's new hotels have also enjoyed a fast-growing convention business that ranked sixth nationwide in number of events and fourth in total attendance by 1978–79.[30]

The similarities of downtown renewal in Portland as well as in Atlanta, Norfolk, Denver, and San Antonio far outweigh the differences in any comparison. At first glance, a visitor may assign high grades to the design values in Portland, with its Forecourt Fountain and its Portland State campus well integrated with the surrounding neighborhoods. One may equally criticize Norfolk and San Antonio for approving sterile arenas and civic centers that are walled off from the rest of the community by arterial roads and glaring concrete pads. What is more important, however, is that each city used the "architectural boosterism" made possible by urban renewal to pursue a common vision of the prosperous metropolis.

For example, common locational patterns in the several cities show the similarity in the purposes of their renewal programs. In each case, the major projects lay between .2 and 1.5 miles from the active business center. They required redevelopment officials to bulldoze shabby districts of lower-income housing and marginal businesses, whose removal presumably made the city instantly more attractive to suburban commuters and shoppers. The sites covered two hundred to three hundred acres with the exception of Atlanta, where the total neared one thousand acres. The redevelopment sites were also areas whose accessibility was dramatically improved in the 1950s and 1960s through freeway construction. The projects in Portland, Denver, San Antonio, and Norfolk lay directly between the old downtown core and the exit ramps of new freeway loops, while the bulk of Atlanta's redevelopment straddled the interstate highway that closely flanks the downtown on the east side. In the minds of investors and planners, all of these locational characteristics meant that the renewal sites were part of their city's "zone of transition"—the ring of mixed, low-density activities around the business core in which growing high-rent activities have historically displaced low-rent uses in an outward ripple. According to such an analysis, urban renewal simply hastened and rationalized a natural transition that was already assured by the new inner-loop freeways.

Planners in all five cities also provided the same sorts of replacement facilities for the transitional renewal zones. Each city offered space for institutional expansion to anchor one side of the central district, using hospitals in Norfolk and San Antonio and universities in Portland, Denver, and Atlanta. The public offices of a civic center complex were used in conjunction with the other institutions in Atlanta and to anchor the opposite side of downtown in Norfolk and San Antonio. The most valuable of the vacant land was set aside for new private offices and hotels to serve the growing sunbelt economy. Other public investment went to auditorium/coliseum/convention center facilities on renewal land in every city except Portland. Until the proper private investors could be found, the renewal agencies were content to hold block after block of cleared land for cheap downtown parking lots.[31]

The results of downtown redevelopment were the same in other southern and western cities. Table 6.1 summarizes available information furnished by redevelopment agencies on thirty-five projects in seventeen cities, including the five discussed above. The typical city has had two downtown projects covering 184 acres each. Sixty percent of the projects have been located within half a mile of the center of the business district, 13 percent between .5 and 1.0 miles from the center, and the remainder between 1 and 2 miles. More than half the projects were started between 1966 and 1969, with 1966 as the median commencement date. The repetitious list of new facilities provides systematic evidence for travelers' impressions of mass-produced renewal downtowns.

Downtown renewal programs were unquestionably the climax of businessmen's government in sunbelt cities. Their success required a municipal leadership that was at home both in city hall and in bank board rooms and that was able to coordinate large amounts of federal, local, and private money in a series of massive mixed-enterprise projects. Success for urban renewal also required a stable base of political support, for the lag between initial planning and completion was usually fifteen to twenty years. The complex blending of public and private entrepreneurship took the talents of the same businessmen, editors, and political operatives who had cooperated in the municipal modernizations of the postwar decade. In cities like Denver and Portland, the business activists were also able to convince many of the local capitalists and bankers who had sat out the postwar reform efforts that downtown renewal offered investment opportunities that were profitable, safe, and respectable.

In evaluating the politics of sunbelt cities, it is striking that local leaders were enormously confident of their urban renewal strategy through the 1960s. By mid-decade, when the typical renewal project in sunbelt cities was just starting, Martin Anderson had already attacked urban renewal for its inefficiency in *The Federal Bulldozer*. Jane Jacobs in *The Death and Life of Great American Cities* had analyzed the often disasterous effects of "cataclysmic money." Herbert Gans, Chester Hartman, and Marc Fried had published the results of extensive research on the destructive impact of renewal on neighborhoods

Table 6.1. *Summary Data from Major Downtown Renewal Projects in Sunbelt Cities*

	Start Date	Acres	Distance from Central Business District	New Facilities
Atlanta	1958	N.A.	0.8 miles	A
	1958	N.A.	0.2	C, H, M, O, PH
	1965	270	1.2	G, O, PH, SH
Birmingham	1966	57	0.4	F, G
	1967	241	0.5	C, M
Denver	1967	113	0.2	O, R
	1969	169	0.6	C
Fresno	1958	86	0	H, O, R
Jacksonville	1969	97	1.5	C, SH
	1972	54	1.5	F, M, O, SH
Los Angeles	1959	136	0.3	G, O
	1967	N.A.	0.7	SH
Little Rock	1968	508	0	C, O
Nashville	1968	40	0	G, O
	1968	317	2.0	C
Norfolk	1955	135	1.0	F, M
	1958	190	0	A, CC, G, H, O, R
Oklahoma City	1966	256	0.8	C, M
	1967	1,258	1.3	M, PH, SH
	1967	199	0	CC, G, O, PH
Portland	1966	115	0.2	O, PH
	1968	47	0.6	C
San Antonio	1962	242	0.8	M, PH
	1962	69	0.4	O, R
	1964	149	0.4	A, CC, F, G
San Francisco	1959	51	0.5	H, O, PH
	1966	87	0.2	CC, H, O, R, SH
Tacoma	1961	9	0.2	G, O
	1963	44	0	O, R

Table 6.1. *(Continued)*

	Start Date	Acres	Distance from Central Business District	New Facilities
Tucson	1968	80	0	A, F, G, H
Tulsa	1965	309	0	G, M, O, R, PH
Winston-Salem	1961	67	1.0	G
	1963	217	1.0	M, SH
	1969	157	1.0	SH
	1969	94	1.0	CC, F, G, H, O

Note: key to facilities:

A	arena or stadium
C	college or university
CC	convention center
F	federal office space
G	local or state government offices/civic center
H	hotel
M	medical facilities
O	private office space
R	retailing
PH	private housing
SH	subsidized housing

N.A.: not available.

and the poor in Boston.[32] Nevertheless, there is almost no evidence that increasing concern with the negative effects of renewal in northern cities had any influence on municipal redevelopment decisions in the South and West. The community self-image in booming sunbelt cities had little place for the concerns about individual elements within the larger urban framework that had emerged in the North.

With every confidence that downtown renewal was in the best interests of themselves and their constituents, sunbelt decision makers also tended to ignore local critics. Renewal advocates wrapped themselves in the flag of civic progress, defining their concern as "the city as a whole." Arguing in the reform tradition, they viewed critics as parochial and particularistic. Renewal advocates claimed the high ground of public interest and argued that the real beneficiaries of urban renewal were not merely downtown department stores and newspapers but rather the entire metropolitan population, since the central business district was the one "neighborhood" that was common to everyone. Small businessmen in renewal zones lacked the resources to respond coherently or to resist programs which were implemented by city governments and trumpeted in the local press. When they did reach the newspapers, they provided human interest stories rather than the occasion for serious debate. Middle-class and working-class taxpayers who worried about the cost of redevelopment programs were usually embarrassed into silence by the prestige of blue ribbon committees.

A more serious source of potential opposition to core area redevelopment was political mobilization through class and ethnic appeals of residents in the run-down neighborhoods that fringed downtown districts. The number of houses and apartments that were leveled by renewal varied widely from project to project, but even limited demolition raised the threat of further community disruption. In Atlanta, Norfolk, San Francisco, and a number of other cities, the redevelopment strategy during the 1950s and 1960s was to buy off potential resistance with public housing and moderate positions on racial integration. That aroused communities in several cities were able to exact a higher price than originally offered in the middle and late 1960s did not change the fact that the urban renewal coalition defined the projects and issues. As chapter nine will describe, however, the short-term solution proved inadequate in the longer term. Changes in the goals of redevelopment agencies in the 1970s had natural roots in the evolution of the renewal process and federal legislation, but they were also related to a new political balance that gave greater weight to neighborhood interests in sunbelt cities.

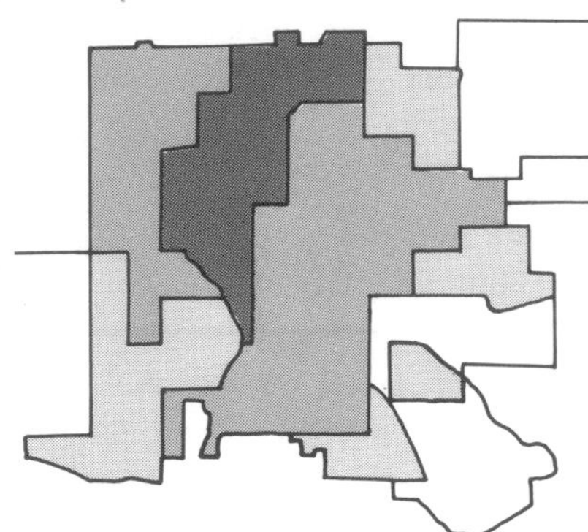

Chapter 7

The Suburban Crisis

Social scientists and planners are as much subject to fads and enthusiasms as are dieters and magazine editors. The time scale may be years rather than weeks or months, but the same process that fills drugstore shelves with protein supplements and brings identical covers on *Time* and *Newsweek* also operates among municipal officials and urban experts. The leading concern for conferences, convention programs, and professional journals for a year or two may be the possibilities of new town development, for another year the revival of ethnic politics, for a third the failure of public housing programs. Only in part do the problems themselves appear and disappear. Rather, it is changes in perceptions and priorities that move attention to one issue or the next.

In the years immediately before World War II, one of the new worries among urban specialists was the "disease of decentralization." The new phrase was heard at the Urban Land Institute, at the United States Housing Authority, and at the Harvard School of Design. The symptoms as discussed by the National Association of Real Estate Boards, among members of the American Society of Planning Officials, and at the New York and Chicago Planning Commissions were straightforward—decay at the urban core and growth only on the periphery. Especially in light of expectations of stable population, suburbanization promised to empty the city center and leave behind abandoned houses, vacant businesses, and deflated land values. "The depopulation of the cores of cities," said Louis Wirth of the University of Chicago, "has been accompanied by blight and physical decay, by declining revenue in the face of increasing costs, and by civic irresponsibility and the increasing impotence of cities to deal with their problems."[1]

The new worry about suburban growth marks a major change in American attitudes. Since the later nineteenth century, urban specialists like Adna Weber and Frederic Howe had viewed the dispersal of population into outlying communities as the great hope for saving the cities from the evils of overcrowding. As late as 1925, when George F. Babbitt was busy selling lots in Floral Heights and Glen Oriole, Harlan P. Douglass argued that "a crowded world must be either suburban or savage." By the 1950s, in contrast, the popular enthusiasm for a "freer, sweeter life" on the edge of the country had been transformed into continual warnings about the dysfunctions of "suburbia," that homogenized environment of tract houses ranked over the suffering landscape like an invading army. Scott Donaldson, in the most complete analysis of the "suburban myth," leaps directly from the mid-1930s to the 1950s and attributes the change of attitude among intellectuals to the snobbish realization that mass suburbanization could scarcely produce the ideal middle landscape that they had dreamed about. It is clear from the previous paragraph, however, that practical planners and public officials had lost their enthusiasm for decentralization several years before the first Levittown. In large part, their objections were not aesthetic but specific and practical, based in particular on fears about the impact of sprawl on city finances already weakened by depression.[2]

The present chapter describes the responses of business and political leaders in sunbelt cities to the surge of suburbanization in the postwar years. The problem seemed particularly acute in many of these cities because much of their wartime growth had exacerbated prewar trends toward unregulated peripheral sprawl. The continuation of such growth promised to disrupt the urban real estate market and ultimately to impose huge public service costs. The common strategy was to re-emphasize one or both of two familiar techniques—the time-honored procedures of annexation and the well-discussed but little-tried alternative of metropolitan planning. In the short run, many southern and western cities showed considerable success in adding territory and establishing the scaffolding for areawide planning. Within approximately fifteen years, however, the growing population and economic independence of suburban areas evened the political balance and effectively blocked further plans for central city control of suburban development.

The census of 1940 provided a specific focus for concern about decentralization. American cities had always been eager to post a good score in the decennial population contest as proof of their prosperity. After a decade of depression, however, eagerness often looked like desperation as many cities struggled to show that they had weathered the crisis without decline. Officials in San Antonio and Albuquerque greeted the spring of 1940 with efforts to annex new suburbs before the census takers arrived. In Portland and Seattle, city employees and chambers of commerce mounted vigorous campaigns during the census period to assure a high count. While sound trucks roamed the streets asking residents to make sure that they had been enumerated, other campaigners copied the tricks of political machines and signed up transient sailors and timberworkers in dark barrooms and musty flophouses.[3]

The published reports showed that many cities had had good cause to worry. As described in chapter three, the 1930s was the decade in which the majority of metropolitan growth occurred for the first time in suburban rings rather than central cities. Individual statistics showed population losses in twenty-seven of the ninety-three American cities with populations of over one hundred thousand. Although all of the losers were located in the Northeast, the minimal gains recorded in Tulsa, Birmingham, Wichita, Tacoma, and Seattle were severe blows to civic pride in communities accustomed to unremitting expansion. San Francisco recorded a gain of a few hundred persons only because the city obtained a recount to refute preliminary data showing a decline. The Charlotte Chamber of Commerce similarly demanded that the Census Bureau accept local supplementary counts when initial returns showed their city short of the one hundred thousand mark.[4]

The census statistics on suburban growth that disturbed many urban boosters recorded a trend that can be dated specifically to the last years of the 1930s. As the United States climbed toward a semblance of prosperity in 1938 and 1939, unsatisfied demand for housing triggered a building boom surpassed previously only in the mid-1920s. The 2.23 million housing units started in the four years from 1938 through 1941 exceeded total construction for the period from 1929 to 1937. During the same years, economic revival also allowed Americans to purchase 12 million new passenger cars and raised total automobile registration to 29.6 million from a depression low of 20.6 million. As a result, Americans sought new sorts of housing to go with their increased mobility. Fully 81 percent of the housing starts from 1938 through 1941 were for single family units, compared with 60 percent for 1921 through 1930. Rural nonfarm units (which included suburban houses in unincorporated areas and small towns under 2,500 population) constituted 35 percent of the new starts as opposed to 21 percent during the twenties.[5]

Five years later, when city officials had time to take stock of municipal problems after the rush of demobilization, it was clear that wartime tire and gas shortages had failed to prevent the continuation of the suburban trend. One interim census study, for example, showed that the suburban growth rate from 1940 to 1947 had doubled that of central cities in the thirteen largest metropolitan areas. In many sunbelt cities, much of the recent growth was makeshift housing scattered around peripheral defense plants and army bases. In addition to private houses, 46 percent of the seven hundred thousand units of federal defense housing had been built in the states of the Sunbelt West and 17 percent in the Sunbelt Southeast. Because rapid construction had required large tracts of open land, many of these emergency defense apartments were grouped in huge new suburbs such as Portland's Vanport and Oakland's San Lorenzo. In slightly broader perspective, the postwar years redoubled the process of population dispersal. From 1946 to 1950, the sale of 21 million new automobiles not only allowed Americans to junk the old Ford or Plymouth that had sputtered through the war but also raised total registration to 40.3 million. During the same period, the postwar boom produced nearly 5 million housing starts, 83 percent in single family units and 42 percent for rural nonfarm families.[6]

If city officials had defined decentralization as a disease in 1940, they viewed it after the war as a virulent epidemic. In one example, the Public Administration Clearing House declared an "emergency" over suburban growth and convened a three-day conference to consider ways to limit the actions of subdividers through state planning boards, metropolitan planning agencies, or the use of eminent domain to assemble large peripheral tracts for planned development. For long-established housing lobbies, the deterioration of central city real estate that often accompanied suburbanization supplied further arguments for expanded public housing programs and helped to justify the Housing Act of 1949. Other organizations and experts with a focus on land-use patterns were equally concerned to develop "unified metropolitan planning," seeking to maintain a primary directive role for the central city through extraterritorial controls, annexation, and consolidation.

Although it was too late to reverse the process of decentralization, wrote Catherine Bauer, the central city still had the opportunity to "assume responsible whole-hearted leadership" for the urban region.[7]

It was the latter trend of thought that seemed especially compelling in many sunbelt cities. Every metropolis that had experienced a wartime boom or postwar prosperity had its haphazard trailer camps, strings of tract houses along unpaved streets, and knotted traffic jams at country crossroads. The immediate response was frequently based on the assumption of primacy for the central city. With peripheral towns hopelessly mired in their new problems and county governments unwilling to abandon attitudes and procedures developed for a rural society, the central city was the only immediately available agent of change. The development of strategies to impose order on suburban chaos by bringing new subdivision under the control of the central city therefore became a major element in the program of urban reformers in Norfolk, San Antonio, Denver, and other sunbelt cities.

Concern in Denver in fact coincided with the worries of national urban specialists. A ten-member delegation from the Denver Planning Commission returned in 1941 from an Urban Land Institute conference held at MIT with its own warning about the "sinister disease" of decentralization. Although Denver was not yet in "so acute a stage of disintegration" as other cities, the metropolis still showed "startling evidence of the flight of Denver residents across corporate boundaries." Suburban growth rates five times that of Denver threatened urban blight, lowered the value of public and private property, and interfered with the rational provision of services. One of the early reactions was the adoption of a model housing code by the city, supposedly to stem the outward tide of migration by preserving Denver's attractiveness. In a complementary action, Denver annexed five square miles from 1941 through 1946.[8]

Initial efforts at metropolitan planning also developed under Denver leadership with the goal of bringing the new suburbs under "unified urban control." The Denver Planning Commission organized the Upper Platte River Regional Planning Commission in 1939. As an informal group of metropolitan officials that met in the Denver Planning Commission offices, the new agency worked to assist outlying communities and to devise regional plans for physical facilities. After some dissatisfaction with the preeminent role assumed by Denver, the

Arapahoe, Adams, and Jefferson counties withdrew near the end of the war to form the short-lived Tri-County Planning Commission (1944–49). Even so, Denver continued to assume the leading role in the region, convening the Denver Metropolitan Area Conference in 1948 to consider an agenda of areawide problems.[9]

Portland was also active in the promotion of regional planning. In the 1930s, Commissioner Ormond Bean had protected the City Planning Commission from budget cutters, had served as chairman of the Oregon State Planning Board, and had represented Portland on the League of Oregon Cities. By the end of the decade, Bean and Portland planning engineer Harry Freeman had placed concern over haphazard sprawl and its effects on city service costs on the list of concerns of both organizations.[10] In one reaction, delegates to the League of Oregon Cities meeting held in Portland in the spring of 1944 noted that "sporadic, scattered, and unregulated growth of municipalities and urban fringes has caused tremendous waste in money and resources" and called for legislation to provide for metropolitan planning agencies in order to allow "orderly growth and development." At the same time, Commissioner William Bowes worried publicly about the growing suburban trend and assigned planning commission staff to work on the problem of metropolitan area organization.[11]

The postwar building boom soon made the problems of suburban sprawl an issue for wide public concern. Portland officials and businessmen both worried about the rapid outward spread of new construction, the bypassing of vacant lots within city limits, and the costs of providing schools, police, utilities, and business facilities for a dispersed population.[12] In one response, Portland took on initial responsibility for assembling data needed for regional planning.[13] William Bowes also chaired a special study commission in 1947 that successfully urged the legislature to provide for county planning commissions. Over the next several years, he urged the establishment of planning activities in Portland's suburban counties and in 1952 was nearly able to arrange the consolidation of staffs for the Portland Planning Commission and the new Multnomah County Planning Commission. Only conflicting personalities and disagreements over salaries rather than explicit resistance by rural and suburban county residents prevented the establishment of a single planning agency for three-fourths of the metropolitan area.[14]

As an alternative to the promotion of metropolitan planning, central city leaders could also choose the strategy of annexation. As chapter two has indicated, more than a score of sunbelt cities undertook extensive annexation programs in the postwar years. In several cases, major motivations were the urban booster's pure joy in large numbers and the general desire to maintain the prominence of the central city and its central business district within the growing metropolis. The Albuquerque *Journal*, for one example, helped to revive the prewar "Greater Albuquerque" campaign in 1946. Rapid growth on the fringes of the city, complained the editors, was becoming "a detriment to health and physical appearances of greater Albuquerque. . . . We need some program whereby we can be brought together in one big municipality." One of the compelling reasons for the series of annexations that tripled the city's area to forty-eight square miles, said the newspaper three years later, was a "bigger census total."[15]

Similar reasons lay behind the annexation campaign that raised the area of Phoenix from seventeen to 187 square miles during the 1950s. From the introduction of the idea of major expansion in 1946 and 1947, discussion largerly ignored specific goals such as increased tax base or reduced per unit service costs. Instead, Phoenix leaders talked in overlapping terms about the need to make their city the center of the Salt River Valley, to take advantage of growth, or to attract new employers by imposing order in metropolitan growth. Indeed, the desire to make the territorial expansion program more acceptable to suburbanites was one of the major causes of charter reform and the establishment of businessmen's government under the Charter Government Committee. In turn, the new city administration in 1951 and 1952 developed an explicit rationale for expansion, appointed an annexation coordinator, and set about to make Phoenix the political and economic center of the metropolis. The mayor who had initiated the modernization of Phoenix government stated the goal of the city leadership directly: "We wanted Phoenix to be the economic center of the Southwest."[16]

In Norfolk and San Antonio, the adoption of annexation strategies is linked by the role of City Manager Charles Harrell. One of his first actions when hired by Norfolk's reform council in 1946 was to hire a professional planning staff and order a report on city expansion. To give greater legitimacy to the in-house recommendations, Harrell also called in the nationally known consultants Thomas and Doris Reed. Their report in November 1948 called for Norfolk to acquire 24 square miles in adjacent Norfolk County and to reach beyond to absorb 25 square miles of Princess Anne County. As Harrell circumspectly described the program in *Public Management* and in a memorandum to the city council, annexation would enlarge the city tax base, make available industrial land, and "eliminate the evils of unregulated urban development" by allowing coordinated planning under a single jurisdiction.[17] The Norfolk City Council agreed on the long-range advantages of linking new suburbs to the city, trying to absorb 40.7 square miles in 1949 (reduced to 11.2 by state courts in 1954) and 33 square miles in 1955 (reduced to 13.5 square miles by court decisions). As Fred Duckworth reinterpreted Harrell's cautious rhetoric for a business luncheon in 1951, the council believed that "unless additional territory is secured, Norfolk will be effectively walled in for all time. We cannot afford not to annex."[18]

Charles Harrell's annexation policy outlasted his career in Norfolk, and he was equally active in his new position as the first city manager of San Antonio. With the defeat of Gus Mauerman in 1947, San Antonio had dropped the expansion program that added 20 square miles at the end of World War II in favor of a five-year war over charter reform. One of Harrell's first acts in January 1952, however, was to advocate a systematic annexation strategy. When the planning commission recommended the addition of 120 square miles (to a city of 74 square miles), suburbanites reacted by starting incorporation procedures for sixteen municipalities with names ranging from Rolling Acres to George Patton. The outcome of vigorous debate and internal disagreement on the city council was a six to two vote in September to annex 80 square miles, a zone that encircled the city on all sides in a ring two to four miles thick.[19]

The experience of Atlanta in the first postwar decade sums up both of the central city strategies for control of suburban growth. In 1947, the Chamber of Commerce, Greater Atlanta Association, Central Atlanta Improvement Association, and other business groups mobilized to rationalize governmental structures for the metropolitan area. Their first accomplishment was to act on a ten-year-old idea by persuading the legislature to authorize a metropolitan planning district to cover Fulton and DeKalb counties. The Atlanta Metropolitan Planning Commission began operation in 1950 with funding shared by Atlanta (55 percent), Fulton County (37 percent), and DeKalb County (8 percent). Between 1952 and 1954, the agency published its basic set of areawide plans for land use, water, sanitation, and transportation. During the next several years it worked particularly to develop detailed plans and to build consensus for a radial expressway system first suggested by a consultant's report in 1946. The continued growth of the metropolitan area was recognized in 1960 by the addition of Cobb, Clayton, and Gwinnett counties.[20]

The second goal of the Chamber of Commerce and its allies was the expansion of Atlanta's boundaries through annexation. Atlanta Mayor William Hartsfield put the goal directly when he argued that the annexation program would determine "whether Atlanta is to be an expanding progressive unit of government, or whether it is to be condemned to slow deterioration, surrounded by suburbs which are themselves unable to do those large things that must be undertaken if a metropolitan area is to grow." When reluctant county residents turned down an initial annexation proposal in 1947, the Atlanta business leadership turned to a more complex campaign. The first step was to persuade the legislature to create a Local Government Commission for Fulton County (which included 89 percent of the city). The Local Government Commission in turn prepared a "Plan of Improvement" that called for the annexation of huge chunks of Fulton County. In an advisory referendum in June 1950, Atlanta itself voted 17,367 to 1,945 in favor of the plan, and areas proposed for annexation voted 6,560 to 4,816 in favor, justifying its adoption by the legislature in 1951.[21]

When the plan of improvement went into effect on 1 January 1952, the city of Atlanta absorbed 82 square miles and one hundred thousand residents from Fulton County. Since most of the new Atlantans were white, the annexation incidentally cut the city's black population from 41 percent to 33 percent of the total. The changes also merged the Atlanta and Fulton County planning commissions, simplified future annexation procedures, and transferred more than a thousand public employees as Atlanta and the remainder of Fulton County traded responsibilities for several services. With a streamlined structure of local government and improved tools for directing the growth of the suburban ring, Atlanta boosters could begin to look toward a metropolis of a million residents even as their city neared the half-million mark.[22]

If the 1950s were years of successful expansion for many sunbelt cities, they were also the era when the balance between city and suburb began to tilt. In one metropolis after another, central city leaders discovered that their strategies for controlling suburbanization had started to fail. By the end of the 1950s or the beginning of the 1960s, it was clear that the attractions of reform governments had been insufficient to hold residents in older neighborhoods, that the process of annexation had failed to keep pace with peripheral growth, and that decisions on regional service distribution had been inadequate to subordinate metropolitan growth patterns to central city needs. Increasingly, divergent interests within the metropolitan area were expressed through the opposition of suburbanites and suburban political units to central city plans.

One of the bitterest conflicts over services developed between Denver and its suburbs. The precondition was the definition of central city interests by the Denver Water Board. Since its formation in 1918, the semiindependent board had taken a conservative stand on the provision of service outside the city despite its access to distant water sources. In part the board and its professional staff were worried about technical problems in supplying water through extensive and poorly engineered suburban systems. Moreover, members of the board (who were appointed by the mayor but were not subject to removal) represented the city's downtown business and real estate interests and were concerned with protecting Denver and Denver investors from suburban sprawl.[23] In the late 1940s, the water board and its bureaucracy maintained their conservative mentality in the midst of political reform, offering little cooperation to Quigg Newton's administration and viewing suburbs as hostile outside interests whose claims constituted threats to Denver. Indeed, the water board assumed considerable powers over growing suburbs. Representatives in 1948 argued that new service should be extended only to those suburbs that the board judged to have adequate zoning and building controls. By giving the water board the right to approve expansion of service areas, water contracts with outlying cities also gave five Denver residents the effective power to veto suburban annexations.[24]

Severe drought in the early 1950s brought water board policies into open conflict with the growing ring of suburbs. On 23 August 1951, the board agreed to assure Denver's supplies by allowing no new water hookups beyond a "blue line" penciled on a map in their downtown Denver headquarters. By the height of the drought in 1954 and 1955, when the entire metropolitan area faced a serious water crisis and suffered through stringent rationing, the board's caution worked to the serious detriment of surrounding communities. Areas that had depended on groundwater were unable to obtain emergency service when their wells ran dry, whereas other growing towns found that Denver would take care only of a fraction of their needs. In turn suburban counties further damaged the possibility of cooperation by rejecting a proposal for the joint development of new transmountain services in 1954. The Denver Water Board and city taxpayers were forced to bear the $115 million cost for the whole Blue River project including Dillon Reservoir and the Roberts Tunnel.[25]

Although the rains returned to the high plains in the later fifties, the water board did not erase the "blue line" until 1960, when the completion of the Blue River diversion was in sight. In the meantime, several suburban towns had reacted to the arrogance of Denver by developing their own water systems under local control. South of the city, Littleton greatly expanded its independent facilities under the impetus of the embargo and Englewood undertook its own diversion system. To the east, the "blue line" cut through the middle of Aurora. Although the city had previously purchased water from Denver, the new policy required that it develop its own wells and supply neighborhoods outside the line from groundwater. With memories of the water crisis still fresh, the city embarked in the early 1960s on a joint $58 million diversion project with Colorado Springs and hostilely rejected Denver inquiries about cooperation. The small suburb of Westminster also developed its own water system after its application for service was rejected by the water board. After bitter debate from 1962 through 1964, the town voted to expand this separate system rather than give up water autonomy in order to buy more cheaply from Denver.[26]

Mutual suspicions engendered or exacerbated by arguments over water supply crippled attempts at intergovernmental cooperation. The Intercounty Regional Planning Commission, which Quigg Newton helped to organize in 1955, elicited little serious cooperation and survived only by catering to the whims of suburban counties. The same four-county metropolitan area by 1962 counted ten city water systems in addition to Denver's and several dozen special water districts. Other public jobs were handled by approximately one hundred fire, sanitation and park districts, twenty-one school districts, and thirty suburban municipalities.[27]

In San Antonio and Norfolk, the first important issue of city-suburban politics was annexation rather than the allocation of services. In both cities, suburban reluctance to accept core city expansion forced a scaling down of expansion plans. The 1952 annexation in San Antonio, for example, met strong resistance from north-side property owners. In particular, two oil tycoons whose estates were covered by the annexation ordinance put up one hundred thousand dollars to bankroll Jack White's successful campaign for mayor in 1953. Although legal difficulties and the chaos of the next two years at San Antonio city hall combined to prevent the deannexation that White had promised, the Good Government League administration after 1955 proceeded much more cautiously on expansion. The city council in December 1959 did adopt a preemptive ordinance declaring an intention to annex 187 square miles (reduced from an initial proposal for 330 square miles). In fact, however, the city followed this action with careful respect for the opinions of Bexar County commissioners and for the interests of major suburban real estate developers such as Ray Ellison Industries. Despite the occasional declaration of major annexation plans from city hall, San Antonio absorbed only 24 square miles from the "frozen zone" during the 1960s.[28]

Resistance to Norfolk's annexation schemes came directly from suburban counties. Under Virginia law, cities function as independent governmental units with responsibility for county as well as city services. Any land annexed by Norfolk would therefore be permanently removed from Norfolk County or Princess Anne County, reducing the county's tax base and the number of voters subject to influence by their political bosses. The major annexation that the city undertook in 1949 was delayed for five years by Norfolk County and by a series of technical mistakes by Norfolk staff. The second major proposal in 1955 to take 33 square miles from Princess Anne County brought the city into conflict with Sidney Kellam and the Democratic organization that had made Princess Anne one of the most reliable components of the Byrd Machine. Even before the annexation was announced, the county had set aside $10 thousand to cover the cost of a court fight. As required by Virginia law, a special annexation court which included a member of the Princess Anne organization met in 1956 and trimmed the city request to 13.5 square miles. Norfolk complained that the reduced award was a "sentence of strangulation" that saddled the city with the service problems of new subdivisions and actually reduced its proportion of developable land. The state supreme court nevertheless upheld the ruling that freed Princess Anne County of major expenses, required Norfolk to assume $2.7 million of the county debt, and protected the county for five years from further annexations.[29]

Increasing suburban resistance to annexation from the later 1950s was a trend found as well in numerous other sunbelt cities. The Phoenix expansion program was seriously slowed in the 1960s by the resistance of Scottsdale, Tempe, and Glendale, and accomplished only one major boundary change after 1961.[30] In Wichita, unhappiness over annexations and annexation proposals among suburban residents and businesses provided the central issue for local politics from 1957 to 1962.[31] Aggregate statistics also show a reduction in the percentage of annexation in the Sunbelt during the 1960s. As Table 7.1 indicates, all parts of the Sunbelt had higher annexation percentages than those for the Northeast and North Central states during both the 1950s and 1960s. However, the South Atlantic states, Oklahoma-Texas, and the Mountain states all had extremely high percentages of territorial growth for the 1950s that were not sustained during the 1960s.

In part, cities like Denver and Norfolk were victims of their own success. Metropolitan growth in most parts of the Sunbelt was so rapid that the methods of regional control that seemed promising in the 1940s had proved insufficient by the 1960s. Increasingly, suburbanites were using independent governmental units to defend their isolation from city residents and city problems, converting spatial distance into political and social distance within the metropolis. As political scientist Oliver Williams has analyzed the emerging pattern of spatial politics, the proliferation of governmental entities within a metropolitan area allows residents to promote and preserve differences in life-style and values. The independent suburban municipality, the suburban county, and the special service district can all be used to preserve attractive and low-density physical environments, residential segregation by economic class, and ethnic segregation of school systems. Indeed, the smaller and more specialized the suburb, the more easily it can promote the preferences of the dominant group. Although suburban governments may be willing to cooperate in addressing "system maintenance" problems on a regional scale (transportation, utilities, water, waste disposal), they jealously guard their control of land use, taxation, social services, and education.[32]

Although Williams focused his analysis on the decentralized postwar metropolis, spatial politics is not new to American cities. Indeed, historians Zane Miller and Richard Wade have described urban politics

Table 7.1. *Percentage of Territorial Expansion for Central Cities of 1970 SMSAs by Region, 1950–1970*

	1950–60	1960–70	Number of Cities
South Atlantic States (Delaware to Florida)	69.1%	27.2%	43
Mid-South States	34.3	36.9	26
Texas-Oklahoma	139.0	45.0	30
Mountain States	95.8	40.2	16
Pacific States	28.5	29.5	28
Northeast / North Central States	14.5	19.5	144

Source: Richard L. Forstall, "Changes in Land Area for Larger Cities, 1950–1970," in *The Municipal Year Book, 1972* (Washington: International City Management Association, 1972), pp. 84–87.

Note: The table omits Jacksonville, Nashville, and Indianapolis, where city-county consolidations during the 1960s involved a process distinct from annexation.

during the progressive era in terms of conflict among different social groups localized in different sections of the city. The introduction of electric streetcars in the 1880s accelerated the residential segregation of American cities by ethnicity and income level. By the turn of the century, the native-born middle class had largely isolated itself in new suburban neighborhoods on the outer end of the trolley lines, while the immigrant poor remained confined to central city slums. It was therefore easy to define political issues in spatial terms. Campaigns against liquor, immigration, and political bosses were all viewed as efforts to maintain order in crowded downtown neighborhoods. With greater or lesser success, residents of the rim neighborhoods also struggled to devise social and political institutions that could preserve their own life-styles in isolation and maintain middle-class control over the growing and disorderly city. Specific techniques in wide use by the end of the progressive era included at-large nonpartisan voting to reduce the political power of ethnic minorities and core neighborhoods, and land use zoning to protect rim communities from undesired development.[33]

The change in metropolitan politics from 1910 to 1960 can be measured by comparing the progressive impulse of the early twentieth century with the neoprogressivism of the postwar Sunbelt. In both cases, much of the leadership came from the local business community in opposition to political machines and city hall gangs. Police corruption and municipal tolerance of illicit enterprises in gambling, prostitution, and the liquor trade provided a focus for moral indignation in both reform movements. In addition, a major element in each reform program was the establishment of efficient and businesslike government. Where the implementation of charter reforms was one of the central goals during the 1910s, the preservation or revitalization of city manager administrations was an important goal after World War II.

Despite the similarities, however, an increasingly important difference of the two reform efforts came from the different political geography of metropolitan areas in the first and second halves of this century. More and more during the 1950s and 1960s, the same sorts of middle-class residents who had so strongly supported urban progressivism in 1905 or 1915 now lived beyond the reach of central city social problems in independent suburbs and unincorporated communities. In the new situation, it became easier to preserve social distance by fending off the city than by trying to dominate it. One consequence during the 1950s was the gradual failure of central city attempts to dominate metropolitan areas through regional planning or annexation. Even in sunbelt states where annexation has remained an available tool, there has been a decline in its use and effectiveness. For the last decade and a half, the tendency toward highly organized political environments in sunbelt cities as described in chapter two has transformed the politics of metropolitan growth into a politics of suburban independence.

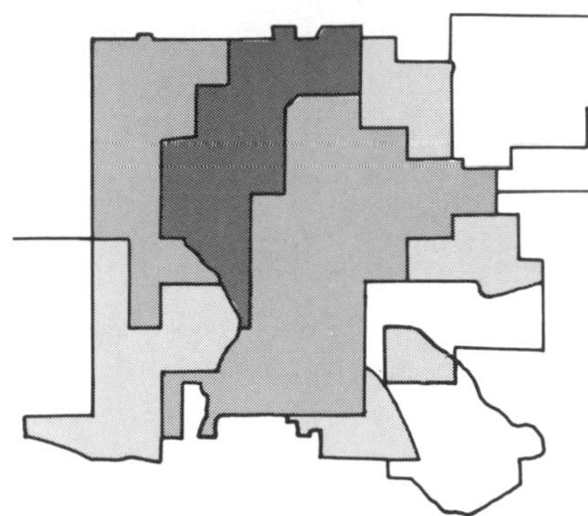

Chapter 8

The Politics of Suburban Equality

The most striking trend during recent years in the social geography of the American metropolis has been the rapidly growing isolation of suburban rings from their core cities. The realization of suburban independence was one of the important ideas to emerge from analysis of the 1970 census. In 1971, reporters for the *New York Times* offered the terms "outer city" and "alternate city" as they described the fast growth of suburban employment and the decentralization of retailing, entertainment, professions, and business services in shopping malls and office parks adjacent to circumferential freeways. During the same years, suburban rings added large quantities of multifamily housing and attracted increasingly heterogeneous populations. The result, in technical jargon, is a "widely dispersed multi-nodal metropolis." In more concrete terms, "urbanized" suburban rings now constitute a centerless substitute for the old central city.[1]

The growth of suburban self-sufficiency provides an additional focus for analyzing the impacts of rapid growth on intrametropolitan politics. Preceding chapters have described aggregate metropolitan growth in sunbelt cities and explored the ways in which central city politicians, planners, and businessmen responded with new initiatives to changing circumstances and new opportunities. In parallel fashion, the present chapter first describes the demographic and economic changes that allow the increasing isolation of sunbelt suburbs from their central cities. The remainder of the chapter then explores in more detail the ways in which the rapid growth and maturation of these suburbs have produced high levels of conflict within metropolitan area governments in Denver, Atlanta, Portland, and Norfolk.

One of the important factors tending to produce these levels of intrametropolitan stress and political conflict has been the speed of metropolitan growth itself. Although the problems of fast growth and population mobility may sometimes force active cooperation in communities with a single governmental entity, such a situation has not obtained even in the youngest auto-airplane metropolis of the postwar Sunbelt.[2] Instead, each area has contained a set of independent taxing and voting units that have had to share decisions relating to huge public investments in the basic physical services necessary to support expanded population. The faster the region's growth, the more often such decisions about the metropolitan infrastructure have been faced in an atmosphere of crisis. The result has frequently been intense disputes between central city and suburbs and among suburbs themselves over the location or allocation of basic services and the attendant tax burdens.[3]

Beyond rapidly expanding suburban populations and suburban service needs, metropolitan growth in the Sunbelt has also involved the reversal of relative socioeconomic status between central city and suburban ring. As chapter three indicated, such shifts are apparent for the 1950s, the decade when the balance of influence between city and suburbs began to tilt. By the end of the 1960s, the continuing reversal of status between city and rim had markedly changed the terms of intrametropolitan politics and provided support for suburban victories. Suburban jurisdictions could rely on growing strength of numbers to win regional or statewide referenda, dominate legislative debates, and intimidate governors. They could also benefit from the political resource represented by high-status residents, who have been just as able as central city leaders to exploit the right connections and the right club memberships. With strong leadership and growing fiscal resources, suburbs can indeed declare independence from each other as well as from the city.

Certainly both points are supported by the specific cases discussed in the following paragraphs. Only in metropolitan Portland has a central city maintained its dominant role in areawide decisions into the current decade, and even here finds itself under repeated challenge. In Denver, Atlanta, and Norfolk, the vitality of suburban politics for the 1960s and 1970s coincides with surges of metropolitan growth and the reversal of relative socioeconomic status in central city and suburbs. Major suburban governments have been able to match the core cities in political sophistication and professional skills and to transform regional politics into a series of complex negotiations. In the process, a number of specific suburbs such as Gresham, Oregon, Aurora and

Lakewood, Colorado, and Virginia Beach and Suffolk, Virginia, have emerged as a new home for aggressive growth policies that have faded in importance for central cities.

The resulting system in which the existence of a variety of geographically localized governmental units within the metropolis allows the expression of a wide range of interests might be summarized under the term "metropolitan pluralism." In general use, pluralism implies the existence of both a variety of political actors and a variety of separable issues. Each political actor can draw on a particular set of political resources and the number of such actors is open-ended. At the same time, each issue will mobilize a distinct group of political actors who are concerned with that issue and who try to influence the outcomes of key decisions. In consequence, it is impossible to define a single structure of power or influence. Instead, political lineups tend to shift from issue to issue as alliances form, dissolve, and reform.

If a pluralist model is applied to intergovernmental relations in the metropolis, the political actors are the central city and the suburban governments that have rapidly been developing independent economic and political resources that enable them to treat the central city as a peer. Continued metropolitan growth promises the emergence of additional participants in the political system as the capacities of newer suburbs expand. With the central city less and less able to dominate regional decisions, intrametropolitan politics becomes an affair of shifting alliances and shifting points of conflict as each jurisdiction follows its own list of concerns. In complex political interchanges, suburban jurisdictions may well present a united front against the city on one issue at the same time that they are fighting each other bitterly on a second question.

The growth of the outer city in the 1970s has largely been self-sustaining. The new resident of a suburban ring is typically a migrant from the suburbs of another metropolis, not a refugee from the central city. Recent census data show that the massive flight from the central city to the suburbs that preoccupied many commentators in the 1940s and 1950s has largely run its course. For the 1960s and 1970s, the new resident of Oak Knoll has no ties to the core city, no sense of responsibility for its problems, and little need for its services that are duplicated in the "main street" of the regional shopping mall.[4] Although there is little specific research, it seems clear that central cities are simply outside the daily orbit of the second generation of postwar suburbanites.

At the same time, suburbs are increasingly self-sustaining as economic entities that are able to generate their own jobs. Spectacular employment increases are only in small measure the result of factories shutting down in the city and reopening in the suburbs. Instead, fringe areas grow by capturing the bulk of new manufacturing facilities constructed by new and fast-growing industries. Especially in the Sunbelt, they also capture new headquarters, warehousing, and business services as national corporations set up branch offices to meet the growing regional markets. The increase in suburban population in addition has provided a market for retailing and personal services that is being met by regional shopping malls. Such service functions in fact offer local employment for a large portion of the suburban labor force.[5]

Models for the new outer city can be found from coast to coast, but as in many suburban trends, its development seems most advanced in the Sunbelt. In metropolitan Washington, the Virginia suburbs of Alexandria-Arlington-Fairfax have a combined population that approaches 1 million. Signs of explosive growth are everywhere. Along the southern bank of the Potomac, the General Services Administration has filled a wall of high-rise offices with tens of thousands of workers who have overflowed the granite bureaus of downtown Washington. Private corporations have lined the I-495 beltway with glass-sided industrial and office buildings. Only a quarter of the 400 thousand workers who lived in northern Virginia in 1970 commuted to jobs within the District of Columbia. Roads that climb from the river into the rolling Virginia hills cut the landscape of subdivisions and garden apartments with ribbons of theaters, discount outlets, and medical buildings. Near expressway nodes are instant minicities such as Tyson's Corner, complete with multilevel shopping mall, movie houses, high-rise hotels, and white-collar office buildings. The entire complex has as much active square footage in retailing and office space as the downtown business district of a Fort Wayne or Topeka. For all elements of everyday life, inhabitants of northern Virginia can live as if the city of Washington did not exist.

Across the continent, Orange County stands as an outer city which has developed from the start without the counterbalance of an inner city. The Bureau of the Census defines the area officially as the Anaheim–Santa Ana–Garden Grove SMSA only because these three towns have the largest populations. A number of other suburban areas now boast their own universities, but Orange County residents can choose between California State-Fullerton and the University of California at Irvine. Indeed, public and private entrepreneurs at Irvine have combined to construct a suburban university and a suburban university town simultaneously. Similarly, the California Angels make Orange County the first suburban area with exclusive claim to its own major league sports team. One Orange County resident interviewed by the *New York Times* described her life in the new centerless city: "I live in Garden Grove, work in Irvine, shop in Santa Ana, go to the dentist in Anaheim . . . and used to be president of the League of Women Voters in Fullerton."[6]

The smaller metropolitan area of Atlanta shows a similar measure of suburban self-sufficiency, with a turning point that can be dated precisely to the end of the 1960s. The great Atlanta building boom of the sixties and early seventies focused national attention on the central business district, but the suburbs were in fact the real beneficiaries. The population of Atlanta itself showed only a 2 percent increase from 1960 to 1970 and a decline from 1970 to 1975, while the suburban ring doubled over the same fifteen years. Retailing followed population very closely, with an explosive growth of outlying shopping centers after 1965. As a result, Atlanta's share of retail sales in the SMSA dropped from 66 percent to 44 percent between 1963 and 1972 and the share in the central business district dropped to 7 percent.[7]

The outward shift in retailing was one facet of a massive suburbanization of employment. Atlanta planners and public officials in the later sixties and early seventies had expected that urban renewal and freeway building would double downtown employment, but recent trends have destroyed that hope. Between 1960 and 1975, the share of total metro area employment in the central business district fell from 20 to 12 percent, with an absolute decrease of two thousand jobs. It is governmental agencies and established local companies such as Coca-Cola, Georgia Power, and Southern Bell that are occupying the new downtown office space. Branch operations of national corporations and business services such as data processing, in contrast, are filling the dozens of office parks that have been built since 1965. By 1973, six such office parks had been located in outlying sections of Atlanta, seventeen between Atlanta's city limits and the I-285 loop, and twenty-three beyond the beltway. The result has been to reduce the proportion of office space in central Atlanta from 90 percent in 1960 to 42 percent by 1980. At the same time, most of the distributive functions of the metropolis are now centered in nearly a hundred industrial parks developed adjacent to suburban freeways.[8]

As in Fairfax County or Orange County, the maturing Atlanta suburbs have little contact with the core of the city. Indeed, the different sectors of the suburban ring have developed considerable independence of each other. Most of the workers at major outlying employment nodes such as Executive Park, the Peachtree Industrial District, the airport, Fulton Industrial Boulevard, and Marietta live and work in the same quadrant of the metropolis. They can also shop at the most convenient of the several regional shopping malls that surround the city. With adjacent hotels, restaurants, theaters, and offices, the most important malls have become the new business districts of the self-sufficient suburbs.[9]

Comparative data on the several SMSAs provide another way to describe the growing independence of sunbelt suburbs. For example, Table 8.1 indicates that flight from the city has played a small and decreasing role in furnishing the suburban population. By 1970, fewer than 10 percent of the residents of suburban Atlanta, Denver, Norfolk, and Portland had moved from the central city within the last five years. The slightly higher proportion in San Antonio reflected the small size of that suburban ring. Except in the military centers with their high rates of population transfer, it was equally likely in 1970 that suburbanites had arrived from outside the metropolis or had moved within the ring of suburbs. With San Antonio again as the exception, the mobility figures for 1965 through 1970 show declines from 1955 through 1960 in the proportion of suburban population with recent experience of the central city.

Table 8.2 contrasts percentages of growth on several economic and demographic indicators for cities and their suburban rings (omitting San Antonio because of its extensive annexations). Between 1960 and 1975, the cities of Atlanta, Denver, Norfolk, and Portland each showed a slight population decline while their suburbs recorded impressive gains. During the sixties, the central cities showed slight increases in number of jobs but their suburbs recorded rates of increase that were from three to seven times greater. There was a similar pattern in retailing between 1963 and 1972, with suburban sales increasing

Table 8.1. *Mobility of Suburban Population in Selected SMSAs, 1955–1960 and 1965–1970*

	Percentage in same house as in 1970	Percentage moved from central city	Percentage moved within suburbs	Percentage moved from other SMSAs or non-metropolitan area
Residence in 1965 of 1970 suburban population aged five years plus				
Atlanta suburbs	40.1	8.9	21.8	21.7
Denver suburbs	40.5	8.2	20.0	24.4
Norfolk suburbs	40.6	8.8	15.5	25.4
Portland suburbs	44.6	9.8	18.5	18.1
San Antonio suburbs	31.3	13.1	8.2	35.9
	Same house as in 1960			
Residence in 1955 of 1960 suburban population aged five years plus				
Atlanta suburbs	40.8	12.7	26.6	19.0
Denver suburbs	31.6	15.0	19.9	31.1
Norfolk suburbs	34.4	14.4	23.7	23.8
Portland suburbs	45.3	10.9	24.9	17.3
San Antonio suburbs	27.9	8.6	10.9	44.3

Sources: 1960 Census of Population, Subject Reports PC (2)-2C, Mobility for Metropolitan Areas, Table 4. 1970 Census of Population, Subject Reports PC (2)-C, Mobility for Metropolitan Areas, Table 15.

three or four times as fast as those in central cities. By the latter date, Atlanta, Denver, and Portland suburbs accounted for the majority of metropolitan retail business.

Among the several sunbelt SMSAs analyzed in detail, Denver offers the most straightforward example of changing political balance between city and suburbs. From 1960 to 1975, the share of metropolitan area population in the central city fell from 53 to 36 percent. During the same years, Denver met repeated opposition on major regional issues from the three adjacent counties, from a half-dozen major suburban cities, and from more than a score of smaller towns. When metropolitan conflict reached the legislature, Denver representatives had to face not only the antiurban bias of rural counties but also the suspicions of smaller cities along the entire Colorado piedmont from Colorado Springs to Fort Collins. Reapportionment simultaneously reduced the relative weight of Denver legislators. During the 1960s, Denver's margin over its suburbs in the state House of Representatives dropped from nine votes to two and in the Senate from four votes to two, with further losses after the 1970 census.[10]

Attention during the sixties centered on efforts to strengthen Denver's position within the metropolitan area by altering the structure of governmental institutions. The only partial success came at the start of the decade with the Metropolitan Capital Improvement District that survived a referendum because of a large majority in Denver only to fall before the justices of the Colorado Supreme Court in 1962. Proposals to create an "urban county," an area government providing six basic services, failed in the legislature in 1965, 1966, and 1967 because of opposition in the affluent suburbs of Jefferson and Arapahoe counties. A "coalition amendment" that would have combined elements of the urban county and service authority plans also failed the next year. While opponents argued that Denver's complaints about inadequate tax base were a ploy for political imperialism, the city's leaders made few friends by advocating the use of its water supply as a bargaining tool at a time when the "blue line" was still recent history. Although Republicans in the legislature led the opposition, allegiance to suburbia in each case outweighed party affiliation. Suburban Democrats happily joined in defending the interests of Jefferson and Arapahoe county residents and politicians.[11]

Denver's response to legislative setbacks was a sudden and aggressive campaign of annexation. Between 1956 and 1958, the city had viewed annexation as a privilege that outlying neighborhoods purchased through a capital improvements fee set at $2,000 per acre. At the end of the decade, however, Denver undertook a rapid expansion effort designed as much to acquire undeveloped land as to supply urban services to established communities. Because Denver has been a consolidated city-county since 1902, its annexations involve the complete transfer of jurisdiction and taxing power from the surrounding counties. To county officials and residents, the Denver program appeared as a blatant grab of potential revenue-rich land whose transfer would raise the tax burden of remaining suburbanites. In addition, suburbanites held the usual fears of conscription into the war against central city programs. Indeed, the situation was especially tense because of an ongoing controversy over intracity busing for racial integration within the Denver school district (coterminous with the city

Table 8.2. *Economic and Population Change in Four Cities and Surrounding Suburbs, 1960–1975*

	Number of Jobs 1970	Percentage of Job Gain 1960–70	Population 1975
Atlanta	313,757	16.7	436,057
Five suburban counties	263,683	119.2	1,078,737
Denver	279,136	19.8	484,531
Four suburban counties	186,914	60.8	911,239
Norfolk-Portsmouth	202,333	8.6	395,368
Two suburban cities	59,562	59.0	318,413
Portland	208,064	11.3	356,732
Four suburban counties	160,149	60.9	726,026

Source: *County and City Data Book*, 1972, 1977.

Note: N.A.: not available.

boundaries) that lasted from the 1969 school board election through the implementation of a court-ordered busing plan in 1974.[12]

The result of the annexation initiative was a five-year period called by one local official "the worst land wars" in the history of the metropolis. The counter move of suburbanites in the middle- and upper-middle income communities west of the city was the quick incorporation of two new municipalities in 1969—Wheatridge with 31,000 residents and Lakewood with 93,000 residents. On the other side of Denver, the city of Aurora replied with its own annexation campaign designed to preempt the central city. Several years of skirmishes over suburban territory led to an informal pact in 1973 in which the two cities partitioned remaining unincorporated areas into spheres of influence. In total, Denver between 1970 and 1974 added about twenty square miles of new land, including tentacles reaching into Jefferson and Arapahoe counties. Further expansion was blocked only by two constitutional amendments adopted by statewide vote in 1974. The citizen-initiated "Poundstone amendment" required that the entire county approve in referendum the annexation of any subarea within its boundaries. An additional compromise amendment formulated in the legislature and backed by suburban county commissions required

ercentage of Population Gain 1960–75	Retail Sales $1,000,000s 1972	Percentage of sales Gain Wholesaling 1962–72
–10.5	1,812	78.5
103.6	2,331	296.5
–2.0	1,367	59.5
109.4	2,150	218.0
–6.0	935	70.1
101.7	443	223.4
–4.3	1,247	N.A.
61.6	1,323	N.A.

majority approval for annexation proposals from a new Metropolitan Boundary Control Commission consisting of three Denver and three suburban members.[13]

The decade of the 1970s has also recorded more failure than success for regional service agencies designed particularly to serve the needs of Denver. Area voters indicated a surprising willingness to assume new responsibilities in 1973 when they authorized the creation of a Regional Transportation Authority and the expenditure of $1,560,000,000 on mass transit facilities. After mid-decade, however, the RTA lost much of its suburban support when detailed study showed that the high-technology alternatives of personal rapid transit and automated rapid transit were in fact impractical. The Denver Water Board, which now provided 40 percent of its service to suburban customers, faced further problems in the 1970s. When the water board in 1973 implemented a moratorium on new suburban connections, the counties of Adams, Arapahoe, and Jefferson sued the board as a collaborator with the Denver annexation program. After removing the moratorium in 1974, the previously arrogant water board has found itself requesting the help of suburban cities as it fights to increase its water supply against west-slope ranchers, Colorado environmentalists, and the Environmental

Protection Agency. Suburban voters in 1973 also defeated an Urban Service Authority for the four-county metropolitan area. When the idea was revived in 1977 by the Denver Metropolitan Area Study Panel, the previous indifference of suburban officials had hardened into an opposition that blocked the proposal. In November, 1980, voters in the five-county area rejected a ballot measure that would have essentially implemented the idea by the creation of a multi-service Metropolitan Council.[14]

In general terms, Denver leaders at the start of the 1960s could fairly expect to prevail on questions of intrametropolitan relations. They could normally expect to lose such contests in the 1970s. As indicated in the discussion, the change is in part the result of shifting population balance giving the suburbs increasing weight in referenda and legislative roll calls. In addition, the rising status of the suburbs relative to Denver has been reflected in increasingly sophisticated suburban governments. The major efforts to maintain social and political isolation from Denver have centered in the high-status counties of Jefferson and Arapahoe rather than the lower-status suburbs of Adams County. With active participation by suburban politicians, the Denver Regional Council of Governments (the successor to the Intercounty Regional Planning Commission) has promoted suburban as much as central city interests, particularly in planning for a west-side loop freeway. Skilled professional staffs and well-informed city councils now help suburban cities such as Lakewood and Aurora to deal with Denver as equals rather than dependents. The city of Boulder, which is included in the SMSA but which is buffered from immediate pressures by twenty miles of prairie, has engaged in sophisticated debate over growth limitations and has adopted a growth ceiling of 100,000 to preserve its insulation from the problems of Denver.

The experience of Atlanta in recent years has paralleled that of Denver. When the *Constitution* declared in March 1975 that Atlanta was a "city in crisis," its editors were responding to two aspects of the suburban trend. One was the shift in the economic balance of power as described in the discussion of suburban self-sufficiency. The other was the hostility of suburbanites who were trying to maintain social and political distance as well as economic distance. This second tendency has perhaps been most apparent in Cobb County, which gained a reputation for adamant social and political conservatism in the later sixties and early seventies. As Atlanta's west-side black district pushed closer to the county line, residents in the new suburban tracts in southern Cobb County adopted "Stop Atlanta" as their primary political slogan. On the other side of the SMSA, DeKalb County voters replaced a relatively progressive county commission of the early 1960s with new leaders increasingly committed to maintaining a clear difference between suburban neighborhoods and the city.[15]

One expression of the growing spirit of suburban isolationism was the reaction to MARTA. As discussed in chapter six, the rapid transit system was designed primarily to preserve the functions and activities of downtown Atlanta by improving access. In the original debates on the MARTA legislation, suburban legislators responded to this core city bias by reducing Atlanta's representation on the eleven-member board from six to four. Anti-Atlanta backlash in 1965 decided that Cobb County would not even participate in the planning phase of the project. Six years later, Clayton and Gwinnet counties also voted by four to one to reject the local sales tax and the benefits of MARTA service. Even in Fulton County, the continuing opposition of suburbanites in the southwestern section of the county came within a few hundred votes of killing the entire project.[16]

Atlanta's suburbanites have also used their local governments to fend off public housing. Most of the jurisdictions in the SMSA have preempted action by the Atlanta Housing Authority by establishing their own public housing agencies, but have refused to establish eligibility for federal funding by adopting a "workable program." County governments have also used zoning regulations to effectively exclude low-income housing by private builders. In one blatant example, Fulton County commissioners in 1972 rezoned a tract for multifamily housing on the expectation that it would be used for "executive apartments" and then refused a building permit when the builder revealed his plans for federally assisted housing. At roughly the same time, efforts by the federal courts to force the dispersal of lower-income housing through the metropolitan area brought intense protests from Congressmen Fletcher Thompson (representing Fulton County suburbanites) and Ben Blackburn (DeKalb), the latter of whom complained that housing dispersal would mean "Middle America . . . losing control of its own country." With the partial exception of several neighborhoods in southern DeKalb County, there is no residential integration in suburban Atlanta. Indeed, public and private discrimination have combined to build a homogenized environment by squeezing existing black residents out of the white suburbs.[17]

Efforts to counter the trend toward suburban isolation by reviving the idea of the 1952 "Plan of Improvement" have been clear failures. Ivan Allen, the Chamber of Commerce, and the *Constitution* all began to talk up annexation in 1964 and 1965, but an effort to absorb the suburban area of Sandy Spring in northern Fulton County failed in 1966. A second effort in 1972 to annex 173 square miles of Fulton County suburbs north of the city was introduced by Mayor Sam Massell as a "Program for Progress" in direct echo of 1952. The proposal was supported by Atlanta banks, the Chamber of Commerce, and other elements of what Lieutenant Governor Lester Maddox called "the establishment crowd." It met even stronger opposition from Fulton County officials, who feared the loss of their tax base, and from suburban residents, who feared higher taxes, land-use restrictions, and school system merger. After months of intense bargaining, the annexation measure failed in the legislature when Maddox used his authority as presiding officer to prevent its consideration by the state Senate. An alternative proposal for the complete consolidation of Atlanta and Fulton County which was presented in 1969–70 received the support of outgoing Mayor Allen but elicited solid opposition from the suburban and rural residents of the county. Since a consolidation would have reduced the proportion of black voters from 40 to 35 percent, it also met opposition from most of Atlanta's black community.[18]

The only promising development for advocates of metropolitan coordination has been the creation of the Atlanta Regional Commission (ARC) in 1971. Its predecessor agency, the Atlanta Region Metropolitan Planning Commission, had largely functioned during the sixties to assist the process of land development through transportation and utility planning. With a board representing political jurisdictions and dominated by the area's five county commission chairmen, the ARMPC had neither the ability nor the inclination to override parochial suburban interests in relation to zoning and housing.[19] The ARC emerged as a milder alternative after the consolidation debate of 1969–70. Established by state legislation, it merged the ARMPC and three other agencies that coordinated federal hospital, law enforcement, and highway grants for the SMSA. The ARC board consists of twelve elected officials and eleven citizens who are appointed by the ex officio board members from districts that cut across jurisdictional boundaries.

On the positive side, the board arrangement does allow reasonable black representation (four of the first twenty-three board members). The agency is also mandated by law to review and comment on any local plan or activity that affects areawide planning or interests. At the same time, its powers are largely the negative ability to block federal grants for ill-conceived projects and to embarrass specific jurisdictions. It does not have the power to operate metropolitan services that is found with Portland's Metropolitan Service District.[20]

In comparison with Denver and Atlanta, the political environment in metropolitan Portland has been biased in favor of the central city. For practical purposes, decision makers in the city of Portland can ignore the 13 percent of SMSA residents who live north of the Columbia River in Vancouver and Clark County, Washington. Within Oregon, the largest suburban community, Beaverton (23,700 in 1976), has been preoccupied with the service demands of rapid growth and with the often repeated conflict between older suburban residents and new arrivals. The result has been frequent referenda on policy questions, high turnover on the Beaverton City Council, and crisis conditions for professional staff. The suburban counties of Washington and Clackamas have also been reluctant to assume responsibility for providing urban services for the rapidly growing population of unincorporated communities. With part-time leadership and inadequate revenues, they have yet to complete the painful transition from rural to suburban government.[21]

With a few exceptions, the major intrametropolitan battles have therefore been fought within Multnomah County between the city of Portland and the East County. Here too, however, the lines of conflict are often blurred by overlapping political structures. The county includes 382,000 Portlanders, 31,000 residents of suburban towns, and 140,000 residents outside municipal boundaries. The county handles tax assessment, welfare, courts, and libraries for all of its residents and provides the additional services of law enforcement, planning, sanitation, and parks for unincorporated areas. Because the county commissioners were elected at large until 1979, there was no formal split between representatives of city and suburban interests, although particular commissioners played to Portland or to suburban voters. Clear polarization is also reduced by the socioeconomic similarities between Portland and outlying parts of the county. The middle-class neighborhoods of northeast Portland and the working-class neighborhoods of southeast Portland blend without perceptible break into similar communities outside the city limits, and the eastern half of Portland and the East County had almost identical scores on indicators of education, income, and occupational status in 1970.[22] The only full-service suburban town is Gresham (23,000), that pursued an active chamber-of-commerce growth policy as a rival of Portland in the early seventies but that more recently has been divided by internal conflict between older and newer residents.

The explicit emergence of city-county conflict can be dated to a new Portland aggressiveness on annexation at the start of the 1960s. In the previous decade, Portland had considered annexation more trouble than it was worth. However, the census of 1960 shocked the Portland leadership when it showed a population decline for the city rather than the expected increase. Reports by the Public Administration Service in 1959 and the local City Club in 1961 also urged annexation on the general argument that it was "essential to the sound development of the core city in a metropolitan area."[23] Under prodding by Mayor Terry Schrunk, the city embarked on a conscious annexation program, soliciting the interest of suburban neighborhoods and developing a timetable for territorial growth. The resulting scare about Portland's ambitions triggered the incorporation of Tigard in Washington County and brought bitter protests from Multnomah County commissioners, who claimed in 1965 to have discovered an unlikely plot to grab several dozen square miles by encircling most of the developed section of the East County with a narrow ribbon of annexed land.[24]

Portland's expansion drive was in fact slow-paced by comparison with many other sunbelt cities, adding only thirteen square miles during the early 1960s. The confusion of charges and countercharges, however, helped to persuade the legislature to establish a Metropolitan Study Commission. Active from 1964 to 1969, the study commission served as a catalyst for several changes in the structure of metropolitan government. On first glance, the only bias of the study commission was to favor areawide solutions to areawide problems. On closer examination, two of the agencies that emerged from its recommendations have reduced the independence of Portland within the metropolitan area. Since 1969, a Metropolitan Boundary Commission has reviewed all annexation proposals. Its major interest is the effect of annexation on the cost and efficiency of service delivery, a criterion that relegates central city desires for increased tax base or population diversification to second place. In May 1970 voters in the metropolitan area also ignored the protests of Portland officials and approved the Metropolitan Service District (MSD), an open-ended regional service agency that some members of the study commission saw as the nucleus for a future general government for the metropolitan area.[25] In general, the creation of the MSD violated Portland's self-image as *the* governmental entity with regional interests and concerns. Specifically, city officials were afraid that the MSD might take over the city water system that supplied Portland and 130,000 outside customers at a profitable markup. In fact, Portland through most of the 1970s was able to limit MSD to solid waste planning and the Washington Park Zoo, which had been a money-loser under city control.[26]

The mixed results of the 1960s have continued to characterize city-suburban relations in the Portland area during the 1970s. As in the earlier decade, Portland has been able to achieve many of its substantive aims, although regional planning has replaced annexation as the salient issue. Battles over several additional proposals for changes in the structure of governmental institutions have also focused on the extent of Portland's influence. Votes on a procession of ballot measures have combined to reduce the influence of Portland residents within Multnomah County and of Portland officials within the metropolitan area.

The most direct conflict of interests among city and suburbs has involved the proposed Mount Hood freeway, an extra radial link in the regional highway grid that would have tied the central business district to a peripheral freeway in eastern Multnomah County. As an approved segment of the federal interstate system and an important element in the state highway program, planning for the Mount Hood freeway had reached the stage of environmental impact assessment preliminary to actual construction decisions at the start of 1974. It also enjoyed strong support from Clackamas County, Gresham, and other residents in eastern Multnomah County who expected to use the road. In contrast, a number of Portlanders objected that the freeway would destroy several viable neighborhoods within the city by displacing 1,750 households and would channel population growth outside the city limits. After a February decision on a suit by southeast Portland residents seriously delayed the construction timetable and introduced the idea of abandoning the freeway, the "Mount Hood" question became the dominant topic for local debate during the spring and summer. Under the leadership of Mayor Neil Goldschmidt, who had won his office two years before on a platform of neighborhood conservation, the Portland council finally voted in July to oppose the freeway. The Multnomah County Commission seconded the Portland vote a month later, following the interests of their city rather than their county constituents. Early in 1975 the governor formally requested the withdrawal of the Mount Hood freeway from the interstate highway system.[27]

More generally, Portland for most of the 1970s dominated metropolitan planning decisions through its influence on the Columbia Region Association of Governments (CRAG). More than other politicians in the SMSA, Neil Goldschmidt has perceived the usefulness of working through the designated regional planning agency and utilized weighted voting on the CRAG board which Portland obtained in 1973 to focus CRAG's attention on problems of special interest to the city. Portland has been especially interested to dominate decisions on the allocation of $150 million in mass transit funds made available by the termination of the Mount Hood freeway. Portland city planners and CRAG staff also maintained a close liaison that limited the input of other jurisdictions on housing, land use, air pollution, and related regional issues. Certainly the common perception in recent years was that CRAG spoke for Portland rather than for the region.

The evolution of the formal structure of governmental institutions, however, has not reflected Portland's continuing influence. Between 1968 and 1973, Multnomah County and Portland made a promising start toward functional cooperation with joint data processing facilities, the consolidation of lower courts, and the merger of health departments. Portland, Gresham, and the county also agreed on areas to be covered by their separate sewer systems.[28] In 1974, however, Neil Goldschmidt took the lead in backing a city-county consolidation measure that proposed to merge Portland, Multnomah County, and forty-two special districts within the county into a single "City-County of Portland-Multnomah." If the ponderous name were not enough, the ballot measure alienated business organizations by providing for partisan elections that could be expected to give Democrats control of the consolidated municipality. In addition, most residents in the East County perceived the measure as a power grab by Portland and by Goldschmidt, who was fresh from his efforts against the Mount Hood freeway. The county commission endorsed the proposal, but many county employees worked against the measure to protect their own jobs and prerogatives. Because it was anticipated that each suburban town would exercise its right to vote against participating in the consolidation, several thousand residents of unincorporated areas also initiated their own annexation to Gresham as a defensive measure. The crashing defeat of the consolidation in November was a product of a mismanaged campaign, specific hostility toward Portland arising from the freeway decision, and a general suburban fear of an aggressive central city.[29]

Reaction to the freeway decision has also taken the form of efforts to alter the county charter. The reformers are primarily unhappy East County citizens who think that at-large voting leaves them underrepresented on the county commission and allows Portland voters to dominate planning decisions affecting areas outside the city. A specific target has been county commission Chairman Don Clark, who opposed the Mount Hood freeway and who has favored consolidation and functional cooperation. In 1976, East County votes were responsible for the narrow passage of charter amendments that established district election of county commissioners. In 1977, Portlanders mobilized a second initiative campaign that reversed the first vote and set up a Charter Review Commission, which in turn submitted successful amendments for a modified district system for the November 1978 election. In the first two years, the commissioner from the suburban East County district clearly articulated the resentment against the Portland orientation of the county administration.[30]

Since Oregonians like nothing better than a crowded ballot, voters in the metropolitan area also agreed in May 1978 to merge CRAG into the Metropolitan Service District, to expand the potential powers of MSD, and to give the agency a board of directors elected from districts within the metropolis. Because both the wording on the ballot and the measure itself were confused and confusing, the change was supported by enemies of Portland, by opponents of regional planning, and by advocates of metropolitan government. The overall effect of placing the MSD under the direction of part-time councilors whose districts cut jurisdictional boundaries will be to undercut the influence of the Portland city government on regional decisions. In its first year, the MSD clearly shifted the bias in local land-use planning toward the extensive patterns of development favored by Washington and Clackamas counties. Several Portland commissioners also hold the underlying fear that the bigger and better MSD may evolve into a general purpose metropolitan government and compete for federal grants and revenue sharing funds.[31]

Tidewater, Virginia, provides the nation's most extreme case of suburban revolt. In the early 1960s, the Norfolk-Portsmouth SMSA experienced a suburban coup that instantly changed the terms of regional politics. Under the authority of new permissive legislation, suburban politicians engineered two city-county consolidations that completely encompassed Norfolk with incorporated territory and almost surrounded Portsmouth. In a vote on 3 January 1962, residents of the oceanfront resort town of Virginia Beach and partially suburbanized Princess Anne County voted by more than four to one to merge into the new city of Virginia Beach effective 1 January 1963. Six weeks later, a similar proposal to form the new city of Chesapeake won overwhelming approval in semisuburban Norfolk County and narrower acceptance in the industrial suburb of South Norfolk.[32]

The central motivation for the two mergers was the desire of political leaders in the counties to preserve their jurisdictions against encroachment from the core cities. Since 1948, Norfolk County had lost thirty-three square miles, 110,000 residents, and $1.9 million in annual revenue to annexations by the two cities, and its politicians faced the constant fear that Norfolk would continue to swallow chunk after chunk on the east side of the county while Portsmouth kept pace on the west side. Indeed, Portsmouth had recently initiated annexation proceedings directed at the northwestern corner of Norfolk County. Princess Anne County had also transferred residents to Norfolk in 1959, and it was common knowledge that Norfolk's leaders planned further eastward expansion when the city became eligible for a new annexation in 1963.[33] Beyond the fears of being consumed by annexation, the established rural families who controlled the counties had few connections and little interest in the central cities. The public arguments in favor of the mergers and the character of the new city charters both support the conclusion that the consolidations were efforts to preserve the political status quo by establishing permanent independence.[34]

Central city reactions to the consolidation plans in the fall of 1961 quickly ranged from astonishment to anger to chagrin. Princess Anne County's plans were particularly embarrassing to the Norfolk City Council. County boss Sidney Kellam the year before had proposed a study of metropolitan area government in return for the informal suspension of Norfolk annexation planning, had maneuvered himself into the chairmanship of the committee, and quietly crippled its operations while he laid plans for consolidation. Certainly the anger of Mayor Fred Duckworth at being bamboozled by Kellam played a part in the ill-advised city decision to purchase a full-page newspaper ad urging Princess Anne and Virginia Beach voters to reject the merger in order to preserve the prosperity of the Tidewater area. In mid-November, a meeting held at Norfolk's suggestion to explore the idea of a three-way merger ended with city representatives raising the threat of a payroll tax. The city council further alienated suburban voters by voting to "gun down" the merger by cutting off water service beyond their city limits as soon as any consolidation became effective (public outcry forced the council to reverse itself a week later). Neither broadsides by a committee of Norfolk businessmen nor protests by Duckworth that the creation of a supersuburb would "prevent for all time the great potential development of this area" carried the stamp of metropolitan statesmanship or swayed suburban voters. Across the Elizabeth River, Portsmouth was equally negative in reaction to the South Norfolk–Norfolk County merger, hurriedly filing an ultimately unsuccessful annexation suit in order to disrupt the proceedings. After the successful merger votes in 1962, Norfolk and Portsmouth were unable even to enlist one-third of the General Assembly members to block approval for the charters of the new cities. Intraparty feuding, resentment of the relative liberalism of Tidewater cities, and memories of Norfolk's recent school crisis all left Norfolk and Portsmouth without friends in Richmond.[35]

The consolidation locked the entire SMSA under the jurisdiction of four municipalities. Because cities over 10,000 residents assume county functions in Virginia, all decisions on local government were centralized in four city councils (and the board of two special districts that operated port facilities and sewers). The result from 1963 to 1973 was the evolution of a metropolitan politics keyed to negotiation and quadrilateral diplomacy. A fifth actor joined the system in 1974 when another major consolidation created the new city of Suffolk from the farm market town of Suffolk and the old County of Nansemond, an area of peanut farms and new subdivisions west of Chesapeake and Portsmouth.[36] Population estimates for 1975 roughly indicate the balance among the five cities, with 287,000 residents in Norfolk,

214,000 in Virginia Beach, 109,000 in Portsmouth, 104,000 in Chesapeake, and 48,000 in Suffolk.[37] As the trend continued, the suburb of Chesapeake passed the central city of Portsmouth in the 1980 census, and the suburb of Virginia Beach drew within a few thousand residents of Norfolk.

Suburban equality is also supported by emerging identities among the new cities. The *Virginian-Pilot*, the area's leading newspaper, altered its masthead on 1 January 1963, to proclaim itself equally the voice of Norfolk, Portsmouth, Virginia Beach, and Chesapeake, adding Suffolk to the list in 1974. In fact, the paper if anything devotes disproportionate space to the new cities. From May to August 1977, a period including city council elections and the adoption of annual budgets, the *Pilot* gave approximately 1,000 column inches to news of Virginia Beach government and politics, 950 inches to Norfolk, 420 inches to Chesapeake, 300 inches to Portsmouth, and 150 inches to Suffolk. Another indicator of changes in regional identities comes from listings in the telephone directory. Excluding city government entries, the phone book in 1960 had 42 inches of listings that started with Norfolk, 1 inch starting with Virginia Beach, and 36 inches starting with the common regional terms Tidewater, Southeastern, Hampton Roads, and Chesapeake. Seventeen years later, the totals were 50 inches for Norfolk, 18 inches for Virginia Beach, 74 inches for the first three regional names, and 15 inches for Chesapeake (which now referred either to city or region).

It is also easy to trace the emerging self-consciousness of residents within specific cities. In Virginia Beach, both the independent weekly *Sun* and the *Beacon*, a local supplement to the *Virginian-Pilot*, have helped to direct attention to the new city's own growth and accomplishments. Under Sidney Kellam's tutelage, the new Virginia Beach City Council was also careful to minimize differences between the old county and the old resort town. It chose to locate city offices at a rural crossroads beyond the fringe of development so that public activities would not be identified with an existing community. As the subdivision frontier creeps steadily southward in the 1970s and 1980s, however, the civic center increasingly will be the natural focus for the emerging supersuburb. Perhaps the most representative effort to nourish a separate municipal identity, however, is a city-sponsored history of Virginia Beach that appropriates the experiences of seventeenth-century settlers to provide an instant heritage for the residents of the instant city.[38]

Certainly by the later 1970s, few Virginia Beachers viewed their city as suburban. City planners, the city manager, and politicians all agree that the bulk of new residents are now direct migrants from other parts of the nation rather than refugees from Norfolk or Portsmouth.[39] Both census data for 1965–70 and a housing survey taken in 1974 confirm that slightly more than 80 percent of the immigrants to Virginia Beach are new arrivals to the SMSA. More than half of the city's labor force also works in Virginia Beach, and new office parks along Virginia Beach Boulevard provide most of the area's new business space.[40] As local officials quickly point out, many of the remaining commuters are military personnel whose work at naval bases in the central cities involves no commitment or interest in the problems of Norfolk or Portsmouth.

In contrast, the new city of Chesapeake was initially plagued by a reservoir of resentment about the merger among politicians and residents of South Norfolk, who had given approval by a margin of only 433 votes out of 3185. The new city council in its first years often split five to five between representatives from the old county and those from the old city. An additional impediment to a common sense of identity was the South Branch of the Elizabeth River, that divided Chesapeake into areas that are suburban to Norfolk and other areas that are tied to Portsmouth.[41] By the 1970s, however, old political feuds had faded with the emergence of a new leadership committed to the development of a viable and diversified city.[42] The development of a civic center at Great Bridge has served the same function as the location of public buildings in Virginia Beach, creating a common center for the city in an area equally accessible to all parts of the scattered city. Indeed, much of the industrial and commercial growth of the decade was centered on highway interchanges close to the civic center. Chesapeake leaders have also sought to promote a separate identity by equipping their community with objects for civic pride and focal points for local activity—a regional shopping center, an unnecessary general hospital.

The strong loyalties in all five Tidewater municipalities have supported directly conflicting civic ambitions. It is frequently suggested that the typical suburban government is interested primarily in preserving the amenities of its residential environment and turns to economic development only as a last resort to bolster a sagging tax base.[43] Neither Virginia Beach, Chesapeake, nor Suffolk, however, is willing to accept a limited role as a bedroom community. At the same time, Norfolk and Portsmouth are struggling to reverse the demographic trends that threaten to turn many central cities into reservations for the poor and the elderly. Instead, each of the cities in the Tidewater system is seeking to achieve and maximize the same goals of broadened economic base and diversified population, competing across the board to be a fully rounded city.

As population spreads westward along the southern side of the James River, for example, the leaders of Suffolk share a developing vision in which new factories and expensive houses crowd its peanut farmers into the far corners of the city. Among the first actions of the new city administration in the mid-1970s were the establishment of an industrial park and the hiring of an industrial development coordinator. City officials were bitterly disappointed in 1977 when a special census failed to confirm hopes that its population had passed the magic mark of fifty thousand.[44] A local politician indicated the emerging attitude of assertiveness when he exploded at one regional meeting that "I'm tired of Suffolk being used . . . I'm tired of people taking our land, taking our water, and giving us nothing in return."[45]

The two other suburbs have also been caught in the excitement of growth during the 1970s. For a decade, Chesapeake has followed a two-pronged development strategy. It has invested heavily in its school facilities in order to attract middle-class residents and has provided roads and sewers in advance of residential construction. It has also tried to supplement its heavy industry along the South Branch by attracting retailing, office activities, and light manufacturing (in particular, an American assembly plant for Volvo).[46] The city council in Virginia Beach has also been a tool of real estate developers. Despite the adoption of a comprehensive zoning ordinance after long debate in 1973, over 90 percent of the new construction undertaken in the last three years has involved the rezoning of agricultural land. The one major advocate of slow growth on the council was defeated for reelection early in the decade, and the city manager now looks forward happily to a population of four hundred or five hundred thousand by the 1990s. In order to reduce the level of commuting to Norfolk and to develop the city's tax base, Virginia Beach has also embarked on vigorous economic growth efforts. It has built industrial parks, started a $16 million convention center to compete directly with Norfolk, and entertained dreams of its own port facilities.[47] The success of these suburban ambitions can be measured by employment estimates for 1970–80 that indicate a 100 percent increase in jobs for Chesapeake and Virginia Beach, a 25 percent increase for Suffolk, and increases of less than 10 percent for Norfolk and Portsmouth.[48]

If the new cities of the Tidewater system are competing vigorously for manufacturing and commercial activities that have traditionally concentrated in central cities, Norfolk and Portsmouth have countered with greater attention to the attractions of their residential neighborhoods. The major efforts of the Norfolk Redevelopment and Housing Authority in the 1970s centered on the provision of $60–$100,000 homes in downtown redevelopment areas and along the downtown waterfront. Portsmouth has similar plans to confront the Norfolk project with a row of high-rise apartments lining its own waterfront. Both sets of projects will compete directly with suburban communities for middle-class newcomers to the SMSA. In addition, Portsmouth has committed itself to new industrial development to support an overburdened local economy. In the short run, its hopes for a $800 million oil refinery on its last large parcel of vacant land have been repeatedly frustrated by environmental concerns. Despite approval by the various permit-granting agencies, antirefinery lawsuits early in 1980 promised to turn the issue into "another complicated, big bankroll, environmental controversy."[49] In the long run, Portsmouth hopes to develop industrial sites on a huge artificial mudbank built by dredge spoils from Hampton Roads harbor.

Each city also has a governmental capacity adequate for pursuing these competitive ambitions. Between 1969 and 1974, municipal spending rose by 100 percent in Portsmouth and 120 percent in Norfolk but climbed by 150 percent in Chesapeake and 175 percent in Virginia Beach. Available figures from 1972–73 indicate that per capita city spending (with welfare costs excluded) was virtually identical in Norfolk, Chesapeake, and Virginia Beach, with Portsmouth slightly higher and the yet unconsolidated governments of Suffolk and Nansemond somewhat lower.[50] It is also clear that the several city budgets are all competently administered by full and qualified staffs. Indeed, managerial equality among the cities has been carried to the extreme that one skilled administrator—Robert House—has served successively as city manager in Chesapeake, Norfolk, and Suffolk; he was succeeded by a subordinate in Chesapeake and more recently saw a protégé from his Norfolk office installed as city manager in Virginia Beach.

The role of the Southeastern Virginia Planning District Commission has been limited to that of broker and facilitator among the several professional staffs. In many metropolitan areas, the central city faces a scattering of small suburban towns that lack the money, staff, or expertise to function effectively across the board. Such towns may frequently cede selected responsibilities to a larger city through service contracts or to the staff of a regional council of governments or planning agency. In Tidewater Virginia, in contrast, the five coequal municipalities carefully guard their influence and interests on every public issue. With a board of directors composed of city councilmen and county supervisors, the Southeastern Virginia Planning District serves as a sort of "league of nations" within the system of municipal diplomacy. When even the location of its offices can become an occasion for intercity jealousy, the regional planning agency has not achieved its goal of coordinating the policies of the "big four" cities. At best, its staff can work with professional counterparts in the several cities to fashion compromises acceptable to elected leaders. At the least, it provides an alternative to the newspapers as a forum for debate on regional problems.[51]

Indeed, almost every issue of regional policy in the last decade and a half has been approached in the spirit of mutual jealousy. The normally emotional problems of life-style such as school integration, land use, law enforcement, and housing are limited to political debate within each city. However, presumably neutral questions involving basic services necessary for maintaining a functioning urban system have proved just as capable of generating passionate conflict among the five full-service cities. In the mid-1960s, for example, Norfolk and Portsmouth together killed a regional transportation plan because its reliance on freeways seemed to threaten downtown business. In turn, suburban hostility blocked the implementation of a later plan for a comprehensive bus system focusing on the old downtowns. The designation of Norfolk's airport as the "regional" facility has also rankled in the other cities that periodically urge the consideration of a second airport in Suffolk or Chesapeake. More recently, Norfolk threatened to cripple a new Tidewater Transportation District by refusing to transfer the city bus system until complex negotiations expanded Norfolk representation on the agency board.[52]

Tidewater politicians and administrators are also in agreement with Robert House that a city must control its own water supply if it hopes to plan its own future. For several decades the metropolitan area has depended on two water systems, with Norfolk supplying Virginia Beach and Chesapeake east of the South Branch and Portsmouth supplying western Chesapeake and Suffolk.[53] In 1969, Chesapeake decided to commemorate its political independence by tapping streams in its southern reaches and constructing its own treatment and distribution facilities. Three years later, Norfolk and Virginia Beach both ignored an interim report by the planning district that favored a regional water system when they entered into bargaining on the renewal of the Virginia Beach water contract. Virginia Beach negotiators wanted Norfolk to agree to expand its distribution network but tried to reserve the right to abrogate the contract if their city could find alternate sources. In August 1972, Norfolk countered by suggesting a moratorium on new hookups that would have quickly closed down the construction industry in Virginia Beach. Virginia Beach officials immediately protested that Norfolk was trying to blackmail the city into a reluctant merger. Even after the newer city accepted terms for a twenty-year contract in the spring of 1973, both sides have continued to maneuver for new advantages. When Norfolk proposed to raise water rates for users in both cities, Virginia Beach Council members protested that any rate hike would violate the spirit of the contract and put their city at the financial mercy of Norfolk. In what was almost surely wishful thinking, Virginia Beach even appropriated one hundred thousand dollars to study the feasibility of a desalination plant to free itself of dependence on Norfolk.[54]

On the western side of the SMSA, Suffolk has agreed with Virginia Beach and Chesapeake that local control of water is a necessary concomitant of political independence. The years from 1968 to 1971 saw debates and legal suits over the water rates that Portsmouth charged customers in the old city of Suffolk and the eventual signing of a new contract that left everyone unhappy. The ill feelings revived in 1975 when the new consolidated city started to develop its own supply and to purchase the parts of the Portsmouth distribution system within its boundaries. In recent years, Portsmouth has accused Suffolk of holding Portsmouth's future hostage by threatening to testify against the oil refinery in environmental hearings. In turn, the mayor of Portsmouth has tried to use the water question to pressure Suffolk toward merger or at least toward consolidation of certain services. Only a large grant from the Economic Development Administration has allowed a solution by enabling Suffolk to duplicate some of the water lines in question with parallel mains.[55] Most recently during a severe drought in the summer of 1980, Suffolk refused Norfolk the right to drill emergency wells within Suffolk city limits.

A final example of intrametropolitan relations involves garbage disposal. In 1977, the Southeastern Virginia Planning District requested seed money from local jurisdictions for the planning and design of an energy recovery system for solid waste. The plan had the general virtue of promoting energy conservation and enjoyed the support of the federal government, which promised to purchase steam generated at the plant for the Norfolk navy yard. At the same time, it would satisfy specific needs of Norfolk and Portsmouth, which were rapidly running out of space for landfill disposal. Without the same immediate problems, Chesapeake withdrew its initial agreement for short-range financial reasons. Virginia Beach initially tried to trade its participation for a renegotiation of its Norfolk water contract and signed the mutual garbage treaty only after months of shuttle diplomacy on the city-suburban expressway.[56]

In summary, intrametropolitan politics in southeastern Virginia involves a process of multilateral bargaining. There has never been a *regional* referendum on any important local issue. Instead, each city tries to use its particular strong points (water supply, industrial land, transit system, space for landfill) as counters in negotiations to fill its most pressing needs, with the unspoken goal of emerging for the next round in a more advantageous competitive position. Beyond the five-sided discussions, moreover, relations are complicated by specific rivalries of special intensity. As the secondary port on the Elizabeth River, for one example, Portsmouth has historically been jealous of the greater size and influence of Norfolk. Every time Portsmouth patriots look across the river from their own boarded-up business district to the new office buildings of downtown Norfolk, the latter city's complaints about pollution from the proposed refinery look like one more version of the old conspiracy to block Portsmouth's growth. Memories of annexation battles in the 1950s, the recurring problems of shared water systems, and habits of retail trade and commuting tie together Norfolk and Virginia Beach as one subsystem on the east side of the metropolis and Portsmouth, Chesapeake, and Suffolk as a second subsystem on the west side.[57] Like partners in a failing marriage, the cities in each subsystem bicker and spar at every turn because each presumes the right to special treatment from the others.[58]

In brief summary, the present chapter has explored the impact of rapid growth and suburbanization during the 1960s and 1970s on the relationships among governmental units within metropolitan Denver, Atlanta, Portland, and Norfolk. The analysis suggests that the rapid pace of sunbelt growth, as described in the opening chapters of the study, has exacerbated intergovernmental conflict by opening or reopening a wide range of questions and requiring quick decisions. It indicates that the decline of central city optimism and the increasing influence of suburbs on metropolitan decisions which has characterized these decades reflect the growing economic independence of suburbs and the reversal of city-suburban status levels described in chapter three. Finally, the experiences of the four cities sketch out the great variety in specific governmental forms that has also marked the sunbelt SMSAs.

As the idea of metropolitan pluralism suggests, suburban cities and a number of suburban counties by the 1970s had the capacity to offer local governments fully as skilled as those of many central cities. Daniel Elazar has suggested that forty to fifty thousand is the minimum population necessary to support sophisticated governmental institutions with professional staffs. Information for the early 1970s from the International City Management Association indicates that the threshold size that assures adequate salaries, trained planners, and the use of automated data processing lies somewhat below fifty thousand.[59] In addition, the expansion of suburban industrial parks, office space, and retailing has increased available taxable wealth. Certainly it would be possible to provide a long list of major suburbs whose governments are as sophisticated as those of any central city. Fairfax and Arlington counties have a national reputation for pioneering efforts in employee relations and land-use planning. Southern California "suburbs" like Glendale and Pasadena have long considered themselves equals of Los Angeles in everything but size, competing for growth and territory and offering a full choice of public services.

Such governments in peripheral cities of the Sunbelt are concerned with every sort of public activity and responsibility. Political scientist Oliver Williams has argued that suburbanites within the metropolitan framework are interested largely to defend life-style differences and willingly leave unexciting "system maintenance" functions to cooperative arrangements. The argument seems to fit only the small bedroom suburb that characterizes the Northeast. In Denver, Atlanta, Norfolk, and Portland, many issues of city-suburban conflict have involved such basic support services as water, waste disposal, and transportation. In each SMSA, the underlying concern of intrametropolitan conflict as it has emerged in the 1970s is the survival or independence of suburban political units. Counties have thus battled against annexations; incorporated suburbs have fought for control of their water supplies; unincorporated subdivisions have clung to independent sewer, water, and fire protection districts. In practical priorities, suburbs and central city battle to defend territorial integrity and to assure the physical well-being of their citizens in order that they may have the chance to promote particular styles of living.

Social isolation, economic independence, and political self-sufficiency all operate to free suburbs of ties to their central city. At a time when many cities themselves are overcoming the arrogance of the 1940s and 1950s and seeking avenues for cooperation rather than control, suburban governments increasingly see little advantage even in cooperation. When most residents of the outer city have no contact, no concern, and no interest in the old core neighborhoods, suburbanites will tend to define their political life without particular reference to the central city. The result in many sunbelt metropolises may well be politics of suburban equality on the model of Norfolk, where the core city is simply one of several actors without special claims to regional leadership or special treatment and where the only strong force compelling regional cooperation is the occasional congruence of specific city interests.[60]

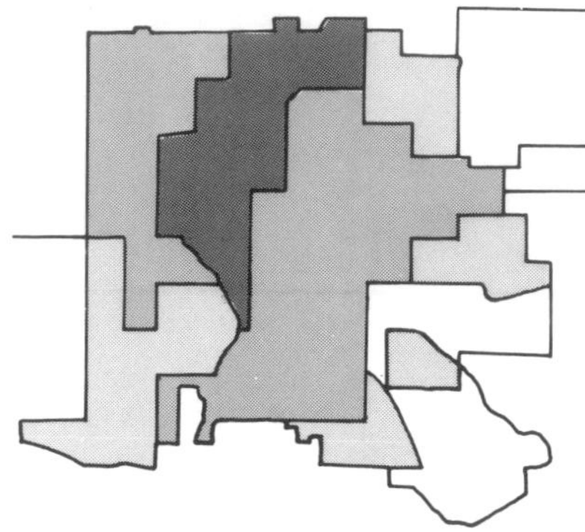

Chapter 9

The Politics of Neighborhood Interest

Time can alter the impact of an old painting. The artist in his workshop in Florence or Amsterdam was interested in the large effects of his composition—light and shade, figures and landscape, foreground and perspective. What often holds our attention, however, is not the large patterns but the fine network of cracks in the layers of pigment and varnish. The deterioration of the canvas and the aging of the paint turn the single large picture into a jigsaw puzzle of chips and fragments.

A parallel process has been occurring within American cities. In the 1940s and 1950s, the broad pattern of competition between core and rim dominated our perceptions. For the 1970s, however, urbanists have sought a new metaphor to describe the character of the metropolis. In particular, Brian Berry has suggested that the postindustrial city should be viewed as mosaic, a set of separate neighborhoods held together in the framework of the metropolitan area. Individuals with different interests and values can avoid day to day conflict by congregating with others of similar life-style in localized communities. Although the component pieces of the metropolitan mosaic form larger patterns, the term places greatest emphasis on the distinctiveness of each neighborhood, whether ghetto or gold coast, bohemia, slum, or family oriented suburb. In our tour of the metropolis as in our walk through the museum, it is now the cracks between the fragments that first draw the eye.[1]

What is new in recent years is not the existence of distinct neighborhoods and communities but rather their increasing prominence as focal points for political action. The businessmen's reforms of the 1940s and 1950s held up the ideal of an overriding common interest for sunbelt cities and their metropolitan areas. As the preceding chapter has described, the attempt to limit the political influence of suburban areas has largely failed. Within central cities, the same reform program explicitly denied the legitimacy of specific minority group interests and repudiated the ward elections that allowed representation of subareas within cities. Here too, however, the development of political independence for suburbs has been paralleled by the new mobilization of neighborhood interests and ethnic groups, the definition of alternative goals for municipal politics, and efforts to establish political forms that represent and protect specific residential neighborhoods or geographical areas within the city.

The consequence of these changes is the extension of the patterns of "metropolitan pluralism" to politics within sunbelt cities. Two distinct tendencies have come together to reemphasize the importance of the spatial dimension in municipal politics. New elements within the white middle class and growing minority populations have both learned from suburbanites that spatial concentration can be a political resource for promoting the interests and independence of individual city neighborhoods. Specifically, the new style of politics in sunbelt cities includes the creation of councilmanic districts, neighborhood associations, and community organizations to serve as an intervening layer between the citizen and city hall.

The common factor in the defection of middle-class urbanites from the urban renewal coalition has been dissatisfaction with mounting costs from the growth program. For some, the trigger for political mobilization has been the desire to defend an older established neighborhood from the encroachment of commercial uses, from rapid racial turnover, or from a planned expressway. Others have embraced the cause of limited growth because they fear that continued development will foul the air, eat up recreational space, raise taxes, and limit the amenities of residential areas. They have responded in some cases by trying to impose new programs on their central city administration. They have also pushed vigorously for the recognition of neighborhood organizations and neighborhood planning as vital elements in municipal policy making.

Many supporters of the new neighborhood politics are members of the "postindustrial" middle class. Scientists, professors, government workers, and executives of national corporations are "cosmopolitan in outlook and pecuniary interest."[2] They depend on statewide or national markets for their talents rather than on local markets for their goods and services. They therefore tend to see the city as a residential environment rather than an economic machine. As salaried employees who have been caught in the inflation of the 1970s, they are also more interested in the availability of affordable and convenient housing in attractive neighborhoods than in the booster's shibboleth of population growth. Leaders for the neighborhood movement are likely to be found in a few clearly defined districts—Northwest Portland, the Fan District in Richmond, Inman Park and Ansley Park in Atlanta, Ghent and Colonial Place in Norfolk. Where citywide structures for neighborhood action have been developed, they are also potential allies with residents of working-class neighborhoods in which the cost-of-living squeeze is even more pressing.

In general terms, the program which these community activists pursue through neighborhood planning and associations can be characterized as "quality-of-life liberalism." They have read Jane Jacobs and have rejected the idea of large-scale interventionist planning in favor of preserving very special local values and advantages of their daily environments. If they lived in the suburbs, they would support the Sierra Club and work to limit community growth on the example of Boulder and Marin County. Within sunbelt cities, the same sorts of people join the Sierra Club and worry about access to recreational land and protection for the urban environment. Their concerns also support efforts to preserve and rehabilitate old housing and old neighborhoods, to slow the rapid turnover of population, and to promote stable racial integration. In recent years, mounting interest in these goals has also interacted with housing rehabilitation and community development programs that require geographically defined target areas.[3]

The growth of political power among black and Hispanic residents in sunbelt cities during the 1970s has complemented and amplified the impact of the middle-class neighborhood activists. During the decades of growth politics, the business establishment in cities from Norfolk to San Antonio to Phoenix tried to satisfy minority demands for participation in public decisions by consulting informally with community leaders and by slating single black or Hispanic leaders on citywide tickets for at-large council elections. Although minority residents were certainly dissatisfied with their subordinate citizenship, they traded their votes and sometimes their neighborhoods for gains in legal treatment, city jobs, and public housing. They also put much of their energy into civil rights issues, where power within city governments was less important than influence on state and national policies.

The late sixties and early seventies brought several changes in the tacit alliances. Younger minority politicans have replaced the generation of older leaders who ratified the deals with the "good government" establishment. As the costs of highway and renewal programs have mounted in minority communities, the newer leaders have argued that token representation brought no real influence on the outcomes of municipal decisions. They have also realized that geographical concentration in ghettos and barrios can work as a political resource. The same programs for targeting community improvement funds on low-income neighborhoods and the same structures of neighborhood decision making that environmental liberals have promoted and utilized can also be used for meeting needs of black and Hispanic citizens. The consequence in several cities has been a change in political allies for minority residents from growth-oriented whites to neighborhood-oriented whites.[4]

In the 1970s, black and Hispanic urbanites have been able to back this rejection of old political patterns with new power at the ballot box. During the forties and fifties, vigorous annexations and white immigration combined to hold the increase in the proportion of minority residents to a few percentage points in a number of cities and actually lowered the black percentage in Norfolk, Charlotte, Tampa, Birmingham, Memphis, Austin, and Tulsa. In the sixties, however, the slowing of annexation efforts and the continuing minority migration have brought sizeable increases in the minority share of central city populations in almost every southern and western metropolis. In addition, the Voting Rights Act of 1965 has provided a new tool for more effectively translating minority numbers into minority votes. One obvious result of the growing minority vote in the Sunbelt has been the election of black mayors in Chapel Hill, Raleigh, Los Angeles, Atlanta, New Orleans, and Birmingham. Another has been a turn or return to ward politics. In San Antonio, Fort Worth, Albuquerque, San Francisco, Atlanta, Richmond, and elsewhere, minority voters have helped to push through new city charters that provide for ward voting.

The remainder of this chapter looks in detail at the growing attention to the politics of neighborhood interest in southern and western cities. For Seattle, Portland, Denver, and several other cities, the neighborhood impulse has centered on the preservation of residential amenities and high-consumption styles of life. In cities like Richmond and Fort Worth, the mobilization of ethnic minorities has been the more important cause. Finally, the cases of Atlanta and San Antonio illustrate the simultaneous operation of neighborhood activism and ethnic assertion. The experiences of these two cities clearly demonstrate that ethnic minorities and quality-of-life liberals have both found it useful to promote and utilize the same political tools in order to challenge the dominance of the postwar growth coalition.

Seattle provides a clear example of the reordering of public goals toward the protection of individual neighborhoods. The characteristic project of the city in the urban renewal era was the World's Fair of 1962, a perfect example of urban boosterism designed to stimulate economic growth and to symbolize the modernity of Seattle with the Space Needle and the monorail. The ideology of growth also dominated city planning. The comprehensive plan of 1957 treated each of 100 neighborhood units as interchangeable components in an expanding city. The plan's chief goals were the expansion of the freeway network and the promotion of high density development. Indeed, the city altered its zoning ordinance in order to facilitate high-rise construction on every ridge and hilltop.[5]

Initial resistance to the growth schemes appeared in the later 1960s as highways and high rises did more and more damage to Seattle neighborhoods. In 1968, advocates of a set of expensive public works bond issues tried to broaden their base of support by earmarking 20 percent of the money for "critical neighborhoods" and organizing community councils to help plan the use of the proceeds. While a deepening economic crisis triggered by the decline of Boeing payrolls undermined confidence in the proponents of continued growth, Seattle residents turned toward the more subdued municipal goal of managed growth. In both black and white neighborhoods, community councils added to the expertise and confidence gained in the bond campaign and evolved from social clubs into partisans for neighborhood preservation.

The result in the first half of the 1970s was a wave of grass roots activity that changed the terms of Seattle politics. Over the protests of professional planners and city officials, the citizen revolt stopped the construction of three extra freeway links and saved the historic Pike Place Market from the wrecking ball through the use of the initiative and referendum. Neighborhood activists also forced the broadening of representation on appointive boards and commissions and dominated the citywide Commission on Goals for Seattle 2000, which met in

1972–73. At a time when sixty thousand workers were unemployed in the Boeing depression, community representatives ignored the official agenda and wrote what they pleased. In June 1973, the city council accepted a document that reversed the policies of the sixties by stressing the need for neighborhood influence on local decisions and the necessity to subordinate the demands of the automobile to the needs of neighborhoods.

The neighborhood revolt also transformed the city's elected leadership. Between 1967 and 1971, political reformers working through CHECC (Choose an Effective City Council) changed the composition of the council by electing members who typified the new quality-of-life liberal—bright and well-educated professionals who enjoyed the amenities of older neighborhoods and the pleasures of a vibrant downtown. The election and reelection of Mayor Wes Uhlman in 1970 and 1974 also reflected the new orientation of Seattle voters. Under Uhlman's direction, the city established nine "little city halls" to bring service delivery into the neighborhoods, created an Office of Neighborhood Planning, and brought housing and transportation planners together in an Office of Policy Planning. The Uhlman administration expanded the area covered by the Model Cities program in 1971, started work on twenty-two neighborhood improvement plans, and implemented neighborhood planning in six other areas with community development funds. The city ordinance that implements the State Environmental Policy Act also adds social and economic sections to the environmental impact statement required of city projects and makes them available to community groups.[6] Mayor Charles Royer has continued the Uhlman program since his election in 1978. A recent effort in the city council to divide the Office of Policy Planning among other agencies largely involved the question of whether bureaucrats or elected officials were the most legitimate spokesmen for the city's liberal policies.

At the least, the reorientation of Seattle government in the 1970s has produced what Roger Sale describes as a consumer's city designed to cater to the wants of the urbane liberal middle class. Certainly the spate of recent articles proclaiming Seattle as America's most livable city recognizes both its physical setting and its range of thriving middle-class neighborhoods. More broadly, Wes Uhlman has argued that the city government has made considerable progress in redirecting its programs to match the desires and perceptions of its citizens and in building self-confidence and competence in lower-status neighborhoods. Neighborhoods that work to develop consensus on issues of local concern now have considerable assurance that their desires will be honored by city officials. The result, he concludes, is a city that has discovered the possibilities of promoting and preserving the individuality of its component neighborhoods.

Neighborhood is as much a catchword in Portland as in Seattle because of the central role of Mayor Neil Goldschmidt. The customary route to membership on the Portland City Council has been to rise through the city hall bureaucracy or to build a career in downtown business. Goldschmidt, in contrast, worked for several years as a legal aid lawyer in the working-class communities of southeast Portland before undertaking successful races for city commissioner in 1970 and mayor in 1972 and 1976. His campaign rhetoric of neighborhood interest, neighborhood planning, and neighborhood preservation was so effective that it defined the theme for Portland politics in the 1970s. Every candidate for commissioner advocated "liveable neighborhoods" or "citizen organizations to keep neighborhood liveable," whereas liberals proposed the creation of a council of neighborhood leaders to function as a sort of lower house of the urban legislature.

Portland under Goldschmidt's direction followed the national trend in turning away from large-scale projects that threaten existing neighborhoods. In addition to the previously discussed decision to block the Mount Hood freeway, his administration shelved plans for the extension of the South Auditorium renewal project into the Victorian neighborhood of Lair Hill, which was designated as one of two historic conservation districts in 1977. The city's new policies emphasize the diversification of housing supply to hold a balanced population and the promotion of citizen participation in municipal decisions. Goldschmidt directly revitalized citizen advisory boards and developed a set of citizen budget advisory committees to work with individual bureaus. He also appointed community activists to the planning commission and added commissioners with a strong commitment to an expanded housing supply to the Portland Development Commission. Instead of massive clearance projects, the development commission is now active in historic preservation in downtown Portland and operates a model housing rehabilitation loan program.

The structure employed for incorporating neighborhood interests into the policy-making process centers on the Office of Neighborhood

Associations. The original idea as proposed for study by a citizen task force in 1971 was to copy the district planning organizations of San Diego and Fort Worth. Goldschmidt responded to the task force report in December 1972 by proposing funding for a bureau of neighborhood associations in the 1973–74 budget. The ordinance which emerged from public debate in 1974 dropped the idea of district organizations, that local activists feared would override the specific interests of individual neighborhoods. The new Office of Neighborhood Associations was designed, in the words of the city ordinance, "to provide standards and procedures whereby organized groups of citizens seeking to communicate with city officials and city bureaus on matters concerning neighborhood liveability may obtain assistance from staff . . . and to provide certain minimum standards for said organizations." The city requires neighborhood associations to be open in membership and to record minority as well as majority opinions. In return, the Office of Neighborhood Associations facilitates local activity, especially by providing a mechanism for introducing neighborhood shopping lists into the city budget process. The planning department also notifies neighborhood associations of zoning change requests and has worked with individual communities on downzoning proposals and district plans.

The office found approximately thirty active neighborhood groups on its establishment in 1974. The Community Action Program of the Office of Economic Opportunity had organized five neighborhoods in southeast Portland, the Model Cities had organized eight more in the black district of northeast Portland, and most other organizations had emerged from freeway or urban renewal fights during the previous decade. The total has doubled in more recent years as the several sections of the city have responded to specific needs and the Office of Neighborhood Associations has established area offices to assist grassroots action. Southeast Portland neighborhoods have concentrated on basic problems of housing rehabilitation and commercial zoning. The area office in northeast Portland operates out of a multiagency community center where it can help with neighborhood housing and economic development programs that carry on the thrust of Model Cities. Larger neighborhood groups in the newer communities of southwest Portland are now splintering into smaller associations to promote public involvement and to work on immediate street, drainage, and service delivery problems. The fiercely independent neighborhoods of north

Portland reflect that area's origin as an independent city and its long-standing feeling of neglect by city hall bureaucrats.[7]

Portland's suburbanites show a similar interest in promoting the individual identity of small communities. The small incorporated suburbs of Clackamas and Washington counties house antiregional newspapers such as the Tigard *Community News* and the Lake Oswego *Review* and elect booster councils that feud with county commissions over services, annexations, and the symbols of local control. Unincorporated communities in all three counties are equally committed to defending their independence from any annexation schemes that might be hatched either in Portland or in suburban cities. During the forties and fifties they followed the advice of antiurban legislatures by organizing special service districts to reduce the need for annexation or incorporation. The thirty-five fire protection districts, twenty-five sanitation districts, and twenty-two water districts created between 1941 and 1961 have provided a nucleus for local community identities. Consolidation of smaller districts into more efficient units in the 1970s under the impetus of the Metropolitan Boundary Commission has strengthened the independence of unincorporated communities by improving their quality of services. Periodic arguments for annexation or incorporation in such communities in Multnomah and Clackamas counties have met adamant resistance from the majority of residents who want to maintain neighborhood integrity.

At its most extreme, the agreement on the importance of neighborhood in metropolitan Portland has led to efforts to promote artificial community identities. The Multnomah County Planning Department in 1977 defined five communities of thirty thousand residents each as units for comprehensive planning and worked diligently to generate public interest in their futures. The expanded Metropolitan Service District is now directed by unpaid councilors elected from twelve districts that have been deliberately drawn to cut across existing political boundaries. Six districts include sections of two counties and three more straddle the line between Portland and Multnomah County. The intention is that the service district respond to the needs of historic or natural communities (of seventy-five thousand inhabitants) rather than to the demands of public bureaucracies. Many of the members of the first council chosen in November 1978 are community activists who have an established record of involvement in neighborhood associations rather than in traditional politics.[8]

The affirmation of neighborhood interest in Denver in the early 1970s was part of a statewide collapse of confidence in the progrowth policies of the 1950s and 1960s. The underlying concerns were mounting fears of California-style sprawl in Denver and other front range cities and of recreational overuse of the Rockies. The pivotal issue in 1972 was Denver's commitment to house the 1976 Winter Olympics. The business community and incumbent politicians including Governor John Love and Mayor William McNichols saw the acquisition of the Olympic Games as a symbol of progress capable of "breaking Denver from the shell of provincialism and catapulting it before the world as a truly international city." Fumbling leadership by the Denver Olympic Committee and cost estimates that rose from $14 million to $92 million, however, raised popular doubts and made it easy to obtain seventy-seven thousand signatures to add to the November ballot a state constitutional amendment and a Denver charter amendment forbidding further public funding for the Olympics. Under the direction of antiwar activist Sam Brown, Jr. and Denver State Senator Richard Lamm, the Citizens for Colorado's Future reiterated three points: that the primary beneficiaries of the Olympics would be the construction and recreation industries; that rising costs would mean higher taxes; and that serious damage would be done to the mountain environment. The margin against the Olympics was three to two statewide and similar in Denver. Two years later, Lamm easily won the governorship by advocating sensible growth to be achieved through land-use controls, the promotion of planned communities, and urban revitalization. He easily won a second term in 1978 against a Republican opponent whose major promise was to stop growth more effectively than Lamm.[9]

Beyond the vote on the Olympics, the effects of statewide quality-of-life rhetoric on Denver city politics have been ambiguous. Mayor McNichols has taken the "wrong" stand on many issues, but he was able to turn back the more liberal District Attorney Dale Tooley in 1971 and 1975 by associating the challenger with intracity busing for racial integration. In this instance, both middle-class Anglo-Americans and Mexican-Americans chose the business-oriented incumbent in order to defend specific neighborhood interests.[10] In the case of men like Bruce Rockwell, bank president and former chairman of the Urban Renewal Authority, members of the downtown establishment have also absorbed new ideas of historic preservation and acknowledge that "the bulldozer days are dead in Denver."[11] More generally, Denver's downtown elite can no longer expect automatically to implement its decisions, but they have not yet had to deal with a strong leader for the quality-of-life liberals comparable to Goldschmidt or Uhlman. Three of the most promising liberal leaders have so far chosen Washington careers, two in the House of Representatives (Patricia Schroeder, Tim Wirth) and one as director of ACTION (Sam Brown).

It is Denver's bureaucrats rather than its politicians who have been the more responsive to new public priorities. Recent planning documents give the sense that Denver is rejecting its mission to be a "continental city" and turning in on itself. The citizen advice program for community development spending is organized by councilmanic districts and gives city council members an explicit role. With growing doubts about their ability to influence land uses on a metropolitan scale, city planners have a greater interest in building on the advantages that the city retains. The planning commission and the community renewal program have both stressed the need to retain the physical amenities of clean air and open space and to protect existing residential neighborhoods. Particular emphasis has been given to conserving older neighborhoods and to rescuing the Platte River corridor from railroad tracks and old warehouses and using it for housing and park land. Perhaps symbolically, voters approved money for mass transit in 1973 while rejecting downtown parking garages beloved by McNichols. Certainly residents have repeatedly declared to pollsters that their most pressing worries are sprawl and air pollution, both of whose solutions involve the promotion of older central city neighborhoods.[12]

San Diego and Charleston have also earned extensive attention for broadly based efforts to establish new priorities among municipal programs. Pete Wilson won election as mayor of San Diego in 1971 and 1975 on a platform of managed growth and long-range comprehensive planning as an alternative to the sprawl of the 1960s. Much like residents of Denver and Portland, San Diegans who fear the transformation of their town into a second "Smogsville" now prefer to forget the old slogan of "City in Motion" and to emphasize residential amenities by calling themselves "America's Finest City." Charleston offers another example where new political leadership in the later 1970s has added a concern for neighborhood planning and participation to a long-standing interest in historic preservation.[13]

As final examples of the fading of growth policies, Albuquerque and San Francisco also show several of the factors involved in the replacement of neoprogressives in city hall by quality-of-life liberals. As early as 1966, the disaffection of Hispanic voters and a lack of imaginative leadership combined to defeat Albuquerque's Citizens Committee after twelve years of control. A shift of attention from metropolitan issues to internal municipal concerns came in 1973, when county voters defeated a proposal to consolidate Albuquerque and Bernalillo County and when city voters replaced their commission-manager charter with a new council-mayor government involving ward elections. The city adopted its first comprehensive plan in 1975 and capped its rejection of the traditional "bigger is better" approach by electing Mayor David Rusk in 1977 on a platform of support for comprehensive planning, downtown revitalization, public transit, neighborhood preservation, and opposition to leapfrog development.[14] In San Francisco, a characteristic "culture of civility" through the 1960s and early 1970s had helped to divert attention from the dominance of city government by a coalition of professional politicians such as Joseph Alioto and urban renewal advocates from San Francisco corporations. Resistance to the Yerba Buena project as described in chapter six anticipated the electoral defeat of the political establishment in 1976, when George Moscone won a narrow victory for mayor with votes from white-collar liberals, homosexuals, Latinos, and blacks. The adoption of district elections for board of supervisors in the same year allowed direct representation for the sections of the city that house its large minority and homosexual populations.[15] The repeal of district representation in a special election in August 1980, was a reaction to the deep social divisions revealed by the city's politics in the last two years.

Given the nature of American society, it is not surprising that the increase of political influence for minority communities has been more stressful than the self-assertion of middle-class white neighborhoods. In Richmond, for example, the superficial appearance of a typical New South city has masked a painful political revolution. Draped on a bluff overlooking the James River, the city presents an impressive skyline with dozens of new downtown buildings. At lunch hour, the crowds of secretaries and junior executives who stream into its downtown streets make it obvious that two-thirds of its jobs come from light industry, government, wholesaling, and finance. Behind the glass and steel surface, however, Richmond is an intensely conservative town whose white residents worship the granite generals of the Confederacy who stand guard over parks and street corners. In the highly mobile United States, Richmond is an anomaly. Only 20 percent of its population in 1970 was born in another state, and most of these newcomers were southerners. The city ranks far behind northern Virginia in average wealth, but within the South it stands third behind Palm Beach and Boca Raton. In the West End of Richmond is Windsor Park, a maze of winding streets and turn-of-the-century mansions, that is the wealthiest neighborhood in urban Virginia. Its average family income in 1970 was nearly fifty thousand dollars, and its residents fill the old clubs and run the city's important institutions.

Downtown and West End define the centers of political power in Richmond. The early 1960s witnessed a limited "managerial revolution" triggered by annoyance with sluggish municipal government and the eight to one defeat of a downtown urban renewal program by the city council in August 1963. Members of the city's business elite—men who worked by day in the rising office towers and who slept by night under the spacious roofs of Windsor Park—organized Richmond Forward to do something about the lack of progress. Backers of the group—major banks, the Chamber of Commerce, the Retail Merchant's Association—advocated expressways, urban renewal, and a downtown coliseum against the opposition of a scattering of liberals and the supporters of the status quo "Richmond philosophy." The new buildings, the scars of redevelopment bulldozers and highway construction, and the continued prosperity of the central business district all bear witness to the success of Richmond promoters in accomplishing their goals.

One of the keys to the success of Richmond Forward was the support of black voters. Since 1958, the Crusade for Voters has attempted to represent the interests of the black community. In return for black seats on the city council (three of nine in 1966), it backed the candidates of the business community in 1964 and 1966. Richmond's middle-class black leadership also exchanged a conciliatory approach for a fair employment ordinance for the municipal government, desegregation of parks and hotels, and initial steps toward integration of public schools. The school board took its first steps toward integration under the leadership of Lewis F. Powell, Jr., now himself a member of the United States Supreme Court. By the middle of the 1960s, editor Virginius Dabney of the Richmond *Times-Dispatch* could point with pride to Richmond's "quiet revolution" as "an example of how sane, level-headed, peaceable and dedicated white and Negro leadership can achieve impressive results on the interracial front in a short time, without stirring up the ferocious animosities that could rob any apparent gains of all meaning."[16]

In the past ten years, the tone of racial relations has changed. While the city's publicists exclaim about its minimal unemployment, black residents look sourly at black unemployment rates over 10 percent. The city elects five delegates to the lower house of the general assembly. None of them is one of the city's 105,000 blacks. For elections to the state Senate, Richmond is split into two districts. The affluent Westenders regularly returned Senator Edward Willey, chairman of the Senate Finance Committee and a pillar of Virginia conservatism in the Senate since 1952. The eastern half of the city since 1970 elected Douglas Wilder, a black lawyer whom the Senate establishment met on arrival with studied snubs.

The most explosive political issue in recent years has also focused on the relations between the two races. The trouble started in 1970, when Richmond annexed 23 square miles of Chesterfield County to incorporate 43,000 whites and 4,000 blacks into the central city. Frightened by what they saw as a Richmond land grab, the suburbanites of Chesterfield and Henrico counties sought incorporation as independent cities at the same time that Richmond requested further annexations. The result the following year was a decision by the General Assembly temporarily to block further changes in boundaries or status. In response the Richmond School Board requested the merger of Richmond, Henrico, and Chesterfield schools into a single district. The merger was decreed on 10 January 1972, by federal Judge Robert Mehrige, who found that only by consolidation of city and suburban schools could integrated education be provided for Richmond school children, 68 percent of whom are black. Although the Supreme Court finally reversed the consolidation order by tie vote in 1974, the controversy aroused bitter fears on the part of white suburbanites.

Richmond blacks at the same time challenged the 1970 annexation in the courts. After a defeat in the 1971 elections for city council, black candidate Curtis Holt filed a suit charging that the addition of thousands of white voters the year before had effectively disfranchised Richmond blacks and assured white control of the city. In 1972 the Supreme Court blocked further city elections until the case could be decided. That action, ironically, confirmed in office the 1971 council, seven of whom were white and most of whom represented the downtown business interests. At the same time that white suburbanites fear to be tied to central city problems and blacks fear the dilution of their own voting power, the Richmond elite advocates the continued expansion of city limits in order to protect downtown investments from an uncertain future. In 1976, federal courts upheld the 1970 annexation but also mandated a system of ward rather than at-large representation on the city council. In March 1977 the first municipal election in seven years gave blacks five of the nine seats and resulted in the choice of Henry L. Marsh as Richmond's first black mayor.[17]

Fort Worth is another sunbelt city in which structural changes in local government have reflected the growing importance of minority residents. Through the 1960s, a number of Negro candidates attempted the city's at-large elections for city council, but none were able to build adequate support in a city that was only one-fifth black and Hispanic. The first step toward greater political involvement by ordinary citizens was the town hall movement of the mid-sixties, a "good government" effort to expand the base of city politics through mass meetings, study committees, and neighborhood conferences. In 1969, the city administration divided Fort Worth into eleven neighborhoods and implemented district planning. The neighborhood planning groups have remained active to oversee implementation even after the acceptance of the last district plan in 1976. The further step in the direction of neighborhood politics in the seventies has been the adoption of single-member districts for city council.

Structural changes have led to significant alterations in the tone of Fort Worth politics. In the fifties and sixties, the "business and professional gentry" set the agenda of issues, even if they were not always able to persuade voters to fund urban renewal efforts. Under the revised charter, the Human Relations Commission has been an equally important access point for political careers. The two black and one Hispanic members of the 1978 council were all former human relations chairpersons, and the city's minority residents are represented on the council roughly in proportion to their 30 percent share of Fort Worth populations. Although the rapidly changing political leadership in the city has not reached consensus on a positive program, the recent resignation of a long-term city manager indicates that Fort Worth has had enough of neutral and businesslike administration in the interests of downtown establishment.[18]

The politics of neighborhood interest in Atlanta emerged directly from dissatisfaction with the spectacular transportation and redevelopment programs of William Hartsfield, Ivan Allen, and their big business colleagues. Very specifically, black Atlantans decided at the end of the sixties that their own establishment of Auburn Street merchants, bank and insurance executives, and university presidents had given up more than they had gained in the urban renewal coalition. Blacks had certainly done well in teaching and government employment and occupied two-fifths of available city positions, but they were also excluded from lucrative unionized jobs on city construction projects. Figures on the reduction of the city's housing supply also showed the problems with closed-door decisions. Between 1957 and 1967, the city erected 5,000 units of public housing. Renewal and public construction simultaneously destroyed 21,000 dwelling units. Most of the 67,000 displaced residents were blacks from core communities who had little choice but to crowd other black neighborhoods or to force racial turnover in previously white communities.[19]

The steady increase in the black share of Atlanta's population from 38 percent in 1960 to 51 percent in 1970 provided the political resource for transforming dissatisfaction into action. The first black alderman was elected under the city's system of at-large voting for district representatives in 1965, the same year as Ivan Allen's overwhelming victory for mayor. The limited black support that helped to defeat the first MARTA referendum in 1968 was also a preview of the mayoral campaign of 1969. Observers initially viewed the victory of Sam Massell over Rodney Cook as the end of a political era in Atlanta. As the lackluster "chamber-of-commerce candidate," Cook was unable to hold together Allen's several bases of support. Massell, who had been active in the promotion of minority interests while vice-mayor, drew 92 percent of the black vote along with 27 percent of the white vote. The city simultaneously increased the number of black aldermen from one to five out of eighteen and elected Maynard Jackson as vice-mayor with the backing of 98 percent of the black voters and 33 percent of the northside whites.[20]

Massell's administration was less revolutionary than expected. During the first three years of the seventies, Massell promoted MARTA, applauded the continued real estate boom, and pushed for the construction of I-485, a freeway connector that promised to gut a half-dozen neighborhoods on the near east side. He also introduced to and lobbied the legislature for the annexation of large parts of Fulton County in order to dilute the city's black electorate with suburban whites. In response to Massell's efforts to reinvigorate the growth program of the sixties, younger black leaders began to identify their own agenda for public action. In particular, they offered to trade support of the annexation for a charter change under which nine of the eighteen aldermen would be elected *in and by* districts. As previously described, they also drove a hard bargain for black support of the second MARTA referendum in 1971.[21]

During the same years of the late 1960s and early 1970s, stubborn advocacy of I-485 by the downtown business establishment helped to generate increasing activism in white neighborhoods. The leaders of the antifreeway campaign since 1965 had been the neighborhood association for Morningside–Lenox Park, an established middle-class community dating from the turn of the century. By delaying the project with court challenges to its environmental impact statement, Morningside–Lenox Park created enough time to add the support of other affected neighborhoods such as Virginia Highlands. Inman Park was another older white community that enjoyed a revival of popularity among quality-of-life liberals at the start of the seventies. Together, these and other affected neighborhoods formed the core for an informal coalition of neighborhoods and were able effectively to kill the freeway in 1973.[22]

As with the development of an independent political agenda for black Atlanta, the increase of neighborhood militancy reflected the demography of the city in the seventies. From Grant Park and Inman Park to Virginia Highlands and Ansley Park, an entire tier of neighborhoods on the east side of Atlanta have become targets for reinvestment by a new generation of urbanites who are attracted by the older homes and amenities of mature trees, parks, and access to downtown. What is striking about these neighborhoods is not that they have attracted suburbanites back to the city, but that they are holding city residents who previously would have moved to the suburbs as they built careers and families. In effect, these quality-of-life liberals have stabilized many Atlanta neighborhoods by replacing earlier residents with a new generation of middle-class homeowners. In turn, however, they expect city policies to meet their own needs by reducing the growth pressures that have historically caused neighborhoods to cycle from middle-class white occupancy to black occupancy to reuse for commercial, institutional, or transportation facilities.[23]

It was the municipal election of 1973 that brought together the trends toward black militancy and neighborhood activism to produce a basic change in Atlanta politics. With a shaky base of support, Sam Massell tried to turn his reelection contest with Maynard Jackson into a confrontation over race. Jackson countered by campaigning on the promise of increased citizen participation and consultation with neighborhoods. Jackson's majority of 59 percent approximately reassembled the same coalition that had elected Massell four years previously, including 95 percent of black voters and 18 percent of white voters. Neighborhood activists also applied their organizing skills to several city council races. The new city charter created a city council of twelve districts with Councilmen elected from each district and six paired districts with Councilmen from each pair elected at large. The new council split evenly among blacks and whites, while the new school board had a majority of five blacks to four whites.[24]

One of the first responsibilities of Maynard Jackson's administration was to implement the new city charter. As shaped by extensive public hearings in 1971 and 1972, the charter rejected the idea of neighborhood councils but did express the goals of community activists by requiring neighborhood roles in the development of one, five, and fifteen year plans for the city. In a first effort to carry out the requirement in 1974, the Department of Budget and Planning identified 190 neighborhoods which met the city's definition as "a geographic area either with distinguishing characteristics or in which the residents have a sense of identity and a commonality of perceived interest, or both." Since the sophistication and degree of organization in these neighborhoods varied widely, the response to an invitation to submit suggestions for incorporation into citywide plans proved too uneven to be useful. After complex bargaining among the mayor, council members, and neighborhoods, the city in 1975 established twenty-four neighborhood planning units that grouped sets of neighborhoods and that cut across the boundaries of council districts. Council members reserved for themselves the job of organizing the twenty-four neighborhood planning committees, most of which have been set up with specific slots for representatives from local businesses and from individual neighborhoods. The Department of Budget and Planning at the same time established a well-staffed Division of Neighborhood Planning to help the planning committees define their needs and to integrate neighborhood plans into the citywide land-use plan and capital budget.[25] Because of the pressures of inflation, unfortunately, the Neighborhood Planning Unit staff has shrunk from twenty members in its first year to six members in 1980.

Atlanta's new charter has also established an ongoing framework for neighborhood politics in providing for the election of two-thirds of the council members by districts. The broad question that remains for the 1980s is whether the city itself will have the resources to promote the stability that is the central goal of the new political agenda. Maynard Jackson proclaimed in 1974 that "in Atlanta . . . the overwhelming concern is the preservation of our neighborhoods," and many of its rehabilitated neighborhoods are national examples. However, whites have continued to move from undiscovered and unfashionable older neighborhoods to the suburbs, lowering the city's population from 495,000 to 425,000 between 1970 and 1976 and raising its black-white ratio toward 60/40. Of all the major sunbelt cities, Atlanta stands at the greatest social and economic disadvantage in relation to its suburban ring. The new administration also had to cope with a temporary collapse of the market for downtown real estate in the middle 1970s and with the implementation problems for MARTA. The opening of MARTA's east-west rail line has recently benefitted downtown retailing, but Jackson at times has found himself suggesting the need for annexations and touring Europe to attract new investment in the best style of the Atlanta sixties.[26]

If the emergence of neighborhood politics in Atlanta was a response to the mounting costs of downtown growth and downtown growth policies, the essential factor in San Antonio has been a breathless drive to develop new communities on the northern edge of the city. The American war in Indochina brought flush times to San Antonio in the later 1960s after two decades of moderate growth. The metropolitan area added 200,000 residents between 1965 and 1974, most of whom found their housing in new subdivisions and apartment complexes around the northern quadrant of interstate loop I-410. The expansion of a suburban medical center including four hospitals and the University of Texas Medical School, the relocation of the city's largest private employer just outside the I-410 loop, a decision in 1970 to build a new University of Texas campus eight miles beyond I-410, and the proposal of a 9,300-acre San Antonio Ranch new town twelve miles outside the freeway loop all focused attention in the early seventies on the far northwestern fringe. Planning department projections in 1976 indicated that a continuation of existing trends through the last quarter of the century could bring a decline of 8,000 residents within I-410 and an increase of 310,000 residents in the outlying sections of Bexar County, four-fifths of whom would locate northeast, north, or northwest of the old core of San Antonio. Retail and office expansion have also concentrated almost exclusively along the northern segment of I-410 since 1970.[27]

The geographical imbalance of growth in San Antonio has provided the central issues for city politics during the past decade. Because of San Antonio's vigorous and successful annexation policy, the entire range of sociospatial conflicts that typically arise in a fast-growing metropolis have been fought within the framework of city politics. Disputes and clashes of interest between downtown property owners and housing developers, between residents of older middle-class neighborhoods and new subdivisions, and between the Mexican-American community of the inner west side and the Anglo-American communities of the north side have all centered on issues of city planning and zoning, the geographical allocation of public services, and the equitable sharing of public costs among different sections of the city. In consequence, the evolution of neighborhood politics in San Antonio has involved not only the demand for participation at the neighborhood level but also bitter battles among the city's neighborhoods and sections over the issues of land use and service levels that lie at the heart of local government. The situation differs significantly from Atlanta, where quality-of-life liberals and blacks were able to agree on a common agenda of structural reforms and substantive policies. In San Antonio the adoption of district elections to facilitate community representation has provided a formal structure through which different sections of the city can pursue widely divergent goals and demands.

One of the unanticipated results of San Antonio's headlong growth was a deep split within the San Antonio business community that destroyed the Good Government League between 1973 and 1975. After twenty years of control, the GGL collapsed under the weight of its own age and its inability to bridge the growing gap between older and newer neighborhoods. Residents of the old north side around Hildebrand Avenue and Breckinridge Park had an interest in preserving the amenities and market value of established Anglo communities. Many of them were also involved in downtown businesses and downtown real estate. Developers, retailers, and homeowners of the new north side around I-410, in contrast, had an insatiable demand for public investment in schools, libraries, roads, sewers, fire stations, and all the other paraphernalia of suburban growth. In the early seventies, businessmen in this new north side organized the North San Antonio Chamber of Commerce to speak for their own particular interests as an alternative to the Greater San Antonio Chamber of Commerce. At the same time, the Good Government League failed to reach out to a younger generation of business and professional leaders or to rethink its proven electoral strategy.[28]

The open break came over two very specific questions of city policy toward peripheral growth. Councilman Charles Becker and Mayor John Gatti, both of whom had been elected on the GGL ticket, split in the fall of 1971 over city approval for the San Antonio Ranch new town, with Becker loudly upholding the virtues of headlong suburban growth. A year later, the city council annexed sixty-five square miles of northside land and 55,000 north-side residents against the bitter opposition of several suburban real estate tycoons. Since the GGL now seemed clearly identified with efforts to control the pace and direction of peripheral growth to the benefit of the old north side, subdividers were more than happy to fund an independent challenge to the GGL ticket by Charles Becker and four of his allies. The election results in April 1973 amounted to a political revolution in which Becker and his running mates took a majority of five council seats, an independent Mexican-American candidate took one seat, and candidates endorsed by the GGL took only three positions. During the next two years, Mayor Becker and his "Texas A&M clique" of enthusiastic land developers kept the door of city hall open for the shopping center magnates and home builders who were busily reshaping the scrublands on the far north side of San Antonio. City Manager Sam Granata, promoted from the Public Works Department by Becker's administration, committed the city to every request for the extension of utilities to serve new subdivisions.[29]

The other remarkable reaction to the boom in San Antonio was a growing demand by the Mexican-American residents of the west side for a fair share in the prosperity. By any standards, many of the west-side neighborhoods were classic examples of low-rise slums. Since the 1930s and 1940s, observers had agreed on a common description of poverty, dilapidated housing, and unemployment. As late as 1970, the thirty-five census tracts with at least 70 percent Mexican-American population (227,864 residents) ranked far below the twenty-five San Antonio tracts with at least 70 percent Anglo population (147,081 residents). In the west-side barrio, 27.1 percent of families were below the poverty level, 13.5 percent of the housing units lacked proper plumbing, and median income was $5,803. In the Anglo neighborhoods of the north side, only 4.8 percent of families were below poverty level, only 1.7 percent of the housing was substandard, and median income was $11,958. Even these census figures overstate the relative wealth of the west side, for the barrio also houses tens of thousands of uncounted and sometimes illegal migrant workers whom public officials find it convenient to ignore.[30]

Beyond the frustrations of poverty and unemployment, west-side residents harbored long-standing grievances about the inadequacy of public services. It was west-side streets that the city had never paved or neglected to repair. It was the low-lying west-side neighborhoods that lacked both storm sewers or sanitary sewers. Although representatives of the Good Government League argued that they had taken serious steps in the late 1960s to deal with the inadequacy of physical facilities, unequal treatment also extended to less obvious aspects of service quality. Parks on the west side were more likely than elsewhere in the city to be poorly maintained fields without recreational equipment. Fire stations on the west side had older equipment and less experienced crews. The zoning commission was more willing to preserve Anglo-American residential neighborhoods against commercial encroachment than to offer the same protection to west-side residents.[31]

The undeniable inequities in the allocation of city services became the issue that mobilized Mexican-American voters in 1974 and 1975. The catalyst was a flash flood on 7 August 1974 that drowned large sections of the west side in the runoff from the Anglo-American highlands. The organization that was available to channel the frustration into a positive program was Communities Organized for Public Service (COPS), a coalition of west-side neighborhood groups and parishes that had slowly grown over the past year with the assistance of the Catholic archdiocese and the facilitation of community organizer

Ernesto Cortes. Following the strategy that Cortes had learned at Saul Alinsky's Industrial Areas Foundation in Chicago, COPS defined a list of very specific grievances, dug out hard supporting data, and pursued its demands through loud and persistent confrontations with decision makers. Its first significant success was to force City Manager Granata to agree to attend a public assembly on the west side by packing a city council meeting. When he arrived at the previously arranged meeting on 13 August Granata found 500 westsiders who were more than ready to talk about the lack of storm sewers. The direct result was the passage in November of a bond issue for $47 million to implement a drainage plan that had mildewed on the shelf since 1945. Over the next several months, COPS took on issues ranging from unsafe street corners to the regulation of junk yards to the allocation of community development funds. Although COPS did not take a direct role, the attenuation of the GGL and the vulnerability of Charles Becker opened the opportunity for the election to the city council in April 1975 of an independent black, two independent Latinos, and a third Mexican-American who soon ignored his GGL endorsement. The Good Government League formally dissolved early in 1976, at the same time that COPS was forcing changes in previously unexamined policies of the city water board.[32]

The keys to the continued success of COPS through the second half of the seventies have been self-respect and respect. The majority of COPS members have come from the Mexican-American middle class. They belong to church-going, achievement-oriented families with steady but limited incomes from small businesses or federal jobs. The organization of COPS as a federation of several dozen community locals that set policies through a monthly congress of delegates is designed to check a tendency toward grandstanding that has weakened Mexican-American leadership. COPS has been particularly successful in utilizing the talents of Hispanic women who would never before have considered public involvement beyond church groups and PTA meetings. As homeowners who may still be paying off mortgages acquired in 1953, COPS members want the same services that are taken for granted in San Antonio's Anglo-American neighborhoods. In a number of its battles with bureaucrats and businessmen, COPS has thought it more important to gain recognition as an equal in the bargaining process than to achieve specific goals.[33] By the end of the decade, professionals in the city government were usually willing to treat COPS representatives as colleagues rather than troublemakers. A noisy dispute in 1977 and 1978 between COPS and the San Antonio Economic Development Foundation, a privately funded industrial recruitment agency, was motivated by a similar desire to break into the closed circle of north-side friends and neighbors who have made all of San Antonio's basic economic decisions.

The council elections of April 1973 and April 1975 introduced the north-side suburbs and an independent west side as powerful political forces offering two sharply differing alternatives to the GGL program for city government. Two months later, the San Antonio Planning Department focused public debate on a single issue by submitting an *Alternative Growth Study* that evaluated the fiscal impacts of different metropolitan growth patterns. The report systematically argued that there was a fundamental conflict between public and private interests, since the bulk of the peripheral land that promised the highest profits to real estate developers also carried the highest capital and operating costs for water supply, bus service, sewage, drainage, gas, and electricity. It also pointed out that the existing trend toward further growth north of I-410 would bring heavy development over the recharge zone for the Edwards Aquifer and thereby threaten to contaminate the groundwater reservoir from which San Antonio drew its water. In careful summation, the report argued that the public costs of contiguous growth are substantially less than leapfrog growth and that Bexar County can house its projected population while protecting its considerable natural and historic resources.[34]

In the short term, north-side developers, the North San Antonio Chamber of Commerce, and construction unions blocked substantive consideration of the *Alternative Growth Study* by the city council. City Manager Granata also fired the report's author, Charles Stromberg, at the suggestion of three council members.[35] In November, however, the same council provided an opportunity for testing public sentiment by voting five to four on a rezoning petition to allow a huge shopping mall to be built in a location that would have promoted growth over the groundwater recharge area. The response was led by the Aquifer Protection Association. The APA membership ranged from retired doctors and military officers to younger quality-of-life liberals, but its greatest strength lay in the older middle-class neighborhoods of the near north side that had supplied the heart of the GGL constituency in the previous generation. A newspaper ad with cutout petitions brought in fifty thousand signatures calling for a special referendum on the rezoning.[36] After a week of debate, COPS also joined the fight for managed growth, since demands for public investment in new suburban neighborhoods reduced the money available to pave west-side streets and build west-side sewers.[37] The result on 17 January 1976 was an overwhelming victory for environmental protection by a margin of 78 percent to 22 percent, giving the council little option but to reverse its decision.

The establishment of district council elections in 1977 was a formal recognition that the locus of power in San Antonio had shifted from a business establishment which claimed to speak for the city as a whole to individual sections and neighborhoods within the city. As early as 1972–73, the Mexican-American Legal Defense and Education Fund (MALDEF) had successfully used the federal courts to replace multimember legislative districts with single member districts in Dallas and San Antonio.[38] Because the GGL had carefully balanced its tickets with safe black and Hispanic candidates, it had been more difficult to prove the discriminatory effects of at-large council elections. In 1975, however, Congress extended the 1965 Voting Rights Act to cover Texas. MALDEF immediately challenged the 1972 annexations on the grounds that the addition of 55,000 Anglo-American residents diluted the influence of Mexican-American voters on their city government. In April 1976 the Justice Department disallowed voting in the annexed areas, an action that not only disfranchised thousands of San Antonians but also threatened the city's ability to market its bonds. Under federal pressure, the city council developed an acceptable ten-one plan under which the mayor would be elected at large and each of ten councilmen from separate districts. The plan passed on 15 January 1977 with 51 percent of the total vote. The organized opposition came from development and real estate interests, the most active support from COPS. The north-side vote was 20–1 against the new charter with every precinct north of Hildebrand voting no. The vote on the west side was 20 to 1 in support. The first election under the new charter in May 1977 resulted in a council evenly balanced among five Mexican-Americans, one black, and five Anglo-Americans (including Mayor Lila Cockrell).[39]

Growth policy and service quality have remained the central issues in San Antonio under the new charter, with positions clearly defined in terms of neighborhood interests. Indeed, the first important action of the new council on 10 June 1977 was to adopt an eighteen-month moratorium on the issuance of building permits, extension of utilities, acceptance of subdivision plans, and zoning changes in the aquifer recharge zone. The vote placed the three north-side districts in opposition to the council majority. When developers responded with lawsuits totaling $1.5 billion, the city engaged an environmental law consultant and replaced the moratorium on 1 September with an interim development control ordinance designed to channel a portion of expected growth away from the northern suburbs. Development control thus meets the needs of San Antonio's Hispanic majority and of its smaller black community on the east side by promising more money for neglected neighborhoods. It also meets the interests of the city's small but growing contingent of quality-of-life liberals by freeing more resources and centering more attention on downtown San Antonio and on a scattering of older neighborhoods that have begun to feel the nationwide rehabilitation boom.

More detailed implementation of growth control policies in the next decade will depend on the acceptance and utilization of the city's proposed comprehensive plan. The detailed plan was written in 1977, 1978, and 1979 within the guidelines of a *San Antonio Growth Sketch* which was adopted by the planning commission and the city council in March 1977. The central goals of the growth sketch meet the basic demands of the city's environmentalists and ethnic communities as articulated in the political battles of 1975 and 1976: "To promote growth for the City maintaining or restoring viability of existing neighborhoods, preventing decline, and encouraging steady, contiguous development. To conserve natural and man-made resources. To revitalize the older neighborhoods in order to maximize use of existing public and private capital improvements and investments, and to preserve and enhance the unique, multicultural historic qualities which have made San Antonio great." To achieve these goals, the growth sketch suggested that most new housing be located inside I-410 (80,000 units) and on the north-side periphery south of the aquifer recharge zone (90,000 units).[40] The plan itself has been prepared in terms of eighteen development sectors that can serve as units for neighborhood planning after the adoption of the plan.

The political process that has led from the aquifer referendum to the growth sketch, development moratorium, and comprehensive plan has clearly been a chain of defeats for north-side development interests. Lila Cockrell's defeat of Charles Becker in the 1979 mayoral election confirmed the loss of direct political power by the northsiders, who can expect over the near future to come up at least one short on crucial votes in the city council. Although the Chamber of Commerce may still decide to oppose the comprehensive plan, the more effective strategy for development-oriented businessmen has been to bypass city elections and consolidate control of independent special-purpose agencies. Through most of the 1970s, for example, San Antonio could expect to decide important decisions made by the Alamo Area Council of Governments (AACOG), the regional planning agency. With the change of direction at city hall that accompanied the new charter, San Antonio's major developers used their statewide influence to remove important regional planning responsibilities from AACOG to ad hoc committees under their own control. In 1977, Governor Dolph Briscoe took regional transportation planning away from AACOG and assigned it to the Steering Committee of the San Antonio and Bexar County Transportation Study, in which development interests have a dominant voice. Briscoe also intervened in a bitter dispute over water quality planning that pitted AACOG and San Antonio against county politicians backed by real estate developers. The authority to influence development patterns by deciding the location of new sewer facilities is now in the hands of another ad hoc committee chaired by H. B. Zachry, the president of the largest construction firm in south Texas.[41]

The issue of service equity has also remained very much alive within the new context of San Antonio's neighborhood politics. In early 1978, a special Bond Steering Committee with one citizen member from each council district put together a $98.4 million package whose essential component was to be funding for west-side and south-side drainage projects. Initial opposition was limited to two north-side council members who complained that their districts were to receive less than an equitable tenth of the funds. By the time of the bond election on 4 March increasingly vehement rhetoric converted the referendum into a vote of confidence in the city's six minority council members. Although north-side opponents explicitly worried about the costs to the city treasury, the underlying theme was racist backlash against the political success of Mexican-Americans. Indeed, the aquifer liberals showed little interest in reciprocal support for the westsiders who had helped with the shopping center referendum and the growth control ordinance. For COPS and for Chicano politicians, the bonds were both a practical proposal and a symbolic issue that linked directly to the flood of 1974. Both sides fought the bond election in terms of effects on neighborhood and sectional interests rather than value for the city as a whole. When the votes were counted, the issue had lost by a three to two margin, with strong support in the ethnic precincts nullified by heavy turnout and solid opposition on the north side.[42]

Over the next decade, San Antonio will have to learn the rules as well as the opportunities of neighborhood politics. With district council elections, the issues of growth and services will continue to be debated in terms of the frequently conflicting desires of older Anglo neighborhoods, west-side neighborhoods, and outlying north-side neighborhoods. If the first two years are an accurate preview, the ten districts will also allow the expression of differing points of view within these broad sociospatial groupings. Especially on the west side, it may be difficult to distinguish issue-based politics from personal politics. In the midst of short-range arguments and shifting alliances within the city council, it will be worth remembering that the politics of neighborhood interest developed in San Antonio as in other cities not only to satisfy specific local needs but also to counterbalance the disproportionate influence of commercial club cliques.

The politics of neighborhood interest has emerged out of deepening concern about the side effects of metropolitan growth. The most obvious problem has been land clearance for downtown renewal and highways that has destroyed old neighborhoods and forced poorer citizens to play a game of "musical houses." The broader desire has been to gain public consideration of interests and values ignored by the urban renewal coalition. Members of the Anglo-American middle class have thus sought small-scale planning and the recognition of neighborhood associations in order to preserve specific advantages of residential communities. Minority leaders have promoted community planning organizations and ward voting to achieve equitable representation in municipal decisions.

The development of new structures for the expression of sociospatial differences within sunbelt cities has meant a partial alteration of the values and structures previously promoted by neoprogressive coalitions. Since most southern and western cities held elections at large in the fifties and sixties, the decision for ward voting has been a specific and explicit reversal of policies. The underlying assumptions of the urban renewal coalition have been challenged by the insistence that there are legitimate localized interests that are not accommodated by the concept of the public good as interpreted by major property owners. At the same time, Atlanta and Portland show that new attention to neighborhoods does not necessarily require the repudiation of city and metropolitan growth.

To carry the contrast further, Zane Miller has recently suggested that the 1970s may mark a fundamental divide in the way Americans view their cities. Since the turn of the century, the dominant conception has been that the metropolis is an organic entity whose citizens have primary responsibility to promote the well-being of the whole. Progressive and neoprogressive beliefs in the importance of efficient metropolitan government and the need to promote the common public interest were the practical applications of this conception. In recent years, however, Miller argues that the recognition of limits to metropolitan growth and public resources has supported a new definition of the city as "a community of advocacy for scarce resources and for personal, group, and local autonomy."[43] In such competition, spatially localized groups have significant advantages over groups that lack a spatial focus. Spatially localized groups that are able to work through a recognized governmental entity such as a ward, a neighborhood planning unit, or a suburban municipality have a further advantage. The result, as indicated earlier, is the emergence of the competitive politics of metropolitan pluralism.

In another point of view, the political developments of the 1970s represent a maturing process that has brought the urban pattern of the Sunbelt closer to older northeastern cities in which the concept of an urban mosaic has been implicit in the geographic segregation of classes and ethnic groups. With increasing age, previously homogeneous southern and western cities also find their internal differences more salient. Because sunbelt cities have relatively few career officeholders, entrenched public employee unions, or long-established bureaucratic fiefdoms, however, their municipal leaders have been more willing than in older cities to welcome the development of neighborhood interests. A number of politicians such as Neil Goldschmidt and Maynard Jackson built citywide careers as advocates of neighborhoods. The evolving profession of neighborhood advocate or planner, as in the National Conference of Neighborhood Organizations, seems to be particularly strong in the South and West.

At the same time, the politics of neighborhood interest has several problematic aspects that await determination in the 1980s. One key for the future will be the degree to which cities will be able to maintain access to sufficient resources to prevent confrontation among their neighborhoods. Recent developments in San Diego and other cities, for example, suggest that "frills" such as neighborhood preservation and neighborhood planning may be early targets for municipal austerity programs. A second key to the future of both neighborhood politics and the politics of suburban independence is the degree to which satisfaction of specific local needs can be integrated with larger metropolitan needs.

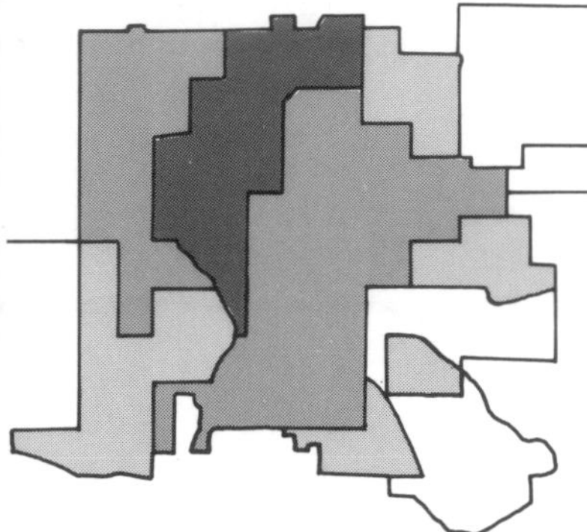

Chapter 10

Urban Growth and Politics in the American Sunbelt

Symbols for the new urban world of the American Sunbelt are available at every hand. The launching pads of Cape Canaveral and the nearby megastructures of Disney World seem to summarize the character of the high-technology and amenities-oriented economy of the new growth zone. The dour grey mushroom of the New Orleans Superdome on the near horizon tells the Bourbon Street tourist something about expectations for growth in sunbelt cities. The looping ribbons and bows of the California freeway system and the infinitely receding line of terminals at Dallas–Fort Worth airport remind us that the Sunbelt has developed without the constraints of rail-bound transportation. The proliferation of major league sports teams in towns like Tampa, Phoenix, and Seattle gives sports fans an easy lesson in the shifting locations of the American population.

The development of higher education offers another mirror for the growth of sunbelt cities. The legions of small colleges and state universities that dotted the landscape of the Mississippi Valley and the West in the nineteenth century were servants of the agricultural economy and symbols of permanence for scores of new towns. The era of urban industrialization around the turn of the century brought the establishment of a new set of research universities and city colleges in New York, Chicago, Pittsburgh, Cleveland, Boston, Worcester, Akron, and Toledo. In response to new trends of regional growth, every southern and western state during the last two decades has similarly created or expanded public universities in the booming sunbelt cities. There are new urban campuses along the South Atlantic coast for Baltimore, Washington, Richmond, Norfolk, Greensboro, Charlotte, Charleston, Atlanta, and Miami. In the Mid-South there are expanded state universities for Nashville, Memphis, Birmingham, New Orleans, and Little Rock. For the western states the list includes Dallas–Fort Worth,

San Antonio, El Paso, Denver, Colorado Springs, Boise, Olympia, Portland, Las Vegas, and a half-dozen California cities.

The sites for the new schools are equally revealing about the patterns of growth within the sunbelt cities. Many of the new campuses have risen out of the rubble of downtown urban renewal projects. Shabby loft buildings and dilapidated housing in Norfolk, Denver, Portland, and other cities have given way to high-rise classroom towers and student parking lots. Just as many of the new universities have been planned and built for suburbanites. California offers higher education in Hayward and Santa Cruz, Fullerton and Riverside, Irvine and La Jolla. Towson State University lies on the far side of the Baltimore beltway, George Mason University among the suburbanizing fields of northern Virginia, and Florida Atlantic University adjacent to the condominiums of Boca Raton. The foundations for the University of Texas at San Antonio were blasted from a limestone ridge in empty scrublands twenty-five miles outside the city. The University of Texas at Arlington serves the super-suburbs of what chambers of commerce have named the Dallas–Fort Worth metroplex.

A survey of the new universities of the South and West provides a quick review of the postwar population trends discussed in the initial chapters of this study. The second postwar generation in the closing decades of the century has every reason to expect the further growth of sunbelt cities and sunbelt suburbs. On the broadest scale, data available for the first half of the 1970s show continued growth in the amenity-rich states of the western and southern rim. The Northeast and the Middle West together showed a net outmigration of 1.5 million between 1970 and 1975 as they ceased to attract new black residents and lost increasing numbers of whites. The outmigration from the old industrial belt contrasts with the 4 million residents gained by the South and West through interregional and international migration. Projections by the federal Bureau of Economic Analysis indicate that the shift of economic activity and income from the older metropolitan areas to the newer cities and towns of the Sunbelt will persist at least through the 1980s.[1]

Within sunbelt states, the 1970s witnessed the continued vitality and expansion of metropolitan agglomerations. Support for this statement requires detailed analysis, for interim census estimates first published in 1974 surprised many experts by revealing that the pace of growth in nonmetropolitan areas had begun to outstrip that of metropolitan America. The growth rate of metropolitan areas as a group fell from 1.5 percent annually between 1960 and 1970 to 0.7 percent between 1970 and 1976. The aggregate growth rate of all nonmetropolitan counties for the same periods increased from 0.7 percent to 1.3 percent.[2] In an effort to pin down the new phenomenon with new terminology, some observers have argued that the United States during the seventies entered a basically new era of "counterurbanization" in which the reassertion of an underlying antiurban bias in the national culture has terminated an aberrant era of industrial urban concentration.[3]

On closer examination, counterurbanization bears a striking similarity to the familiar process of suburbanization. In the age of the interstate highway system, the official redefinition and expansion of SMSAs has failed to keep pace with the outward sprawl of population. Most of the rapid nonmetropolitan growth therefore involves areas outside SMSA boundaries that maintain substantial ties to the metropolis through daily commuting and participation in a single market for retailing and services. Calvin Beale has shown that counties adjacent to existing SMSAs received five-eighths of the net migration into nonmetropolitan areas in the early seventies. Other data show that the fastest growing parts of the country are the suburban rings of metropolitan areas and the nonmetropolitan counties in which more than 20 percent of the workers commute to metropolitan areas.[4]

Population data analyzed by region indicate the continuing prosperity of smaller and middle-sized metropolitan areas in the Sunbelt. In the northeastern and north central states, the five largest metropolitan complexes lost population between 1970 and 1974 and the other metropolitan areas grew by only 1.3 percent, a rate far below the 4.1 percent for the regions' nonmetropolitan population. In the South and West, the three largest metropolitan complexes grew more slowly than the nonmetropolitan areas. Taken as a group, however, the SMSAs with populations under 3 million equaled the nonmetropolitan growth rate in the West and surpassed it in the South. The western figure also exceeded that region's nonmetropolitan rate if depression-damaged Seattle is omitted. The fastest growing individual urban areas during the early seventies were smaller sunbelt SMSAs with populations in the one hundred fifty to five hundred thousand range. Santa Cruz and Santa Rosa, Tucson, Colorado Springs and Fort Collins, Killeen and

Bryan, and a host of SMSAs in Florida have the size to offer a diverse and skilled labor pool and to support a full range of services but retain the attractions of smaller communities.

Over the next decades the ongoing growth of existing SMSAs and the expansion of population in intervening towns and rural areas in the sunbelt states may support the growth of a series of low-density urbanized regions. One example is the Colorado piedmont region that stretches 120 miles from Colorado Springs through Denver to a constellation of smaller towns including Boulder, Longmont, Loveland, Greeley, and Fort Collins. A similar region with its center in Portland may reach along the Columbia River to Vancouver, Longview, and Kelso and southward along the Willamette River to Salem and Eugene. A third example is the twelve-county "metrolina" complex in the Carolinas that centers on Charlotte and extends to Rock Hill, Gastonia, Kannapolis, Salisbury, and Statesville. On the model of the East Coast megalopolis as described by Jean Gottman, the several communities in each region will be linked by increasing levels of commuting over interstate highways and will develop some specialization in economic functions. At the same time, they will retain independent identities and remain separated by large tracts of open space.[5]

The persistence of regional and metropolitan growth trends will reinforce the Sunbelt's emerging characteristics. The idea of a Sunbelt developed in the early 1970s in an effort to summarize certain aspects of the contemporary South and West that set them apart from the rest of the United States. As the preceding analysis has shown, the evolution of a distinct sunbelt region began with the impacts of World War II. For nearly four decades, the growth histories of cities in the Southeast and West record growing dependence on federal spending for defense, for civilian administration, and for urban redevelopment. In more general terms, the sunbelt economy since World War II has been differentiated from that of the industrial belt by the growth of white-collar jobs and the role of the military-technological complex.

World War II also ushered in an era during which urban growth in the Sunbelt has taken distinctive forms. Most basic has been the extraordinary pace of metropolitan growth. Between 1940 and 1970, all of the southeastern and western SMSAs with 1970 populations over three hundred thousand grew more rapidly than the national average for all metropolitan areas; only thirteen of forty-seven large SMSAs in the northern states surpassed the same average. In addition, the newer metropolitan areas of the Sunbelt have been especially affected by the postwar surge to the suburbs. With relatively underdeveloped downtown districts and low population densities even in 1940, they have offered little to counterbalance the contemporary landscape of shopping centers and single-family houses.

In addition to describing the emerging character of sunbelt cities, this book has also explored the political patterns that have developed in response to the pressures of metropolitan growth. The particular interest has been to describe the ways in which rapid growth in total population and its shifting distribution between central cities and suburban rings have affected the success of different programs for public action and the construction of alliances among groups and interests within the metropolis. The historical analysis has found three roughly successive stages in patterns of metropolitan politics that can be summarized as the politics of urban initiative, the politics of city-suburban conflict, and the politics of community independence. Older industrial cities also display elements of the same pattern at points in their recent development, but the SMSAs of the Sunbelt have a much greater tendency to match the descriptive model.

In more detail, it was a combination of wartime crisis and postwar opportunities that brought similar sorts of political change to at least a dozen sunbelt cities. Just as the success of the New Deal changed American attitudes about public responsibility for individual economic security and about the role of government in the economy, the response of most southern and western cities to the defense boom of 1940–43 helped to restore confidence in the capabilities of municipal governments after the lean years of the 1930s. The growing body of professional public administrators viewed defense housing and postwar planning efforts as a dry run for more ambitious programs of civic improvement. For other sunbelt residents, the same programs demonstrated the ability of city governments to assist in providing the services necessary to support the growth of private business.

Despite the new lessons that the war years had offered, the established leaders in many southern and western cities showed every intention in 1945 to run their cities by the same "book" they had followed in 1926 or 1933. Among the bankers of San Antonio and Denver, the source of conservatism may have been simple lack of vision or memories of overextension in the 1920s. On the part of Billy Prieur in Norfolk or Ben Stapleton in Denver, it was fear of altering a carefully tended political equilibrium which made them unwilling to use public authority to assist local entrepreneurs in taking advantage of the shift of population and wealth toward the South and West. The immediate result in 1946 and 1947 was a wave of "G.I. revolts" in which bright young candidates marched against corrupt or inept city hall cliques under the banner of progress.[6] Over a slightly longer period, the later forties and early fifties brought a large number of efforts in sunbelt cities to modernize the formal or informal structure of government by adopting new charters and upsetting old machines.

The immediate aim of postwar reformers was to throw the rascals out and to stencil new names on the doors at city hall, but their broader goal was to define and implement a single set of policies to guide the development of the entire metropolitan area. The frequently expressed worries about the disease of decentralization arose from an early concern about the possible development of intrametropolitan conflict. Ambitious mayors and planners in the optimistic years of the later forties and early fifties therefore offered programs of annexation and regional planning in order to preserve the dominant role of the central city in local decisions and to block the development of independent political influence in suburban areas. Business and political leaders in the city halls and downtown clubs also expected that rapid economic growth under central city leadership would prevent the emergence of dissatisfaction in peripheral areas by bringing prosperity to individual suburbanites and an expanding tax base to suburban governments.

A decade of reform campaigns, charter review commissions, and charismatic candidates gave way in the 1950s to the urban renewal era in sunbelt cities. As postwar reformers consolidated their hold on city governments, they implemented their agenda of administrative modernization and economic development. Businesslike government meant new budgeting, purchasing, and personnel practices, the restructuring of operating departments, and the recruitment of professional workers from a national pool. It also meant the creation of businesslike housing and redevelopment agencies whose semiindependent status made it easy to provide public services without worrying about the satisfaction of specific interests. Government partnership with the private sector meant new freeways, port and airport improvements, downtown office space and enticements to new manufacturing industries.

The men in the foreground during the 1950s and 1960s were the same people who could be found in the Chamber of Commerce board room or at the monthly meetings of the Jaycees, for the sunbelt reform movements operated with the assumption that leadership should come from certain groups within the local business community. In the Virginia of Jefferson and Washington, the gentleman freeholders who owned the large plantations took it as a matter of course that their stake in the economy entitled them to control public decisions. Two centuries later, local market businessmen in Norfolk and Richmond drew the same conclusion, stepping from private to public offices as naturally as the Lees and Randolphs had accepted the call to Williamsburg. From one ocean to the other, it was difficult to distinguish the members of the Good Government League in San Antonio, the Charter Government Committee in Phoenix, or the Myers Park clique in Charlotte from the crowd in the country club lounge.

The natural allies of the downtown businessmen were the municipal bureaucrats. Programs of economic growth promised a large tax base with which to implement new initiatives, while the promotion of administrative efficiency allowed opportunities to establish reputations among their professional peers. Along with Cincinnati and Kansas City, the showcases for ambitious city managers were large sunbelt cities like San Diego, Dallas, Fort Worth, Richmond, and Norfolk where an organized business community offered a stable base of support. The same years were also a golden age for the planners, housing experts, public health specialists, and redevelopment officials who filled the operating bureaus and agencies. As Lester Salamon has recently stated, urban planning on a broad scale "has never been more effective than when it was harnassed to the goals of that powerful coalition of progressive business elements and activist chief executives that took shape in city after city following the Second World War and that exploited the potent planning tools made available by the federal urban renewal and highway programs to lay claim to the decaying urban core for the administrative activities required in an increasingly technological society."[7]

The sunbelt states in the 1950s and 1960s easily offer more than a score of examples of booster governments. The homogeneous, middle-American populations of most western cities made it easy for civic leaders to construct agreement around the related goals of population growth and a white-collar economy. New residents had moved to San Jose, Albuquerque, and Denver precisely because of their range of high-status jobs, while established businessmen enjoyed the resulting booms in retailing and real estate. The tightly guarded political systems of many southern cities achieved the same consensus by excluding dissident voices and admitting minorities on carefully defined terms. Indeed, one of the significant differences between the booming cities of the Sunbelt Southeast during the urban renewal era and the less successful cities of the Mid-South lies in the area of political accomodation between whites and blacks. Particularly prosperous cities such as Norfolk, Charlotte, and Atlanta developed a tacit contract that traded white backing for substantial public housing programs and expanded municipal jobs in return for black acceptance of downtown renewal and freeway programs that often disrupted black neighborhoods. The white business community in deep south cities like Little Rock, Memphis, New Orleans, and Birmingham was unwilling or unable to offer black residents the same sort of junior partnership in city politics until the end of the 1960s.[8]

Despite their broad support within sunbelt cities, the leaders of businessmen's administrations were increasingly unsuccessful in extending consensus on their political goals through entire metropolitan areas. Tentatively during the 1950s and more strongly during the 1960s, governments within the suburban ring raised the basic question of equity in the allocation of the benefits and burdens of local government. Indeed, the same rapid growth that demonstrated the success of central city reform movements also exacerbated intrametropolitan conflict by forcing quick decisions and quick action on the service needs of new suburbs. With little time for careful debate and inadequate institutions for areawide decision making, residents of each metropolis had to apportion limited public resources between the competing demands of suburban development and urban redevelopment.

The result, with growing frequency, was a politics of confrontation between older and newer areas over taxes and services. Because of the rapid sorting of metropolitan population by socioeconomic status, conflicts between older and newer areas were often conflicts as well between poorer and richer communities. Both city and suburban officials scrambled to make sure that decisions on highway construction, bus routes, sewers, and other metropolitan service networks met the specific needs of their own constituents. Suburbs looked jealously at water systems and other physical services that remained under control of city agencies at the same time that they worked to fend off the extension of city school districts. Residents on both sides of the boundary markers argued loudly that they were being gouged by the tax collectors but shortchanged on the services that their taxes purchased.

The third stage in the cycle of urban reform in the postwar Sunbelt has been the gradual weakening or breakup of the businessmen's coalitions during the past fifteen years. In part, the decline has stemmed from problems among the reformers themselves. The neoprogressives in many cities by the 1970s were as tired as the original progressives had been in 1920. A decade or two decades of political control had allowed the reformers to achieve many of their goals in restructuring city administrations, installing modern management practices, and rebuilding sections of downtowns. More and more of the old leaders preferred a graceful exit from the public arena to further years of strenuous effort to accomplish a dwindling list of reforms. Most of the reform efforts also failed to recruit successors as the original leaders dropped out of politics or moved to new jobs. Even the highly organized Good Government League forgot to replace sixty-year-old and seventy-year-old members with men and women in their thirties and forties. As a consequence, younger businessmen and lawyers with political ambitions tended to develop new issues and to build careers outside the reform context.

The rapid growth of suburbs relative to central cities also weakened business-oriented coalitions in many SMSAs. In particular, the suburbanization of retailing, recreation, and construction opened a gap between businessmen dependent on inner-city markets and real estate values and those whose prosperity was tied to peripheral growth. In San Antonio, the split among locally oriented businesses was a major element in the collapse of the Good Government League. In Charlotte, a similar split helped to defeat a city-county consolidation proposal in 1971. The new charter was developed and supported by the Chamber of Commerce and the downtown business interests that had pushed urban renewal and economic development programs in the later fifties and sixties. It mobilized the opposition of suburban voters who feared the creation of a single school system and of suburban businessmen who saw it as a tool for maintaining downtown dominance of local growth patterns. In the new Charlotte of the middle 1970s, the old elite has shown little ability to deal with the problems of race relations in housing and schools. Instead of lunching with country club colleagues, city officials must negotiate with a host of community organizations with relatively specific concerns.[9]

The step beyond the splintering of downtown and suburban business interests has been the evolution of suburban independence. As chapter seven has described, suburban rings in the 1970s are becoming self-sufficient as social and economic units. Many of the suburban counties and municipalities within these peripheral rings are also as capable as central cities in providing efficient government for their citizens. As outmigration of population and business reduces the resources available to core cities, suburban politicians may find that their most powerful rivals within the metropolis are now other suburbs. The vitalization of suburban governments and politics has simultaneously provided the context for the evaporation of political consensus within core cities. The common failure of annexation plans and of efforts to dominate regional planning during the 1960s demonstrated to many city residents the need to develop new policies to replace the faded vision of the postwar reformers. The usual choice has been to meet the needs of increasingly heterogeneous populations by accentuating the virtues and interests of individual neighborhoods. In combination, the trends of the 1970s have replaced the simple dichotomy of city and suburb with more complex patterns of spatial politics based on the self-interests of numerous subareas within central cities and suburban rings.

For many central cities, the decline of the reform consensus has meant a change of political tone and the establishment of new priorities among municipal programs with new prominence for such goals as historic preservation and growth management. It has also meant increasing belief that the specific interests of geographical subareas are more important than a concept of public interest that turns out to serve particular business interests. A number of sunbelt cities have developed new governmental structures to match the slogans about community control and humane planning. The previous chapter thus reviewed the rise of community planning organizations and neighborhood lobbies in Portland and Seattle and the adoption of ward voting in Richmond, Fort Worth, San Antonio, and Albuquerque.

Despite its importance, the cycle of postwar reform and the evolution of spatial politics in the large cities of the South and West has received little attention. For most urban experts, references to an "urban renewal era'' or modern ''civic renaissance'' call to mind a list of cities in the old industrial belt. The editors of *Fortune* in 1957 and 1958 defined what is still a commonly accepted list of cities that benefitted from reinvigorated leadership after 1945. One article described a ''new breed'' of big-city mayors who were not so much politicians as public entrepreneurs interested in the promotion of economic growth. Examples included Richard Daley of Chicago, Richardson Dilworth of Philadelphia, David Lawrence of Pittsburgh, Robert Wagner of New York, Charles Taft of Cincinnati, Raymond Tucker of Saint Louis, and Frank Zeidler of Milwaukee. Another editorial called attention to the ''businessman's city,'' with particular reference to the Greater Philadelphia Movement and Saint Louis Civic Progress. In a list that seems sadly dated in the 1970s, *Fortune* also cited Cincinnati, New York, Philadelphia, Milwaukee, Pittsburgh, Baltimore, Detroit, and San Francisco as evidence that large cities were among the best-run organizations in the country.[10]

Historians and political scientists who have examined the civic renaissance of the 1950s have tended to start with general propositions and to end with examples drawn from the Northeast and Middle West. In 1964, for instance, Robert Salisbury argued that a ''new convergence of power'' was reshaping American urban politics as strong mayors, professional planners, and businessmen combined their efforts to promote economic growth. His cases in point were Chicago, Saint Louis, Pittsburgh, and New Haven. Three years later, Jeanne Lowe argued that New York, New Haven, Pittsburgh, Philadelphia, and Washington were the cities that were winning their ''race with time.''[11] Several studies in the 1970s summarize the experience of the same sorts of cities. New Haven, Boston, Chicago, Pittsburgh, Philadelphia, Saint Louis, and New Orleans appear on every list; Wilmington, Newark, Syracuse, Baltimore, Cleveland, and San Francisco appear on occasion.[12]

If the postwar decades in fact brought a ''burst of civic reform activity not seen since the progressive era,'' the focus of change was more properly the emerging Sunbelt rather than the Northeast. In the first place, the spirit of civic optimism in the Northeast scarcely survived the 1960 census of population and the 1963 censuses of business and manufactures. In combination with the high unemployment of the 1959 recession, minimal population gains or losses in the older cities were a painful shock to their activist leadership. Data on business locations similarly showed that heroic revitalization programs in cities like Pittsburgh had failed to modernize the economic base or to counteract the national tilt toward the South and West.[13]

In the second place, reform-minded businessmen in many northern cities were as much front men for regular political organizations as they were independent actors. In Chicago, Richard Daley was not a representative of a new breed of civic leaders but a canny politico who reinvigorated the Democratic party with the assistance of businessmen and establishment institutions like the University of Chicago. Mayor Lee of New Haven similarly used the local Democratic machine as a tool for urban redevelopment and as an independent power base for negotiations with business interests. In Pittsburgh and Saint Louis, the civic renaissance involved a sometimes uneasy partnership between regular party politicians and central city business interests. Pittsburgh's Mayor David Lawrence and his Democratic organization worked as senior partners with the Alleghany Conference on Community Development, which represented Richard Mellon and other major industrialists. The smoke abatement, housing, and urban renewal programs that made Pittsburgh everyone's favorite example of a city on the move in the middle fifties depended first on the votes that Lawrence could deliver and second on the prestige and financial backing of local banks and businesses. Without the same tight central control, progressive government in Saint Louis depended on constant negotiations between the "good government" mayor and the professional politicians based in county offices and ward committees.[14]

The "renaissance coalition" in the North also involved the customary mobilization of labor unions and European ethnic groups. No matter how shiny the new buildings looked to a visitor or how new the rhetoric sounded in *Harpers* or *Fortune*, local residents viewed urban redevelopment as another manifestation of traditional city politics. Scholars generally agree that urban machines and politicos from the 1930s to the 1960s were able to use the new programs of state and federal aid to preserve their own influence. Certainly Richard Lee and Richard Daley sold their programs to the voters not in terms of general issues but as a way of satisfying a package of specific interests. In short, the new progressivism in northern cities with strong ethnic communities and established party organizations was an effort to use new tools to assemble the same sort of public investment coalition that historians associate with turn-of-the-century bosses.

The postwar reform movements in sunbelt cities as described in this study differ from those of the northern cities on each of the points described. As chapter two indicates, sunbelt cities on the average have smaller European ethnic communities and weaker unions. They are also likely to have city manager administrations and nonpartisan elections. Both characteristics helped the civic-minded businessmen who had assumed control after 1945 to make their decisions without worrying about other interests within the city. Indeed, if the editors of *Fortune* had really wanted to find the "businessman's city" in its pure form in 1957, they should have looked to Dallas, San Antonio, Norfolk, Denver, and San Jose.

Even though northern and sunbelt cities differed in the character of their participants in postwar revitalization efforts, however, they have shared the fundamental similarity of limited success. In a frostbelt city such as Philadelphia, the end of the civic renaissance is spectacularly represented by the transition at city hall from Chestnut Hill sophisticates, Joseph Clark and Richardson Dilworth, in the fifties to old-line politician James Tate in the sixties and to modern know-nothing Frank Rizzo in the seventies. In most sunbelt cities, the shift in political balance has been less blatant but just as real. Southern and western cities emerged from the challenges of World War II with exciting opportunities to build new metropolitan communities without the accumulation of mistakes and hostilities that burdened older cities. Their first generation of postwar leaders matched the opportunities with strong ambitions for metropolitan growth under unified direction. Nevertheless, the theme of the last two decades has been the ineffectiveness of integrative institutions whether the focus is the fate of reform administrations or the rise of intrametropolitan conflict. Despite the promise of common goals, the trend in sunbelt SMSAs has been increasing variety and fragmentation in governmental structure. Efforts to sell the entire metropolis on common policies have failed to prevent the proliferation of concern for small areal units. Regional planning, annexation, and deference to core city leadership have all been weakened by the outward tide of population that advanced the status of suburban rings and by smaller eddies that created socioeconomic differences among neighborhoods and among suburbs.

The history of metropolitan politics in the Sunbelt since 1940 confirms the importance of underlying patterns of social geography. In summary, spatial politics in southern and western cities has meant the development of metropolitan pluralism. A wide range of groups, defined variously by ethnicity, social class, or residential location, have developed the capacity and willingness to pursue parochial goals through formal and informal political entities that are considerably smaller than the metropolis as a whole. The common element in the political geography of many SMSAs is therefore the complexity of competition among central cities, their neighborhoods, and their suburbs. The same metropolitan area may illustrate the problems of neighborhood rivalries, intersuburban competition, sectoral disputes within regional agencies, and traditional city-suburban conflicts.

For the future, sunbelt citizens can expect that increasing political fragmentation of their metropolitan areas will gradually erode their advantages over older cities, and exacerbate inequities in the intrametropolitan allocation of the benefits of growth and government. When entire SMSAs are considered, sunbelt cities still have the resources to provide decent jobs and adequate public services. They can expect a second generation of economic prosperity to attract new residents with high levels of education and skills. However, governmental fragmentation and suburban independence will mean that many metropolitan resources will be unavailable for the central cities of these same SMSAs. The immediate crises of depopulation and bankruptcy that have made headlines in the seventies are still confined to the older cities of the industrial belt, but New Orleans, Jacksonville, Washington, Denver, Portland, Seattle, San Francisco, Oakland, and Los Angeles all show danger signs that promise increased financial vulnerability in the eighties.[15]

In more general terms, the residents of sunbelt SMSAs can expect to face increasingly difficult problems of urban maturity during the 1980s even while they enjoy the continuation of extraordinary growth. Although the urban renewal era lasted longer in the South and West than in the Northeast, the final decades of the century do not necessarily promise the same distinctiveness for the central cities of the Sunbelt that characterized the first postwar generation. Southern and western cities which have lost their battle for continued territorial growth will increasingly find themselves faced with the same problems of obsolescence that haunt New York and Chicago. It is too early to predict the replication of the South Bronx or Chicago's Woodlawn in the Gulf and Pacific cities, but it is not too early to worry about the results of blocked growth. A recent study by Richard Nathan, for example, examined the degree of social and economic disparity between central cities and suburbs in 1970. Most of the highly disadvantaged cities were found in the industrial belt, with Newark and Cleveland heading the list. However, Atlanta ranked seventh on the hardship scale (above Gary and Rochester), Richmond ranked thirteenth (above Philadelphia), and Miami, New Orleans, and San Jose also had high levels of economic and social problems relative to their suburbs. Los Angeles also looks more and more like an older rather than a younger city. While the suburban world of Orange and Ventura counties has continued to grow, Los Angeles itself has experienced net outmigration, increasing population densities, a shift toward multifamily housing, and a rising proportion of minority residents during the 1970s.[16] In a symbolic indication of the relative fortunes of the city and its suburbs, the Los Angeles Rams announced a move to Orange County only two years after the New York Giants skipped from the Bronx to New Jersey.

The response of many city dwellers and city politicians to their loss of special status within the metropolis has been to turn in on themselves. Residents defend their own wards and neighborhoods from rapid change while city officials scramble to locate new housing or new factories on remaining parcels of vacant land within the city limits. Unfortunately, the well publicized return to the city, which has been widely hailed in South Atlantic cities such as Baltimore, Washington, Richmond, Charleston, and Savannah, and western cities such as Seattle, Portland, and Denver, is unlikely to have significant long-range impact on the aging process. Beyond the admitted aesthetic attractions of older neighborhoods, the rediscovered advantages of the central city are the availability of housing suitable for one- and two-member households and convenience to downtown office jobs. The former can be supplied just as easily in well-planned suburbs. The latter in itself furnishes a limited market in most cities.[17] As a case in point, Norfolk is hoping to fill perhaps fifteen hundred new middle-class housing units in redeveloped neighborhoods over a two-decade span from 1970 to 1990. A middle-class counterflow to core neighborhoods is scarcely a gleam in a planner's eye in San Antonio. In addition, new rapid transit systems for Washington, Atlanta, San Francisco, Portland, and other cities will reduce the competitive advantage of older neighborhoods by enhancing the access of suburbanites to downtown business districts. Enthusiasts for downtown revival and central city living might well take warning from the recent history of the United Kingdom. The citizens of Great Britain greeted their freedom from the worries of empire with a decade of high living and cultural excitement that parallels the experience of sunbelt cities as they turned away from the metropolitan arena. The limitations of internal resources in an aging society, however, quickly transformed the swinging England of the 1960s into the battered Britain of the 1970s.

Over the past generation, the most exciting aspects of metropolitan politics in the Sunbelt have been the inclusive vision of the 1940s and the willingness in many cities to accept new interests during the 1970s. If they can draw on the same sorts of positive leadership for the 1980s, the central cities of the South and West still have the opportunity to participate in shaping the future of the larger metropolis. One possible form for such participation might be formation of an alliance between the stranded city and its stranded suburbs that have also been left behind the wave of outward growth. As older communities within suburban rings find themselves with the problems of a maturing population and an aging housing stock and physical plant, they may make common cause with their central city to influence decisions on regional services and programs. Despite the rise of suburban independence, residents of the Sunbelt also retain the option of experimenting with new forms of government for metropolitan areas. Encouraging examples include the continued success of Miami-Dade County Metro, the Seattle Metro service district, the Atlanta Regional Commission, and the recent expansion of the Metropolitan Service District in Portland.

The postwar growth coalitions of the sunbelt cities failed in large part because of their arrogance. Central city leaders of the 1940s and 1950s generated their own oppositions by assuming the right to make decisions for their own constituents and for the larger metropolis. Before the relatively recent patterns of intrametropolitan conflict become permanent habits of metropolitan politics, there is still at least a decade in which to try an alternative style of spatial politics based on negotiation among geographical subareas treated as equals. Neither neighborhood politics nor the politics of suburban independence need to involve confrontation if the residents of sunbelt cities can develop integrative institutions that recognize the distinctiveness of the separate communities within the metropolitan framework.

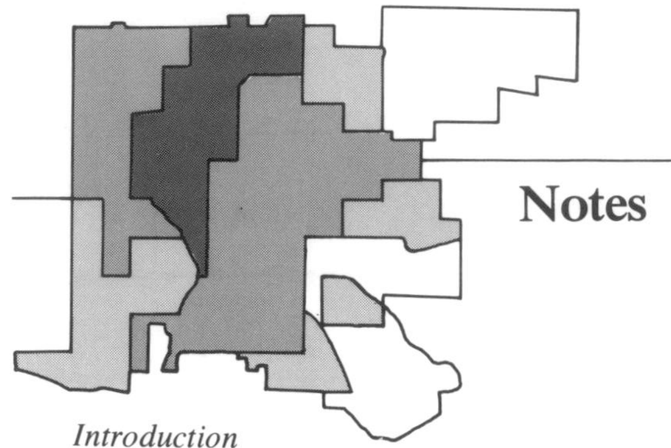

Notes

Introduction

1. Phillips, *Republican Majority*; Lubell, *Hidden Crisis*, p. 269.

2. Seventy nationally syndicated political journalists were surveyed by letter and telephone during August–October 1977. Replies were obtained from eighteen.

3. Sale, Kirkpatrick, *Power Shift*, p. 270; *New York Times*, 8, 9, 10, 11, and 12 February 1976.

4. *New York Times*, 9 February 1976; "Second War Between the States," pp. 82–114; "Federal Spending: The North's Loss is the Sunbelt's Gain," pp. 878–90.

5. Havemann and Stanfield, "Frostbelt Strikes Back," p. 1031.

6. *New York Times*, 12 September, 22 November, and 18 December 1977; Havemann and Stanfield, "Frostbelt Strikes Back," pp. 1028–37; Robert Scott and David Boren, speaking at Symposium on "Alternatives to Confrontation: A National Policy Toward Regional Change," Austin, Texas, September 1977.

7. David Boren, E. Blaine Liner, and Michael Harrington, speaking at "Alternatives to Confrontation"; *New York Times*, 12 September and 18 December 1977; Jusenius and Ledebur, *Myth in the Making*.

8. Breckenfeld, "Business Loves the Sunbelt," p. 142; George Peterson, speaking at "Alternatives to Confrontation."

9. Rostow, "Regional Change," pp. 9673–77.

10. Breckenfeld, "Business Loves the Sunbelt," pp. 132–46.

11. Kevin Phillips, letter to author, 28 July 1977.

12. Jusenius and Ledebur, *Myth in the Making*.

13. *New York Times*, 9 February 1976.

14. Sale, Kirkpatrick, *Power Shift*, p. 18; Phillips, *Republican Majority*, pp. 273–74, 438; *New York Times*, 8 February 1976.

15. Riesman and Glazer, "Intellectuals and the Discontented Classes," pp. 87–113; Phillips, *Republican Majority*, p. 437.

16. *New York Times*, 8 February 1976; Phillips, letter of 28 July 1977.

17. A metropolitan population of 300,000 in 1970 is taken as the lower cutoff for the group of cities considered in this study both for convenience

(there were 100 such SMSAs in 1970) and because it serves as a rough threshold above which metropolitan characteristics are likely to occur. See Duncan, *Metropolis and Region*, p. 275.

18. Wade, "Agenda for Urban History," pp. 54–57; Miller, *Boss Cox's Cincinnati*, pp. 57–73.

19. Wilson, "Los Angeles," pp. 129–32.

Chapter 1

1. Nash, *American West*, pp. 110–18; Pomeroy, *Pacific Slope*, pp. 215–52; Sale, Roger, *Seattle*, pp. 136–72; Abbott, Carl, *Colorado*, pp. 215–32.

2. Berge, *Economic Freedom*, pp. 7–14, 74; Pacific Coast Board, *Economic Outlook*, pp. 1, 32; Perloff, *Regions*, pp. 43–44, 471–77.

3. Ullman, "Amenities as a Factor in Regional Growth," pp. 119–32; Shryock, *Population and Mobility*, p. 404.

4. Berry, *Growth Centers*, p. 5; Perloff, *Regions*, pp. 464–66.

5. Stegner, "The West Coast," pp. 15–17, 41; Pomeroy, "What Remains of the West?" pp. 37–56.

6. Morgan, *Westward Tilt*, pp. 16, 26; Nash, *American West*, p. 296.

7. McWilliams, *California*, pp. 10, 363; Morgan, *Westward Tilt*, pp. 3–12; Perloff, *Regions*, p. 273.

8. Rand, *Los Angeles*, p. 3; Threnstrom, "Growth of Los Angeles," pp. 3–19; Hirsch, "Los Angeles," pp. 237–41; Roszak, "Life in the Instant Cities," pp. 63–83; Grey, "Los Angeles," pp. 232–42; Thompson, *Edge of History*, pp. 3–23; Elman, *Ill-At-Ease*, p. 4.

9. Clotfelter and Naylor, *Strategies for Change*, p. 28; Nichols, "The South as a Developing Area," pp. 25–27; Southern Growth Policies Board, *Growth Management Policies*, pp. 9–10; Niemi, *Gross State Product*; Hoover and Ratchford, *Economy of the South*.

10. Perloff, *Regions*, p. 278.

11. Simpson and Nosworthy, "Changing Occupational Structure," pp. 204–5; Noland, "Technological Change," pp. 170–71; Clotfelter and Naylor, *Strategies for Change*, pp. 30–31; Shryock, *Population and Mobility*, p. 416; Niemi, *Gross State Product*, pp. 49–51; *New York Times*, 6 February 1971.

12. Reissman, "Social Development," pp. 102–3; Nichols, "South as a Developing Area," p. 24.

13. Brownell, "Urbanization in the South," pp. 105–20; Brownell and Goldfield, *City in Southern History*, pp. 5–22.

14. Key, *Southern Politics*, pp. 3–12, 664–75; Bartley and Graham, *Southern Politics*, p. 19; Sundquist, *Dynamics*, pp. 254–59.

15. Connery and Leach, "Southern Metropolis," pp. 60–81; Mayo, "Social Change," pp. 1–10; Thompson, "New South," pp. 7–19; Reissman, "Social Development," pp. 102–3.

16. Perloff, *Regions*, pp. 28–32.

17. Hamilton, "Southern Migration," pp. 58–61; Shryock, *Population and Mobility*, p. 416.

18. U.S., Bureau of the Census, *Current Population Report*, Series P-25, No. 640 (November 1976).
19. Cater, "How Different is the South?"; *New York Times*, 18 December 1977.
20. Nelson and Clark, *Los Angeles Metropolitan Experience*, p. 63; de Torres, "Economics and Geography," pp. 51–56; Breckenfeld, "Business Loves the Sunbelt," pp. 136, 146; "Second War Between the States," p. 97; U.S., Bureau of the Census, *Current Population Report*, Series P-25, No. 640 (November 1976).
21. Keen, "San Diego," pp. 10–15.
22. de Torres, "Economics and Geography," pp. 51–56.
23. *Survey of Current Business* 55 (November 1975), pp. 14–21.
24. Pack, "Frostbelt and Sunbelt," pp. 8–15; Jusenius and Ledebur, *Myth in the Making*.
25. Perloff, *Regions*, pp. 34–35, 39, 47, 475–77, 484; Ullman, "Amenities as a Factor in Regional Growth," pp. 119–32; Shryock, *Population and Mobility*, pp. 416–18.
26. Morrison and Wheeler, "Rural Renaissance in America?" p. 2.
27. Duncan, *Metropolis and Region*, p. 155; Vance and Smith, "Metropolitan Dominance and Integration," pp. 114–34; Winsborough, "Changing Regional Character," pp. 44–47.
28. Meinig, *Imperial Texas*, pp. 110–21; Paul, *Mining Frontiers*, pp. 1–11, 48–55.

Chapter 2

1. Sale, Kirkpatrick, *Power Shift*, p. 51; "Houston Is Where They're Moving," pp. 83–91; "New No. 1 City," p. 82; King, "Bright Lights," p. 84.
2. Ashby, "Supercities: Houston," p. 16; *New York Times*, 9 and 15 February 1976; Muller, Thomas, *Growing and Declining Urban Areas*.
3. Briggs, *Victorian Cities*, pp. 51–52.
4. Berry and Kasarda, *Contemporary Urban Ecology*, p. 167.
5. Brownell, Blaine, *Urban Ethos*, pp. 80–93, 135–39.
6. Schlegel, *Conscripted City*, p. 3; U.S., Department of Labor, *Impact of World War II*, Part I, pp. 23, 49, Part II, pp. 14–17, 25, 28.
7. Neuberger, "Cities of America: Portland," p. 23; Tilden, "Portland," pp. 34–40; Perkin and Graham, "Denver," pp. 280–317; Chapman, "San Antonio," pp. 39–40; Texas Writers' Project, *San Antonio*, p. 41; Gunther, *Inside USA*, pp. 88–91, 213–25.
8. Marsh, *Hampton Roads*, pp. 69, 178; U.S., Department of Labor, *Impact of World War II*, Part I, pp. 60, 78, 126.
9. Marsh, *Hampton Roads*, pp. 76–77, 314; U.S., Department of Labor, *Impact of World War II*, Part I, p. 58.
10. Moses, *Portland Improvement*; U.S., Bureau of the Census, *Wartime Changes in Population*.

11. "Portland Stalks Postwar Specter," pp. 17–20; "Detour Through Purgatory," pp. 238, 240.

12. Ennor, "Portland Voters," pp. 430–31; Oregon Bureau of Municipal Research, *Basic Factors*, pp. 32–34.

13. Denver Research Institute, *Economic Forces*, pp. 94–97, 111–17; Bogue and Beale, *Economic Areas*, pp. 202, 581–82.

14. Landolt, *Mexican-American Workers*, p. 92; "San Antonio," pp. 2–20.

15. Abbott, Carl, *Colorado*, pp. 235–39.

16. Trillin, "U.S. Journal: Denver," pp. 75–79; Haselbush, "Denver," pp. 81–104.

17. Bevins, "Atlanta's Staggered Plan," p. 93.

18. "Atlanta Bulwark," pp. 43–45.

19. Duncan, *Metropolis and Region*, pp. 369–70; Bogue and Beale, *Economic Areas*, pp. 614–15; Perry, "Cities of America: Atlanta," pp. 26–27; Tharpe, "Atlanta," pp. 67–82.

20. Portland Planning Bureau, *Economic Development*, p. 40; Duncan, *Metropolis and Region*, pp. 363–68.

21. Bennett and Zlatkovich, "San Antonio," pp. 144–49; San Antonio Planning Department, *Economic Analysis*, pp. 5–6, 27–31; San Antonio Comprehensive Planning Division, *Report on Population*, pp. 2–23; Landolt, *Mexican-American Workers*, p. 222.

22. See technical memoranda on regional employment prepared regularly by the Southeastern Virginia Planning District Commission and Tsuchigane and Whaley, "Selected Economic Impacts," pp. 14–21.

23. The regional capitals, according also to Duncan, *Metropolis and Region*, were New Orleans, Birmingham, Louisville, Fort Worth, Houston, Richmond, Oklahoma City, Jacksonville, Memphis, and Nashville.

24. The data from which location quotients were calculated were furnished by the Bureau of Economic Analysis, U.S. Department of Commerce. The manufacturing centers in the West are the chemical- and oil-town of Beaumont and the space-age city of San Jose, while the manufacturing cities in the South are Wilmington; Greensboro; Greenville, South Carolina; and Louisville. The TVA towns of Knoxville and Chattanooga are the cities that combine government and manufacturing. The data used in Table 2.2 combine Fort Worth and Dallas as a single metropolitan economy. Fresno does not appear in the table because its only concentrations of activity were in farm employment and "other industries."

25. Alternative data confirm the importance of government employment for sunbelt cities. Total federal civilian and military employment for the large SMSAs of the Southeast, Mid-South, and West can be compared to that for all SMSAs in 1970. The large metropolitan areas of the West, with 3.36 percent of their population in federal jobs, and those of the Southeast, with 3.08 percent, were more heavily dependent on federal jobs than the typical American metropolis. The large SMSAs in the Mid-South at 2.44 percent fell below the

two sunbelt regions but exactly matched the national metropolitan average. The data are taken from the U.S. Bureau of the Census, *County and City Data Book* (1972). To calculate the proportion for all SMSAs, 75 percent of federal civilian employment nationwide was allocated to metropolitan areas (a figure slightly above their 69 percent share of total population and their 71.5 percent share of military employment).

26. Browning and Gesler, "Sun Belt—Snow Belt," pp. 68–74.

27. Jackson, Kenneth, "Metropolitan Government," pp. 442–62; Dye, "Urban Political Integration," pp. 430–44; Connery and Leach, "Southern Metropolis," p. 70; Advisory Commission on Intergovernmental Relations, *Challenge of Local Government Reorganization*, pp. 83–86; Forstall, "Annexation," pp. 60–61.

28. McCorkle, *Municipal Annexation*; Advisory Commission on Intergovernmental Relations, *Challenge of Local Government Reorganization*, pp. 82–86.

29. Berry and Kasarda, *Contemporary Urban Ecology*, p. 184.

30. Hawley, "Understanding Metropolitan Political Integration," p. 133; Hawkins, "Life Style," pp. 325–37; Connery and Leach, "Southern Metropolis," pp. 67–78; Advisory Commission on Intergovernmental Relations, *Challenge of Local Government Reorganization*, pp. 92–93.

31. Marando and Whitley, "City-County Consolidation," pp. 181–204.

32. Temple, *Merger Politics*, pp. 18–22, 52–55, 106.

33. Bernard, *Metro Denver*, pp. 22–23, 38–40; Pratt, "Counties' Role Grows," pp. 397–402.

34. Jacksonville, Nashville, Memphis, Houston, Dallas, Tulsa, Oklahoma City, El Paso, Albuquerque, San Antonio, Tucson, Phoenix, San Diego, and Honolulu.

35. Miami, Orlando, Fort Lauderdale, West Palm Beach, Oxnard, San Bernardino, and Bakersfield.

36. Greensboro, Tampa, and San Francisco.

Chapter 3

1. Muller, Peter, *Outer City*, p. 2; Berry, "Counterurbanization Process," pp. 17–30.

2. Berry and Kasarda, *Contemporary Urban Ecology*, p. 173; Sternlieb and Hughes, *Current Population Trends*, p. 75. The percentage data are calculated only for the counties included within SMSAs at the start of each decade, omitting new SMSAs and added counties. Total population figures include all areas within SMSAs at each census year.

3. Dobriner, *Class in Suburbia*, pp. 5–27; Donaldson, *Suburban Myth*, pp. 1–22.

4. Stein, *Eclipse of Community*; Seeley, *Crestwood Heights*; Whyte, *Organization Man*; Spectorsky, *Exurbanites*.

5. Gans, *Levittowners*; Danielson, *Politics of Exclusion*; Clark, S. D.,

Suburban Society; Wirt, *On the City's Rim*; Hadden and Masotti, *Urbanization of the Suburbs*; Kramer, *North American Suburbs*; Berry, *Human Consequences*, pp. 56–73.

6. Kahn, *American People*, p. 120.

7. *New York Times*, 30 May 1971.

8. Whyte, "Urban Sprawl," pp. 103–9, 194–200; Gruen, *Heart of Our Cities*, pp. 65, 69–70; Roszak, "Life in the Instant Cities," pp. 63–83; *New York Times*, 18 December 1955 and 2 February 1957.

9. Nelson and Clark, *Los Angeles Metropolitan Experience*, pp. 60–63.

10. Kopkind, "Modern Times in Phoenix," pp. 14–16; Meinig, *Southwest*, pp. 103–5; *New York Times*, 14 March 1974.

11. Clotfelter and Naylor, *Strategies for Change*, p. 232; Reissman, "Urbanization in the South," pp. 90–96.

12. King, "Bright Lights, Big Cities," p. 84; Huxtable, "Deep in the Heart of Nowhere."

13. Berry, "Counterurbanization Process," p. 23; Muller, Thomas, *Growing and Declining Urban Areas*, pp. 75–79; Harvey and Clark, "Nature and Economics of Urban Sprawl," pp. 1–9.

14. U.S., Bureau of the Census, *County and City Data Book*, Table 3.

15. Lillard, "Revolution by Internal Combustion," pp. 84–99; Banham, *Los Angeles*, pp. 213–22.

16. U.S., Bureau of the Census, *County and City Data Book*, Table 3.

17. Schnore, *Class and Race*, p. 20; Quinn, "Dispersing the Urban Core," pp. 545–54; Schwartz, "Images of Suburbia," pp. 325–39.

18. Schnore, "On the Spatial Structure of Cities," pp. 347–98; Sjoberg, *Preindustrial City*, pp. 96–98.

19. Schnore, *Class and Race*, p. 21. Also see Goldsmith and Stockwell, "Interrelationship of Occupational Selectivity Patterns," pp. 194–205; Schnore, "Urban Structure and Suburban Selectivity," pp. 164–76; Pinkerton, "City-Suburban Residential Patterns," pp. 500–502; Schnore, "Socioeconomic Status of Cities and Suburbs," pp. 76–85; Schnore and Winsborough, "Functional Classification," pp. 124–51.

20. Glenn, "Suburbanization in the United States," pp. 66–70, 75; Farley, "Components of Suburban Population Growth," pp. 16–21; Pinkerton, "City-Suburban Residential Patterns," pp. 504–5, 510–11; Schnore, *Class and Race*, pp. 70–91.

21. Advisory Commission on Intergovernmental Relations, *Metropolitan Social and Economic Disparities*, pp. 11–12, 22; Colman, *Cities, Suburbs, and States*, pp. 45, 50.

22. The substandard or slum zone for Denver was defined as the areas that a 1939 housing study found to have 40 percent or more substandard housing and median dwelling age of at least 30 years (*Housing in Denver, University of Denver Reports*, 17 [1941]). For Portland, the slum zone includes the "most blighted areas" in 1960 as determined by the Columbia Region Association of Governments in *Derivation of Indices of Residential Blight for the Greater Portland-Vancouver Area* (1972); the zone includes all but two of the census tracts that in 1960 had 95 percent or more of their housing dating from before

1940. In Atlanta and Norfolk, the slum zone included census tracts that in 1950 showed two of the following: average rent under city median; percentage of housing built prior to 1919 above city median; and percentage of housing dilapidated or lacking private bath above city median. Since Portsmouth was not tracted until 1960, the same criteria were applied to that city's wards in 1950 and the ward boundaries matched to the 1960 tracts. In San Antonio, the slum zone was defined as those census tracts that in 1960 had both substandard housing and low value housing. A tract was placed in the first category if at least 44 percent of its housing was unsound (twice the SMSA figure of 22 percent) or if 40 percent of its housing units had more than one inhabitant per room (SMSA figure 20 percent). It was placed in the second category if the median value of owner-occupied housing was less than $5,000 (SMSA median $9,300) or if the median contract rent was $33 or less (SMSA median $49).

23. For more information on Denver growth patterns, see Abbott, Carl, "Suburb and City," pp. 53–71.

24. It is important to describe the use of growth zones and their limitations in more detail. First, the analysis used the median of census tract values in each zone and therefore aggregates data on groups rather than individuals. All tracts are weighted equally in taking the median values for each zone, although their populations in 1970 ranged from fewer than 100 to more than 10,000. Second, the census withholds information on the socioeconomic variables for small tracts in order to preserve the anonymity of individuals. Such cases were treated as missing values and omitted from the calculation of that particular median. Third, the zones were defined in terms of 1970 tract boundaries. In some cases, a single 1960 tract was broken into two or more tracts that fell into different zones in 1970. When this problem arose, the indicator values for the single 1960 tract were counted in the computations of 1960 medians for both zones in which its segments were found in 1970.

25. Denver Regional Council, *Changing Region*, p. 11.

26. In part because of the city's vigorous annexation policy that quintupled its area from 1940 to 1970, there is no clear contrast between San Antonio and Bexar County. San Antonio had a higher income level than the county as a whole from 1950 to 1970, a higher educational level in 1940 and lower since 1950, and virtually an identical percentage of high-status workers since 1940.

27. Hoyt, *Structure and Growth*, pp. 112–22; Douglass, *Suburban Trend*, pp. 74–122; Ogburn, *Social Characteristics*, pp. 47–60; Harris, "Suburbs," pp. 1–13.

28. Hadden and Masotti, *Urbanization of the Suburbs*, p. 17; Clark, S. D., *Suburban Society*, pp. 12–14; Kramer, *North American Suburbs*, pp. xi–xxi.

29. Taeuber and Taeuber, *Negroes in Cities*, pp. 6, 48–51; Schnore and Evanson, "Segregation in Southern Cities," pp. 58–67.

30. Picnot, *Economic and Industrial Survey*, p. 349; *San Antonio Express*, 10 October 1965.

31. Alamo Area Council, *Overall Economic Development Program*, pp. 18–20; San Antonio Committee on Slum Clearance, *Comprehensive Master Plan*, pp. 31–34.

32. In 1970, there were 22,421 residents in Universal City, Converse, Live Oak, Selma, Cibola, Schertz, Windcrest, and Kirby City.

33. Portland Planning Department, *Portland's Residential Areas*, pp. 41–74; Staehli, *Preservation Options*, pp. 6–75.

34. Portland Planning Department, *Portland's Residential Areas*, pp. 41–74.

35. Oregon Legislative Interim Committee, *Problems of the Urban Fringe*, p. 77.

36. The following are comparative figures for Washington, Clackamas, and Multnomah counties:

	Washington	Clackamas	Multnomah
Percentage of workers commuting to central city, 1960	30.0	43.0	63.9
Percentage of workers commuting to central city, 1970	35.1	36.4	54.6
Percentage of workers employed in county of residence, 1960	55.5	51.5	31.7
Percentage of workers employed in county of residence, 1970	50.8	42.4	28.3

37. Ratios of unrelated individuals to families in each county were as follows: Adams, .212; Arapahoe, .239; Boulder, .689; Denver, .653; and Jefferson, .200.

38. Denver Community Renewal Program, *Strategy*, pp. 24–25.

39. Denver Unity Council, *Spanish-Speaking Population*, pp. 4–6; Denver Area Welfare Council, *Spanish-American Population*, pp. 10–15.

40. Abbott, Carl, *Colorado*, pp. 260–62.

41. Colorado Writers' Project, *Colorado*, pp. 125–26; Abbott, Carl, "Boom State and Boom City," p. 219.

42. Doeppers, "Globeville Neighborhood," pp. 506–22.

43. Joyner, "Tucson," pp. 165–95.

44. Reed and Reed, *Report on Annexation*.

45. Southeastern Virginia Regional Planning Commission, *Basic Data*, p. XVII–12.

46. The line roughly follows the Western Branch of the Elizabeth River, the Lafayette River, and Virginia Beach Boulevard–Laskin Road.

47. The ratios on socioeconomic status measures of the north-side tracts in metropolitan Norfolk to the entire SMSA are as follows:

	Education	Income	Occupation
1960	1.14	1.53	1.32
1970	1.04	1.53	1.30

48. White and Crimmins, "Urban Growth: Atlanta," pp. 231–52.

49. The sector figures omit tract 301 at the northwest corner of Cobb County and tracts 105, 115, and 116 at the extreme ends of Fulton County.

50. Haar, *President's Task Force*, pp. 2, 27–41.

Chapter 4

1. "City Planning: Battle of the Approaches," pp. 164–68.

2. Lamb, "Mobilization of Human Resources," p. 326.

3. Shryock, "Wartime Shifts," p. 275; Hauser, "Wartime Population Changes," p. 239.

4. Myers, "Defense Migration," pp. 69–76; Lamb, "Mobilization of Human Resources," p. 324.

5. Bauer, "Cities in Flux," pp. 73–75; Wirth, "Urban Community," p. 67; Bratt and Wilson, "Regional Distortions," pp. 9–15; Hauser, "Wartime Population Changes," pp. 239–41.

6. Shryock, "Wartime Shifts," p. 282; Hauser, "Wartime Population Changes," p. 242. Portland fell in the second category according to Hauser's analysis. Atlanta and San Antonio fell in the highest subgroup within the first category (superior postwar prospects) and Denver and Norfolk in a middle group of the first category (excellent prospects).

7. Pomeroy, Hugh, "Impact of the War," p. 31; Cookingham, "Effect of War," pp. 15–26; Blum, *V Was for Victory*, pp. 93, 103; U.S., National Resources Planning Board, Part 2, *Wartime Planning*, p. 102; Wirth, "Urban Community," p. 70.

8. The cities were Louisville, Nashville, Oakland, Portland, Richmond, San Diego, and Spokane. Walker, *Planning Function*, pp. 357–66.

9. Martin, *William Berry Hartsfield*, p. 26; Allen, *Our Fair City*, pp. 118–19; Portland *Oregonian*, 9 November 1938; Ormond Bean and Ernest Culligan, radio transcript, 2 November 1938, Bean Papers.

10. Funigello, *Challenge to Urban Liberalism*, pp. 44–110, 220.

11. Bauer, "War-Time Housing," p. 33; "Boom Town: San Diego," pp. 64–69; "Boom Town Inquiry," pp. 30–31; "Westward Empire," pp. 86–96.

12. Scott, *American City Planning*, pp. 373–74; Funigello, *Challenge to Urban Liberalism*, p. 34; Bauer, "War-Time Housing," p. 33.

13. Marsh, *Hampton Roads*, pp. 76–77.

14. Springer, "Growing Pains of Defense," pp. 5–8; Van Urk, "Norfolk," pp. 144–51; "Norfolk, Virginia," pp. 368–74; Davenport, "Norfolk Night," p. 17; Mezerik, "Journey in America," pp. 617–19. The papers of Norfolk's wartime mayor Joseph Wood contain numerous letters from other parts of the nation expressing concern over the city's reputation.

15. U.S., House of Representatives, *Hearings: Hampton Roads*, pp. 19–30, 173–75, 203–5; Norfolk *Ledger-Dispatch*, 23 March 1943; Joseph Wood to James Shields, 31 March 1941, Wood Papers; Schlegel, *Conscripted City*, pp. 32–33, 51–60, 171–91, 250–57.

16. U.S., House of Representatives, *Hearings: Hampton Roads*, testimony of Manley Simons, p. 30 and of Arthur Owens, pp. 175, 310–11; Joseph Wood to James Shields, 31 March 1941 and to unidentified correspondent, 9 August 1943, Wood Papers.

17. Klutznick, "Impact of the War," p. 39; Schlegel, *Conscripted City*, pp. 250–56; Norfolk *Ledger-Dispatch*, 23 March 1943. Moses also investigated San Diego, San Francisco, Newport, and Portland, Maine.

18. U.S., House of Representatives, *Hearings: Hampton Roads*, testimony of Arthur Owens, pp. 310–11.

19. Ibid., testimony of W. E. Hudgins, Jr., pp. 203–5, of H. C. Borland, pp. 19–21, 62, and of J. H. Bain, p. 57.

20. Joseph Wood to Edward Izac, 1 April 1943, Wood Papers.

21. H. C. Borland to City Council, 30 September 1941 and 11 November 1942, Central Files, Norfolk City Hall.

22. Norfolk *Ledger-Dispatch*, 20 October 1943; H. C. Borland to City Council, 1941 (undated) and 27 June 1942, Central Files, Norfolk City Hall; Jewish Family Welfare Bureau to City Council, 28 March 1944, Norfolk City Council Minutes.

23. Meyer, *Journey*, pp. 202–13; Menefee, *Assignment USA*, pp. 51–56; Tindall, *Emergence of New South*, pp. 694–703; Baumhauer, "Municipal Services of Mobile," p. 66; Lane, *Ships for Victory*, pp. 438–40.

24. Dos Passos, *State of the Nation*, pp. 92–93.

25. Reed, "The FEPC," pp. 446–67.

26. U.S., Bureau of the Census, *Wartime Changes in Population*; Portland City Club, "Negro in Portland," p. 60; Lane, *Ships for Victory*, pp. 248–49; Menefee, *Assignment USA*, pp. 75–77.

27. Janeway, "Trials and Errors," p. 26.

28. Portland City Council Proceedings, 7 October 1942; William Bowes to Earl Riley, 8 April 1941, Bowes Papers.

29. Portland *Oregonian*, 22 August 1943; Housing Authority of Portland, *From Roses to Rivets*; Harry Freeman to Earl Riley, 11 July 1942, Riley Papers.

30. Scott, *San Francisco Bay Area*, pp. 244–48; Lotchin, "Metropolitan-Military Complex," pp. 19–30; Hauser, "Wartime Population Changes," p. 241.

31. "Richmond Took a Beating," pp. 264–65; Lane, *Ships for Victory*, pp. 442–45; Scott, *San Francisco Bay Area*, pp. 249–55.

32. Scott, *San Francisco Bay Area*, pp. 246–48.

33. Scott, *American City Planning*, pp. 400–407.

34. Funigello, "City Planning," pp. 91–104; Funigello, *Challenge to Urban Liberalism*, pp. 173–76; U.S., National Resources Planning Board, Part 2, *Wartime Planning*, p. 77; Hetherton, "State and Local Planning Boards," pp. 194–99; Puget Sound Regional Planning Commission, *Puget Sound Region*, p. 153.

35. U.S., President's Committee for Congested Production Areas, *Final Report*.

36. Funigello, *Challenge to Urban Liberalism*, pp. 188–235.

37. American Society of Planning Officials, *Newsletter*, February 1945, pp. 14–16; Ballard, "Shock of Peace," p. 178; Portland *Oregonian*, 9 April, 8 and 10 July 1943 and 3 August and 1 November 1945; *The Portland Realtor* 26 (4 June 1943).

38. U.S., National Resources Planning Board, Part 2, *Wartime Planning*, p. 97; American Society of Planning Officials, *Newsletter*, February 1945, p. 15; Funigello, *Challenge to Urban Liberalism*, p. 173; Fleischman, "Sunbelt Boosterism," p. 153.

39. H. C. Borland to Norfolk Association of Commerce, 19 September 1944, Central Files, Norfolk City Hall; Norfolk City Council Minutes, 27 July and 12 and 19 October 1943.

40. The executive committee included Aaron Frank (Meier and Frank Department Store), Paul Dick (president of the U.S. National Bank), L. T. Merwin (president of the Northwest Electric Company), David Simpson (president of the Chamber of Commerce and a commercial real estate broker), Jack Smith (Hawley Pulp and Paper Company), and William Bowes. McVoy, "How Cities Are Preparing," pp. 78–80; "Portland Area Post-War Development Committee" (1944), Bowes Papers.

41. Moses, *Portland Improvement*, pp. 13–16.

42. Meyerson, "Post-War Plans," p. 10; Tunnard, "Portland Improvement," p. 21; Moses, *Portland Improvement*, p. 6.

43. William Bowes to Robert Moses, 16 November 1943, to City Club, 7 February 1944, to Multnomah County Commission, School District No. 1, and Port of Portland, all 9 February 1944, Bowes Papers; William Bowes, transcript of radio talk, 15 November 1943, Bowes Papers; Portland Area Post-War Development Committee, Minutes, 3 January 1944, Bowes Papers.

44. Keen, "Sewerage for San Diego," pp. 56–58; U.S., National Resources Planning Board, Part 2, *Wartime Planning*, p. 97; Bauer, "War-Time Housing," pp. 33–34; "California County Plans for Peace Era," p. 77; "San Diego Faces Post-War Transition," p. 95; "Blueprint for San Diego," pp. 36–37.

45. Carhart, "Denver Makes a Plan," pp. 80–82; Dorsett, *Queen City*, p. 226.

46. U.S., National Resources Planning Board, Part 2, *Wartime Planning*, p. 74; Feiss, "How Cities are Preparing," pp. 46–50; Denver Regional Association, *Facing the Challenge*.

47. "Dallas Meets a Challenge," p. 41; American Society of Planning Officials, *Newsletter*, February 1945, p. 15; "Dydamic Men of Dallas," pp. 98–103; Funigello, *Challenge to Urban Liberalism*, p. 223.

48. W. H. Taylor to Committee for Economic Development, 21 December 1943, to Norfolk Chamber of Commerce, 21 December 1943, Central Files, Norfolk City Hall; Norfolk City Council, Minutes, 17 May 1944; Norfolk *Ledger-Dispatch* 20 October 1943.

49. Scott, *San Francisco Bay Area*, pp. 259–68.

50. Earl Riley to William Bowes, 16 April 1946, Bowes Papers.

Chapter 5

1. Pomeroy, *Pacific Slope*, pp. 300–302; Garnsey, *America's New Frontier*, p. 119; Scott, *Metropolitan Los Angeles*, p. 40; Hoover and Ratchford, *Economic Resources*, pp. 130–32.
2. Meyer, *Journey Through Chaos*; Janeway, "Trials and Errors," p. 26.
3. Mezerik, *Revolt*, pp. xi–xiv, 207–14, 281–90; Hoover and Ratchford, *Economic Resources*, pp. 43–88.
4. Berge, *Economic Freedom*, pp. 1–12; Garnsey, *America's New Frontier*, pp. 3–38, 267–99.
5. West, *Rocky Mountain Cities*.
6. Committee for Effective City Government, "Council-Manager Government for Portland: A Plan for 1958," Bowes Papers.
7. Portland *Oregonian*, 20 June and 22 August 1950 and 10 and 16 January 1952; Mayor's Committee of Municipal Reorganization, Minutes, 1949–50.
8. Portland *Oregonian*, 3 March 1965.
9. Public Administration Service, *City Government of Portland*.
10. Portland *Oregonian*, 24 August 1957 and 15 February 1958; Portland *Oregon Journal*, 2 May 1958; Terry Schrunk, "Statement on Council-Manager Proposal for Portland, November 21, 1957," Bowes Papers; and Multnomah Labor Council, "Arguments and Information Regarding the Council-Manager Plan," Bowes Papers.
11. Citizens for Good Government, minutes and campaign materials, Bowes Papers.
12. Charles Buxton, Vincent Dwyer, and Jack McCandless, interview transcripts, Oral History of Colorado.
13. Gunther, *Inside USA*, p. 244; Flemming, "Denver," pp. 287–89; Perkin and Graham, "Denver," p. 291.
14. Fleming, "Denver," pp. 290–91; Perking and Graham, "Denver," pp. 281–91.
15. Morgan, *Westward Tilt*, pp. 276–77; Garnsey, "Rise of Regionalism," p. 19; Max Brooks, interview transcript, Oral History of Colorado.
16. George Cranmer, interview transcript, Oral History of Colorado; Gunther, *Inside USA*, p. 224; Flemming, "Denver," pp. 292–93; Perkin and Graham, "Denver," p. 281.
17. Perkin, *First Hundred Years*, p. 581; Morgan, *Westward Tilt*, p. 271.
18. George Cavender, interview transcript, Oral History of Colorado; Gray, *Report on Politics in Denver*, p. II–9; *New York Times*, 30 November 1947.
19. Hautaluoma, "Organizational Influence," pp. 11–17; Charles Buxton and Max Brooks, interview transcripts, Oral History of Colorado.
20. Dorsett, *Queen City*, p. 265; John Love, interview transcript, Oral History of Colorado.
21. Chambers, *Salt Water*, pp. 376–77; Norfolk *Virginian-Pilot*, May-June 1946; Pretlow Darden, interview, April 1978.
22. Norfolk Housing Authority, *This Is It*, pp. 3–6; Wertenbacker and Schlegel, *Norfolk*, p. 349.

23. See City of Norfolk, City Council Minutes and Central Files, City Hall.

24. Norfolk *Virginian-Pilot*, 4 June 1950 and 8 November 1951; Pretlow Darden, interview, April 1978; Wertenbacker and Schlegel, *Norfolk*, pp. 368–72; Norfolk City Manager, *Norfolk Story*, 1947–51.

25. Norfolk's sister city of Portsmouth did not experience such a spectacular political upheaval as Norfolk. The postwar years were marked, however, by the establishment of a planning commission in 1945, the completion of a major city plan by Harland Bartholomew and Associates in 1947, and a series of annexations in 1948–49. See Marsh, *Hampton Roads*, p. 246.

26. Henry Howell to Calvin Childress, 1 April 1961, and Henry Howell, "Memorandum of Interference of William L. Prieur in Councilmanic Election," 17 May 1961, in Howell Papers.

27. A remonstrance by a committee of leading businessmen who had been active in support of the People's Ticket failed to save Harrell's job. Eight of the fourteen persons who sought Harrell's retention later appeared as members of the Committee of 100 in 1959. See Norfolk *Virginian-Pilot*, 13, 14, and 15 December 1951.

28. Roy Martin, Francis Crenshaw, and Forrest White, interviews, April 1978; Forrest White, "Will Norfolk's Schools Stay Open?" pp. 29–33; Carter, "Desegregation in Norfolk," pp. 507–20.

29. Norfolk *Virginian-Pilot*, 26 and 27 January 1959; Norfolk *Ledger-Dispatch*, 26 January 1959.

30. Chambers, *Salt Water*, p. 387; Pretlow Darden, interview, April 1978; Lewis Powell to Stuart T. Saunders, 15 March 1959, Bemiss Papers.

31. Data from Norfolk city directories and Norfolk and Princess Anne County Land Books, 1958.

32. Henry Howell to Margaret White, 30 April 1959, and to Robert Kennedy, 10 November 1960, Howell Papers; President's Report to Norfolk Committee for Public Schools, 26 May 1960, White Papers; Minutes of Executive Board, Virginia Committee for Public Schools, 26 October 1959 and 23 January 1960, Virginia Committee for Public Schools Papers; Norfolk *Virginian-Pilot*, 16 November 1960, 7 July 1961; Norfolk *Ledger-Dispatch*, 12 July 1961. The total vote in City Council elections rose from 3,300 in 1956 and 8,000 in 1958 to more than 20,000 in 1960, 1962, and 1964. The to' vote in the Democratic legislative primary rose from 10,731 in 1957 to 2? in 1959 and 25,115 in 1961.

33. Norfolk *Virginian-Pilot*, 25 July 1961.

34. Peyton, *San Antonio*, pp. 177–83.

35. Henderson, *Maury Maverick*, pp. 47–51, 188–91; Granneberg, "Maury Maverick's San Antonio," pp. 421–26; Peyton, *San Antonio*, pp. 186–91.

36. Walter McAllister, interview, April 1978; Henderson, *Maury Maverick*, pp. 226–31.

37. *San Antonio Express*, 6–14 and 28 May 1947; "Businessmen Take Over San Antonio," p. 104; Robert Sawtelle and Kemper Diehl, interviews, April 1978.

38. *San Antonio Express*, 3–11 May 1949; Robert Sawtelle and Walter McAllister, interviews, April 1978.

39. Peterson, *Day of the Mugwump*, pp. 196–98; *San Antonio Express*, 4–10 May 1950.

40. Kemper Diehl, interview, April 1978; *San Antonio Express*, 6–10 May, 13–14 October, and 11 and 14 November 1951.

41. Sam Bell Steves, quoted in *San Antonio Express*, 6 April 1953.

42. Good Government League, "In Search of Good Government," quoted in Gibson and Ashcroft, "Political Organizations," p. 4.

43. Peterson, *Day of the Mugwump*, pp. 198–99; *San Antonio Express*, 5–6 April 1955; Robert Sawtelle, interview, April 1978.

44. Cottrell, *Municipal Services*, p. 12; Crane, "San Antonio," pp. 134–37; Gibson and Ashcroft, "Political Organizations," p. 6.

45. Lineberry, *Equality and Urban Policy*, pp. 55–56.

46. Chance, "Relations of Selected City Government Services," pp. 24–34; Cottrell, *Municipal Services*, pp. 12–16; Lineberry, *Equality and Urban Policy*, pp. 55–57; Gibson and Ashcroft, "Political Organizations," pp. 15–21.

47. Shelley, "Revitalizing a City," pp. 1–4; "San Antonio Liberals," p. 5.

48. Cobb, "Colonel Effingham."

49. Haas, "Southern Metropolis," pp. 162–63; Haas, *De Lesseps S. Morrison*; "Old Girl's New Boy," pp. 26–28.

50. Cline and Wolf, "Albuquerque," pp. 14–15; Goodall, "Phoenix," pp. 114–22; Goodall, "Political Patterns," pp. 38–39.

51. Stone, Price, and Stone, *City Manager Government*, pp. 55–62, 152–72, 352–55; Thometz, *Decision-Makers*, pp. 28–41; Leslie, *Dallas*, pp. 60–85; Wilcox, "San Diego," pp. 155–63; Banfield and Wilson, *City Politics*, pp. 180–82; Lubell, "Charlotte," pp. 32–33.

52. Banfield, *Big City Politics*, pp. 133–42; Bender, *Report on Politics in Seattle*, pp. II–46–51, V–10, VI–20–23.

53. The early 1950s also witnessed the modernization of informal rather than formal political structures in two Mid-South cities that remained on the periphery of the sunbelt boom. From 1910 to 1948, politics in Memphis meant Edward Crump, the undisputed boss of the city and of the Tennessee Democratic party. Between 1948, when the election of Estes Kefauver to the United States Senate broke Crump's control of state politics, and his death in 1954, Crump faced increasing challenges at home from Edmund Orgill and local reform interests. Although Orgill succeeded as mayor in 1955, his Good Local Government League lost the next election and faded from the scene. Even if the post-Crump reformers failed to consolidate their control on the model of Phoenix or Albuquerque, however, they did open Memphis to debate on basic issues of race relations and economic development. Two hundred miles to the east, Mayor Ben West similarly redefined the terms of local politics in Nashville. After his election in 1951, the hard-driving liberal revitalized a sleepy city administration, promoted urban renewal, and advocated consolidation and annexation programs. See Wright, *Memphis Politics*, and Hawkins, *Nashville Metro*.

54. Gosnell, "Fulton County," pp. 60–62; Darmstadter, "Metropolitan Atlanta," pp. 258–63; "Forty Million Dollar Bond Issue," p. 120; Martin, *William Berry Hartsfield*, pp. 18–24.

55. Portland *Oregon Journal*, 7 July 1953.

56. Hays, "Politics of Municipal Reform," pp. 157–69.

Chapter 6

1. Trillin, "U.S. Journal, Kansas City," pp. 94–101.

2. Charles Agle in Norfolk *Virginian-Pilot*, 14 August 1956.

3. Silver, "Urban Planning and Urban Development"; Joyner, "Tucson," pp. 185–94; Adde, *Nine Cities*, p. 88.

4. Frank Shull to Carvel Linden (Portland Chamber of Commerce), 26 June 1953; Redevelopment Advisory Board of Housing Authority of Portland, Minutes, 4 June 1952; transcript of radio address by Guy Jacques, 8 August 1952; transcript of testimony from Marc Bowman to Portland City Council, 13 October 1953; transcript of unidentified address to National Association of Housing Officials Chapter Meeting, 11 December 1952; all items in Portland Chamber of Commerce Papers.

5. Housing Authority of Portland, *Vaughan Street*; Redevelopment Advisory Board of Housing Authority of Portland, Minutes, 19 November 1952 and 2 February 1953, in Portland Chamber of Commerce Papers.

6. Molotch, "City as Growth Machine," pp. 314–17.

7. Hansen, "Tulsa," pp. 210–16.

8. Scott, *San Francisco Bay Area*, pp. 288–90; Wirt, *Power in the City*.

9. Hartman, *Yerba Buena*, pp. 22–203; San Francisco Redevelopment Agency, *San Francisco Redevelopment*, pp. 61–65.

10. Davis, "An Analysis of Human Resource Development," pp. 37–51.

11. "Politics of Hemisfair," pp. 1–7; "This World's Fair Has a Long Future," pp. 66–71.

12. Wertenbacker and Schlegel, *Norfolk*, pp. 372–76.

13. Norfolk *Virginian-Pilot*, 23 July 1961; Norfolk *Journal and Guide*, 25 August 1951, and 10 August 1957.

14. Norfolk *Virginian-Pilot*, 11 January 1958.

15. "Vision in Virginia," p. 46; Richmond *Times-Dispatch*, 16 October 1959, and 25 June 1961; Norfolk *Virginian-Pilot*, 6 January 1957, 22 December 1963, and 14 June 1965; Norfolk *Ledger-Dispatch*, 8 February 1960, and 3 December 1963.

16. Real Estate Research, *Downtown Denver*, p. 67; Adde, *Nine Cities*, pp. 165–92.

17. Moore, *Downtown Denver*; Downtown Denver Master Plan Committee, *Development Guide*; Gray, *Report on Politics in Denver*, pp. VI–11–12.

18. J. Robert Cameron, interview transcript, Oral History of Colorado; Hackenstaff, *Memories*, p. 39.

19. J. Robert Cameron, quoted in Haselbush, "Denver," p. 85.

20. Martin, *William Berry Hartsfield*, p. 126; Jennings, *Community Influentials*, pp. 140–52.

21. White and Crimmins, "How Atlanta Grew," pp. 13–14; Hebert, *Highways*, pp. 99–101; Haverty, "Atlanta Story," pp. 13–15.

22. Hartshorn, *Metropolis in Georgia*, p. 186; *Journal of Housing*, 23 (August 1966), p. 458.

23. Jennings, *Community Influentials*, p. 29; Hartshorn, *Metropolis in Georgia*, p. 165.

24. Hein, "Image of a City," pp. 209, 212; Cater, "Atlanta," pp. 18–21; Thompson, Lewis, and McEntire, "Atlanta and Birmingham," p. 21; Martin, *William Berry Hartsfield*, pp. 51, 68, 100, 112, 187.

25. Powledge, "Profiles: New Politics in Atlanta," pp. 31–32; Freedgood, "Life in Buckhead," p. 109.

26. Jennings and Ziegler, "Class, Party and Race," pp. 391–407; Hardon, "Statistical Analysis of Black-White Voting," pp. 20, 45–50, 62.

27. Ippolito and Levin, "Public Regardingness," pp. 628–34; Hebert, *Highways*, pp. 110–22.

28. Hebert, *Highways*, p. 130.

29. Henley, "New Town," pp. 271–72; Barnett, "Concern and Comprehensive Planning," pp. 414–16.

30. Judd, *Politics*, pp. 373–80; White and Crimmins, "How Atlanta Grew," pp. 14–15; Hartshorn, *Metropolis in Georgia*, p. 168.

31. The patterns of development match even more closely if public construction outside urban renewal areas in also considered. Portland thus built a coliseum in the 1950s immediately across the Willamette River from downtown, and Denver supplemented an existing civic center on the edge of the business district opposite the renewal zone with new cultural facilities including a library, art museum, and historical museum.

32. Anderson, *Federal Bulldozer*, pp. 52–90, 216–30; Jacobs, *Death and Life*, pp. 291–317; Gans, *Urban Villagers*, pp. 281–335; Hartman, "Housing of Relocated Families," pp. 266–86; Fried, "Grieving for a Lost Home," pp. 167–70; Gans, "Failure of Urban Renewal," pp. 27–39; Wilson, *Urban Renewal*, pp. xiii–xix.

Chapter 7

1. Wirth, "Urban Community," p. 64; Hoyt, "Structure of American Cities," pp. 475–81; Tugwell, "San Francisco," pp. 186–87; Fugard, "What's Happening," p. 107; Greer, *Problems of Cities and Towns*; Greer, *Your City*, p. 9; Scott, *American City Planning*, pp. 364, 369.

2. Weber, *Growth of Cities*, p. 475; Howe, *The City*, p. 204; Douglass, *Suburban Trend*, p. 327; Donaldson, *Suburban Myth*, pp. 23–44.

3. *San Antonio Express*, 14 May 1940; Rabinowitz, "Growth Trends in Albuquerque SMSA," pp. 64–65; Northwest Regional Council, *Pacific Northwest Problems*, pp. 1–3.

4. Lubell, "Charlotte," p. 32; Scott, *American City Planning*, p. 378.

5. U.S., Bureau of the Census, *Historical Statistics*, pp. 393, 462.

6. U.S., Bureau of the Census, *Statistical Abstract of the United States: 1946*, p. 786; Greer, *Your City*, p. 43; Scott, *American City Planning*, pp. 452–57.

7. Bauer, "Cities in Flux," p. 80; Greer, *Your City*, p. 129.

8. Denver Planning Commission, *Preliminary Outline*, p. 8, *Problem of Centralization*, pp. 5–6.

9. Kurtz, "Tri-County Regional Planning Commission," pp. 113–22; Denver Metropolitan Area Conference, *Proceedings*.

10. Freeman, "Public Utility Problems," pp. 56–57; ibid., "Local Planning," pp. 134–37.

11. "Resolutions of the Third Wartime Conference of the League of Oregon Cities, May 1944," World War II Agencies Papers; William Bowes, transcript of radio talk, 1943, Bowes Papers; McVoy, "Post-War Period: Portland," pp. 78–80.

12. Fred Meyer to William Bowes, 27 April 1946, and Harry D. Freeman to William Bowes, 23 April 1946, Bowes Papers.

13. Clark and Associates, *Portland Housing Survey*.

14. *Oregon Journal*, 10, 17, and 24 February 1957; William Bowes, "County Planning and Zoning," address at Oregon City, 2 December 1947, Bowes Papers; Special Committee on Rural Planning and Zoning, Report to Governor Earl Snell, 7 January 1947, Bowes Papers.

15. *Albuquerque Journal*, 9 January 1946, quoted in Rabinowitz, "Growth Trends in Albuquerque SMSA," p. 65.

16. Wenum, *Annexation*, p. 51.

17. Harrell, "Norfolk," pp. 16–17; *Norfolk Ledger-Dispatch*, 15 June 1950.

18. Norfolk *Virginian-Pilot*, 15 May 1951; *Norfolk Ledger-Dispatch*, 15 June 1950 and 6 March 1951.

19. *San Antonio Express*, 5 October 1952; *San Antonio News*, 24 June 1952.

20. Scott, *American City Planning*, p. 442.

21. "Atlanta Annexation Try Fails," p. 93; Heddan, "Atlanta Breaks Through Its Boundaries," pp. 106–7.

22. Hughes, "Annexation and Relocation," pp. 26–30; "Georgia Legislature Streamlines City-County Government," p. 113.

23. League of Women Voters, *Colorado's Water*, p. 24; Bernard, *Metro Denver*, p. 54; Cox, *Metropolitan Water Supply*, pp. 94–107; Gray, *Report on Politics in Denver*, pp. VI–9–10.

24. *Rocky Mountain News*, 18 March 1946; Denver Metropolitan Area Conference, *Proceedings*, p. 19; Denver Planning Commission, *Preliminary Outline*, pp. 10, 23–24; Cox, *Metropolitan Water Supply*, pp. 96, 102, 114.

25. Bernard, *Metro Denver*, p. 55; League of Women Voters, *Colorado's Water*, p. 26.

26. Cox, *Metropolitan Water Supply*, pp. 105, 123–26, 134–35, 140–47; *Rocky Mountain News*, 3 January 1960.

27. Furniss, "Response of the Colorado General Assembly," pp. 754–65; Bernard, *Metro Denver*, pp. 52, 58, 61–66; Cox, *Metropolitan Water Supply*, p. 22.

28. *San Antonio Light*, 18 November 1962 and 24 March 1963; Peterson, *Day of the Mugwump*, p. 198; Kemper Diehl, interview, April 1978.

29. *Norfolk Ledger-Dispatch*, 16 August 1955; Norfolk *Virginia-Pilot*, 24 April 1948, 18 May 1955, 26 August 1956, 10 April 1957, and 16 June 1958.

30. Wenum, *Annexation*, pp. 85–88, 103.

31. Carpenter, "Wichita," pp. 224–43.

32. Williams, "Life Styles," pp. 299–317.

33. Wade, "Agenda for Urban History," pp. 43–69; Miller, *Boss Cox's Cincinnati*, pp. 57–73.

Chapter 8

1. Muller, Peter, *Outer City*, pp. 1–2, 12, 29–40; Greer, "Predictions That Came True," pp. 505–14; *New York Times*, 30 May 1971.

2. Hawley, "On Understanding," pp. 123–24.

3. Urbanists who have considered the question of intrametropolitan relations in sunbelt cities have offered at best an untested suggestion that areas of rapid growth are likely to show relatively little antagonism between city and suburb. In the first place, they argue, a large proportion of residents in fast-growing metropolitan areas are newcomers who are unlikely to be bound by old loyalties, to worry over past conflicts, or to hold strong convictions about the merits of one or another municipality. In the second place, suburbs in such areas are seen as immature communities that have not yet developed the clear identities or stable political structures necessary to maintain sociospatial segregation. The relatively greater willingness of southern and western suburbanites to accept annexation and consolidation is cited as partial evidence in support of the theory of metropolitan harmony in the Sunbelt. See Lineberry, "Suburbia," p. 7; Scott, "Implications of Suburbanization," p. 38; Williams, "Life Styles," pp. 299–310.

4. Zikmund, "Sources of the Suburban Population," pp. 27–44; Fava, "Beyond Suburbia," pp. 14–15; Muller, Peter, *Outer City*, p. 45.

5. Birch, "From Suburb to Urban Place," p. 29; Muller, Peter, *Outer City*, pp. 29–40.

6. *New York Times*, 30 May 1971.

7. Hartshorn, *Metropolis in Georgia*, pp. 190–92; Dent, "Challenge to Downtown Shopping," p. 31.

8. Wright, "Office Market," pp. 34–36; Hartshorn, "Getting around Atlanta," pp. 43–44; Hartshorn, *Metropolis in Georgia*, p. 187.

9. Hartshorn, "Getting around Atlanta," pp. 48–50.

10. John Fuhr, interview transcript, Oral History of Colorado; Furniss, "Response of the Colorado General Assembly," pp. 754–65.

11. Bernard, *Metro Denver*, pp. 50, 58, 61–66; Furniss, "Response of the Colorado General Assembly," pp. 754–65.

12. Jackson, "Discrimination and Busing," pp. 101–8; Abbott, *Colorado*, pp. 250–51; Bernard, *Metro Denver*, p. 23.

13. Robert Farley quoted in Stromberg and Wilcox, *Urban Manager*, p. 173.

14. *Rocky Mountain News*, 13 July 1972 and 1 January 1974; *Denver Post* 8 August 1973; *New York Times*, 22 August 1976; Stromberg and Wilcox, *Urban Manager*, pp. 168–80; Ellis Rawls, interview, June 1974; Charles Stromberg, interview, April 1978.

15. Hebert, *Highways*, p. 104; Hartshorn, *Metropolis in Georgia*, p. 193.

16. Holland, "Widening the Scope," p. 390; Hebert, *Highways*, p. 112.

17. Cleghorn, "Atlanta," p. 36; Danielson, *Politics of Exclusion*, pp. 98, 161, 185; Hartshorn, *Metropolis in Georgia*, p. 203.

18. Leach, "Atlanta Area," pp. 555–57; "Fulton-Atlanta Merger," pp. 97–98; "Atlanta-Fulton Study," p. 156; Moore, "Annexation Atlanta."

19. Spector, "Fact and Fiction," pp. 4–7, 46–47; American Society of Planning Officials, *Atlanta Region*, pp. 1–2, 23.

20. Buckner, "Atlanta," pp. 144–46; Honey, "Metropolitan Governance," pp. 447–48.

21. Oregon Legislative Interim Committee, *Problems of the Urban Fringe*, p. 11; Martin Cramton, interview, December 1977; Ronald Saroff, interview, December 1977; Robert Stacy, interview, August 1978.

22. In the 1970 Census, Multnomah County outside Portland had a median income of $9,582 for families and unrelated individuals, 9.5 percent of its residents in professional-managerial jobs, and 12.3 years median schooling for adults. The forty eastern census tracts of Portland had median values on these indicators of $9,235, 9.15 percent, and 12.3 years.

23. Portland City Club, "Report on Portland City Government"; Public Administration Service, *City Government of Portland*.

24. Portland *Oregonian*, 14 March 1965; Don Carlson, interview, December 1977.

25. A. McKay Rich, Ronald Cease, and Don Carlson, interviews, December 1977.

26. Portland *Oregonian*, 25 September 1969; Portland *Oregon Journal*, 13 September 1969; David Eccles to Frank Consalvo, 10 December 1969, Eccles Papers.

27. Douglas Wright, interview, August 1978.

28. Portland State Urban Studies Center, *Municipal Annexation*, p. 61; Don Clark, files on "City-County Coordinating Committee," 1965–70, Clark Papers.

29. Ron Buel, interview, August 1978; A. McKay Rich and Don Carlson, interviews, December 1977.

30. Portland City Club, "Report on County Charter"; E. Kimbark MacColl, interview, December 1977; Ron Buel, interview, August 1978.

31. Portland *Oregonian*, 25 August 1978; Keisling, "Making New Local Government."

32. Temple, *Merger Politics*, pp. 73–92.

33. Norfolk *Ledger-Star*, 1 January 1963; Temple, *Merger Politics*, p. 18. Virginia law required a five-year wait after the 1 January 1958 annexation before Norfolk could adopt another annexation ordinance.

34. Sidney Kellam, Ivan Mapp, and John V. Fentress, interviews, April 1978; Temple, *Merger Politics*, pp. 22, 69, 106.

35. Norfolk *Virginian-Pilot*, 28 October, 17 November, and 5 December 1961 and 1 and 31 January and 1 February 1962; Temple, *Merger Politics*, pp. 73–92, 102–3.

36. In 1972, voters converted the old County of Nansemond into a City of Nansemond as a prelude to the merger.

37. Comparable figures for 1960 were 305,000 in Norfolk, 85,000 in Virginia Beach, 115,000 in Portsmouth, 74,000 in Chesapeake, and 44,000 in Suffolk.

38. Sidney Kellam, Joan Coates, and James Hambright, interviews, April 1978.

39. Norfolk *Ledger-Star*, 23 June and 14 July 1977; Sidney Kellam, interview, April 1978.

40. Real Estate Research, *Regional Housing Study*.

41. Analysis of migration patterns using 1970 census tract data shows three streams of population movement into Chesapeake: from Portsmouth into the west-northwest section of Chesapeake, from Portsmouth into the west central section, and from Norfolk into the northeast section.

42. Ziemba, "Power in Chesapeake," pp. 23–25.

43. Scott, "Suburban Governmental Structures," p. 237; Williams, "Life Styles," pp. 299–310.

44. John Rowe, interview, May 1978.

45. Norfolk *Virginian-Pilot*, 5 and 28 May and 16 June 1977.

46. Durwood Curling, interview, June 1978; Norfolk *Virginian-Pilot*, 16 December 1973; Norfolk *Ledger-Star*, 14 July 1977.

47. Fates, "CZO," pp. 22–27; Sam Clay, Reid Ervin, and Robert Scott, interviews, May 1978.

48. Southeastern Virginia Planning District, *Population and Employment Forecasts*.

49. Carter, "Virginia Refinery," pp. 668–71; *New York Times*, 27 April 1980.

50. The spending figures are $465 for Chesapeake, $454 for Norfolk, $509 for Portsmouth, $345 for Suffolk-Nansemond, and $448 for Virginia Beach.

51. Robert Foeller, interview, April 1978; Norfolk *Virginian-Pilot*, 26 April 1963.

52. Norfolk *Ledger-Star*, 17 September 1965 and 25 August 1970; Norfolk *Virginian-Pilot*, 30 June and 11 September 1965 and 20 February 1975.

53. Southeastern Virginia Regional Planning Commission, *Basic Data*, p. XVI–2.

54. Norfolk *Virginian-Pilot*, 18 April, 30 July, and 19 and 30 August 1972, and 1 October 1977.

55. Norfolk *Virginian-Pilot*, 29 June and 10, 12, and 13 August 1977.

56. Abbott, Margery, "Energy Recovery"; Norfolk *Virginian-Pilot*, 9 June 1977.

57. In 1970, Virginia Beach sent 24,000 commuters to Norfolk each day and only 2,000 to Portsmouth, while Chesapeake sent 12,000 to Norfolk and 6,000 to Portsmouth. Even patterns of newspaper readership reflect the split. Although both now serve the entire SMSA, the *Virginian-Pilot* was originally a Norfolk paper and the *Ledger-Star* emerged from the consolidation of a Norfolk and a Portsmouth paper. In 1977, the *Pilot* was more popular in Norfolk and Virginia Beach and the *Ledger* was more popular in Portsmouth and Chesapeake.

58. The discussion has implicitly accepted Mathew Holden's suggestion that metropolitan political systems are analogous to the international political system. In recent years, several review articles have argued that Holden's comparison is inadequate to account for metropolitan political phenomena. The thrust of the critique is that governments within the metropolitan area are not independent actors, but are linked together by and subordinated to areawide interest groups, areawide special districts, state programs, federal programs, and professional managers with national constituencies. For Tidewater Virginia, the criticisms can be answered point by point. First, the five cities have certainly retained their independence as political and economic units with competing ambitions. Second, the Tidewater area lacks significant areawide public interest groups to override the process of negotiation among independent governments. The nearest example, the antirefinery pressure group, in fact consists almost entirely of Norfolk residents. Third, there are few special districts in the SMSA. The special districts created to deal with transportation and garbage in the mid-1970s have not been activated until every municipal interest has been satisfied. Fourth, the professionalizing and routinizing of intergovernmental relations within the SMSA has not depoliticized municipal affairs. The only difference is that political battles can be fought in conference rooms and newspaper stories rather than in electoral campaigns. As in international politics, the professional staffs negotiate to find areas of agreement that the political leaders can then ratify. See Holden, "Governance," pp. 627–47; Friesma, "Cities," pp. 239–52; Scott, "Suburban Governmental Structures," pp. 213–38.

59. Elazar, *Cities of the Prairie*, p. 438; Elazar, "Suburbanization," pp. 69–71.

60. Daniel Elazar has examined the same trend toward suburban autonomy with more positive conclusions than described here. He has noted that the boundaries of large metropolitan areas "hide" several score of substantial cities that maintain thoroughly separate political and social lives. Such "civil communities" with populations ranging upward from forty thousand have the available human and economic resources to "provide the range of talents necessary to operate a sophisticated local government and the fiscal wherewithal to do so." In turn, the medium-size suburb may make a contribution to better metropolitan coordination. Citing the San Francisco Bay area as an ex-

ample, Elazar argued that "inter-local cooperation in matters of areawide concern has come easier in metropolitan areas which have many cities within the same medium size range . . . which can join forces without fearing for their very existence." See Elazar, "Suburbanization," pp. 66, 69–71, 78.

Chapter 9

1. Berry, *Human Consequences*, pp. 59–66.
2. Molotch, "City as a Growth Machine," p. 317.
3. Abbott and Abbott, "Colonial Place," pp. 1–17.
4. Altschuler, *Community Control*, p. 53.
5. For general discussions of evolving city growth policy in Seattle, see Bender, *Report on Politics in Seattle*; Sale, Roger, *Seattle*; Uhlman, "Neighborhood Preservation."
6. Woods, "Seattle's Friday Afternoon Massacre," pp. 6–7.
7. Staehli, *Preservation Options*; Pedersen, "Neighborhood Organization" and "Citizen Participation"; Mary Pedersen, interview, December 1977; Ron Buel, interview, August 1978.
8. Portland *Oregonian*, 26 June 1978; Don Clark to City-County Charter Commission, 25 June 1972, Clark Papers; David Seigneur, interview, June 1978; Ronald Saroff, Martin Cramton, and Ronald Cease, interviews, December 1977.
9. Foster, "Colorado's Defeat," pp. 163–68.
10. Abbott, Carl, "Plural Society," pp. 250–51.
11. Rockwell, "Thoughts on Preservation," pp. 123–25.
12. Denver Planning Commission, *Denver 1985*; Denver Community Renewal Program, *Strategy*; Dorsett, *Queen City*, pp. 269–70; Schler, "Citizen Participation."
13. Hallman, *Organization and Structure*, pp. 8, 48, 88–89; Keen, "San Diego," pp. 10–11; Colburn, "Underside of Paradise," p. 17.
14. Wrinkle, "New Mexico," p. 126; Rabinowitz, "Growth Trends in Albuquerque SMSA," pp. 68–72; Cline and Wolf, "Albuquerque," pp. 13–20.
15. Wirt, *Power in the City*; Lee and Rothman, "San Francisco's District System," p. 173.
16. Dabney, "Richmond's Quiet Revolution," p. 28; Rankin, "Richmond Crusade for Voters"; *Richmond Times-Dispatch*, 30 December 1962; Wheaton, "Renovators," pp. 25–26.
17. The voting rights case is traced in the *New York Times*, 11 August and 13 November 1976 and 3, 7, and 9 March and 30 July 1977; in the *Washington Post*, 17 December 1974; and in Zimmerman, "Federal Voting Rights Act," pp. 278–83.
18. Spain, "Fort Worth," pp. 50, 54, 60–64; Hallman, *Organization and Structure*, pp. 8, 89–90, 94.
19. Hartshorn, *Metropolis in Georgia*, p. 198; Hein, "Image of a City," pp. 215–19; Hebert, *Highways*, p. 105.

20. Hardon, "Statistical Analysis," pp. 18, 20, 46; Hein, "Image of a City," pp. 220–21; Hebert, *Highways*, p. 126.

21. Moore, "Annexation Atlanta," pp. 40–41, 47, 55; Schemmel, "Atlanta's Power Structure," pp. 62–65; Jones, "Black Political Empowerment," pp. 98–103.

22. Little, "Atlanta Renewal," pp. 100–108; Hebert, *Highways*, pp. 115–16.

23. Hutchinson and Beer, "In-Migration," p. 11.

24. Powledge, "Profiles: New Politics," p. 30; Jones, "Black Political Empowerment," p. 105.

25. Hallman, *Organization and Structure*, pp. 9, 32–33, 54, 58, 73; Little, "Atlanta Renewal," pp. 100–108.

26. Nathan and Adams, "Understanding Central City Hardship," p. 51; U.S. Senate, Committee on Public Works, *Transportation Planning and Priorities*, p. 4.

27. San Antonio Comprehensive Planning Division, *Report on Growth Policy Issues*, defines the north side as those areas north of Culebra Road and I-10. Also see San Antonio Community Renewal Program, *Economic Analysis*, White, "San Antonio," pp. 103–10, and Robert Green, interview, April 1978.

28. Robert Sawtelle, interview, April 1978.

29. Kemper Diehl, interview, April 1978; Catherine Powell, interview, September 1977; Charles Stromberg, interview, April 1978; Watterson and Watterson, *Politics of New Communities*, pp. 18–26.

30. Cottrell, *Municipal Services Equalization*, pp. 9–11; Catherine Powell, interview, September 1977.

31. Walter McAllister, interview, April 1978; L. Tucker Gibson, interview, September 1977; Cottrell, *Municipal Services Equalization*, pp. 17–30. Lineberry, *Equality and Urban Policy*, reaches somewhat different conclusions in an analysis of San Antonio data.

32. Yoes, "COPS Takes on City Hall," pp. 1–5; Yoes, "COPS Proves Effective," pp. 7–11; Trillin, "U.S. Journal, San Antonio," pp. 92–100; Burka, "Second Battle of the Alamo," p. 139; *Wall Street Journal*, 31 July 1977.

33. Beatriz Gallegos, Maury Maverick, Jr., and Jan Jarboe, interviews, April 1978.

34. San Antonio Planning and Community Development, *Alternative Growth Study*; Jan Jarboe, interview, April 1978.

35. Charles Stromberg, interview, April 1978.

36. Lanny Sinkin, interview, September 1977.

37. Councilman Henry Cisneros and COPS earlier in the year had fought specific telephone and water rate increases with the argument that higher charges in developed areas were subsidizing the extension of service to new subdivisions. See Burka, "Second Battle of the Alamo," and Casey, "Henry Cisneros," p. 33.

38. Charles Cottrell, testimony in U.S. House of Representatives, Committee on the Judiciary, *Hearings: Extension of the Voting Rights Act*, pp. 401, 418, 424–38.

39. Cottrell and Stevens, "1975 Voting Rights Acts," pp. 79–100; Gibson and Ashcroft, "Political Organizations."

40. San Antonio Planning Department, *San Antonio Growth Sketch*, p. 5.

41. *San Antonio Light*, 10 September 1977; Casey, "Politics of Sewage," pp. 44–47; Kemper Diehl, interview, April 1978.

42. Beatriz Gallegos and Jan Jarboe, interviews, April 1978.

43. Miller, "Scarcity," pp. 131–56.

Chapter 10

1. Sternlieb and Hughes, "Wilting of the Metropolis," pp. 4–7; ibid., *Current Population Trends*, p. 65.

2. Ibid., *Current Population Trends*, p. 75.

3. Berry, "Counterurbanization," pp. 17–30.

4. Beale, *Revival of Population Growth*, pp. 6–7; Morrison and Wheeler, "Rural Renaissance in America?" pp. 12–13; Sternlieb and Hughes, *Current Population Trends*, p. 75. The annual growth rates more precisely are: (1) central cities (1970–76) 0.6 percent; (2) suburban rings (1970–76) 1.6 percent; (3) nonmetropolitan counties with 20 percent or more commuting to SMSAs (1970–74) 2.0 percent; and (4) other nonmetropolitan counties (1970–74) 1.1 to 1.4 percent.

5. Clay and Orr, *Metrolina Atlas*; Zuiches and Fuguitt, "Residential Preferences," pp. 491–504.

6. Bartley, "Limits of Urban Reform," pp. 253–55.

7. Salamon, "Urban Politics," pp. 418–28.

8. Jennings, *Community Influentials*; Wright, *Memphis Politics*; Moye, "Charlotte-Mecklenburg."

9. Moye, "Charlotte-Mecklenburg."

10. "New Strength in City Hall," pp. 156–59, 251–64; "Businessman's City," pp. 93–96.

11. Lowe, *Cities*; Salisbury, "Urban Politics," pp. 775–97.

12. Gelfand, *Nation of Cities*, pp. 158–64; Miller, *Urbanization of America*, pp. 181–97; Mollenkopf, "Post-War Politics," pp. 273–80; Barnekov and Rich, "Privatism and Urban Development," pp. 431–60.

13. Adrian, "Metropology," pp. 148–53; Miller, *Urbanization of America*, pp. 196–97.

14. Lubove, *Twentieth Century Pittsburgh*; Wolfinger, *Politics of Progress*; Banfield and Wilson, *City Politics*, pp. 135–36.

15. Stanley, *Cities in Trouble*, pp. 1–5.

16. Nathan and Adams, "Understanding Central City Hardship," pp. 51–62; Nelson and Clark, *Los Angeles Metropolitan Experience*.

17. Goldfield, "Limits of Suburban Growth," pp. 83–102.

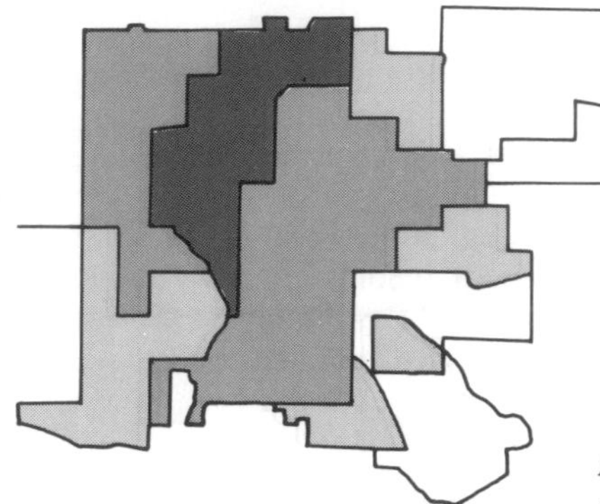

Bibliography

A reasonably complete bibliography on the growth of sunbelt cities from the 1940s through the 1970s would be as long as the present study. The following list of references is therefore limited to sources and collections that have been directly cited. However, several additional comments might be of use to others interested in pursuit of similar topics.

Many of the key events in the economic and political development of American cities are chronicled in periodicals edited for audiences of businessmen and government officials. *American City, Business Week, Fortune, Journal of Housing, National Civic Review* (*National Municipal Review* through 1958), *National Real Estate Investor, New York Times, Planning, Public Management, Urban Land*, and *Wall Street Journal* offer national coverage. They are complemented by local publications with similar readerships such as the *Atlanta Economic Review, City Club Bulletin* (Portland), and *Texas Business Review*. Among academic journals, *Land Economics, Phylon, Publius, Social Science Quarterly*, and *Urban Affairs Quarterly* proved most valuable for this study.

The major metropolitan dailies in the five case-study cities provide general coverage of growth and politics. In Portland, the *Oregonian* has long offered more depth in local news than the *Oregon Journal*. The *Virginian-Pilot* has held the same edge over the *Ledger-Star* in Norfolk. There is less basis for choosing between the *Denver Post* and *Rocky Mountain News*, the *San Antonio Express* and *San Antonio Light*, and the *Atlanta Journal* and *Atlanta Constitution*. Regional and city general-audience magazines that have flourished in the 1970s have usually lost their interest in significant analysis of urban growth and politics as their circulations and advertising budgets have grown. Cases in point are *Atlanta* (1962–), *Metro* (Norfolk area, 1970–), *Oregon Magazine* (1971–), and *SA: The Magazine of San Antonio* (1977–).

Manuscript resources for the study of metropolitan politics during the last generation are impressively rich in Portland. The Oregon Historical Society and the University of Oregon have had active collection programs and the City of Portland records have been carefully preserved and made accessible. The Old Dominion University Archives in Norfolk has also begun to preserve local political manuscript materials. At the other extreme, available collections for San Antonio are distressingly sparse.

Reports and studies issued by local government agencies are perhaps the most valuable source of information on patterns and trends in metropolitan growth. Under one name or another, every city has its departments of planning, economic development, and community development and its housing and redevelopment agencies. With both carrot and stick brandished by the federal government, every metropolitan area during the past two decades has also supported a growing regional planning agency—Southeastern Virginia Planning District Commission, Alamo Area Council of Governments, Denver Regional Council of Governments, Atlanta Regional Commission (Atlanta Regional Metropolitan Planning Commission), Metropolitan Service District (Columbia Region Association of Governments), and their equivalents.

The major difficulty with reports and documents from such agencies is that they are hard to locate. For a practicing planner, few things are of less interest than a ten-year-old report that gathers dust on the shelves if it escapes periodic housecleanings. For a librarian, few items are more trouble than a poorly bound, mimeographed report from a local agency that carries no predetermined Library of Congress catalog number. The line separating internal memoranda and working reports from documents formally issued for public consumption is also difficult to define. Unless the researcher comes across the rare agency that has conscientiously kept and cataloged its reports, his or her research will depend on the random collections of public and university libraries and the individual bookshelves of agency employees.

The situation is somewhat better in the case of documents issued by state agencies and special study commissions. Because reports of study commissions are limited in number and receive special public attention, they are relatively easy to find in libraries. Reports from the federally sponsored Urban Observatory program in the 1970s likewise are relatively accessible. In addition, governmental research institutes at major state universities are valuable sources of newsletters and monographs dealing with issues of metropolitan government. For this study, the specific organizations are the Institute of Government at the University of Virginia, the Institute of Public Affairs at the University of Texas, the Bureau of Governmental Research and Service at the University of Colorado, and the Bureau of Municipal Research at the University of Oregon.

Books and Reports

Abbott, Carl. *Colorado: A History of the Centennial State*. Boulder: Colorado Associated University Press, 1976.

Adde, Leo. *Nine Cities: The Anatomy of Downtown Renewal*. Washington: Urban Land Institute, 1969.

Allen, Robert. *Our Fair City*. New York: Vanguard, 1947.

Altschuler, Alan. *Community Control*. New York: Pegasus, 1970.

American Society of Planning Officials. *The Atlanta Region Metropolitan Planning Commission: The Years Ahead*. Chicago: 1967.

Anderson, Martin. *The Federal Bulldozer*. Cambridge: MIT Press, 1964.

Banfield, Edward. *Big City Politics*. New York: Random House, 1965.
______, and Wilson, James Q. *City Politics*. New York: Vintage, 1966.
Banham, Reyner. *Los Angeles: The Architecture of the Four Ecologies*. New York: Harper and Row, 1971.
Bartley, Numan V., and Graham, Hugh D. *Southern Politics and the Second Reconstruction*. Baltimore: The Johns Hopkins Press, 1975.
Beale, Calvin. *The Revival of Population Growth in Nonmetropolitan America*. Washington: Economic Development Division, Economic Research Service, Department of Agriculture, 1975.
Bender, Charles. *Report on Politics in Seattle*. Cambridge: Harvard-MIT Joint Center for Urban Studies, 1961.
Berge, Wendell. *Economic Freedom for the West*. Lincoln: University of Nebraska Press, 1946.
Bernard, William C. *Metro Denver: Mile High Government*. Boulder: Bureau of Governmental Research and Service, 1970.
Berry, Brian. *Growth Centers in the American Urban System*. Cambridge, Mass.: Ballinger Publishing Co., 1973.
______. *The Human Consequences of Urbanization*. New York: St. Martin's Press, 1973.
______, and Kasarda, John. *Contemporary Urban Ecology*. New York: Macmillan Co., 1977.
Blum, John M. *V Was for Victory: Politics and American Culture During World War II*. New York: Harcourt, Brace, Jovanovich, 1976.
Bogue, Donald J., and Beale, Calvin. *Economic Areas of the United States*. New York: The Free Press, 1961.
Briggs, Asa. *Victorian Cities*. New York: Harper and Row, 1963.
Brownell, Blaine. *The Urban Ethos in the New South, 1920–1930*. Baton Rouge: Louisiana State University Press, 1976.
______, and Goldfield, David, eds. *The City in Southern History: The Growth of Urban Civilization in the South*. Port Washington, N.Y.: Kennikat Press, 1977.
Chambers, Lenoir. *Salt Water and Printers Ink: Norfolk and Its Newspapers 1865–1965*. Chapel Hill: University of North Carolina Press, 1967.
Clark, Dan E., II and Associates. *Portland Housing Survey*. Portland: City of Portland and State of Oregon, 1950.
Clark, S. D. *The Suburban Society*. Toronto: University of Toronto Press, 1966.
Clay, James W., and Orr, Douglas M., Jr. *Metrolina Atlas*. Chapel Hill: University of North Carolina Press, 1972.
Clotfelter, James, and Naylor, Thomas H. *Strategies for Change in the South*. Chapel Hill: University of North Carolina Press, 1975.
Colman, William. *Cities, Suburbs, and States: Governing and Financing Urban America*. New York: The Free Press, 1975.
Colorado Writers' Project. *Colorado: A Guide to the Highest State*. New York: Hastings House, 1941.
Cottrell, Charles. *Municipal Services Equalization in San Antonio, Texas:*

Explorations in "Chinatown." San Antonio: St. Mary's University, 1976.

Cox, James L. *Metropolitan Water Supply: The Denver Experience*. Boulder: Bureau of Governmental Research and Service, 1967.

Danielson, Michael. *The Politics of Exclusion*. New York: Columbia University Press, 1976.

Denver Area Welfare Council. *The Spanish-American Population of Denver*. Denver: 1950.

Denver Metropolitan Area Conference. *Proceedings of the Denver Metropolitan Area Conference*. Denver: 1948.

Denver Regional Association. *Facing the Challenge of War and Post-War Problems in the Denver Area*. Denver: 1943.

Denver Research Institute. *Economic Forces behind Colorado's Growth, 1870–1962*. Denver: Colorado Department of Employment, 1963.

Denver Unity Council. *The Spanish-Speaking Population of Denver: Housing, Employment, Health, Recreation, Education*. Denver: 1946.

Dobriner, William. *Class in Suburbia*. Englewood Cliffs, N.J.: Prentice-Hall, 1963.

Donaldson, Scott. *The Suburban Myth*. New York: Columbia University Press, 1969.

Dorsett, Lyle. *The Queen City: A History of Denver*. Boulder: Pruett Publishing Co., 1977.

Dos Passos, John. *State of the Nation*. Boston: Houghton Mifflin, 1944.

Douglass, Harlan P. *The Suburban Trend*. New York: The Century Co., 1925.

Downtown Denver Master Plan Committee. *Development Guide for Downtown Denver*. Denver: 1963.

Duncan, Otis D., et al. *Metropolis and Region*. Baltimore: The Johns Hopkins Press, 1960.

Elazar, Daniel. *Cities of the Prairie*. New York: Basic Books, 1970.

Elman, Richard. *Ill-At-East in Compton*. New York: Pantheon, 1967.

Funigello, Phillip J. *The Challenge to Urban Liberalism: Federal-City Relations During World War II*. Knoxville: University of Tennessee Press, 1978.

Gans, Herbert. *The Levittowners*. New York: Pantheon, 1967.

———. *The Urban Villagers*. New York: The Free Press, 1962.

Garnsey, Morris. *America's New Frontier: The Mountain West*. New York: Alfred A. Knopf, 1950.

Gelfand, Mark. *A Nation of Cities: The Federal Government and Urban America, 1933–65*. New York: Oxford University Press, 1975.

Gray, Kenneth. *Report on Politics in Denver*. Cambridge: Harvard-MIT Joint Center for Urban Studies, 1959.

Greer, Guy, ed. *The Problems of Cities and Towns: Proceedings of the Conference on Urbanism, March 5–6, 1942*. Cambridge: Harvard University Press, 1942.

———. *Your City Tomorrow*. New York: Macmillan Co., 1947.

Gruen, Victor. *The Heart of Our Cities: The Urban Crisis, Diagnosis and Cure*. New York: Simon and Schuster, 1964.
Gunther, John. *Inside USA*. New York: Harper and Row, 1947.
Haar, Charles, ed. *The President's Task Force on Suburban Problems: Final Report*. Cambridge, Mass.: Ballinger Publishing Co., 1974.
Haas, Edward. *De Lesseps S. Morrison and the Image of Reform: New Orleans Politics, 1946–1961*. Baton Rouge: Louisiana State University Press, 1974.
Hackenstaff, Cyrus. *Memories of Cyrus Hackenstaff*. Denver: 1976.
Hadden, Jeffrey, and Masotti, Louis, eds. *The Urbanization of the Suburbs*. Beverly Hills: Sage Publications, 1973.
Hallman, Howard. *The Organization and Structure of Neighborhood Councils*. New York: Praeger Publishers, 1977.
Hartman, Chester. *Yerba Buena: Land Grab and Community Resistance in San Francisco*. Berkeley: National Housing and Economic Development Law Institute, Earl Warren Legal Institute, University of California, 1974.
Hartshorn, Truman. *Metropolis in Georgia: Atlanta's Rise as a Transaction Center*. Cambridge, Mass.: Ballinger Publishing Co., 1976.
Hawkins, Brett. *Nashville Metro: The Politics of City-County Consolidation*. Nashville: Vanderbilt University Press, 1966.
Hebert, Richard. *Highways to Nowhere: The Politics of City Transportation*. New York: Bobbs-Merrill, 1972.
Henderson, Richard B. *Maury Maverick: A Political Biography*. Austin: University of Texas Press, 1970.
Hoover, Calvin B., and Ratchford, B. U. *Economic Resources and Policies of the South*. New York: Macmillan Co., 1951.
______. *The Economy of the South: Report of the Joint Committee on the Economic Report. 81st Congress, First Session*. Washington: Government Printing Office, 1949.
Housing in Denver. University of Denver Reports, Vol. 17. Denver: University of Denver, 1941.
Howe, Frederic. *The City: The Hope of Democracy*. New York: Charles Scribner's Sons, 1906.
Hoyt, Homer. *The Structure and Growth of Residential Neighborhoods in American Cities*. Washington: Federal Housing Administration, 1939.
Jacobs, Jane. *The Death and Life of Great American Cities*. New York: Random House, 1961.
Jennings, M. Kent. *Community Influentials: The Elites of Atlanta*. New York: The Free Press, 1964.
Judd, Dennis. *The Politics of American Cities: Private Power and Public Responsibility*. Boston: Little, Brown and Co., 1979.
Jusenius, Carol, and Ledebur, Larry. *A Myth in the Making: The Southern Economic Challenge and Northern Economic Decline*. Washington: Economic Development Administration, 1976.

Kahn, E. J., Jr. *The American People: The Findings of the 1970 Census*. New York: Weybright and Talley, 1974.

Key, V. O. *Southern Politics in State and Nation*. New York: Alfred A. Knopf, 1949.

Kramer, John. *North American Suburbs*. Berkeley, Calif.: Glendessary Press, 1972.

Landolt, Robert. *The Mexican-American Workers of San Antonio, Texas*. New York: Arno Press, 1976.

Lane, Frederic C., et al. *Ships for Victory: A History of Shipbuilding Under the U.S. Maritime Commission in World War II*. Baltimore: The Johns Hopkins Press, 1951.

League of Women Voters of Colorado. *Colorado's Water Resources*. Denver: 1958.

Leslie, Warren. *Dallas Public and Private*. New York: Grossman Publishers, 1964.

Lineberry, Robert L. *Equality and Urban Policy: The Distribution of Municipal Public Services*. Beverly Hills: Sage Publications, 1977.

Lowe, Jeanne. *Cities in a Race with Time*. New York: Random House, 1967.

Lubell, Samuel. *The Hidden Crisis in American Politics*. New York: W. W. Norton and Co., 1970.

Lubove, Roy. *Twentieth Century Pittsburgh: Government, Business, and Environmental Change*. New York: John Wiley, 1969.

McCorkle, Stuart. *Municipal Annexation in Texas*. Austin: University of Texas Institute of Public Affairs, 1965.

McWilliams, Carey. *California: The Great Exception*. Westport, Conn.: Greenwood Press, 1971.

Marsh, Charles F., et al. *The Hampton Roads Communities in World War II*. Chapel Hill: University of North Carolina Press, 1951.

Martin, Harold. *William Berry Hartsfield: Mayor of Atlanta*. Athens: University of Georgia Press, 1978.

Meinig, Donald. *Imperial Texas*. Austin: University of Texas Press, 1969.

______. *Southwest: Three Peoples in Geographical Change*. New York: Oxford University Press, 1971.

Menefee, Selden. *Assignment: USA*. New York: Reynal and Hitchcock, 1943.

Meyer, Agnes. *Journey Through Chaos*. New York: Harcourt, Brace and Co., 1944.

Mezerik, A. G. *The Revolt of the South and West*. New York: Duell, Sloan, and Pearce, 1946.

Miller, Zane. *Boss Cox's Cincinnati: Urban Politics in the Progressive Era*. New York: Oxford University Press, 1969.

______. *The Urbanization of America*. New York: Harcourt, Brace, Jovanovitch, 1973.

Moore, Mechlin D. *Downtown Denver*. Technical Bulletin No. 54. Washington: Urban Land Institute, 1965.

Morgan, Neil. *Westward Tilt: The American West Today*. New York: Random House, 1963.

Moses, Robert. *Portland Improvement*. New York: William Rudge's Sons, 1943.

Muller, Peter. *The Outer City: Geographical Consequences of the Urbanization of the Suburbs*. Washington: Association of American Geographers, 1976.

Muller, Thomas. *Growing and Declining Urban Areas*. Washington: The Urban Institute, 1975.

Nash, Gerald. *The American West in the Twentieth Century*. Englewood Cliffs, N.J.: Prentice-Hall, 1973.

Nelson, Howard J., and Clark, William A. V. *The Los Angeles Metropolitan Experience: Uniqueness, Generality and the Goal of the Good Life*. Cambridge, Mass.: Ballinger Publishing Co., 1976.

Niemi, Albert. *Gross State Product and Productivity in the Southeast*. Chapel Hill: University of North Carolina Press, 1975.

Northwest Regional Council. *Pacific Northwest: Problems and Materials*. Portland: 1940.

Ogburn, William F. *Social Characteristics of Cities*. Chicago: International City Managers Association, 1937.

Oregon Bureau of Municipal Research and Service. *Basic Factors Relating to the Financial Problems of the City of Portland*. Eugene: University of Oregon, 1946.

Pacific Coast Board of Intergovernmental Relations. *Economic Outlook for the Pacific Coast, 1950–1960*. San Francisco: 1950.

Paul, Rodman. *Mining Frontiers of the Far West*. New York: Holt, Rinehart and Winston, 1963.

Perkin, Robert. *The First Hundred Years: An Informal History of Denver and the Rocky Mountain News*. Garden City, N.Y.: Doubleday and Co., 1959.

Perloff, Harvey, et al. *Regions, Resources, and Economic Growth*. Baltimore: The Johns Hopkins Press, 1960.

Peterson, Lorin. *The Day of the Mugwump*. New York: Random House, 1961.

Peyton, Green. *San Antonio: City in the Sun*. New York: McGraw-Hill Book Co., 1946.

Phillips, Kevin. *The Emerging Republican Majority*. New Rochelle, N.Y.: Arlington House, 1969.

Picnot, T. N. *An Economic and Industrial Survey of San Antonio, Texas*. San Antonio: City of San Antonio, 1942.

Pomeroy, Earl. *The Pacific Slope: A History of California, Oregon, Washington, Idaho, Utah, and Nevada*. New York: Alfred A. Knopf, 1965.

Portland State College Urban Studies Center. *Annexation, Incorporation and Consolidation in the Portland Metropolitan Area*. Portland: Portland Metropolitan Study Commission, 1968.

Public Administration Service. *The City Government of Portland, Oregon: A Survey Report*. Chicago: 1959.

Rand, Christopher. *Los Angeles: The Ultimate City*. New York: Oxford

University Press, 1967.

Real Estate Research Corporation. *Economic Survey and Market Analysis of Downtown Denver*. Chicago: 1962.

———. *Regional Housing Study: 1974*. Norfolk: Southeastern Virginia Planning District Commission, 1974.

Reed, Thomas H., and Reed, Doris D. *Report on Annexation: City of Norfolk and Environs*. Norfolk, 1948.

Sale, Kirkpatrick. *Power Shift: The Rise of the Southern Rim and Its Challenge to the Eastern Establishment*. New York: Random House, 1975.

Sale, Roger. *Seattle: Past to Present*. Seattle: University of Washington Press, 1976.

Schlegel, Marvin. *Conscripted City: Norfolk in World War II*. Norfolk: Norfolk War History Commission, 1951.

Schnore, Leo. *Class and Race in City and Suburbs*. Chicago: Markham, 1972.

Scott, Mel. *American City Planning Since 1890*. Berkeley: University of California Press, 1969.

———. *Metropolitan Los Angeles*. Los Angeles: The Haynes Foundation, 1949.

———. *The San Francisco Bay Area: A Metropolis in Perspective*. Berkeley: University of California Press, 1959.

Seeley, John R., Sim, R. Alexander, and Loosley, Elizabeth W. *Crestwood Heights: A Study of the Culture of Suburban Life*. New York: Basic Books, 1955.

Shryock, Henry S., Jr. *Population and Mobility Within the United States*. Chicago: University of Chicago Community and Family Study Center, 1964.

Sjoberg, Gideon. *The Preindustrial City*. New York: The Free Press, 1960.

Southern Growth Policies Board. *Growth Management Policies for the South*. Research Triangle Park, N.C.: 1974.

Spectorsky, Auguste C. *The Exurbanites*. Philadelphia: Lippincott, 1955.

Staehli, Alfred. *Preservation Options for Portland Neighborhoods*. Portland: Neighborhood History Project, 1974.

Stanley, David T. *Cities in Trouble*. Columbus, Ohio: Academy for Contemporary Problems, 1976.

Stein, Maurice. *The Eclipse of Community*. Princeton, N.J.: Princeton University Press, 1960.

Sternlieb, George, and Hughes, James. *Current Population Trends in the United States*. New Brunswick, N.J.: Center for Urban Policy Research, 1978.

Stone, Harold A.; Price, Don K.; and Stone, Kathryn H. *City Manager Government in Nine Cities*. Chicago: Public Administration Service, 1940.

Stromberg, Charles, and Wilcox, Robert, eds. *The Urban Manager as an*

Agent of Planned Change. Denver: University of Colorado at Denver, 1977.

Sundquist, James. *Dynamics of the Party System*. Washington: Brookings Institution, 1973.

Taeuber, Karl E., and Taeuber, Alma F. *Negroes in Cities*. New York: Atheneum, 1972.

Temple, David. *Merger Politics: Local Government Consolidation in Tidewater Virginia*. Charlottesville: University of Virginia Press, 1972.

Texas Writers' Project. *San Antonio: An Authoritative Guide to the City and Its Environs*. San Antonio: The Clegg Co., 1938.

Thometz, Carol E. *The Decision-Makers: The Power Structure of Dallas*. Dallas: Southern Methodist University Press, 1963.

Thompson, William Irwin. *At the Edge of History*. New York: Harper and Row, 1971.

Tindall, George. *The Emergence of the New South, 1913–1945*. Baton Rouge: Louisiana State University Press, 1967.

Urban Studies Center, Portland State College. *Municipal Annexation, Incorporation, and Consolidation in the Portland Metropolitan Area*. Portland: Metropolitan Study Commission, 1968.

Walker, Robert. *The Planning Function in Urban Government*. Chicago: University of Chicago Press, 1941.

Watterson, Wayt T., and Watterson, Roberta S. *The Politics of New Communities: A Case Study of San Antonio Ranch*. New York: Praeger Publishers, 1975.

Weber, Adna F. *The Growth of Cities in the Nineteenth Century*. New York: Macmillan Co., 1899.

Wenum, John. *Annexation as a Technique for Metropolitan Growth: The Case of Phoenix*. Tempe: Arizona State University, 1970.

Wertenbacker, Thomas J., and Schlegel, Marvin. *Norfolk: Historic Southern Port*. Durham: Duke University Press, 1962.

West, Ray B., ed. *Rocky Mountain Cities*. New York: W. W. Norton and Co., 1949.

Whyte, William H. *The Organization Man*. New York: Simon and Schuster, 1956.

Wilson, James Q., ed. *Urban Renewal: The Record and the Controversy*. Cambridge: MIT Press, 1966.

Wirt, Frederick, et al. *On the City's Rim: Politics and Policy in Suburbia*. Lexington, Mass.: D. C. Heath, 1972.

———. *Power in the City*. Berkeley: University of California Press, 1975.

Wolfinger, Raymond. *The Politics of Progress*. Englewood Cliffs, N.J.: Prentice-Hall, 1974.

Wright, William E. *Memphis Politics: A Study in Racial Bloc Voting*. New York: McGraw-Hill Book Co., 1962.

Articles

Abbott, Carl. "Boom State and Boom City: Stages in Denver's Growth." *The Colorado Magazine* 50 (Summer 1973): 207–30.

———. "Plural Society in Colorado." *Phylon* 39 (September 1978): 250–60.

———. "Suburb and City: Changing Patterns of Socioeconomic Status in Metropolitan Denver Since 1940." *Social Science History* 2 (Fall 1977): 53–71.

Abbott, Margery Post. "Energy Recovery from Solid Waste: Planning in Southeastern Virginia." *Tidewater Economic Report* 5 (April 1978): 2–3.

———, and Abbott, Carl. "Colonial Place, Norfolk: Residential Integration in a Southern Urban Neighborhood." *Urban Affairs Papers* 1 (Fall 1979): 1–17.

Adrian, Charles. "Metropology: Folklore and Field Research." *Public Administration Review* 21 (Summer 1961): 148–53.

Ashby, Lynn. "The Supercities: Houston." *Saturday Review* 3 n.s. (4 September 1976): 16–19.

"Atlanta Annexation Try Fails." *American City* 62 (September 1947): 93.

"Atlanta Bulwark." *Business Week* (15 September 1945): 43–45.

"Atlanta-Fulton Study Issues." *National Civic Review* 59 (March 1970): 156.

Barnekov, Timothy, and Rich, Daniel. "Privatism and Urban Development: An Analysis of the Organized Influence of Local Business Elites." *Urban Affairs Quarterly* 12 (June 1977): 431–60.

Barnett, Robert. "Concern and Comprehensive Planning." *Journal of Housing* 35 (August 1978): 414–16.

Bartley, Numan V. "The Limits of Urban Reform in the New South." *Journal of Urban History* 2 (February 1976): 253–55.

Bauer, Catherine. "Cities in Flux." *American Scholar* 13 (Winter 1943–44): 70–84.

———. "War-Time Housing in Defense Areas." *Architect and Engineer* 151 (October 1942): 33–35.

Baumhauer, Charles. "Municipal Services of Mobile Overtaxed by Defense Activity." *American City* 57 (February 1942): 66.

Beiman, Irving. "Birmingham: Steel Giant with a Glass Jaw." In *Our Fair City*, edited by Robert Allen, pp. 99–122. New York: Vanguard, 1947.

Bennett, Carol, and Zlatkovitch, Charles. "San Antonio: A Military, Trade and Service Center." *Texas Business Review* 51 (July, 1977): 144–49.

Berry, Brian. "The Counterurbanization Process: Urban America Since 1970." In *Urbanization and Counterurbanization*, edited by Brian Berry, pp. 17–30. Beverly Hills: Sage Publications, 1976.

Bevins, Carl. "Atlanta's Staggered Plan." *American City* 58 (November 1943): 93.

Birch, David. "From Suburb to Urban Place." *Annals of the American Academy of Political and Social Science* 422 (November 1975): 25–35.

"Blueprint for San Diego." *Business Week* (31 March 1945): 36–37.
"Boom Town Inquiry." *Business Week* (21 June 1941): 30–31.
"Boom Town: San Diego." *Life* 11 (28 July 1941): 64–69.
Bratt, Elmer C., and Wilson, D. Stevens. "Regional Distortions Resulting from the War." *Survey of Current Business* 23 (October 1943): 9–15.
Breckenfeld, Gurney. "Business Loves the Sunbelt (and Vice Versa)." *Fortune* 95 (June 1977): 132–46.
Brownell, Blaine. "Urbanization in the South: A Unique Experience?" *Mississippi Quarterly* 26 (Spring 1973): 105–20.
Browning, Clyde, and Gesler, Will. "The Sun Belt—Snow Belt: A Case of Sloppy Regionalizing." *Professional Geographer* 31 (February 1979): 66–74.
Buckner, Bill. "Atlanta Broadens Its Regional Base." *Planning* 38 (August 1972): 144–46.
Burka, Paul. "The Second Battle of the Alamo." *Texas Monthly* (December 1977): 139–43, 218.
"The Businessmen's City." *Fortune* 57 (February 1958): 93–96.
"Businessmen Take Over San Antonio." *Business Week* (12 January 1952): 104–12.
"California County Plans for Peace Era." *American City* 58 (August 1943): 77.
Carhart, Arthur. "Denver Makes a Plan." *City Planning* 6 (August 1930): 80–82.
Carpenter, Dwight M. "Wichita: Cowboys, Crises, and Tuesday Night Fights." In *Urban Politics in the Southwest*, edited by Leonard Goodall, pp. 224–43. Tempe: Arizona State University Institute of Public Administration, 1967.
Carter, Luther. "Desegregation in Norfolk." *South Atlantic Quarterly* 58 (Autumn 1959): 507–20.
______. "Virginia Refinery Battle: Another Dilemma in Energy Facility Siting." *Science* 199 (10 February 1978): 668–71.
Casey, Rick. "Henry Cisneros: He Wants to be San Antonio's Philosopher/Mayor." *SA: The Magazine of San Antonio* 1 (October 1977): 27–38.
______. "The Politics of Sewage, or Vice-Versa." *SA: The Magazine of San Antonio* 2 (February 1979): 44–47.
Cater, Douglas. "Atlanta: Smart Politics and Good Race Relations." *The Reporter* 17 (July 1957): 18–21.
______. "How Different is the South?" *Washington Post* (10 December 1976).
Chapman, John. "San Antonio." *Southwest Review* 22 (Autumn 1936): 16–40.
"City Planning: Battle of the Approaches." *Fortune* 28 (November 1943): 164–68, 222–23.
Cleghorn, Reese. "Atlanta." *City* 5 (January-February 1971): 35–37.
Cline, Dorothy, and Wolf, T. Phillip. "Albuquerque: The End of a Reform

Era." In *Urban Politics in the Southwest*, edited by Leonard Goodall, pp. 7–22. Tempe: Arizona State University Institute of Public Administration, 1967.

Colburn, George A. "The Underside of Paradise." *Planning* 43 (April/May 1977): 16–20.

Connery, Robert H., and Leach, Richard H. "Southern Metropolis: Challenge to Government." In *The American South in the 1960s*, edited by Avery Leiserson, pp. 60–81. New York: Praeger Publishers, 1964.

Cookingham, L. P. "The Effect of War upon Cities." In *Planning: 1943*, pp. 15–26. Chicago: American Society of Planning Officials, 1943.

Cottrell, Charles, and Stevens, R. Michael. "The 1975 Voting Rights Acts and San Antonio, Texas: Toward a Federal Guarantee of a Republican Form of Government." *Publius* 8 (Winter 1978): 79–100.

Crane, Bill. "San Antonio Pluralistic City and Monolithic Government." In *Urban Politics in the Southwest*, edited by Leonard Goodall, pp. 127–42. Tempe: Arizona State University Institute of Public Administration, 1967.

Dabney, Virginius. "Richmond's Quiet Revolution." *Saturday Review* 47 (29 February 1964): 18–19, 28.

"Dallas Meets a Challenge." *American City* 58 (October 1943): 41.

Darmstadter, Doris. "Metropolitan Atlanta." *National Municipal Review* 30 (May 1941): 258–63.

Davenport, W. "Norfolk Night." *Colliers* 109 (28 March 1942): 17–18.

Dent, Borden. "The Challenge to Downtown Shopping." *Atlanta Economic Review* 28 (January-February 1976): 29–33.

de Torres, Juan. "Economics and Geography: The West Coast." *Across the Board* 14 (July 1977): 51–56.

"Detour Through Purgatory." *Fortune* 31 (February 1945): 181–84, 234–40.

Doeppers, Daniel. "The Globeville Neighborhood in Denver." *Geographical Review* 57 (October 1967): 506–22.

Dye, Thomas. "Urban Political Integration: Conditions Associated with Annexation." *Midwest Journal of Political Science* 8 (November 1964): 430–44.

"The Dydamic Men of Dallas." *Fortune* 39 (February 1949): 98–103, 162–66.

Elazar, Daniel. "Suburbanization: Reviving the Town on the Metropolitan Frontier." *Publius* 5 (Winter 1975): 53–80.

Ennor, Howard R. "Portland Voters Approve Public Works Program." *National Municipal Review* 31 (September 1944): 430–31.

Farley, Reynolds. "Components of Suburban Population Growth." In *The Changing Face of the Suburbs*, edited by Barry Schwartz, pp. 3–38. Chicago: University of Chicago Press, 1976.

Fates, Linda. "CZO: The Virginia Beach Land Use Hassle." *Metro Magazine* (August 1973): pp. 22–27.

Fava, Sylvia. "Beyond Suburbia." *Annals of the American Academy of Political and Social Science* 422 (November 1975): 10–24.

"Federal Spending: The North's Loss is the Sunbelt's Gain." *National Journal* 8 (26 June 1976): 878–90.

Feiss, Carl. "How Cities are Preparing for the Post-War Period: Denver." In *Planning: 1944*, pp. 46–50. Chicago: American Society of Planning Officials, 1944.

Fleischman, Arnold. "Sunbelt Boosterism: The Politics of Postwar Growth and Annexation in San Antonio." In *The Rise of the Sunbelt Cities*, edited by David C. Perry and Alfred J. Watkins, pp. 151–68. Beverly Hills: Sage Publications, 1977.

Fleming, Roscoe. "Denver: Civic Schizophrenia." In *Our Fair City*, edited by Robert Allen, pp. 277–98. New York: Vanguard, 1947.

Forstall, Richard. "Annexation and Corporate Changes, 1970–74." In *The Municipal Yearbook 1976*, pp. 59–61. Chicago: International City Management Association, 1976.

"Forty Million Dollar Bond Issue Voted for Atlanta and Fulton County Improvements." *American City* 61 (September 1946): 120.

Foster, Mark. "Colorado's Defeat of the 1976 Winter Olympics." *The Colorado Magazine* 53 (Spring 1976): 163–86.

Freedgood, Seymour. "Life in Buckhead." *Fortune* 64 (September 1961): 108–14.

Freeman, H. D. "Local Planning and Economic Opportunity." In *Proceedings of the Fifth Annual Pacific Northwest Regional Planning Conference*, pp. 134–37. Portland: Pacific Northwest Regional Planning Commission, 1939.

———. "Public Utility Problems in Fringe Areas." In *The Urban-Rural Fringe: Proceedings of the Commonwealth Conference*, pp. 56–58. Eugene: University of Oregon, 1942.

Fried, Marc. "Grieving for a Lost Home." In *The Urban Condition*, edited by Leonard J. Duhl, pp. 151–71. New York: Basic Books, 1963.

Friesma, H. Paul. "Cities, Suburbs, and Short-Lived Models of Metropolitan Politics." In *Urbanization of the Suburbs*, edited by Jeffrey Hadden and Louis Masotti, pp. 239–52. Beverly Hills: Sage Publications, 1973.

Fugard, John R. "What's Happening to Our Central Business Districts." In *National Conference on Planning: 1940*, pp. 107–10. Chicago: American Society of Planning Officials, 1940.

"Fulton-Atlanta Merger Debated." *National Civic Review* 59 (February 1970): 97–98.

Funigello, Phillip J. "City Planning in World War II: The Experience of the National Resources Planning Board." *Social Science Quarterly* 53 (June 1972): 91–104.

Furniss, Susan. "The Response of the Colorado General Assembly to Metropolitan Reform." *Western Political Quarterly* 26 (December 1973): 754–65.

Gans, Herbert. "The Failure of Urban Renewal." *Commentary* 40 (April 1965): 29–37.

Garnsey, Morris. "The Rise of Regionalism in the Mountain West." *The*

Nation 163 (21 September 1946): 18–20.

"Georgia Legislature Streamlines City-County Government." *American City* 66 (May 1951): 113.

Glenn, Norval. "Suburbanization in the United States Since World War II." In *Urbanization of the Suburbs*, edited by Jeffrey Hadden and Louis Masotti, pp. 51–78. Beverly Hills: Sage Publications, 1973.

Goldfield, David R. "The Limits of Suburban Growth: The Washington, D.C. SMSA." *Urban Affairs Quarterly* 12 (September 1976): 83–102.

Goldsmith, Harold F., and Stockwell, Edward G. "Interrelationship of Occupational Selectivity Patterns Among City, Suburban and Fringe Areas of Major Metropolitan Centers." *Land Economics* 45 (May 1969): 194–205.

Goodall, Leonard E. "Phoenix: Reformers at Work." In *Urban Politics in the Southwest*, edited by Leonard Goodall, pp. 110–26. Tempe: Arizona State University Institute of Public Administration, 1967.

______. "Political Patterns in Southwestern Cities." In *Urbanization in the Southwest: A Symposium*, edited by Clyde Wingfield, pp. 33–41. El Paso: University of Texas at El Paso, 1968.

Gosnell, Cullen. "Fulton County and Atlanta Survey Bears Fruit." *National Municipal Review* 29 (January 1940): 60–62.

Granneberg, Audrey. "Maury Maverick's San Antonio." *Survey Graphic* 28 (July 1939): 421–26.

Greer, Ann L. "Predictions That Came True: The Suburbanized Metropolis." *Urban Affairs Quarterly* 13 (June 1978): 505–14.

Grey, Arthur L., Jr. "Los Angeles: Urban Prototype." *Land Economics* 35 (August 1959): 232–42.

Haas, Edward. "The Southern Metropolis, 1940–1976." In *The City in Southern History*, edited by Blaine Brownell and David Goldfield, pp. 159–213. Port Washington, N.Y.: Kennikat Press, 1977.

Hamilton, C. Horace. "Southern Migration." In *The South in Continuity and Change*, edited by John C. McKinney and Edgar T. Thompson, pp. 53–78. Durham: Duke University Press, 1965.

Hansen, Bertil. "Tulsa: The Oil Folks at Home." In *Urban Politics in the Southwest*, edited by Leonard Goodall, pp. 196–223. Tempe: Arizona State University Institute of Public Administration, 1967.

Harrell, Charles. "Norfolk Considers Annexing Large Area." *Public Management* 31 (January 1949): 16–17.

Harris, Chauncey. "Suburbs." *American Journal of Sociology* 49 (July 1943): 1–13.

Hartman, Chester. "The Housing of Relocated Families." *Journal of the American Institute of Planners* 30 (November 1964): 266–86.

Hartshorn, Truman. "Getting Around Atlanta: New Approaches." *Atlanta Economic Review* 28 (January-February 1978): 43–51.

Harvey, R. O., and Clark, W. A. V. "The Nature and Economics of Urban Sprawl." *Land Economics* 41 (February 1965): 1–9.

Haselbush, Willard. "Denver: Activity Remains Strong in Both Downtown and Suburban Markets." *National Real Estate Investor* 21 (September 1979): 81–104.

Hauser, Philip M. "Wartime Population Changes and Postwar Prospects." *Journal of Marketing* 8 (January 1944): 238–48.

Hautaluoma, Jacob, Loomis, Ross, and Viney, Wayne. "Organizational Influence in Denver: Structure and Process." *Rocky Mountain Social Science Journal* 7 (October 1970): 11–17.

Havemann, Joel, and Stanfield, Rochelle. "A Year Later, the Frostbelt Strikes Back." *National Journal* (2 July 1977): 1028–37.

Haverty, Rawson. "The Atlanta Story." *Atlanta Economic Review* 17 (June 1967): 13–15.

Hawkins, Brett. "Life Style, Demographic Distance, and Voter Support of City-County Consolidation." *Social Science Quarterly* 48 (December 1967): 325–37.

Hawley, Willis D. "On Understanding Metropolitan Political Integration." In *Theoretical Perspectives on Urban Politics*, edited by Willis D. Hawley and Michael Lipsky, pp. 100–145. Englewood Cliffs, N.J.: Prentice-Hall, 1976.

Hays, Samuel. "The Politics of Municipal Reform in the Progressive Era." *Pacific Northwest Quarterly* 55 (October 1964): 157–69.

Heddan, Paul Van T. "Atlanta Breaks Through Its Boundaries." *American City* 66 (November 1951): 106–7.

Hein, Virginia H. "The Image of a City 'Too Busy to Hate': Atlanta in the 1960s." *Phylon* 33 (Fall 1972): 205–21.

Henley, James W., Jr. "New Town in Town Downtown." *Journal of Housing* 32 (July 1975): 271–72.

Hetherton, P. "State and Local Planning Boards and Defense." In *Proceedings of the National Conference on Planning: 1941*, pp. 194–99. Chicago: American Society of Planning Officials, 1941.

Hirsch, Werner Z. "Los Angeles: A Leading City." In *Los Angeles: Viability and Prospects for Metropolitan Leadership*, edited by Werner Z. Hirsch, pp. 237–41. New York: Praeger Publishers, 1971.

Holden, Mathew, Jr. "The Governance of the Metropolitan Area as a Problem in Diplomacy." *Journal of Politics* 26 (August 1964): 627–47.

Holland, Lynwood M. "Widening the Scope." *National Civic Review* 56 (July 1967): 385–91.

Honey, Rex. "Metropolitan Governance." In *Urban Policymaking and Metropolitan Dynamics*, edited by John S. Adams, pp. 425–62. Cambridge, Mass.: Ballinger Publishing Co., 1976.

"Houston Is Where They're Moving." *Fortune* 83 (February 1971): 83–91.

Hoyt, Homer. "The Structure of American Cities in the Post-War Era." *American Journal of Sociology* 47 (January 1943): 475–81.

Hughes, Clyde M. "Annexation and Relocation of Functions." *Public Management* 34 (February 1952): 26–30.

Hunt, Don. "Tidewater: Shortage of Office Space Predicted as Occupancies, Rental Rates Rise." *National Real Estate Investor* 22 (February 1980): 95–99.

Hutchinson, John D., Jr., and Beer, Elizabeth T. "In-Migration and Atlanta's Neighborhoods." *Atlanta Economic Review* 28 (March-April 1978): 7–14.

Huxtable, Ada Louise. "Deep in the Heart of Nowhere." *New York Times*, 15 February 1976.

Ippolito, Dennis S., and Levin, Martin L. "Public Regardingness, Race, and Social Class: The Case of a Rapid Transit Referendum." *Social Science Quarterly* 51 (December 1970): 628–34.

Jackson, Harold E. "Discrimination and Busing: The Denver School Board Election of May, 1969." *Rocky Mountain Social Science Journal* 8 (October 1971): 101–8.

Jackson, Kenneth. "Metropolitan Government versus Political Autonomy: Politics on the Crabgrass Frontier." In *Cities in American History*, edited by Kenneth Jackson and Stanley Schultz, pp. 442–62. New York: Alfred A. Knopf, 1972.

Janeway, Elliott. "Trials and Errors: Trouble on the Northwest Frontier." *Fortune* 26 (November 1942): 24–32.

Jennings, M. Kent, and Ziegler, Harmon. "Class, Party and Race in Four Types of Elections: The Case of Atlanta." *Journal of Politics* 28 (May 1966): 391–407.

Jones, Mack H. "Black Political Empowerment in Atlanta: Myth and Reality." *Annals of the American Academy of Political and Social Science* 439 (September 1978): 90–117.

Joyner, Conrad. "Tucson: The Eighth Year of the Seven Year Itch." In *Urban Politics in the Southwest*, edited by Leonard Goodall, pp. 165–95. Tempe: Arizona State University Institute of Public Administration, 1967.

Keen, Harold. "San Diego: From Navy Town to 'America's Finest City.' " *Planning* 43 (April-May 1977): 10–15.

———. "Sewerage for San Diego for National Defense." *American City* 58 (September 1943): 56–58.

Keisling, Phil. "Making a New Local Government." *Willamette Week* (25 September 1978).

King, Larry. "Bright Lights, Big Cities." *Atlantic* 235 (March 1975): 84–88.

Klutznick, Philip M. "Impact of the War on Communities." In *Proceedings of the National Conference on Planning: 1942*, pp. 36–40. Chicago: American Society of Planning Officials, 1942.

Kopkind, Andrew. "Modern Times in Phoenix." *New Republic* 153 (6 November 1965): 14–16.

Kurtz, Maxine. "The Tri-County Regional Planning Commission." *Public Administration Review* 7 (Spring 1947): 113–22.

Lamb, Robert K. "Mobilization of Human Resources." *American Journal of Sociology* 48 (November 1942): 323–30.

Leach, Richard. "Atlanta Area Faces Problems of Growth." *National Civic Review* 53 (November 1964): 555–57.

Lee, Eugene C., and Rothman, Jonathan S. "San Francisco's District System Alters Electoral Politics." *National Civic Review* 67 (April 1978): 173–78.

Lillard, Richard. "Revolution by Internal Combustion." In *The California Revolution*, edited by Carey McWilliams, pp. 84–99. New York: Grossman Publishers, 1969.

Lineberry, Robert. "Suburbia and the Metropolitan Turf." *Annals of the American Academy of Political and Social Science* 422 (November 1975): 1–9.

Little, Charles. "Atlanta Renewal Gives Power to the Communities." *Smithsonian* 7 (July 1976): 100–108.

Lotchin, Roger. "The Metropolitan-Military Complex in Comparative Perspective." *Journal of the West* 18 (July 1979): 19–30.

Lubell, Samuel. "Charlotte, North Carolina." *Saturday Evening Post* 223 (23 June 1951): 32–33, 46.

McVoy, Arthur. "How Cities are Preparing for the Postwar Period: Portland." In *Planning: 1944*, pp. 78–80. Chicago: American Society of Planning Officials, 1944.

Marando, Vincent, and Whitley, Carl. "City-County Consolidation: An Overview of Voter Response." *Urban Affairs Quarterly* 8 (December 1972): 181–204.

Mayo, Selz C. "Social Change, Social Movements, and the Disappearing Sectional South." *Social Forces* 43 (October 1964): 1–10.

Meyerson, Martin. "Post-War Plans: A Survey." *Task* 5 (Spring 1944): 9–12.

Mezerik, A. G. "Journey in America." *New Republic* 111 (13 November 1944): 617–19.

Miller, Zane. "Scarcity, Abundance, and American Urban History." *Journal of Urban History* 4 (February 1978): 131–56.

Mollenkopf, John. "The Post-War Politics of Urban Development." *Politics and Society* 5 (1975): 247–96.

Molotch, Harvey. "The City as a Growth Machine." *American Journal of Sociology* 82 (September 1976): 304–32.

Morrison, Peter, and Wheeler, Judith. "Rural Renaissance in America?" *Population Bulletin* 31 (October 1976): 1–29.

Myers, Howard. "Defense Migration and Labor Supply." *Journal of the American Statistical Association* 37 (March 1942): 69–76.

Nathan, Richard, and Adams, Charles. "Understanding Central City Hardship." *Political Science Quarterly* 91 (Spring 1976): 51–62.

Neuberger, Richard. "The Cities of America: Portland, Oregon." *Saturday Evening Post* 219 (1 March 1947): 22–23, 104–8.

"The New No. 1 City in the Southwest." *Business Week* (12 June 1971): 82–86.

"New Strength in City Hall." *Fortune* 56 (November 1957): 156–59, 251–64.

Nichols, William H. "The South as a Developing Area." In *The American South in the 1960s*, edited by Avery Leiserson, pp. 22–40. New York: Praeger Publishers, 1964.

Noland, E. William. "Technological Change and the Social Order." In *The South in Continuity and Change*, edited by John C. McKinney and Edgar T. Thompson, pp. 167–97. Durham: Duke University Press, 1965.

"Norfolk, Virginia." *Architectural Forum* 76 (June 1942): 368–74.

"Old Girl's New Boy." *Time* 50 (26 November 1947): 26–28.

Pack, Janet Rothenburg. "Frostbelt and Sunbelt: Convergence over Time." *Intergovernmental Perspective* 4 (Fall 1978): 8–15.

Perkin, Robert, and Graham, Charles A. "Denver: Reluctant Capital." In *Rocky Mountain Cities*, edited by Ray B. West, pp. 280–317. New York: W. W. Norton and Co., 1949.

Perry, George S. "Cities of America: Atlanta." *Saturday Evening Post* 218 (22 September 1945): 26–27, 47–52.

Pinkerton, James R. "City-Suburban Residential Patterns, by Social Class: A Review of the Literature." *Urban Affairs Quarterly* 4 (June 1969): 499–519.

"The Politics of HemisFair—And of San Antonio." *Texas Observer* (30 September 1966): 1–7.

Pomeroy, Earl. "What Remains of the West?" *Utah Historical Quarterly* 35 (Winter 1967): 37–56.

Pomeroy, Hugh. "Impact of the War on Communities." In *Proceedings of the National Conference on Planning: 1942*, pp. 27–38. Chicago: American Society of Planning Officials, 1942.

Portland City Club. "The Negro in Portland." *City Club Bulletin* 26 (20 July 1945).

———. "Report on County Charter Review Commission." *City Club Bulletin* 58 (21 October 1977).

———. "Report on Portland City Government." *City Club Bulletin* 41 (19 May 1961).

"Portland Stalks Postwar Specter." *Business Week* (11 November 1944): 17–20.

Powledge, Fred. "Profiles: A New Politics in Atlanta." *New Yorker* 48 (31 December 1972): 28–40.

Pratt, Henry J. "Counties' Role Grows in Urban Affairs." *National Civic Review* 61 (September 1972): 397–402.

Quinn, Michael. "Dispersing the Urban Core: Recent Studies of the City in Suburbia." *Urban Affairs Quarterly* 11 (June 1976): 545–54.

Rabinowitz, Howard. "Growth Trends in the Albuquerque SMSA, 1940–1978." *Journal of the West* 18 (July 1979): 62–74.

Rankin, Robert A. "The Richmond Crusade for Voters: The Quest for Black Power." *University of Virginia Newsletter* 51 (September 1974).

Reed, Marl E. "The FEPC, the Black Worker, and Southern Shipyards." *South Atlantic Quarterly* 74 (Autumn 1975): 446–67.

Reissman, Leonard. "Social Development and the American South." *Journal of Social Issues* 22 (February 1966): 101–16.

______. "Urbanization in the South." In *The South in Continuity and Change*, edited by John C. McKinney and Edgar T. Thompson, pp. 79–100. Durham: Duke University Press, 1965.

"Richmond Took a Beating." *Fortune* 31 (February 1945): 264–65.

Riesman, David, and Glazer, Nathan. "The Intellectuals and the Discontented Classes." In *The Radical Right*, edited by Daniel Bell, pp. 87–113. Garden City, N.Y.: Doubleday and Co., 1963.

Rockwell, Bruce. "Thoughts on Preservation, Past and Future." In *Economic Benefits of Preserving Old Buildings*, pp. 123–25. Washington: Preservation Press, 1975.

Rostow, Walt W. "A National Policy Towards Regional Change." *Congressional Record–Senate* (14 June 1977): 9673–9677.

Roszak, Theodore. "Life in the Instant Cities." In *The California Revolution*, edited by Carey McWilliams, pp. 53–83. New York: Grossman Publishers, 1969.

Salamon, Lester. "Urban Politics, Urban Policy, Case Studies, and Political Theory." *Public Administration Review* 37 (August 1977): 418–28.

Salisbury, Robert. "Urban Politics: The New Convergence of Power." *Journal of Politics* 26 (November 1964): 775–97.

"San Antonio." *Federal Reserve Bank of Dallas Business Review* 44 (June 1959): 2–20.

"San Antonio Liberals: Piecing it Together." *Texas Observer* (27 May 1966): 5.

"San Diego Faces Post-War Transition with Confidence." *American City* 60 (July 1945): 95.

Schemmel, Bill. "Atlanta's Power Structure Faces Life." *New South* 27 (Spring 1972): 62–68.

Schnore, Leo. "On the Spatial Structure of Cities in the Two Americas." In *The Study of Urbanization*, edited by Phillip Hauser and Leo Schnore, pp. 347–98. New York: John Wiley, 1965.

______. "The Socioeconomic Status of Cities and Suburbs." *American Sociological Review* 28 (February 1963): 76–85.

______. "Urban Structure and Suburban Selectivity." *Demography* 1 (1964): 164–76.

______, and Evanson, Phillip C. "Segregation in Southern Cities." *American Journal of Sociology* 72 (July 1966): 58–67.

______, and Winsborough, Hal H. "Functional Classification and the Residential Location of Social Classes." In *City Classification Handbook*, edited by Brian Berry, pp. 124–51. New York: Wiley-Interscience, 1971.

Schwartz, Barry. "Images of Suburbia: Some Revisionist Commentary and Conclusions." In *The Changing Face of the Suburbs*, edited by Barry Schwartz, pp. 325–39. Chicago: University of Chicago Press, 1976.

Scott, Thomas. "Implications of Suburbanization for Metropolitan Political Organization." *Annals of the American Academy of Political and Social Science* 422 (November 1975): 36–44.

———. "Suburban Governmental Structures." In *The Urbanization of the Suburbs*, edited by Jeffrey Hadden and Louis Masotti, pp. 213–38. Beverly Hills: Sage Publications, 1973.

"The Second War Between the States." *Business Week* (17 May 1976): 82–114.

Shelley, B. Jack. "Revitalizing a City: The San Antonio Experience." *Public Affairs Comment* 12 (July 1966): 1–4.

Shryock, Henry S. "Wartime Shifts of the Civilian Population." *Milbank Memorial Fund Quarterly* 25 (July 1947): 269–82.

Simpson, Richard L., and Nosworthy, David B. "The Changing Occupational Structure of the South." In *The South in Continuity and Change*, edited by John C. McKinney and Edgar T. Thompson, pp. 198–224. Durham: Duke University Press, 1965.

Spain, August O. "Fort Worth: Great Expectations—Cowtown Hares and Tortoises." In *Urban Politics in the Southwest*, edited by Leonard Goodall, pp. 46–67. Tempe: Arizona State University Institute of Public Administration, 1967.

Spector, Samuel. "The Fact and Fiction of Planning, Zoning, and Discrimination." *Atlanta Economic Review* 21 (December 1971): 4–7, 46–47.

Springer, Gertrude. "Growing Pains of Defense." *Survey Graphic* 30 (January 1941): 5–8.

Stegner, Wallace. "The West Coast: A Region with a View." *Saturday Review* 42 (2 May 1969): 15–17, 41.

Sternlieb, George, and Hughes, James. "The Wilting of the Metropolis." In *Toward a National Urban Policy*, U.S., House of Representatives, Committee on Banking, Finance and Urban Affairs, Subcommittee on the City, pp. 1–18. Washington: Government Printing Office, 1977.

Sutton, Horace. "Sunbelt vs. Frostbelt: A Second Civil War?" *Saturday Review* 5 (15 April 1978): 28–37.

Tharpe, Gene. "Atlanta: Major Announcements Herald Resurgence of Downtown Market." *National Real Estate Investor* 21 (May 1979): 67–82.

Thernstrom, Stephen. "The Growth of Los Angeles in Historical Perspective." In *Los Angeles: Viability and Prospects for Metropolitan Leadership*, edited by Werner Z. Hirsch, pp. 3–19. New York: Praeger Publishers, 1971.

"This World's Fair Has a Long Future." *Business Week* (30 March 1968): 66–71.

Thompson, Daniel C. "The New South." *Journal of Social Issues* 22 (February 1966): 7–19.

Thompson, Robert A.; Lewis, Hylan; and McEntire, Davis. "Atlanta and Birmingham: A Comparative Study in Negro Housing." In *Studies in*

Housing and Minority Groups, edited by Nathan Glazer and Davis McEntire, pp. 13–83. Berkeley: University of California Press, 1960.

Tilden, Freeman. "Portland, Oregon: Yankee Prudence on the West Coast." *World's Work* 60 (October 1931): 34–40.

Trillin, Calvin. "U.S. Journal: Denver." *New Yorker* 53 (23 January 1978): 75–79.

———. "U.S. Journal, Kansas City, Missouri: Reflections of Someone Whose Home Town Has Become a Glamour City." *New Yorker* 50 (8 April 1974): 94–101.

———. "U.S. Journal, San Antonio: Some Elements of Power." *New Yorker* 53 (2 May 1977): 92–100.

Tsuchigane, Robert, and Whaley, John. "Selected Economic Impacts of the Navy in Southeastern Virginia." *Virginia Social Science Journal* 15 (April 1980): 14–21.

Tugwell, Rexford. "San Francisco as Seen from New York." In *National Conference on Planning: 1940*, pp. 182–88. Chicago: American Society of Planning Officials, 1940.

Tunnard, Christopher. "Portland Improvement." *Task* 5 (Spring 1944): 21–22.

Ullman, Edward. "Amenities as a Factor in Regional Growth." *Geographical Review* 44 (January 1954): 119–32.

Vance, Rupert, and Smith, Sara. "Metropolitan Dominance and Integration in the Urban South." In *The Urban South*, edited by Rupert Vance and Nicholas Demerath, pp. 114–34. Chapel Hill: University of North Carolina Press, 1954.

Van Urk, J. B. "Norfolk: Our Worst War Town." *American Mercury* 56 (February 1943): 144–51.

"Vision in Virginia." *Newsweek* 54 (14 December 1959): 46.

Wade, Richard C. "An Agenda for Urban History." In *The State of American History*, edited by Herbert Bass, pp. 43–69. Chicago: Quadrangle, 1970.

"The Westward Empire." *Fortune* 26 (July 1942): 86–96.

"What's a War Boom Like." *Business Week* (6 June 1942): 22–32.

Wheaton, M. L. "The Renovators." *Commonwealth: The Magazine of Virginia*. 40 (December 1973): 25–26.

White, Dana, and Crimmins, Timothy. "How Atlanta Grew: Cool Heads, Hot Air, and Hard Work." *Atlanta Economic Review* 28 (January-February 1978): 7–15.

———. "Urban Growth: Atlanta." *Journal of Urban History* 2 (February 1976): 231–52.

White, Forrest P. "Will Norfolk's Schools Stay Open?" *Atlantic* 204 (September 1959): 29–33.

White, Ron. "San Antonio: Realty Market Marches to Cadence of Sunbelt Prosperity." *National Real Estate Investor* 21 (May 1979): 103–10.

Whyte, William H. "Urban Sprawl." *Fortune* 57 (January 1958): 103–9, 194–200.

Wilcox, Robert F. "San Diego: City in Motion." In *Urban Politics in the Southwest*, edited by Leonard Goodall, pp. 143–64. Tempe: Arizona State University Institute of Public Administration, 1967.

Williams, Oliver. "Life Styles, Values, and Political Decentralizatior in Metropolitan Areas." *Social Science Quarterly* 48 (December 1967): 299–317.

Wilson, James Q. "Los Angeles Is—and Is Not—Different." In *Los Angeles: Viability and Prospects for Municipal Leadership*, edited by Werner Z. Hirsch, pp. 119–32. New York: Praeger Publishers, 1971.

Winsborough, Hal H. "The Changing Regional Character of the South." In *The South in Continuity and Change*, edited by John C. McKinney and Edgar T. Thompson, pp. 34–52. Durham: Duke University Press, 1965.

Wirth, Louis. "The Urban Community." In *American Society in Wartime*, edited by W. F. Ogburn, pp. 63–77. Chicago: University of Chicago Press, 1943.

Woods, Julia. "Seattle's Friday Afternoon Massacre." *Planning* 45 (April 1979): 6–7.

Wright, Alexander S., III. "The Office Market: Central City versus Suburbs." *Atlanta Economic Review* 28 (January-February 1978): 34–36.

Wrinkle, Robert. "New Mexico." In *Rocky Mountain Urban Politics*, edited by JeDon A. Emenheiser, pp. 113–26. Logan: Utah State University, 1971.

Yoes, E. D., Jr. "COPS Proves Effective." *Texas Observer* (26 November 1976): 7–11.

———. "COPS Takes on City Hall." *Texas Observer* (12 November 1976): 1–5.

Ziemba, Joan. "The Power in Chesapeake." *Metro Magazine* (November 1972): 23–25.

Zikmund, Joseph, II. "Sources of the Suburban Population, 1955–1960 and 1965–1970." *Publius* 5 (Winter 1975): 27–54.

Zimmerman, Joseph. "The Federal Voting Rights Act: Its Impact on Annexation." *National Civic Review* 66 (June 1977): 278–83.

Zuiches, J. J., and Fuguitt, G. V. "Residential Preferences and Population Distribution." *Demography* 12 (1975): 491–504.

Public Documents

Advisory Commission on Intergovernmental Relations. *The Challenge of Local Government Reorganization: Substate Regionalism and the Federal System*. Vol. III, Report No. A–44. Washington: Government Printing Office, 1974.

———. *Metropolitan Social and Economic Disparities: Implications for Intergovernmental Relations in Central Cities and Suburbs*. Report A–25. Washington: Government Printing Office, 1965.

Alamo Area Council of Governments. *Overall Economic Development Program*. San Antonio: 1976.

Columbia Region Association of Governments. *Derivation of Indices of Residential Blight for the Greater Portland-Vancouver Area*. Portland: 1972.

Denver Community Renewal Program. *A Strategy for Community Renewal*. Denver: 1973.

Denver Planning Commission. *Denver 1985: A Comprehensive Plan for Community Excellence*. Denver: 1967.

———. *The Problem of Centralization and Decentralization*. Denver: 1941.

———. *Preliminary Outline for a Regional Plan*. Denver: 1937.

Denver Regional Council of Governments. *The Changing Region: A Report on Population Change in the Seventies*. Denver: 1976.

Housing Authority of Portland. *From Roses to Rivets: Being an Account of the Housing Authority of Portland, Oregon*. Portland: 1946.

———. *Vaughan Street Redevelopment Project: Preliminary Report*. Portland: 1952.

Norfolk City Manager. *The Norfolk Story: City Manager's Annual Report*. Norfolk: City of Norfolk, 1947–51.

Norfolk Housing Authority. *This Is It*. Norfolk: 1946.

Oregon Legislative Interim Committee on Local Government. *Problems of the Urban Fringe: Portland Area*. Salem: State of Oregon, 1956.

Portland Planning Bureau. *Economic Development in Portland, Oregon: Opportunities, Constraints and Policy Issues*. Portland: 1977.

Portland Planning Department. *Portland's Residential Areas: An Initial Appraisal of Blight and Related Factors*. Portland: 1965.

Puget Sound Regional Planning Commission and Washington State Planning Council. *Puget Sound Region: War and Post-War Development*. Washington: Government Printing Office, 1943.

San Antonio Committee on Slum Clearance and Urban Redevelopment. *San Antonio Comprehensive Master Plan*. San Antonio: City of San Antonio, 1951.

San Antonio Comprehensive Planning Division. *A Report on Growth Policy Issues: Growth Sketches for San Antonio*. San Antonio: Community Development Department, 1976.

———. *A Report on Population: San Antonio and Bexar County*. San Antonio: Community Development Office, 1973.

San Antonio Planning and Community Development Department. *Alternative Growth Study*. San Antonio: 1975.

San Antonio Planning Department. *Economic Analysis: San Antonio*. San Antonio: Community Renewal Program, 1972.

———. *San Antonio Growth Sketch*. San Antonio: 1977.

San Francisco Redevelopment Agency. *San Francisco Redevelopment Program, 1979: Survey of Project Data*. San Francisco: 1979.

Southeastern Virginia Planning District Commission. *Population and Employment Forecasts*. Research Memorandum No. 58. Norfolk: 1976.

Southeastern Virginia Regional Planning Commission. *Basic Data for Planning: Southeastern Virginia Region*. Norfolk: 1962.

U.S., Bureau of the Census. *County and City Data Book*. Washington: Government Printing Office, 1972.

———. *Current Population Report*, Series P-25, No. 640 (November, 1976).

———. *Wartime Changes in Population and Family Characteristics, Portland-Vancouver Congested Production Area*, Series CA-2 and CA-3, No. 6, May 1944.

———. *Historical Statistics of the United States*. Washington: Government Printing Office, 1960.

———. *Statistical Abstract of the United States*. Annual Volumes, 1940–79. Washington: Government Printing Office, 1940–79.

U.S., Department of Labor, Bureau of Labor Statistics. *The Impact of World War II in the Hampton Roads Area*. Industrial Area Study No. 23. Washington: 1944.

U.S., House of Representatives, Committee on the Judiciary, Subcommittee on Civil and Constitutional Rights. *Hearings: Extension of the Voting Rights Act*. 94th Congress, First Session, 1975.

U.S., House of Representatives, Naval Affairs Committee. *Hearings: Hampton Roads Naval Affairs Subcommittee on Congested Areas*. Washington: 1943.

U.S., National Resources Planning Board, *National Resources Development Report for 1943*. 2 parts. Part 1, *Post War Plan and Program*. Part 2, *Wartime Planning for War and Post War*. Washington: Government Printing Office, 1943.

U.S., President's Committee for Congested Production Areas. *Final Report*. Washington: 1944.

U.S., Senate, Committee on Public Works, Subcommittee on Transportation. *Transportation Planning and Priorities for the Seventies: Hearings, May 10, 1974*. 93rd Congress, Second Session, 1974.

Unpublished Studies and Papers

Ballard, Jack S. "The Shock of Peace: Military and Economic Demobilization after World War II." Ph.D. dissertation, University of California, Los Angeles, 1974.

Boren, David. Address to Symposium on Alternatives to Confrontation: A National Policy Toward Regional Change, Austin, Texas, 1977.

Chance, Truett Lamar. "The Relationship of Selected City Government Services to Socio-Economic Status Characteristics of Census Tracts in San Antonio, Texas." Ph.D. dissertation, University of Texas, 1970.

Cobb, James C. "Colonel Effingham Crushes the Crackers: Political Reform in Postwar Augusta." Paper delivered at Conference on the Urban South, Norfolk, 1977.

Davis, Howard. "An Analysis of Current Patterns of Human Resource Development in San Antonio, Texas." Ph.D. dissertation, University of Texas, 1966.

Gibson, L. Tucker, and Ashcroft, Robert R. "Political Organizations in a Nonpartisan Election System." Paper delivered to Southwestern Social Science Association, 1977.

Hardon, Berdie Ricks. "A Statistical Analysis of the Black-White Voting Coalition in Atlanta, 1949–1970." M.S. thesis, Georgia State University, 1972.

Harrington, Michael. Address to Symposium on Alternatives to Confrontation: A National Policy Toward Regional Change. Austin, Texas, 1977.

Liner, E. Blaine. Address to Symposium on Alternatives to Confrontation: A National Policy Toward Regional Change. Austin, Texas, 1977.

Moore, Lawrence Ellis. "Annexation Atlanta—1972: A Look at the Political Issues." M.S. thesis, Georgia State University, 1972.

Moye, William. "Charlotte-Mecklenburg Consolidation: Metrolina in Motion." Ph.D. dissertation, University of North Carolina, 1975.

Pedersen, Mary. "Citizen Participation in Portland, Oregon." Paper delivered at National Conference of Neighborhood Coordinators, 1976.

———. "Neighborhood Organization in Portland, Oregon." Unpublished reports, 1974–75.

Peterson, George. Address to Symposium on Alternatives to Confrontation: A National Policy Toward Regional Change. Austin, Texas, 1977.

Schler, Daniel J. "Citizen Participation: Title I of the Housing and Community Development Act in Denver." Paper delivered to Western Social Science Association, 1979.

Scott, Robert. Address to Symposium on Alternatives to Confrontation: A National Policy Toward Regional Change. Austin, Texas, 1977.

Silver, Christopher. "Urban Planning and Urban Development in the New South: Richmond, Virginia, 1900–1960." Paper delivered at Conference on the Urban South, Norfolk, 1978.

Uhlman, Wes. "Neighborhood Preservation in Seattle." Paper delivered at conference on A Sense of Place in the City, Portland, 1978.

Newspapers and Periodicals

American Society of Planning Officials *Newsletter*
Denver Post
Journal of Housing
New York Times
Norfolk *Journal and Guide*
Norfolk *Ledger-Dispatch*
Norfolk *Ledger-Star*
Norfolk *Virginian-Pilot*
Portland *Oregonian*
Portland *Oregon Journal*
Richmond *Times-Dispatch*
Rocky Mountain News
San Antonio Express
San Antonio Light
San Antonio News
Survey of Current Business
The Portland Realtor
Wall Street Journal
Washington Post

Manuscript Collections

Charlottesville, Va.
- University of Virginia
  - Harry Byrd Papers
  - Virginia Committee for Public Schools Papers

Denver, Colo.
- Colorado Historical Society
  - Oral History of Colorado Project
    - Max Brooks transcript
    - Charles Buxton transcript
    - J. Robert Cameron transcript
    - George Cavender transcript
    - George Cramner transcript
    - Vincent Dwyer transcript
    - John Fuhr transcript
    - John Love transcript
    - Jack McCandless transcript

Eugene, Oreg.
- University of Oregon
  - Portland Chamber of Commerce Papers

Norfolk, Va.
- Kirn Memorial Library
  - Norfolk Redevelopment and Housing Authority File
- Norfolk City Hall
  - City Council Minutes
  - Central Files
- Old Dominion University
  - Henry Howell Papers
  - Forrest White Papers
  - Joseph Wood Papers

Portland, Oreg.
- City of Portland Archives
  - City Council Proceedings
  - Planning Commission Minutes
- Housing Authority of Portland
  - Minutes
- Multnomah County Library
  - Mayor's Committee of Municipal Reorganization Minutes
- Oregon Historical Society
  - Ormond Bean Papers
  - William Bowes Papers
  - Don Clark Papers
  - David Eccles Papers
  - Housing Authority of Portland Papers
  - Earl Riley Papers
  - World War II Agencies Papers

Richmond, Va.
- Virginia Historical Society
  - Bemiss Papers

Interviews

Buel, Ron. *Willamette Week*. Portland, August 1978.

Carlson, Don. Portland Metropolitan Area Boundary Commission. Portland, December 1977.

Cease, Ronald C. Portland, December 1977.

Clay, Sam. City of Virginia Beach. Virginia Beach, May 1978.

Coates, Joan. *Virginia Beach Sun*. Virginia Beach, April 1978.

Cottrell, Charles. San Antonio, September 1977.

Cramton, Martin. Multnomah County. Portland, December 1977.

Crenshaw, Francis. Norfolk, April 1978.

Curling, Durwood. City of Chesapeake. Chesapeake, June 1978.
Darden, Pretlow. Norfolk, April 1978.
Davis, Wendell. City of San Antonio. San Antonio, September 1977 and April 1978.
Diehl, Kemper. *San Antonio Express*. San Antonio, April 1978.
Ervin, Reid. City of Virginia Beach. Virginia Beach, May 1978.
Fentress, John V. City of Virginia Beach. Virginia Beach, April 1978.
Foeller, Robert. Southeastern Virginia Planning District Commission. Norfolk, April 1978.
Gallegos, Beatriz. Communities Organized for Public Service. San Antonio, April 1978.
Gibson, L. Tucker. San Antonio, September 1977.
Green, Robert. Bexar County. San Antonio, April 1978.
Guerra, Claude. Alamo Area Council of Governments. San Antonio, September 1977.
Hambright, James. *Virginia Beach Beacon*. Virginia Beach, April 1978.
Hoyt, L. Palmer. *Rocky Mountain News*. Denver, April 1978.
Jarboe, Jan. *San Antonio Light*. Washington, April 1978.
Kellam, Sidney. Virginia Beach, April 1978.
Kent, Denton U. Columbia Region Association of Governments. Portland, December 1977.
McAllister, Walter. San Antonio, April 1978.
MacColl, E. Kimbark. Portland, December 1977.
Mapp, Ivan. City of Virginia Beach. Virginia Beach, April 1978.
Martin, Roy. Norfolk, April 1978.
Maverick, Maury, Jr. San Antonio, April 1978.
Monaghan, Jay. Colorado Open Space Council. Denver, June 1974.
Osborne, Patricia. City of San Antonio. San Antonio, September 1977.
Pedersen, Mary. City of Portland. Portland, December 1977.
Powell, Catherine. San Antonio, September 1977.
Rawls, Ellis. Denver Regional Council of Governments. Denver, June 1974.
Rich, A. McKay. Portland, December 1977.
Rowe, John. City of Suffolk. Suffolk, Virginia, May 1978.
Saroff, Ronald. City of Beaverton. Beaverton, Oregon, December 1977.
Sawtelle, Robert. San Antonio, April 1978.
Scott, Robert. City of Virginia Beach. Virginia Beach, May 1978.
Seigneur, David. Clackamas County. Oregon City, Oregon, June 1978.
Sinkin, Lanny. Aquifer Protection Association. San Antonio, September 1977.
Stacy, Robert. 1000 Friends of Oregon. Portland, August 1978.
Standing Patrick. City of Virginia Beach. Virginia Beach, May 1978.
Stromberg, Charles. Denver, April 1978.
White, Forrest P. Norfolk, April 1978.
Wright, Douglas. City of Portland. Portland, August 1978.

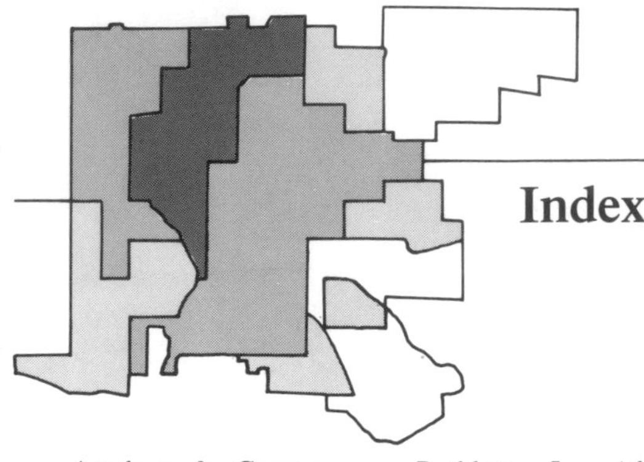

Index